LOYAL TO EMPIRE

General Sir Charles Monro. (Surrey Infantry Museum)

LOYAL TO EMPIRE

THE LIFE OF GENERAL SIR CHARLES MONRO, 1860–1929

PATRICK CROWLEY

FOREWORD BY GARY SHEFFIELD

The
History
Press

This book is dedicated to the memory of Professor Richard Holmes – the inspiration for this tome – and to the Surrey Infantry Museum at Clandon House, Surrey, which was sadly destroyed by fire in April 2015.

By the same author:
Kut 1916
The Infantry Regiments of Surrey
Afghanistan – The Three Wars
A Guide to the Princess of Wales's Royal Regiment

First published 2016

The History Press
The Mill, Brimscombe Port
Stroud, Gloucestershire, GL5 2QG
www.thehistorypress.co.uk

British Library Cataloguing in Publication Data.
A catalogue record for this book is available from the British Library.

ISBN 978 0 7509 6599 6

Typesetting and origination by The History Press
Printed and bound in Great Britain by TJ International Ltd

CONTENTS

ACKNOWLEDGEMENTS

It has taken some time to write and construct this book, as it has been written over a period when I have left the Regular Army after thirty-four years' service and taken on a new appointment championing the cause of the reserves and cadets in the south-east of England. Main thanks go to my wife, Jane, for being so patient as it was being written, and to Lynne Gammond, who kindly spent time proofreading and making suggestions as it progressed. Special thanks also go to Colonel John Powell, who was working in Gibraltar and researched Monro's time there for me. In terms of research help, once again Prince Consort's Library in Aldershot and their head librarian, Tim Ward, have been outstanding and I am extremely grateful to the staff of the Surrey History Centre, Imperial War Museum, Liddell Hart Centre for Military Archives at King's College London, National Army Museum, National Archives, the British Library, Joint Services' Defence College Library and Sherborne School for their helpfulness. Finally, I am very fortunate that Professor Gary Sheffield, an internationally renowned First World War expert, has done me the honour of writing the foreword.

Patrick Crowley

FOREWORD

General Sir Charles Monro is a difficult subject for a biographer. Unlike fellow Great War generals Douglas Haig and Henry Rawlinson, Monro did not leave a voluminous body of papers. The only previous biography is over eighty years old and is sadly inadequate from the point of view of the modern historian. Nor is there much in the way of modern work on Monro: at best, he has a walk-on role in accounts of Gallipoli and Fromelles. John Bourne's chapter length biographical sketch from 2006 is one of the few exceptions.

Patrick Crowley, in his biography, is making bricks with inadequate amounts of straw in places, but by placing Monro in a wider context reduces this as a problem. The more senior Monro became, the greater his visibility in the sources, and so from the Boer War onwards, Monro the man increasingly comes to the fore, although we often see him through the eyes of others. Patrick Crowley's achievement is to make Charles Monro a somewhat less shadowy figure, although in the absence of fuller sources, in some respects Monro remains frustratingly elusive.

And yet Monro, as Colonel Crowley demonstrates, was a significant figure. Two roles stand out: his tenure as a senior commander (at divisional, corps and army level) in the First World War; and as commander-in-chief (C-in-C) India. As commander of 2nd Division in the original British Expeditionary Force (BEF), Monro had a key leadership position at a crucial time. Whilst he was not regarded by successive Cs-in-C, French and Haig, as a 'top tier' general, Monro still had a hugely responsible and vital role to play. He was fated not to command in the great attritional battles of 1916–17, the Somme, Arras or Passchendaele, nor in the desperate defensive actions of 1918 that proved to be the prelude to the advance to victory from August to November of that year. Thus it is impossible to judge how Charles Monro would have adjusted to the learning process that characterised both the BEF as a whole and its commanders. It is probably unfair to judge him purely on his handling of the Battle of Fromelles in July 1916.

The fact that Monro was selected to become C-in-C India in 1916 is noteworthy, not just because it says something about his reputation as a field commander, but also it is a clear statement of how highly he was regarded as an administrator. This was no sinecure. India was a vital part of the British Empire's war effort, and it needed a strong and energetic C-in-C. This period saw Monro's greatest contribution to the British state, which remains remarkably unheralded. Monro had already shown his powers of decision – and moral courage – in taking the decision to abandon the Gallipoli campaign. This was undoubtedly the right call, but it earned him the enmity of Winston Churchill, from whose ever-fertile brain the original scheme had emerged.

There are still many areas of the history of the British Army of the Great War in which much research remains to be done. Surprisingly, high command is one of them. We still know too little about many of the men who commanded major formations. But we now know more about Charles Monro. Undoubtedly, there is more to be done, but Patrick Crowley's admirable book is an important step in the right direction.

Gary Sheffield
Professor of War Studies, University of Wolverhampton

GLOSSARY

AAG:	Assistant Adjutant General
ADC:	Aide de Camp
ANZAC:	Australian and New Zealand Army Corps
Bart.:	Baronet
BEF:	British Expeditionary Force
BG RA:	Brigadier-General Royal Artillery
CB:	Companion of the Bath
CGS:	Chief of the General Staff
CIGS:	Chief of the Imperial General Staff
C-in-C:	Commander-in-Chief
CRE:	Commander Royal Engineers
DAAG:	Deputy Assistant Adjutant General
DMO:	Director Military Operations
DSO:	Distinguished Service Order
GCB:	Knight Grand Cross of the Most Honourable Order of the Bath
GCMG:	Knight Grand Cross of the Most Distinguished Order of Saint Michael and Saint George
GCSI:	Knight Commander of the Star of India
GHQ:	General Headquarters
GOC:	General Officer Commanding
GSO 1:	General Staff Officer 1 or Chief of Staff
KCB:	Knight Commander of the Order of the Bath
LHCMA:	Liddell Hart Centre for Military Archives
MEF:	Mediterranean Expeditionary Force or Mesopotamia Expeditionary Force

MGC:	Machine Gun Corps
NCO:	Non-Commissioned Officer
PSC:	Passed Staff College
QMG and AA:	Quartermaster General and Assistant Adjutant or Deputy Chief of Staff
RMA:	Royal Military Academy
TNA:	The National Archives
VC:	Victoria Cross
VCO:	Viceroy-Commissioned Officer

PREFACE

Kitchener, Haig, French, Robertson, Plumer, Allenby and Smith-Dorrien, along with some other personalities, are relatively well-known commanders, but Charles Monro is probably the least familiar of the senior generals of the First World War; it is about time that this situation was rectified, particularly as the centenary of the conflict is remembered.

However, Monro avoided publicity, was a humble man, left few papers for analysis and had no direct family descendants, so investigating his life is quite a challenge. That is probably why no academic has attempted to study him in detail since General Sir George Barrow's biography of 1931 and why this book is not a definitive biography – the gauntlet is certainly thrown down to anyone who can achieve the perfect analysis of his life from the reference material available.

Barrow was close to Monro and knew him very well, serving as his chief of staff in the 1st Army during 1916 and in India later. His informative book touches many aspects of his career, particularly Monro's role in Gallipoli and India, though he avoids any balanced criticism and does not even mention Monro's role in the controversial Battle of Fromelles on the Western Front. Nor does he provide any defined sources for his comment.

Otherwise, John Bourne has provided an excellent short summary of his career in Beckett & Corvi's *Haig's Generals*, though his experience of regimental duty and his time in India and Gibraltar does not receive great attention. There is also a good summary of Monro's career by Cassar in the *Oxford Dictionary of National Biography*.

However, none of these more recent references have gone into such depth as *Loyal to Empire*. This book goes beyond recent short summaries of his military life and deliberately contextualises certain aspects of his career. Whilst knowledge of his detailed personal contribution to operations in the North-West Frontier of India and in South Africa is scarce, these events helped shape his life and attitude. Therefore, they are worth summarising from the perspective of his regiment, the Queen's Royal Regiment (West Surrey), and the army formations in which he served.

Monro was instrumental in reshaping musketry tactics before the war at a time of great change within the British Army, yet his role has barely been mentioned in previous histories. He was also one of a few chosen officers to serve as divisional, corps and army commander on the Western Front, was critical in the decision to evacuate the disastrous beaches at Gallipoli and was the senior military commander in India at a particularly crucial and fragile period. This was a loyal and extremely professional officer who was definitely no 'donkey' and just 'got on with the job'.

Patrick Crowley

1

THE EARLY YEARS

Not every future general is born on a ship, but on 15 June 1860 that was Charles Carmichael Monro's introduction to the world. The *Maid of Judah*, a wooden sailing ship, was on her way from Melbourne, Australia, to London. On board were his parents, Scotsman Henry Monro, a successful entrepreneur in Australia, but not in good health, and his mother, Catherine (née Power), originally from Clonmult, County Cork, Ireland, and five of his Australian-born siblings, four brothers and one sister.

The *Maid of Judah* was one of twenty-nine ships that sailed as part of the Aberdeen White Star Line in the period 1842–70: 'No ships that ever sailed the seas presented a finer appearance than these little flyers … They were always beautifully kept and were easily noticeable amongst other ships for their smartness.'[1] The *Argus* newspaper of Melbourne advertised the journey in the previous March; William C. Mitchell being the captain:

> This vessel has earned a first rate reputation, while in the Sydney trade, as one of the celebrated Aberdeen Line for her quick passages, as well as for the excellent condition in which she has always discharged her cargo. She is now alongside the Hobson Bay Railway Pier, and the attention of intending passengers is called to her excellent accommodations, which have been expressly fitted for the Australian trade, her 'tween decks being lofty and well ventilated, and specially adapted for the comfort of second and third class passengers.

The advertisement records the cost of first-class travel as 'per agreement' and that the ship 'carries an experienced surgeon'.[2] This was fortunate for Catherine Monro, about to deliver her next son. There are no clues about

Maid of Judah. (Author's collection)

how advanced her pregnancy was, but she travelled, perhaps knowing that her next child's arrival was imminent. Charles was born two months out, northbound from Australia, off the Cape of Good Hope. Perhaps the future general's character was being formed; the combination of an unusual birth, his place in the family and the fact that his father was to die when he was only 9 years old helped to form a very robust character.

His biographer and one of his close staff officers on the Western Front, General Sir George Barrow, referring to his parental background commented that he 'was Scotch when on duty and Irish when off duty',[3] suggesting a certain formality and stiffness in character, tempered by great imagination and the ability to tell fascinating and captivating stories.

The Monros were, and still are, an illustrious and successful family. Charles' great-uncle, Major General Sir James Carmichael-Smythe, commanded the Royal Engineers at the Battle of Waterloo in 1815. One ancestor, Alexander Munro of Bearcrofts, was on the Royalist side at the Battle of Worcester in 1651, entered Parliament and was knighted. His eldest son, George, took over the estate of Auchenbowie, near Stirling, and had helped defeat the Jacobites at Dunkeld in 1689; he also fought at the siege of Namur in 1695. One of Alexander's other sons, John, was the first of eight generations of extremely successful physicians, helping to establish the Edinburgh University of Medicine. The last of these, another Alexander Monro ('Tertius' as he was the third Alexander), was the future general's grandfather. He became president of the Royal College of Physicians and had twelve children – six boys and six girls.

His fourth son, David, the future general's uncle, was another member of the family who qualified as a doctor of medicine from Edinburgh, but he was to choose politics in New Zealand as his main career. He was eventually the second Speaker of the House of Assembly and was knighted. One of David's seven children, Charles John, was credited with introducing rugby to New Zealand in 1870.

Alexander Tertius' third son, Henry, the future general's father, went to Australia as a 24-year-old in 1834. His first wife, Jane Christie (née Whittle), whom he may have met on the voyage over, died tragically only one year after their marriage. His ten children were borne by his second wife, Kate. Charles was her sixth child. Though Charles was not to be blessed with children, other branches of the Monro family tree have flourished in various professions over the years and bred two major generals in recent times.[4]

The family spent a short time in England and Edinburgh, then moved to St Servan in Brittany, France. Charles and his brother, George, were taught French, an extremely useful skill for the future general on the Western Front. The family was then struck by another tragedy, as the boys' father, Henry, who had headed to Malaga for health reasons, died at the early age of 59. Kate

had to cope with the nine children – the three eldest were old enough to be reasonably independent, however the remaining two sons and four daughters were 15 years old and under.[5] Charles, now 11, and his slightly older brother, George, were sent to public boarding school at Sherborne in Dorset in 1871, a school their three elder brothers had also attended prior to 1867.[6]

Charles Monro, aged 7. (Barrow)

Sherborne School

Sherborne School was to be a safe and natural second home for the boys. The school had been founded under the auspices of King Edward VI in 1550 and still has the motto '*Dieu et mon droit*' (God and my right). It embodied the best of British traditional privileged education and was used to producing future army officers for the Empire. As one of the school's histories states, 'The Crimean War and the Indian Mutiny passed by the school without visible memorial; yet twenty Shirburnians served in the former and twenty-four in the latter, and six of them lost their lives.'[7]

A sense of duty would have been drilled into the boys. This, together with a high level of discipline, were strong characteristics of Charles Monro, as commented on by both Field Marshal Herbert Plumer and George Barrow in later years.[8] Barrow quotes that Charles had 'a smile for everyone' at school and enjoyed cricket, though he does not seem to have particularly thrived academically. He goes on to say, 'There was nothing in Charles Monro's boyhood to mark him as likely to outstrip any of his contemporaries in the race of life.'[9] That may be true, but the circumstances of one's upbringing and experiences at school provide a foundation that affects everyone's destiny.

Charles and George had arrived at Sherborne at a time when its most legendary reforming headmaster, Hugo Harper, was running the school. He made considerable improvements to the education, both in standards and variety of subjects, whilst expanding the real estate and its size. The curriculum was modernised, the three-term system instigated and science was introduced for the first time. By the time Harper left in 1877, after twenty-seven years in post, there were 248 boarders and eighteen staff and the school was ranked one of the best public schools in the country. When he died in 1895, the School History quoted *The Educational Review*, describing Harper as 'the last of the really great headmasters of this century'. One of his wider and longest lasting achievements was helping to establish an independent universities examination board.[10] It is doubtful whether the two boys would have appreciated all this, but they would have benefited.

We do know that Charles and George were pupils in School House, like their three brothers.[11] The 'house' was very much the close family within the school, as it is today.[12] Sherborne now has eight houses, including School House, which was established in 1860, the same year that the railway came to Sherborne town.

Conditions were spartan by today's standards. School accommodation that was adequate for 300 boys at the time of Charles' stay 'was stigmatised as not good enough for 200 in 1901',[13] and the ninety boys of School House shared only four baths. Internal lighting was dim and hot water was scarce. Discipline was tough and often meted out by the senior boys, there were no trained matrons and only limited medical support at hand. One had to be strong to survive these conditions, but the environment was normal for Charles' strand of society and there are no known references to him being unhappy.

The public school system provided the perfect and typical upbringing for a future senior army officer from the Victorian and Edwardian eras. The emphasis was on producing 'gentlemen'. As Moore-Bick's excellent analysis of junior officers on the Western Front states:

> Gentlemen were a social elite, identified by precise codes of deportment and conduct. The deferential way in which they were typically treated was balanced by the expectation that they would conform to those standards. Their supposed moral standing and innate authority meant that gentlemen were seen as naturally suited to leadership roles. [14]

Charles Monro was proud of his connection with Sherborne School and the school magazine proudly tracked his progress through the army. He returned to the annual 'Commemoration', or Speech Day, in 1921. The Bishop of Dover preached from the words, 'Behold I make all things new' and acknowledged that the post-Great War audience 'wanted this England – which they loved more than ever because of the sacrifices made for it – to be a better England and the world to be a better world'. General Sir Charles Monro, who was handing out the prizes, was typically more practical after watching physical training and horsemanship skills; the *Western Gazette* reported:

> General Monro impressed the value of physical training, not only for the development of the body, but as a means of inculcating qualities of leadership. The combination of intellectual activity and physical health and energy would, he said, produce that good all-round citizen of which the Empire never stood in greater need than at the present time. [15]

The emphasis on recruiting potential officers from public schools continued well into the First World War, as the experience was seen to provide a 'social passport' and breed appropriate leadership. However, Sherborne School was not one of the main providers of officers to Sandhurst. During the period from 1878 to 1899, most came from Eton, Bedford Grammar School, Harrow, Clifton, Wellington, Winchester, Cheltenham and the United Services School at Westward Ho! [16] Also, most of the boys' fathers were army officers, unlike the Monros. The system of recruiting officers may have suited the period, but does not escape criticisms from later historians. Barnett wrote that as a result of the system 'the control of the Army remained in the hands of men out of touch with, and out of sympathy with, the social and technical changes of the age'.[17]

At these schools, paternalistic concern for others was encouraged, but professionalism appears to be less important than contacts and personality; a person's character was critical. Sherborne School's move away from just teaching the classics and encouraging sport, to introducing the sciences was relatively radical for the times. There was little radical social change when Charles Monro was at school, but professions were beginning to alter their recruitment policies and open greater opportunities for the middle classes in Britain's main institutions; the armed forces, Parliament and the Church. For example, the year that Charles began school, 1871, was the same year that the Cardwell Reforms included the abolition of the purchase of army commissions, so even the military system was changing, albeit slowly.

Robbins has analysed the background of 700 senior officers who served on the Western Front at the higher levels of the army in the First World War. Charles Monro, like most of the others, was born in the period 1854–94, with an Anglo-Saxon, Protestant and professional background. Fellow divisional commanders in 1914 were all within six years of Charles Monro's age and had been schooled at similar institutions to Sherborne School – Eton (Charles Fergusson), Haileybury (Hubert Hamilton) and Marlborough (Henry Wilson), for example. Robbins reinforces the point that 'the British Army's elite shared an Establishment and Victorian upbringing, which provided a common social background and elaborate social ties'.[18] Old established families like the Monros continued that tradition of service.

It is not known whether the two brothers had much choice but to join the army, however the next step for Charles and his brother, George, was an army 'crammer' run by the Reverend G. Brackenbury at Wimbledon. It seems remarkable that, after the high-quality education at Sherborne, a crammer was needed. However, the extra effort was reluctantly required by most candidates for officer training: 'Detested by universities and colleges, despised by those parents who paid his fees, and scorned often by those who sat under him, the crammer none the less despatched many a famous soldier and empire-builder on the way to immortality.'[19] English history, German, French and Latin, mathematics, drawing and geometry were the subjects covered.[20]

Despite comments by many authors of the amateur nature of Victorian soldiering, this was not the attitude of Captain G. J. Younghusband in 1891: 'To be a successful soldier requires just as much application and hard work as to be a successful lawyer; and the earlier a young fellow realises the importance of this hard fact, the more likely he is to succeed.'[21] He extolled the value of crammers, saying that they gave 'boys five times as much individual tuition and made them work twice as hard as they had had to at school'.[22]

The extra individual attention was seen to be worth the effort. Winston Churchill and the future General Sir Hubert Gough went to Captain James 'Jimmy', a retired Royal Engineer in Kensington, for their crammer; Lord Kitchener went to Mr George Frost at Greenwich. The future General Sir Ian Hamilton, whom Charles Monro would later succeed at Gallipoli, went to Captain Lendy at Sunbury.[23]

Charles Monro passed the examinations and entered the Royal Military College, Sandhurst, on 1 September 1878.

Sandhurst

Today, all British Army potential officers are trained at Sandhurst. This was not the case in 1878; future Royal Engineers and Royal Artillery officers attended the Royal Military Academy, Woolwich, whilst all other branches had their officers trained at the Royal Military College, Sandhurst. Candidates for the latter establishment had to be aged between 17 and 20, younger than today's recruits.

Captain Younghusband had strong views about which institution provided the best future, though his comment would not be appreciated by modern sappers and gunners:

> It is almost as hard for a 'Sapper' or a 'Gunner' to become a brigadier-general as it is for a camel to go through the eye of a needle. They are both specialists, and a life of specialism is judged to be, rightly or wrongly, an indifferent training for a man who has to command large bodies of men in the future.[24]

It should be noted that at the time of writing, the Chief of the General Staff is a sapper! Even 'The Story of Sandhurst' booklet, issued to the author 100 years later, states, 'The RMA (Woolwich) generally attracted Gentlemen Cadets slightly lower in the social scale than the RMC (Sandhurst), for the reason that the Artillery and Engineers tended to be less fashionable than the Line (Infantry).'[25]

One hundred and fifty gentlemen cadets were admitted to Sandhurst in September 1878, including Charles. His brother, George, was on a slightly earlier course.[26] Charles joined other cadets, who had arrived in May of the same year and would pass out in December. They 'were divided into ten divisions of thirty each, with five instructors (as commanders) and five under-officers'.[27]

Royal Military College, Sandhurst. (Author's collection)

The course was for one year – eight months of work divided into three terms. The syllabus included, 'Queen's Regulations, regimental interior economy, accounts and correspondence, military law, elements of tactics, field fortifications and elements of permanent fortifications, military topography and reconnaissance and riding'.[28] Remarkably, 'musketry was an optional subject until 1892', however riding was critical.[29] Unofficial activities were described as 'some bullying, some ragging, some drinking, some learning', and long-term friendships were made.[30]

Charles Monro's report is not in the Sandhurst archives, but Barrow records that he did not set the world alight whilst he was there. He was known for unpunctuality and 'rather below the average of the cadet at his time'.[31] He is reported as being a poor horse rider, but Barrow states that he was captain of the cricket team. Evidence for the latter achievement cannot be found, though he was certainly in the team – in the Sandhurst versus Woolwich match of 4 July 1879, C. C. Monro was bowled out by Crampton for a duck![32]

The future general passed out very near the bottom of his intake at the 120th position, on 13 August 1879, unlike his future corps commander, Douglas Haig, who was commissioned top of his intake six years later, earning the Anson Memorial Sword.[33] Thomas records that the only notable event at Sandhurst in that year was the opening of the new chapel, which still exists today.[34] Monro had not peaked early in his military career and this story shows how one should not write people off when they are young.

His age group was to be an important one; as Thomas pointed out, 'the men of the late seventies and early eighties were the strategists, army or corps commanders, who were to pass the First World War at general headquarters'.[35] In the meantime, Charles Monro was commissioned as a second lieutenant into 1st Battalion, the Queen's (Second) Royal Regiment. It is recorded that the commanding officer, Lieutenant Colonel Francis Hercy, was a friend of the family.[36]

An interesting year in which to be commissioned, in 1879 Charles would have followed the fortunes of Lieutenant General Chelmsford as he invaded Zululand in that January. There followed the British disaster at Isandlwana on the 22nd, and the unfortunate death in the war of the French Prince Imperial, Louis Napoleon, whilst serving with the Royal Artillery in June. Better news from that front would have arrived in England just before his commissioning, as the incredibly brave action of Rorke's Drift was fought, earning eleven Victoria Crosses for the army and the decisive battle against the Zulus was won at Ulundi. In the same year, another South African conflict, the 'Gun War', was being fought in Basutoland, and in India the Second Naga Hills Expedition was taking place. Meanwhile, the Second Afghan War was being fought and Kabul was occupied in October, followed by the forced resignation of the Emir Mohammed Yakub.

At home, Gilbert & Sullivan's *HMS Pinafore* received its debut and Oxford University accepted its first female degree students. Whilst a great deal was going on within the Empire, Second Lieutenant Charles Monro was to start his career inauspiciously, in the garrison town of Colchester.

Regimental Duty

He was joining a proud regiment to which, as a general in much later years, he would be appointed 'Colonel of the Regiment'. The 1st Battalion had fought during 1838–39 in the First Afghan War, but last had operational experience during 1860 with the war in China, fighting with distinction at Taku Forts. It had only been in Colchester a few months when Charles Monro joined, having just returned from thirteen years in India. The 2nd Battalion was in Bengal, India, but was later to become involved in the Third Burma War. Recruits for both organisations were trained at the brigade depot in Guildford, Surrey.

The regiment had been raised on Putney Heath in 1661, as the Tangiers Regiment in order to garrison Tangier in North Africa, which had passed to the British Crown as part of Catherine of Braganza's dowry upon marrying King Charles II. It was extremely proud of being England's senior infantry regiment of the line, taking seniority after the Guards regiments and

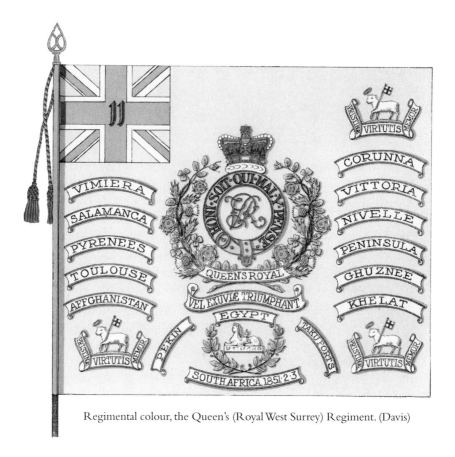

Regimental colour, the Queen's (Royal West Surrey) Regiment. (Davis)

becoming the 2nd Foot – the 1st Foot were the Royal Scots.[37] It had served with distinction around the world and gained a number of battle honours, including Tangier (1662–80), Namur (1695), Afghanistan (1839), South Africa (1851–53), Taku Forts and Pekin (1860).

Its Peninsular War experience took place between 1811 and 1814; it included Vimiera, Corunna, Salamanca, Vittoria, Pyrenees, Nivelle and Toulouse. It had also helped put down the Duke of Monmouth's rebellion in 1685, the rebellion in Ireland four years later and had served on ship as marines in the naval Battle of the Glorious First of June, in 1794 off Ushant. Charles Monro would have learned the regiment's two mottoes, *Pristinae Virtutis Memor* (remembering their gallantry in former days) and *Vel Exuviae Triumphans* (even the spoiled have their hour of triumph).

The badge of the regiment was the Paschal Lamb. There is no genuine recorded historical reason for this emblem. It is claimed that it was adopted as a Christian symbol in the fight against the Moors at Tangier. Another distinction was the cipher of Queen Catherine – two 'Cs' interlaced, with a crown over it. This badge was displayed on the regiment's unique third colour.[38] The colours also displayed the Sphynx, superscribed 'Egypt', to commemorate the regiment's participation in the Egyptian campaign of 1801.

Cap badge, the Queen's (Royal West Surrey) Regiment. (Author's collection)

It is important to mention these badges and regimental heritage, as it was amongst this tradition and unique 'tribe' that Charles Monro gained his initial experience in the army. The regiment and its brother officers and soldiers would help set his standards and professionalism in future years. He had joined a unique 'band of brothers' with their own particular *esprit de corps* within the regimental system.

This system has altered over the years and received both negative and positive comment. At its best, it promotes unit cohesion and motivation in battle. This is brought about by fostering a sense of loyalty and developing an obligation to a corporate identity and reputation. This would have been particularly acute in Charles Monro's battalion after its long service together overseas, its fine history and traditions. This sense of belonging, sharing common experiences, continuity and regional connections providing a focus for recruiting, traditions and *esprit de corps* are acknowledged attributes for a regiment as much today as they were then. However, there was, and still is, the danger that people's potential and initiative are not capitalised within such a small insular organisation, which can be inflexible and generate inefficient rivalry between units.[39]

As a young subaltern, Charles Monro was about to see significant changes to this system as a result of the Cardwell-Childers reforms to the British Army, which were implemented from 1870 to 1881. These were described as 'the first in the century to amount to a root and branch reorganisation of the British Army'.[40] Some changes had already occurred just before he joined the army, as more battalions became based at home, the drafting methods were improved and length of regular service for soldiers had been reduced from ten years to six years, followed by six years in the Army Reserve; this established a regular reserve for the first time. Thus, just under two years after his commissioning, his regiment's two battalions became 'county regiments' alongside the rest of the infantry of the line. This involved a slight name change, so his unit became 1st Battalion, the Queen's (Royal West Surrey) Regiment, establishing a special relationship with the county of Surrey.

Cardwell divided the country into sixty-six brigade sub-districts, each of which had a depot and two regular battalions, one of which would normally be abroad.[41] Recruits were to be primarily taken from an allocated territorial region and the training depot was located within the same area. For Charles Monro's regiment, this was to be the county of Surrey with the depot at Stoughton Barracks, Guildford. Each regiment was allocated a militia battalion and one or more volunteer battalions (the equivalent of today's Territorial Army/Army Reserve). For the two Queen's (Royal West Surrey) Regiment battalions, this meant joining with the 3rd Militia Battalion and four volunteer battalions – the 1st at Croydon, the 2nd based at Guildford, the 3rd in Bermondsey and the 4th in Southwark.[42] Regulars and militia received their initial training at the Guildford depot. The regular soldiers then joined the home 1st Battalion which was responsible for providing drafts to the linked 2nd Battalion overseas in India.

The changes in the army were not perfect, as they rarely are; the home battalions were not necessarily happy with their role and sometimes shunned their new relationship with the militia and volunteers. The shorter lengths of service were not ideal for overseas, and home battalions that had to be deployed abroad in an emergency still had to take recruits from outside their areas.[43] Lord Roberts was to blame the developing new recruiting system for the concentration of too many young and immature recruits sent to Zululand in 1879. However, territorial connections were established that still exist today and this helped generate cohesion within regiments.[44] 'The distinguishing points of the new army were short service and a Reserve, linked battalions, and localization of half the Army in Britain.'[45]

'Professionalisation' was one of the reasons for the various changes going on around Second Lieutenant Charles Monro. Whilst the purchase of officers' commissions had ceased in 1871, in 1881 Childers was improving non-commissioned officers (NCOs) 'pay, prospects and pensions'.[46] Corporals were to be able to extend their service, in stages, to twenty-one years and gain a pension, whilst sergeants were able to serve the same length of time, were guaranteed a pension and were given separate accommodation. Junior NCOs became responsible for discipline in barrack blocks for the first time and the most senior NCOs, the regimental sergeant majors and regimental quartermaster sergeants gained a new status as intermediary ranks between NCOs and officers.

Simultaneously, compulsory retirement ages and set pensions at those ages were introduced for officers, and more field officers, specifically majors, were established in units to encourage junior officers' aspirations for promotion. Childers also introduced an Army Act to improve and modernise disciplinary procedures. Charles Monro was learning his trade at a time of

Second Lieutenant Monro (standing, fourth from the right) with 1st Battalion Queen's, Colchester, c. 1879/80. (Surrey History Centre. QRWS 2-13-2-5)

great modernisation in the army, though service based in the quiet garrison town of Colchester for nearly three years must have been a little frustrating compared with imperial soldiering elsewhere in the world.

Lieutenant Colonel Thomas Kelly-Kenny took command of the 1st Battalion, the Queen's (Royal West Surrey) Regiment in 1882 just as this major army reorganisation was still taking place.[47] He had seen operational service in the China War of 1860 and in the Abyssinian Expedition of 1867–68 and had a successful career leading to the very senior appointment of adjutant general in 1901. Charles Monro seemed to flourish under his tutelage as, despite his poor Sandhurst results, after two years he was appointed adjutant, the key staff officer within his battalion. This post was, and still is, the right-hand man to the commanding officer. Thomas Kelly-Kenny must have liked what he saw, as Charles Monro was to serve again as one of his key staff officers in the Boer War, when Kelly-Kenny was a divisional commander.

The battalion was sent to Ireland in 1883, where it remained at various locations for the next seven years. This period of its history is not marked by any significant events, though some aspects of the British Army's role in the country do not appear to have changed much from modern times. According to this quotation from the battalion's deployment to Belfast in 1886, 'Here they were employed for several months in the difficult and unpleasant duty of piqueting the streets to prevent disturbances between the Orangemen and the Nationalists.'[48] One soldier was murdered by a revolver bullet 'by mistake'.

Meanwhile, Charles Monro relinquished his adjutancy in July 1886 and was selected for the Staff College entry in February 1889 after ten years of relatively quiet soldiering in England and Ireland.

The Staff College

To be selected for the Staff College, Camberley, which was in the same grounds as the Royal Military College of Sandhurst, was a major step forward for Charles Monro. Attendance on the two-year course was increasingly being seen as important for higher command, though not essential. A student could have had a steady and perhaps nondescript military career up to that point, but with a good performance at the Staff College behind them the opportunities were opened up for a more rewarding future.

Not everyone in the army thought that this elitist and professional approach was necessarily the right way to develop a career. Some regiments were not keen on sending their officers on the course, so Lord Allenby, for example, 'was the first officer of the 6th Inniskilling Dragoons to go there – in 1896', just seven years after Charles Monro.[49] Charles Monro's biographer, Barrow, who also attended the 1896 course along with the future Field Marshal Sir Douglas Haig, commented about the attitude of his own commanding officer, who was:

> ... one of the many senior officers of those days who, having an unreason-able antipathy to the Staff College, regarded the staff with hostility, labelled all who were entitled to the letters Passed Staff College (PSC) after their names as Staff College pundits, and considered polo, hunting, shooting and a knowledge of drill all the education necessary to produce a thoroughly efficient officer.[50]

Attendance was not essential for future high command, but it helped. Robbins points out that in the First World War General Sir Henry Horne 'would be the only gunner to command an army in France but also the only one of the ten Army Commanders not to have passed Staff College'.[51]

There were normally thirty-two spaces on the course each year, so sixty-four students were in the college at any one time. For the February 1889 intake, twenty-eight were awarded by competition, including four for the Royal Artillery, two for officers of the Royal Engineers, three for the Indian Army and one Royal Marine.[52] Charles Monro gained one of the eighteen competition vacancies designated to the cavalry and infantry combined. The remaining four places were nominations.

For most candidates, commanding officer's reports were critical, alongside successful examination results. Charles Monro passed his exam in June 1888, though sixteen of the sixty-eight applicants failed. He scored 2,655 points, earning the creditable sixteenth highest mark out of the fifty-two who did pass and proving his intelligence.[53] The subjects tested were mathematics, fortification, military topography, tactics, a language (French, German or Hindustani), military history, geography and military law.

The average age of students at the Staff College was 30 years old and most were captains or promoted captain whilst on the course. On entry, Charles Monro was a 28-year-old lieutenant who received his promotion to captain on 24 July 1889.

There were two terms in each year and during the Easter and summer leaves battlefield study tours on the Continent took place. The curriculum consisted of military art and history, fortification and artillery, field fortification and minor tactics, military administration and staff duties, military topography, reconnaissance and practical field work, military law, a modern language (French or German were compulsory for the British Army students, Hindustani for the Indian Staff Corps; Russian was also an option), natural sciences and, of course, riding. Sport was encouraged, particularly the college drag hounds, coach driving, squash, golf, boating, polo and cricket. Charles Monro certainly played for the cricket XI, as proven by an existing picture in the Staff College archives, and Barrow and Godwin-Austen state that he was their captain.[54]

Younghusband had clear views about the importance of balancing academic studies and sport:

> Every manly sport, and pastime, is thoroughly encouraged, and supported; on the admirable principle that no man can have clear head, and steadfast nerves, unless he is in sound health, and excellent bodily training, a consideration which is often overlooked in the modern craze for competitive examinations.[55]

Monro was an active proponent of this philosophy, both in riding and cricket.

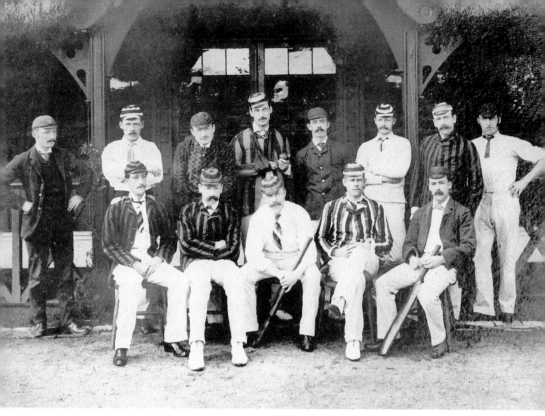

Staff College cricket, 1889. Monro is seated, second from the left. (Defence Academy Archives)

Once graduated, officers were then attached to unfamiliar branches of the army for four months. Quite a lot of the study was practical, though perhaps at too low a level, and there were two main sets of exams – one at the end of the first year and one at the end of the course. For example, the military topography exam in the second year included:

Rapid Sketch on horseback – 100 marks available.
Field Sketch, and making use of maps on the ground – 100 marks.
Theoretical Paper, embracing the whole subject – 100 marks.[56]

Reconnaissance abilities were important in those days, as now, but technology was limited. Without high-quality cameras or electronic gadgetry, intelligence in the field usually relied on verbal line-of-sight reporting supported by hand-drawn sketches.

The commandant of the Staff College during Charles Monro's time was Brigadier General Cornelius Francis Clery, who held the post from 1888–93. He was also an infantryman, who had seen active service in the Zulu War of 1879, Egypt in 1884 and the Sudan in 1884–85.[57] Although he had written a book on minor tactics, he has been described as 'a distant character who was only rarely seen by the students'.[58]

The main professor in military art, history and geography was Colonel John Frederick Maurice, who had assumed the appointment in 1885. He had been commissioned into the Royal Artillery and served as personal secretary to Sir Garnet Wolseley in the Ashanti Campaign of 1873–74. He had also taken part in the Zulu War in 1880 and the Egyptian expedition of 1882. He was chosen as part of the 'Wolseley Ring' for his clear brain, experience and hard work, yet was also known for being absent-minded, impractical and of 'a violently argumentative nature'.[59] However, 'he had a gift for making the subject of military history absorbingly interesting' and encouraged officers to think for themselves and to study military campaigns in depth.[60] Laudably, he wanted his students to establish the facts of a military event and the causes behind those facts and then identify conclusions useful for the future. This analytical approach would put Monro in good stead in later years.

The 'Report on the Final Examinations' at the Staff College, held in December 1891, provides the evidence that Charles Monro passed the final tests.[61] Lieutenant General Biddulph's comments include the list of officers who passed, though Captain Charles Monro is not given any special mention for his performance in any subject, unlike some of the others. An example of a typical comment concerns military topography results:

> The horseback sketches were decidedly the more accurate and reliable, although the attempt to combine rapidity of execution with accuracy and completeness of detail, generally resulted in some sacrifice of the two latter essentials. Captain F. N. Maude, Royal Engineers, executed his sketch in remarkably quick time (four hours and fifteen minutes),[62] but at the expense of both neatness and accuracy; while Captain N. B. Inglefield, Royal Artillery,[63] took twenty-five minutes longer, but at a sacrifice of completeness of detail.[64]

Interestingly, F. N. Maude, who was an outspoken character, later commented adversely on the style of teaching. Despite Colonel Maurice's efforts, Maude believed that 'instead of making the Staff College into a true University, for experimental and original research, we made it a kind of repetition school for the backward'.[65]

The military art and history paper concentrated on questions related to the Franco-German War of 1870, the benefits for and against the use of the rifle or lance by cavalry, the increase of artillery in the German Army and principles of infantry in the attack from 1866 to 1891.

The 1891 graduates were to include one general of the future (Charles Monro), two lieutenant generals (Robert Broadwood and Ernest De Brath) and two major generals (J. H. Poett and Montagu Stuart-Wortley), but they were also mixing with a batch of other future senior officers from the year before and the following course.[66] Charles Monro was, therefore, part of a relatively well-educated elite when he graduated from the Staff College, despite some of the criticisms of its methods. Two years' professional study must have added value to his capability, compared with others who did not receive the opportunity. Brian Bond summed up his findings from comments made by students in the 1880s: 'The general impression of those who were students in the 1880s is that these were two very happy years, that they were of some professional value, but that the work did not make very rigorous demands.'[67]

Colonel John Maurice had worked hard to improve the course and it was to become more practical after Charles Monro's time at the college. More reforms were to take place under the stewardship of the new 'professor', Colonel George Henderson, from 1892, and the new commandant, Colonel Henry Hildyard, from 1893. On handover to Henderson, Maurice stated, 'I am deeply conscious that at present the Staff College produces a monstrous deal of bread for very little sack. The able men benefit greatly but from the ruck we have turned out I fear me some cranks and not a few pedants.'[68]

Field Marshal Sir William Robertson, who had joined the army as a private soldier in 1877 and was appointed the commandant of the Staff College in 1910, had a more positive view of the college's value as an institution:

> Another advantage of the course is that the students are taught the same basic principles of strategy and tactics, and are accustomed to employ the same methods of administration. It is necessary in any business that the men responsible for its administration should abide by the same rules, follow the same procedure, and be fully acquainted with the best means for ensuring smoothness and despatch; and nowhere is the necessity greater than in the business of war, where friction, delay and misapprehension are fraught with so many possibilities of mischief. It is only by the establishment of a sound system with which all officers are thoroughly familiar that these rocks can be avoided.[69]

He goes on to state the importance of a 'common school of training' and the fact that when he became Chief of the Imperial General Staff there was a common understanding between him and different commanders around the world, including Charles Monro in India. He wrote, 'That the mutual agreement and excellent comradeship established between Staff College graduates during the twenty years previous to 1914 were of inestimable value to the Empire throughout the Great War is, in my humble belief, beyond contradiction.'[70]

In a similar vein, Barrow, of the class of 1896 which included a number of future famous commanders, emphasised in his autobiography the importance of the Staff College in creating bonds of understanding and friendship:

> In one other way, combining pleasure and education, the Staff College course has a value not to be found in educational establishments outside the services. It consists in the comradeship of men and diverse characters and opinions but speaking the same professional language, holding the same views on all matters of conduct, and trained in the same school of military honour. Lastly, it is at the Staff College that many a permanent friendship is formed.[71]

Professor Brian Holden Reid's *War Studies Paper* of 1992 is an excellent assessment of the Staff College from 1890–1930, catching the end of Charles Monro's attendance there. Whilst acknowledging that reconstructing what was taught there at a given date is not easy and that there was a lot of criticism in the 1920s about the pre-First World War syllabus, he notes, 'in many ways the heyday of military history at the Staff College' was in the period 1880–1914.[72]

Staff College, 1889–90. Monro is standing, third row up, fifth from the left. (Defence Academy Archives)

British staff officers were not generally criticised for their administrative failures in the First World War, but lack of leadership and an obsession with parochial detail rather than universal strategic analysis. The great military forward thinkers of the 1920s, Captain Basil Liddell Hart and Major General J. F. C. Fuller, criticised the detail. Liddell Hart wrote, 'And the method of study was one of excessive concentration on detail rather than an inquiry into the broad principles of the leader's art and comparison of the great captains of all ages.'[73] And J. F. C. Fuller:

> At present we are controlled, through no fault of its individual members, by a hierarchy which, though autocratic, is sterile. It fears initiative, it is terrified at originality and it suppresses criticism. Thus 'a new spirit' was required at the Staff College, 'the spirit of loyalty to truth'.[74]

Holden Reid deduces that 'these failings clearly reflected the mode of instruction which produced mentally unadventurous graduates' and 'the Staff College produced sound technical staff officers rather than imaginative, reflective commanders'.[75] However, this was not Field Marshal Robertson's view; he was a believer in the need for detail.

It has been necessary to dwell on the Staff College experience, as two years of study for Charles Monro was to critically influence the rest of his career, both for professional reasons and for the personal contacts that he made. The evidence shows that some effort was made to shape intellectually the future high-level commanders of the First World War, which did involve intelligence, initiative and application. Instruction was gradually improving as the years progressed, through the efforts of some key 'professors'. However, there may have been too much of a concentration of low-level tactics and detailed procedures, rather than the practical writing of orders and the wider study at the operational and strategic levels of war. With hindsight it is easy to be critical, and the author, who has been both a student and a teacher at the Staff College, is well aware of how critical bright students can be of any syllabus, no matter how well considered it may be. At this time, the army was generally engaged in small wars where knowing the details of reconnaissance, movement, logistics etc. were seen to be more important than the strategic forward thinking needed for a major European war.

SERVICE OVERSEAS AND OPERATIONAL EXPERIENCE

The time had come for overseas service and operational experience for the 31-year-old Captain Charles Monro. This was, and still is, an essential prerequisite for any future senior commander. Most of his next nine years were overseas, starting with garrison duties in Malta and India, but more excitingly with company command on the Mohmand and Tirah expeditions in the North-West Frontier region of the Indian Empire and then as a key staff officer in the South African Boer War.

He had re-joined his original infantry unit, 1st Battalion, the Queen's (Royal West Surrey) Regiment, and was posted with the other 800 officers and men to Malta at the end of 1892. According to the Regimental History, this was a pretty uneventful three-year garrison posting.[1] He was one of the five battalion captains with limited duties in that environment. However, he was obviously seen as an officer who needed opportunities as he temporarily filled two important roles there, away from

Caricature of Captain Monro, company commander, F Company. (Surrey History Centre. QRWS 1-16-9-4)

the battalion – as a temporary aide-de-camp (ADC) to the governor, and as the acting brigade major to the local infantry brigade commander.[2] Both of these posts were 'right-hand man' appointments, particularly the latter, so he was starting to be given trusted key authority. ADCs do pick up some basic tasks, though, and his initial reaction to that attachment was that he was 'no good at carrying ladies' cloaks'.[3]

India

In February 1895, his battalion arrived at its garrison location in India: Amballa (now Ambala). There were fifty-two British infantry battalions in India at the time, out of a total of 141, and thirteen were in the Punjab command. Ambala is a long way from Surrey. Situated in the far north of India, now in the state of Haryana, bordering with the Punjab, it is still an important Indian Army and Air Force base.

The battalion's eight companies were quickly despatched across the region in order to show presence and keep law and order where necessary. Apart from a short time as brigade major to Brigadier General William Penn Symons, Charles Monro, as one of the company commanders, had a great deal of local authority and independence away from battalion headquarters – the company level of operations was critical.

The Indian Army, which worked side by side with the British Army, was going through a significant reorganisation in the same year his battalion arrived. In October 1895, the new Indian Army was formed, the three old Presidency armies being absorbed later in 1903. It was organised into four new commands: the Punjab, Bengal, Madras and Bombay.

The period 1894–99 in India has been described as 'five years of natural calamities, troubles on the Frontier, and symptoms of political unrest under a weak, colourless Viceroy, Lord Elgin'.[4] An import duty had been imposed back home on Indian cotton in 1894 and there was widespread drought in 1896–97, which mainly affected central provinces but also parts of the Punjab. This famine was later followed by an even worse one in 1899–1900, which affected one-third of the country and resulted in many human lives and cattle lost. In addition, bubonic plague broke out in Bombay in 1896 and spread to parts of the country, including the Punjab – 193,000 people died in India and there was little medical knowledge about its cause or treatment, though it was known that isolation helped stem its advance.[5]

A key political decision was made during this period that still affects politics in the region today; the establishment of the Durand Line, a demarcated boundary between India and Afghanistan. This came about from two joint Afghan and Indian commissions of 1894–96, the Indian Mission being led by Sir Mortimer Durand. For the first time, the no-man's-land between the two countries was formally split. This resulted in different tribes falling into each of the two countries' spheres of influence, though due to the nomadic nature of many of the tribes, the line ended up splitting some of them. At the time, it was thought that this would stabilise the region – it had the opposite effect.

The regiment, like much of the British Army, had experienced service in India before. The 1st Battalion had been there for twenty years from 1825–45, including deployment during the First Afghan War, whilst the 2nd Battalion was in India, including two years in Burma, from 1878–94. This latest tour would last thirteen years, from 1895–1908, though Charles Monro would only be with the 1st Battalion for the first four.

Captain Monro was remembered as a professional, selfless company commander who looked after his men in F Company. He generally had a good boyish humour, but occasionally displayed a fiery temper. He was always sympathetic to subordinates and was not afraid of responsibility.

The British military presence had been adjusted since the Indian Mutiny of 1857. The ratio of British soldiers to Indian was significantly increased, following a recommendation of an 1859 royal commission, which led to 'the maximum reached being 62,000 (British) to 135,000 (Indians)', though 30,000 more troops were available in the 1880s, due to North-West Frontier threats.[6] Also, brigades were deliberately mixed British and Indian units to ensure a 'backbone' of reliability.

Any new weaponry went to the British first and artillery was carefully controlled. For example, the new bolt-action, magazine-fed Lee–Metford rifle, sighted to 2,800 yards and quick firing, was issued to British battalions, whilst the older slower firing single-loading Martini-Henry was the standard Indian infantryman's personal weapon. One relatively new weapon was the Maxim gun, an early machine gun fed by ammunition belts of 250 rounds and sighted to 2,500 yards. One was issued to each British infantry battalion and some cavalry regiments. Eight soldiers looked after each gun, including the immediate three-man crew. Their fire could be very effective, particularly in defensive positions, though they were not very reliable. Even so, they could cause havoc amongst concentrated groups of enemy, leading to the historian Hilaire Beloc writing, 'whatever happens, we have got the Maxim gun, and they have not'.[7] The British did not want a repeat of the Indian Mutiny, so the best weaponry was placed in the most trusted hands.

Life in India's garrisons varied and was easier than conditions earlier in the nineteenth century, when many soldiers and their wives and families succumbed to various diseases at an alarming rate. However, the 1890s famine and plague risks have already been mentioned. Unsurprisingly, the environment still claimed some British victims, often to cholera, typhoid or malaria. Here is one verse from that period:

> We little thought when he left Peshawar
> His race was so near run
> But alas death called him
> Before he did return.[8]

Along with the animated beginning of Kipling's 'Cholera Camp':

> We've got the cholerer in camp – it's worse than forty fights;
> We're dyin' in the wilderness the same as Isrulites.
> It's before us, an' we cannot get away,
> An' the doctor's just reported we've ten more to-day![9]

Efforts had been made to build airier barracks at great cost and soldiers' diets had been better balanced and appropriately supervised in an attempt to improve hygiene and sanitation. In addition, a great deal of sport, including hunting, fishing and pig-sticking, was encouraged to also improve health. Officers, in particular, had unique sporting and hunting opportunities, which reveal how attitudes about wild animals have changed. Lieutenant William Birdwood, a future field marshal who would serve briefly under Charles Monro at Gallipoli in 1915, wrote about his first tiger:

> In those times the Government kept a few elephants at Dehra for transport purposes, and we were occasionally able to borrow these for *shikar* [hunting]. I borrowed one, and set out into the forests with a small party to shoot stag and bear, but reliable news of a 'kill' at once switched me to tiger. From a *machan* [raised platform] in a tree I got sight of the tiger and wounded him, whereupon he got off into cover in the thick jungle. I then transferred myself to the elephant and proceeded to walk up to the wounded beast, with exciting results. The tiger charged. I hit him again with one barrel but missed with the other, and he then sprang on the elephant, seizing the pad with his teeth. Had I had a revolver I could have placed the barrel in his mouth. As it was, I reloaded quickly and despatched him. He turned out to be only a moderate-sized brute with a large forearm, but he certainly gave me more satisfaction than any of the others shot in later years.[10]

Day-to-day temptations in the 'Shiny', as the troops called India, were drink and women. Methodism and the Temperance Movement had grown in

F Company, 1st Battalion Queen's, Dagshai, 1895. Monro is seated, second row up, centre.
(Surrey History Centre. QRWS 2-13-3-17)

strength, including the Army Temperance Association set up by Lord Roberts, and coffee and tea rooms were established in barracks. However, alcohol was cheap and prevalent and would, inevitably, lead to trouble. Up until the time of Charles Monro's battalion's arrival in Amballa, there had been regimental brothels, with full health checks, but due to Quaker activists and action by the Women's Christian Temperance Union these were banned, leading to a massive rise in venereal disease. One Quaker had visited 2nd Battalion the Buffs before the change in policy: 'The tents of the government harlots confront the troops from morning to night, separated from their own tents by only a public thoroughfare, without any buildings or trees intervening.'[11]

There was still some confusion about the effects of the sun – sunburn, heat exhaustion and heat stroke. It was an offence to go into the sun without wearing a pith helmet or 'solar topi'. The helmet, adopted in the 1860s, was designed to keep the head cool by providing a space between the top of the head and sunlight, with another gap at the back at the neck. Many people believed that sunstroke was caused by the sun's rays hitting the spine, so a 'spine pad' had to be worn, a lint pad secured by tapes along the spine. In practice, this encouraged prickly heat. Meanwhile, to supposedly help combat cholera, 'flannel cholera belts were issued to be worn round the abdomen'.[12]

Apart from the heat and health hazards, life for the British soldier in India was generally not that arduous. He had a higher standard of living than in England and had a steady workload of training and guarding, with plenty of time to himself, cheap labour to do his chores, lots of sport and not a great deal to spend his money on. The British Army in India very much lived by itself, separated from the local community and living an isolated life with its training, sports and officers' and sergeants' mess activities – described by one historian as 'a village community in exile'.[13] Troops entertained themselves trying to speak 'Soldier Bat', a mixture of Hindustani and English, understood around the cantonments. This tradition of constructing some sentences with the occasional Indian word is still sometimes evident in today's British Army, for example, 'Where is my dhobi [washing]?'

There were also some difficult race relations and, as Barthop comments, 'The soldier of a hundred years ago did not usually consort with Indians, and his attitude towards the indigenous population would horrify today's liberal conscience.'[14]

The ultimate experience of being in India was 'going to war', with some real dangers. For the men of Captain Monro's company, the normal monotony of routine was about to be broken by the excitement of action.

The North-West Frontier

One Regimental History sums up the situation in the North-West Frontier as follows: 'The British Government in India had much the same difficulty with the turbulent North-West Frontier as Hercules had with the Hydra: no sooner had one situation been brought under control than trouble flared up elsewhere.'[15]

The various tribes in the North-West Frontier region of the Indian Empire, now split between Pakistan and Afghanistan, have always been proud, independent and belligerent. They have not wanted to be beholden to anyone. Many were, and are, nomadic, and their homes have been amongst a tangle of inhospitable hills with a few vulnerable routes running through them. The key passes being, from north to south, the Khyber and Kurram, Tochi and Gomal, Bolan and Kojak, linking British India to Afghanistan.

The tribes' various names included, from north to south, Yusufzai, Mamund, Mohmand, Afridi, Orakzai, Turi, Wazir and Mahsud. They were named, collectively, 'Pathans' by the British. This is generally defined today as members of a Pashto-speaking people of eastern Afghanistan and north-west Pakistan, but is not a name or collective grouping that is recognised by everyone, even now.

Officers of 1st Battalion Queen's, 1897. Monro is in the back row, third from left. (Surrey History Centre. QRWS 30WRIGWD-1-12)

The different tribes all had varying reputations. For example, a 'lessons learned' booklet of the 1930s states:

> The people differ less than do the parts they live in. All are men to reckon with. I place the Mahsud highest as a fighter along with the Mamund, a little folk but stark. The Afridi probably comes third – his blood feuds and sectional quarrels make him somewhat less ready to die. But all are apt in war, and taken all in all are probably the finest individual fighters in the east, really formidable enemies, to despise whom means trouble.[16]

The same booklet refers to the tribes' great mobility, even at night, over rocks and boulders, their patience and their camouflage skills, describing them as 'hard as nails'. The advice given to deal with this threat is to be tough and mobile as well, but to make the most of British 'discipline and firepower', combining both for effective fire and movement. Another manual's advice states, 'when fighting against him, troops must keep extremely wide awake and wounded men must never be allowed to fall into his hands'.[17] This was poetically expressed in Rudyard Kipling's final verse of 'The Young British Soldier':

> When you're wounded and left on Afghanistan's plains.
> And the women come out to cut up what remains,
> Jest roll to your rifle and blow out your brains
> An' go to your Gawd like a soldier.[18]

In this campaign, Captain Monro's company was to face the Mohmands, Afridis and Orakzais. From an account of the time:

> Of all the Pathan tribes dwelling on the North-West Frontier of India, the Afridis are the most numerous, powerful, and possibly the most war-like [and] no tribesmen on the North-Western frontier of India are of finer physique or better armed ... They are perpetually at war with each other. Every tribe and section of a tribe has its internecine wars, every family its hereditary blood-feuds, and every individual his personal foes. There is hardly a man whose hands are unstained; every person counts up his murders.[19]

All quite a challenge, perhaps, for an average 20-year-old regimental soldier from Surrey. Discipline and firepower were to be key.

The latest hostilities in the North-West Frontier broke out in the middle of June 1897, with an unexpected ambush on a British political officer and his Indian Cavalry escort in the Tochi Valley, in what was considered a quiet area. A brigade was sent to deal with the situation. This was followed in July by another attack on two forts, Malakand and Chakdara, in the Swat Valley some 200 miles to the north. Both the Tochi and Malakand areas had been garrisoned following previous expeditions, including one to Chitral only two years before.

The Pathans did not appreciate these garrisons or the recent Durand Line, seeing annexation by British India and their independence threatened. More widely, the Muslim world had witnessed the encouraging success of the Turks in their victory over Greece in 1897. Regionally, the Amir of Afghanistan helped to agitate the situation and the powerful local Muslim priests feared a loss of status and succeeded in stirring up antipathy. As a recent Tribal Analysis Center report has stated, there was and still remains resistance to centralised secular control:

> Over a rural, tribal periphery where the uneducated population could be rallied quickly to the support of the emerging opportunist mullahs claim-ing to represent God's will to people prone to believe their messages. Added to the susceptible population, these practised orators frequently claimed a heritage derived from religious, respected ancestors and claimed an ability to perform miracles to demonstrate that they were the 'instruments of God's Will'.[20]

Various names were attributed to these local mullahs, 'Saidullah', 'Lewani Fakir', 'Mullah Mastan', 'the Great Fakir', 'Mad Fakir' or 'Mad Mullah' (not to be confused with the Mad Mullah who fought the British in Somaliland). Saidullah claimed that he had been visited by a long-dead priest who had told him to evict the British from Swat and Peshawar. The same Tribal Analysis Center report claims that this has had a lasting effect, despite his failure, managing to 'inoculate the Pashtuns living there with the belief that their homeland was a special "domain of Islam" requiring defence against occupation by infidels'.[21]

These were influential individuals; the attack on the Malakand Fort involved an assault by 1,000 tribesmen led by a fakir and the enemy force was to rise to 20,000 in the area. However, both the Malakand and Chakdara forts survived the initial attacks and were relieved at the beginning of August, though the minor detachments on the Khyber Pass were swept aside by the Afridis and the town of Peshawar threatened by Hadah Mullah. This was the worst uprising for fifty years.

What of Captain Monro and 1st Battalion the Queen's (Royal West Surrey) Regiment, located at Amballa? The next four and a half months were to be spent on operations; firstly in the Malakand Field Force and later in Tirah. The battalion, under the command of Lieutenant Colonel John Stratford Collins, was to be the only British infantry unit during these actions that was deployed in both regions. As one of the eight company commanders, he is recorded as being particularly conscientious about looking after his soldiers, at the expense of his own comfort. He is said to have had a 'stern sense of discipline' and a strong temper, which was mainly kept under control. As for his company officers, 'any little weaknesses or faults of manner which they possessed were corrected by means of a constant flow of good-humoured chaff'.[22] This was a highly respected officer ready to take his company to war.

The Malakand Field Force

The 800-strong battalion moved from its barracks in Amballa to Jullundur to relieve a battalion of the Buffs on 5 August 1897. On the 10th, it was mobilised, passed through Rawalpindi and Nowshera, where it was issued with camels and then moved to the Malakand Pass. It was joining the reserve brigade, which became the 3rd Brigade of the Malakand Field Force, under the command of Brigadier General J. Wodehouse. By 31 August, it comprised:

1st Battalion the Queen's (Royal West Surrey) Regiment
39th Garwhal Rifles
22nd Punjab Infantry

Number 1 Mountain Battery, Royal Artillery
Number 3 Company, Bombay Sappers and Miners
Two squadrons 11th Bengal Lancers

Major General Bindon Blood and staff. (Hobday)

Major General Sir Bindon Blood. (Hobday)   Brigadier General Wodehouse. (Hobday)

This is a good example of the deliberate mixed balance of British and Indian units within a typical brigade, with the artillery controlled by British troops.

The overall commander of the 12,000-strong Malakand Field Force was Major General Sir Bindon Blood, a very experienced Royal Engineer officer who had served in South Africa, Egypt, Afghanistan and India. He was a descendant of Colonel Thomas Blood who attempted to steal the crown jewels in 1671. He had been canvassed to take a young subaltern, Winston Churchill of the 4th Hussars, on the expedition by both Winston and his mother, Lady Jennie Churchill. Although Major General Blood had no room on his staff, he agreed that Winston Churchill could deploy as a war correspondent. Churchill took up the offer, joined the force and wrote for the *Pioneer* and *Daily Telegraph*. He was also inspired to write and publish a book on the campaign, called *The Story of the Malakand Field Force: An Episode of Frontier War*, in 1898. His motivation for this foray is explained by a letter to his mother:

> I have considered everything and I feel that the fact of having seen service with British troops while still a young man must give me more weight politically – must add to my claims to be listened to and may perhaps improve my prospects of gaining popularity with the country.[23]

A more recent contributor to the *Daily Telegraph*, its defence editor Con Coughlin, has commented, 'The Malakand campaign was the war that made Churchill's name' and it 'was a pivotal moment in Churchill's rise to greatness'.[24] There is no doubt that he gained low-level combat experience, showed bravery, was mentioned in despatches and made his name as an author for the first time. He was to earn greater publicity later in South Africa. In addition, he was to share some of his experiences with 1st Battalion the Queen's (Royal West Surrey) Regiment – Monro's regiment.

The battalion marched along dusty roads in the heat, though often in the cooler nights and sometimes in drenching cold rain as they headed over the mountainous terrain of the Malakand Pass, to Khar and then Chakdara. One obstacle was a 1,500ft-long suspension bridge which would only take one man at a time and therefore took many hours to cross. The 3rd Brigade continued their advance to Sado, the limit of wheeled transport. Intelligence was limited about the ground they were about to cross and there were no detailed maps, so progress was cautious and slow.

The plan against the Mohmands was for Major General Sir Bindon Blood, with the 2nd and 3rd Brigades, to move on Nawagai, ready to enter Mohmand territory from the north on 15 September. Meanwhile, Major General Edmond Elles, based at Peshawar with his force, was to

Durbar with the Mohmand *Jirgahs*. (Hobday)

simultaneously occupy the territory from a different direction, then unite with the other column to carry out punitive action against the tribe. Brigadier General Wodehouse's 3rd Brigade, equipped with camels to carry its supplies, followed the 2nd Brigade, using mules as it advanced.

Logistics were a major consideration as so little was known about the terrain and the availability of water en route. Some success was achieved as they advanced, because the brigade, supported by its political officers, managed to persuade some of the tribal groupings to hand over weapons. Winston Churchill commented on the stoicism of Captain Monro's regiment:

> Not one had fallen by the way. They looked strained and weary, but nothing would induce them to admit it. 'An easy march', they said. 'Should have been here long ago if the native troops had not kept halting'. This is the material for Empire building.[25]

After receiving some minor harassing fire on 12 September, the 3rd Brigade established a camp 1 mile south of the village of Nawagai on 14 September. Elsewhere that night the first substantial attack by tribesmen on the 2nd Brigade was repulsed, but only at the price of 150 casualties. Bindon Blood decided to allow the 2nd Brigade to deal independently with the local enemy, whilst the 3rd Brigade waited at Nawagai for Major General Elles' column to arrive. However, Nawagai became an isolated position in a flat valley, where the Khan was of doubtful loyalty and there was no immediate opportunity for reinforcement. It is no surprise that Captain Monro's soldiers rapidly reinforced their position, 'the trenches being deepened, traverses formed, communications improved, and earth cover arranged so as to give protection against fire delivered from any direction'.[26]

Winston Churchill, who had been with Major General Bindon Blood's column since 2 September, had spent some time with reconnaissance patrols sent out by the 11th Bengal Lancers, experienced meetings (*jirgas* – assembly of elders) with local tribesmen and gathered useful material for his newspaper articles. He had also experienced action on 16 September at Shahi-Tangi, bravely fighting alongside the Buffs and Sikhs of the 2nd Brigade. As a result, he received his mention in despatches.

He often witnessed nineteenth-century 'counter-insurgency' techniques that had nothing to do with the more modern ideas of 'hearts and minds'. The British and Indian forces isolated villages and often removed all of their stored crops and then destroyed the buildings in retribution. As Winston Churchill commented in a letter to a friend, 'After today we begin to burn villages. Every one. And all who resist will be killed without quarter.' In contrast, he also told his mother about the enemy tribesmen, 'they kill and

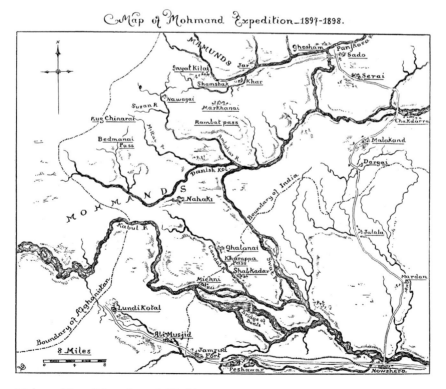

Mohmand Expedition, 1897–98. (Davis)

mutilate everyone they catch and we do not hesitate to finish their wounded off'.[27] In addition, he commented on the effectiveness of the 'dum-dum' bullet in British hands. The bullet expanded on contact with a body, increasing the size of the exit wound; only a year later, the German Government brought pressure to bear against this type of bullet, calling it inhumane and excessive and against the laws of war. The dum-dum bullet was banned for use in war by the Hague Convention of 1899, but was very effective against the tribesmen in this campaign.

The 11th Bengal Lancers sent out another patrol from Nawagai on 17 September. Contact with the enemy was made and some friendly casualties taken, and 1st Battalion the Queen's (Royal West Surrey) Regiment and an artillery mountain battery were despatched to aid their extraction – a successful three-hour operation. Once returned from their foray the battalion lost a soldier the following night to a swordsman, one of the regimental histories commenting that he was 'probably looking for a night latrine'.[28]

Some 3,000 Mohmand tribesmen formed up to threaten the 3rd Brigade at Nawagai on 19 September. They made a great deal of noise and poured derision at the defending force, whose artillery fired at them but had no effect as they were out of range. Enemy sniping continued that evening and one of the battalion's soldiers was wounded during what was referred to as the 'little' night attack. Star shells were fired by 1 Mountain Battery to help illuminate enemy firing positions.

The main enemy assault was to occur the following day and fortunately there was some sound intelligence obtained by the brigade's political officers warning of the attack. The troops prepared bonfires, 100ft from the trenches, to light the area as it became dark, whilst piquets were placed in dips in the ground 50 yards in front of the defensive position, to provide early warning of any trouble. This started at 2030 hours, as the bonfires were lit and enemy musketry fire began:

> On the first fire being lighted, a heavy discharge of musketry opened from three sides of the camp from every bit of rising ground and cover within reach. Tents were struck at once, and volleys and star shell began, with occasional rounds of case by the battery into the *nullah* (ravine or gully), where the enemy swordsmen collected for their rushes.[29]

The firing continued until 0230 hours and there was a series of determined enemy assaults on three sides of the position, though most of their attention was directed at the Queen's in the south-west corner, who had the greater firepower and effect with their dum-dum bullets. Perhaps the tribesmen surmised that if they could break the sole British battalion, they could take the

Nawagai Fort and village. (Hobday)

Night attack on the camp of the Queen's, 20 September 1897. (Davis)

Night attack at Nawagai, 19 September.
(Hobday)

No 1 Mountain Battery, Nawagai.
(Hobday)

position. Winston Churchill, who was in the camp, commented that success
was ensured by the fast-firing, magazine-fed Lee–Metford rifles and provides
a vivid description of the performance by Captain Monro's battalion and its
steadiness under attack:

> The fire of the British was, however, crushing. Their discipline was admi-
> rable, and the terrible weapon with which they were armed, with its
> more terrible bullet, stopped every rush. The soldiers, confident in their

power, were under perfect control. When the enemy charged, the order to employ magazine fire was passed along the ranks. The guns fired star shell. These great rockets, bursting into stars in the air, slowly fell to the ground shedding a pale and ghastly light on the swarming figures of the tribesmen as they ran swiftly forward. Then the popping of the musketry became one intense roar as the ten cartridges, which the magazine of the rifle holds, were discharged almost instantaneously. Nothing could live in front of such a fire. Valour, ferocity, fanaticism, availed nothing. All were swept away. The whistles sounded. The independent firing stopped, with machine-like precision, and the steady section volleys were resumed. This happened not once, but a dozen times during the six hours that the attack was maintained.[30]

Whilst the transport drivers sheltered behind the battalion's lines, some of the enemy musketry fire was directed at the command tents in the centre of the area. Unfortunately, at about midnight, Brigadier General Wodehouse was wounded in the leg and during the night 120 animals were killed or injured. The attacks were all repulsed at the expense of one man killed and nearly thirty wounded; the dead soldier and three of the wounded belonged to the battalion. Two hundred enemy bodies were found, though their total casualties were assessed at about 700. Major General Sir Bindon Blood also commented on the battalion's success:

> The steadiness of the troops during this somewhat trying action was quite perfect, and the safety of the camp was never in the slightest degree doubtful, though the enemy's swordsmen were so determined that many of them were shot down close to the entrenchment. The fire discipline of the infantry was shown to be excellent, especially that of the Queen's, under Lieutenant Colonel Collins, who are, in all respects, an example of what an infantry battalion should be.[31]

The battalion was proud of its achievement, especially as the success at Nawagai seemed to break the back of the Mohmand's offensive spirit, 'taking the heart out of the enemy'.[32] The victory was followed by an advance that secured the mountainous Bedmanai Pass.

After a number of punitive skirmishes, during which the local violence was suppressed and the battalion had two more men wounded, 1st Battalion the Queen's (Royal West Surrey) Regiment was redeployed to Peshawar, following its six weeks of marching, to join the Tirah Expeditionary Force. Total casualties in the battalion were three killed and four wounded.

Tirah Expeditionary Force

The new enemy, the Afridis and Orakzais, were a more determined and numerous enemy than the Mohmands and needed a greater force to defeat them. Around 50,000 tribesmen could be mustered and it was to be a few months before their humiliating seizure of the Khyber Pass forts and the capture of 50,000 rounds of small-arms ammunition at the Landi Kotal outpost could be avenged.

An example had to be made to dissuade other tribes from revolting. The Tirah Expeditionary Force was placed under the command of Lieutenant General Sir William Lockhart, who had 'unrivalled experience of hill warfare'.[33] He was an Indian Army officer who had experience from various campaigns including Bhutan, Abyssinia, Hazara, the Second Afghan War and the Third Burma War. He had even had responsibility for the security of the Khyber Pass in his career, so this was, theoretically, the right commander for the task, though Miller has unkindly described his character as 'a rather colourless, deadpan, ramrod product of the Victorian military mould'.[34]

His orders came from army headquarters in Simla:

> The general object of this expedition is to exact reparation for the unprovoked aggression of the Afridi and Orakzai tribes on the Peshawar and Kohat borders, for the attacks on our frontier posts, and for the damage to life and property which has thus been afflicted on British subjects and on those in British service. It is believed that this object can best be attained by the invasion of Tirah, the summer home of the Afridis and Orakzais, which has never before been entered by a British force.[35]

The Tirah terrain and the enemy were to be a challenge. The landscape was even more rugged than that experienced by the Malakand field force, 'It was a land of narrow gorges and steep declivities, of jagged hill-tops and hidden nullahs.'[36] Any communication and logistic activity, including dealing with the wounded, was extremely difficult and a large number of the enemy were equipped with accurate breech-loading rifles.

The campaign was described as 'the first example of regular troops engaging in operations against savage antagonists armed with modern weapons of precision'.[37] Many of the Afridis, who were recorded as being 'hardy, alert, self-reliant, and active, full of resource, keen as hawks and cruel as leopards', were also reported as being 'fairly well armed with the Martini-Henry rifle', as well as some Sniders and even a few modern Lee–Metfords.[38]

The tribesmen exploited the mountainous terrain using their excellent fieldcraft skills, whilst their guerrilla 'hit and run' techniques made any decisive engagement and victory by the British and Indian troops very unlikely. Soldiers used to firing volleys at charging swordsmen had a much greater challenge in engaging scattered tribesmen amongst the rocks. Again, detailed maps were not available and intelligence gained locally non-existent.

The largest expeditionary force used in the North-West Frontier was assembled, mainly in the Kohat area. It consisted of two divisions of two brigades each, a line of communication brigade, the separate moving Peshawar and Kurram columns and a reserve Rawalpindi brigade. This amounted to 12,000 British and 23,000 Indian troops and 20,000 Indian followers. It included 10,000 horses and ponies, 15,000 mules and 160 bullocks. In all, 45,000 animals kept the force moving and supplied.[39]

Captain Monro and his battalion had joined Brigadier General Alfred Gaselee's 2nd Brigade of the 1st Division, under Major General William Penn Symons, in October 1897. This was the same Penn Symons Monro had supported as brigade major, two years before. For this campaign, the battalion was grouped as follows:

2nd Brigade
　　1st Battalion the Queen's (Royal West Surrey) Regiment
　　2nd Battalion Yorkshire Regiment
　　2nd Battalion 4th Gurkhas
　　3rd Sikhs
　　Sections A and B of 8 British Field Hospital
　　Sections A and C of 14 British Field Hospital
　　31 Native Field Hospital

Artillery, cavalry and engineers were grouped in supporting divisional troops.

Surgeon Captain A. E. Masters had joined the Queen's Battalion and wrote to his wife:

> I was suddenly ordered to prepare to accompany the Queen's who were to march next day at 7 a.m. We set off by three marches going through some peaceful Afridi country and down here on the third day, settling down for four or five days in camp whilst the brigades were getting together and getting transport, which is to be entirely mule … The actual peace garrison here is a very small one, a couple of forts and outlying defensive posts. This regiment has just returned from the Mohmand expedition where they were in the brigade that had five hours of the hottest night firing from the enemy that has been known for a long time in frontier warfare. They seem a very nice lot of fellows.[40]

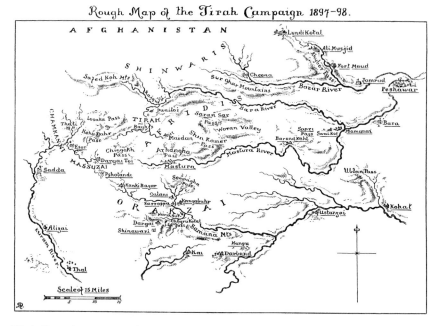

Tirah Campaign, 1897–98. (Davis)

The advance began in October 1897, from Kohat, taking the four-day march to Shinwari, with the 2nd Division leading. The advance had been delayed because of the transport and logistic challenges and the fact that some of the gathering troops, like Captain Monro's battalion, had to be reconstituted after the Malakand expedition. This was Afridi territory, but the locals had been paid to keep the Kohat Pass open.

Intelligence had suggested that the Afridis and Orakzais were going to make a stand at the Sempagha Pass, beyond Shinwari. However, it soon became evident that the enemy had also placed themselves in forward harassing positions at Dargai and Narik Suk. The plan was to drive the enemy off these two positions on 18 October. The attack was mainly conducted by 2nd Division units, and was to be the first significant action by the Tirah Expeditionary Force. This did not include 1st Battalion the Queen's (Royal West Surrey) Regiment, but deserves a mention as the action was seen to personify Empirical heroism.

Dargai was at the end of a small plateau, but in order to reach it an exposed bare ridge had to be crossed using a single track as an axis. The whole area was strewn with rocks, easy for the tribesmen to hide behind, and they were looking down on the ridge. Artillery engaged the enemy as best it could and a frontal daylight attack was launched by the 3rd Gurkhas, the King's Own Scottish Borderers and the Northamptonshire Regiment, as an additional flanking attack was launched.

Dargai was taken with surprisingly few casualties, but it is the attack two days later which is most memorable. Unfortunately, despite the bravery of the first assault, the position had to be abandoned in the face of overwhelming numbers of tribesmen rushing towards the feature and a failure to anticipate the threat. It was not possible to 'seize and hold' the Dargai position with the numbers of friendly troops immediately available. Instead, a withdrawal in contact occurred, resulting in friendly forces losing six killed and thirty-four wounded. Many more of the tribesmen were casualties, but the British had lost ground – and face.

The second attack on Dargai took place on 20 October. This time, more artillery and infantry were brought to bear on the position, which again had a frontal assault launched at it. The 2nd Gurkhas and the Dorsets, Derbyshires and Gordon Highlanders were to feel the brunt of the fighting. The attack began at 1000 hours, as the artillery began their barrage, though it was difficult to bring down accurate fire amongst the rocks. The ridge began to fill with casualties as each battalion tried to move forward under a hail of fire. Two hours later, Brigadier General Kempster was told to take the position at all costs.

The commanding officer of the Gordon Highlanders, Lieutenant Colonel Henry Mathias, is said to have called, 'Highlanders! The general says the position must be taken at all costs. The Gordons will take it!'[41] The Gordon Highlanders and the 3rd Sikhs led this latest assault, as the other battalions were pinned down on the ridge, with 25-year-old Scottish Piper George Findlater reputedly playing either 'Cock o' the North' or 'Haughs of Cromdale'. He was hit in the foot, then the ankle, but carried on playing, propping himself on a boulder under heavy enemy fire. He was to earn the Victoria Cross, along with Private Edward Lawson of the same battalion and Private Samuel Vickery of 1st Battalion the Dorsetshire Regiment. Private Lawson was again wounded twice and managed to rescue an officer and a soldier under fire. Private Vickery also rescued a soldier under fire, then distinguished himself the following month by killing three enemy tribesmen, whilst separated from his company.[42] General Sir William Lockhart commented on the Highlanders:

> The Gordon Highlanders went straight up the hill without check or hesitation. Headed by their pipers and led by Colonel Mathias, with Major Macbean on his right and Lieutenant A. F. Gordon on his left, this splendid battalion marched across the open. It dashed through a murderous fire, and in forty minutes had won the heights, leaving three officers and thirty men killed or wounded on the way.[43]

Dargai was taken, but at a total cost of 193 casualties, including thirty-seven dead. The tenacity and effectiveness of the enemy was not to be underestimated after this first significant and costly action.

The 1st Battalion the Queen's (Royal West Surrey) Regiment was to experience the next major contact in this campaign, at Sempagha Pass. Captain Monro's battalion had reached Dargai, with the rest of 2nd Brigade, 1st Division, two days after the battle. The Regimental History recorded, 'All ranks were in high spirits at the prospect of adding to the laurels gained in the Mohmand country.'[44] As they moved further into enemy territory, they quickly discovered the importance of proper defences at night, as they were continually harassed by sniping fire. They also had a reminder of how the enemy treated captives. On the same night a staff officer lost his arm to the sniping and 'two British soldiers and four native followers were found outside the camp, so cut up as to be quite unrecognisable'.[45]

The attack on Sempagha was planned for 29 October. Sempagha was at 7,000ft, approached by a valley ¾ mile across and overlooked by a series of steep slopes and spurs. The plan was for the 1st Brigade to seize the spurs in order to secure ground for the artillery and protect and support the assault by the 2nd Brigade, supported by the 3rd and 4th Brigades. Lessons had been learned from Dargai; this was to be a more systematic attack, making best use of artillery.

The 1st Brigade successfully secured the flanks for Brigadier Gaselee's 2nd Brigade to advance, alongside the divisional commander. In addition, 1st Battalion the Queen's (Royal West Surrey) Regiment was left centre, 4th Gurkhas to the left, the Yorkshire Regiment to the right centre and 3rd Sikhs far right. As the artillery barrage continued, Captain Monro's battalion was the first up on the enemy's position after a 3,000ft climb. Major Robert Hanford-Flood was commanding the battalion as Lieutenant Colonel Collins was ill. Despite the fact that the tribesmen had prepared sangar positions, they could not withstand the artillery fire of six mountain batteries and assault, so the position was taken by 1130 hours. 'The feebleness of the opposition offered was most unexpected.'[46] There were twenty-four friendly casualties, including one soldier of the Queen's killed and eight wounded, which included the acting commanding officer.

The Tirah Expeditionary Force pushed further into enemy territory. A basic technique when advancing or launching an attack was to ensure that heights around objectives were secured and piqueted. Captain Monro's battalion had this task for the next successful attack on the Arhanga Pass; another officer and soldier were wounded this time.

One of the constant challenges was protecting the many baggage columns going to and from the field force and on 1 November most of the battalion was piqueting the recently captured Arhanga Pass, carrying out this important task. The previous night, the Afridis had successfully ambushed one of those columns; sixty Sikh mules with all their stores were captured and nine drivers killed or wounded. They were, however, partially thwarted on the night of the 1st, when they launched a similar ambush. Though more mules were lost, thanks to the initiative shown by Lance Corporal Simpson of the Queen's the enemy were not as successful as they might have been. He collected a dozen men with their bayonets fixed, established a fire position on a slope and in the dark beat off the Afridis with well-controlled volley fire, described by a Northamptonshire officer as 'so good that the men might have been on inspection parade'.[47] He was promoted sergeant for his coolness and the steadiness of his men. Captain Shadwell reported that:

> It is improbable that the physical damage done by this firing in the dark was very great, but the moral effect was enormous, for it kept other men in good heart, made the tribesmen imagine they were dealing with a much larger body of men than was really the case and greatly tended to lessen the general confusion inseparable from an attack on a convoy in the dark.[48]

The Tirah was now occupied and every effort was made to pacify the two tribes, by demanding monetary retribution and the handing in of weapons whilst simultaneously launching punitive strikes at villages. The Orakzais responded most positively to the negotiations, but the Afridis remained belligerent. The occupying forces, including the Queen's Battalion, continued to be sniped at and some of the units were regularly attacked. On 9 November, a reconnaissance took place of Saran Sar Pass, used as a line of communication by the Afridis; within the participating troops, another twenty-three were killed and forty-four wounded. Two days later, on another reconnaissance of the pass, the Queen's were on a spur covering the withdrawal of the rest of the force, when Lieutenant Wallace Wright was wounded and a private soldier killed.[49]

The battalion was commended for its action that day, reducing casualties within the rest of the brigade because of their accurate fire support. One of the greatest challenges in this form of warfare came when friendly troops withdrew from positions; competent rearguard actions were often the deciding factor on whether each operation had been a success or not.

Unfortunately, elsewhere in the Maidan area on 16 November, waves of tribesmen launched a successful night attack which resulted in heavy casualties for the Dorsetshire Regiment: thirteen killed, including two officers, and eight wounded. The enemy's guerrilla tactics, making the most of their strengths and avoiding the maximum effect of artillery in daylight was successful. This was not an easy campaign, despite the general superiority of friendly firepower. As Colonel Callwell later analysed:

> It was the martial instinct of the Afridis and their excellent arms, which brought into play in a theatre of war presenting unprecedented difficulties to a disciplined army, made the Tirah campaign one of the most dangerous and arduous struggles which British troops have been engaged in since the Indian Mutiny.[50]

As the weather grew cooler, 1st Battalion the Queen's (Royal West Surrey) Regiment became involved in 2nd Brigade punitive operations against villages in various valleys and were next engaged by the enemy on 26 November. This time, Lieutenant Herbert Engledue received the praise. The brigade was coming under fire from a number of snipers, firing from thickly wooded spurs, so they were difficult to identify and dislodge. Lieutenant Engledue launched an effective attack with twenty men, pinning the enemy down with half of them, whilst the remainder outflanked the position. The tribesmen were completely surprised in their sangar by the direction of the assault; his men bayoneted six and shot six, resulting in two killed, the others wounded and the capture of four rifles, though Lieutenant Engledue lost one soldier killed. As a result of this simple action, the brigade was able to move forward unmolested.

The battalion took part in a typical punitive action a few days later in the Chamkani Valley. Winning 'hearts and minds' was not a priority in that period, as already illustrated by the actions of the Malakand field force. Village stores of food were destroyed and buildings burned in reprisal to maintain the coercive nature of the campaign. Attitudes were summed up by Reuter's special correspondent, Lionel James:

> One of the most magnificent sights that one could wish to see was the destruction of that valley by 'fire and sword' as the evening waned into night. The camp was ringed with a wall of fire – byres, outhouses, homesteads, and fortresses one mass of rolling flame, until the very camp was almost as light as day. Then the actual fury of the fire subsided, and the wooden structures of the houses and uprights of the towers stood in outline glowing in the pitchy darkness: a warning to the skulking camp prowler who sneaks up to within the limit of his rage to shoot the sleeping soldier and the harmless camp follower.[51]

December 1897 and January 1898 were relatively quiet for the battalion, but the men had to live uncomfortably in the open amidst rain, sleet and snow.

Officer group, 1st Battalion Queen's, Peshawar, 1898. Monro is the back row, third from the left. (Surrey History Centre. QRWS 30HAMIEO-18-16)

Final negotiations took place with the tribes and the Tirah Expeditionary Force was withdrawn. The jury is probably out concerning the success of the mission. Some reparation had occurred, according to the original plan, and many tribesmen and their families had been punished by the punitive actions. The Orakzais had submitted, but the Afridis had not and the Indian Government had to spend a great deal of money both on the expedition and keeping troops available for further deployment for months afterwards.

Colonel Callwell commented that the final march out of the region by 2nd Division with 'the men all "drawn, pinched, dishevelled, and thoroughly worn" into Swaikot – was in fact far from completely successful'.[52] He believed that eight weeks was not enough time to complete the mission. Winston Churchill had the same sentiments about the Tirah experience, writing to his mother:

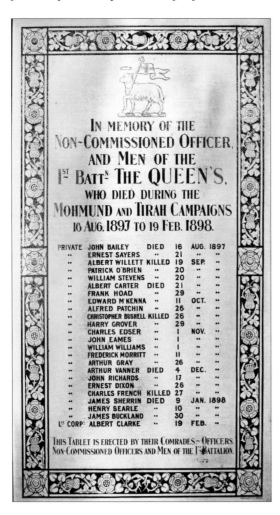

IN MEMORY OF THE
NON-COMMISSIONED OFFICER
AND MEN OF THE
1ˢᵗ BATTᴺ THE QUEEN'S,
WHO DIED DURING THE
MOHMUND AND TIRAH CAMPAIGNS
16 AUG. 1897 TO 19 FEB. 1898.

PRIVATE	JOHN BAILEY	DIED	16	AUG. 1897
"	ERNEST SAYERS	"	21	" "
"	ALBERT WILLETT	KILLED	19	SEP. "
"	PATRICK O'BRIEN	"	20	" "
"	WILLIAM STEVENS	"	20	" "
"	ALBERT CARTER	DIED	21	" "
"	FRANK HOAD	"	29	" "
"	EDWARD M KENNA	"	11	OCT. "
"	ALFRED PATCHIN	"	26	" "
"	CHRISTOPHER BUSHELL	KILLED	26	" "
"	HARRY GROVER	"	29	" "
"	CHARLES EDSER	"	1	NOV. "
"	JOHN EAMES	"	1	" "
"	WILLIAM WILLIAMS	"	1	" "
"	FREDERICK MORRITT	"	11	" "
"	ARTHUR GRAY	"	26	" "
"	ARTHUR VANNER	DIED	4	DEC. "
"	JOHN RICHARDS	"	17	" "
"	ERNEST DIXON	"	26	" "
"	CHARLES FRENCH	KILLED	27	" "
"	JAMES SHERRIN	DIED	9	JAN. 1898
"	HENRY SEARLE	"	10	" "
"	JAMES BUCKLAND	"	30	" "
Lᶜᵉ CORPˡ	ALBERT CLARKE	"	19	FEB. "

THIS TABLET IS ERECTED BY THEIR COMRADES ~ OFFICERS
NON-COMMISSIONED OFFICERS AND MEN OF THE 1ˢᵗ BATTALION.

Memorial to the Queen's.
(Emmanuel Church, Stoughton,
Guildford)

The whole expedition was a mistake, because its success depended on the
tribesmen giving in when their country was invaded and their property
destroyed. This they have not done. We have done them all harm possible
and many of them are still defiant.[53]

The overall friendly casualties since mid-October were nearly 300 dead and
850 wounded; these were seen as high figures for such a short space of time.

What of Captain Monro and his battalion? Fortunately, they had conducted
an ordered withdrawal from the operation. Casualties had been relatively light
compared with some other units, at eight killed and fourteen wounded, and
morale was high. They had never lost a battle and had contributed to a series
of successful actions against the enemy. Major General Symons spoke to the
commanding officer, Lieutenant Colonel Collins, and his men in May 1898:

I cannot permit you and your Regiment to leave the Khyber Force without giving you an expression of my thorough appreciation of your brilliant services since you have been under my command in the field. Whilst you were in cantonments in Amballa, I formed a high opinion of the efficiency of the Battalion. It has been more than justified in the Tirah campaign. No matter what the occasion, whether on piquet duty, foraging, advancing or retiring, we all had sure confidence that if the Queen's were in it there need be no anxiety. The great care taken by the officers of the men, good discipline especially on the march, sound instruction of all ranks in their profession as soldiers, all combine, with esprit de corps, to make you the smartest and best Infantry Battalion that I know.[54]

This was a proud and proficient battalion, which was to gain the battle honour 'Tirah' on its regimental colour. The battalion and its company commander (now Major Monro, having been promoted in February 1898 just before the end of the deployment) had gained a great deal of valuable experience in the two campaigns. It had suffered the rigours of the environment, withstood enemy assaults and demonstrated high levels of discipline and initiative. Major Monro had experienced his first command under enemy fire in India. He had no inkling that he would return to the country as the C-in-C eighteen years later.

His first staff appointment, as brigade major, was to Gibraltar in October 1898. This must have seemed very civilised and quiet compared with his previous operational tour. Indeed, he first met his future wife, the Honourable Mary Townley O'Hagan, on the Rock. Within a year, however, he had served as the deputy assistant adjutant general (DAAG) in Guernsey and then given the same appointment in Aldershot. These were all key posts at his level, working to the senior officer in each location. The DAAG assisted what was the equivalent of a modern deputy chief of staff, primarily responsible for the administration and logistics of all the local units and their headquarters on behalf of the commander.

Excitement and danger were on the horizon again, however, as the South African War began. This time he would deploy as a key staff officer with Headquarters 6th Division, rather than on regimental duty with his battalion.

3

SOUTH AFRICA

The Boer War (1899–1902) between the British Empire and the people Conan Doyle described as 'the most formidable antagonists who ever crossed the path of Imperial Britain', was to significantly influence Major Monro's generation and was to prove a much greater challenge than dealing with the tribesmen of the North-West Frontier.[1]

The Afrikaner Volk were descendants of Dutch, German and French immigrants to South Africa, many of whom had emigrated in the seventeenth century. They were a formidable race, who were determined to keep their independence, particularly within the republics of the Orange Free State and Transvaal, rather than be totally dominated and controlled by the British-occupied South Africa surrounding them. They were a population used to a tough life on the veldt, with excellent survival, marksmanship and horse-riding skills, and they wanted to preserve their way of life.

Animosity between the Afrikaner and the British was deep-rooted; they had already been to war, following the threat of a British-imposed South African Federation within the Empire and a declaration of independence by the Boers in 1880. This had led to an embarrassing defeat for the British at the Battle of Majuba Hill in 1881 and a quickly negotiated peace, which left the Transvaal with a substantial amount of independence and the Boers with a great deal of confidence. This new conflict was, from their perspective, trying to achieve similar results as that 'First War of Independence'.

Since the First Boer War, two activities had threatened the peace. One was the imperial ambition of Cecil Rhodes, prime minister of Cape Colony, with his diamond mining interests in Kimberley, and the other was the discovery of gold in the Transvaal. The latter generated a huge influx of *uitlanders* (foreigners/outlanders), as the Boers called them, into the Transvaal, creating what they thought was a threat. The *uitlanders*, who started to outnumber local Boers and demand concessions, had many restrictions placed upon them, being denied the rights of full citizens, yet the Boers were making enormous amounts of money from their taxes. This helped to generate further animosity. Meanwhile, in 1895, the Cecil Rhodes' inspired Jameson Raid had not generated an *uitlander* uprising as intended, but had created even more distrust between the two sides and generated further support to the Boers from Germany.

As the Boer republics became increasingly threatened, more and more arms and ammunition were imported from Germany and France to help ensure their security – this included modern Mauser rifles and Krupp artillery. Stability was not helped by the appointment of Sir Alfred Milner as high commissioner in South Africa. A highly intelligent man who was extremely jingoistic and ambitious, he wanted to create a new federation, incorporating the Boer republics within the British Empire. Whilst Milner was away in London explaining his case, the pragmatic Major General William Butler was appointed C-in-C of British forces in South Africa. He believed that South Africa needed 'a rest cure and not an operation' and did his best to placate the *uitlanders* and discourage conflict.[2]

Ironically, the main military man seemed to be avoiding war, whilst Milner, the civilian, sought it. The Boer President, Paul Kruger, attempted to control the situation too and provide some concessions to the *uitlanders*. However, the shooting of a British mining engineer in December 1898 exacerbated the rising tensions.

The *uitlanders'* cause was again highlighted by Alfred Milner's 'Helot's Despatch', which stated:

> The case for intervention is overwhelming … The spectacle of thousands of British subjects kept permanently in the position of helots, constantly chafing under undoubted grievances, and calling vainly to Her Majesty's Government for redress, does steadily undermine the influence and reputation of Great Britain and the respect for the British Government, within its own dominions.[3]

Alfred Milner demanded a show of force to pursue his ambitions and he asked for an extra 10,000 troops in South Africa. In England, the C-in-C Field Marshal Sir Garnet Wolseley, a former high commissioner for South Africa, planned for an expeditionary force of 35,000, including mobilised reservists and consisting of an army corps and cavalry division to deal with the worsening situation, all under the command of General Sir Redvers Buller. He also suggested a demonstration of force on Salisbury Plain.

Both plans, however, were opposed by the Secretary of State for War, who thought that they would aggravate the situation. Meanwhile, talks took place between Milner and Kruger in early June 1899, but broke down and the bellicose rhetoric continued with the colonial secretary, Joseph Chamberlain, stating that the Transvaal should no longer threaten the peace and prosperity of the world. Major General Butler was forced to resign in August 1899 because of Milner's dissatisfaction with his lack of loyalty. The Empire was confident and, arguably, at the height of its power – the army stood by for hostilities.

Despite Field Marshal Wolseley's aspirations and the concerns expressed about the readiness of forces by General Buller, the politicians did not want to react too quickly and aggravate the growing threat of war. However, sixty artillery pieces and 27,000 troops were available in South Africa when conflict

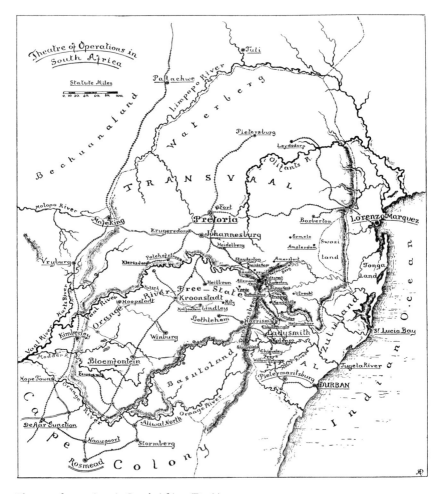

Theatre of operations in South Africa. (Davis)

began in October 1899, as local troops had just been doubled in number at the last moment with reinforcements from Great Britain, Malta, Egypt, Crete and Mauritius. This was not going to be enough, however. Before Major General Butler's dismissal, he had predicted that 200,000 would be needed to pacify the Boers.[4] Boer numbers were estimated at about 50,000, and by the end of this war the British Empire had to field nearly 450,000 troops to bring victory. As Field Marshal Lord Carver has written, 'The British Army was ill-prepared for the war it was about to wage.'[5]

At the strategic level, the reforms suggested by the Lord Hartington Royal Commission of 1890 had not been executed nor the reform measures suggested by Spencer Wilkinson. These would have included a reorganisation of the War Office and the setting up of a General Staff helping to make preparation for war more efficient; this did not happen until after the Boer War. This stagnation and lack of modernisation was seen at the tactical level as well.

At first glance, the British seemed all-powerful. Regular Army strength was around 227,000, with about 148,000 infantry and 19,000 cavalry; 108,000 were in the United Kingdom, 68,000 in India and the rest spread as garrisons throughout the rest of the Empire. However, this was going to be a form of war that the British had not experienced before. As one history commented in the 1930s, 'Though individually formidable, the Afghans, Zulus, Sudanese and frontier tribesmen had played into our hands by launching massed attacks against which our usual superiority of armament had its natural effect.'[6]

British tactics were still based on dealing with rushes of enemy tribesmen, rather than dealing with 'hit and run' tactics by very mobile marksmen. It has been written that 'the British soldier of 1899 himself was no more than a mindless brick in a moving wall of flesh'.[7] A lack of initiative and firing volleys in close ranks was not the way to defeat the Boer. A great deal of the equipment was poor and most British soldiers were not armed with the latest Lee–Enfield rifles; their Lee–Metfords were outgunned by the Boers' more accurate and faster-shooting Mauser. Even when the new rifle was issued, it was discovered that the sights were inaccurate. The 1903 Royal Commission on the war condemned the performance of virtually the whole army, from top to bottom, and the 1902 Akers-Douglas Committee heavily criticised officers' lack of professional education.

The British were to be confronted by an intelligent and very capable enemy and it was the first time they had been faced by Europeans since the Crimean War of 1854–56. South Africa was a big country and lines of communication were long and therefore vulnerable. Initially, British logistics were poor and the requirement for mobility and plenty of horses was not appreciated. In addition, the British forces were hastily assembled, never having worked or grouped with each other before. Regular soldiers, reservists and colonial troops were thrown together and expected to fight efficiently when there had been only limited investment in their training before the conflict. They were also predictable, as movement was generally along the railways because roads and tracks were so poor. The Boers were extremely capable and determined; they also knew the country, whilst the British did not even have detailed maps.

General Buller's force started to receive orders to move to South Africa from late September. A cavalry division, an army corps of three infantry divisions and eight infantry battalions for lines of communication began to embark and Regular Army reservists were called up.

Meanwhile, an ultimatum to the British Government was issued on 9 October 1899 by the South Africa Republic:

> British troops should be withdrawn from the borders of Natal.
> Reinforcements landed in South Africa in 1899 should be withdrawn.
> All troops en route to South Africa by ship should be turned back.

The British ultimatum followed, which demanded Boer disarmament, legal concessions for the *uitlanders* and surrender. Both ultimatums being ignored, war began on 11 October 1899. The conduct of the Second Boer War can be divided into five main phases:

> The Boer offensive in October 1899.
> The British counter-offensive under General Buller from November 1899 to early February 1900.
> The British offensive under Lord Roberts from mid-February 1900 to mid-March 1900.
> Guerrilla and conventional war from mid-March 1900 to September 1900.
> Guerrilla warfare from September 1900 to May 1902 when the peace treaty was signed.

The Boers seized the initiative immediately during the first phase and the second phase led to a series of disasters for the British. The British colony of Natal was invaded, the field force beaten and driven into Ladysmith. Other troops were trapped in Mafeking and Kimberley. In response, General Buller split his forces and the subsequent actions led to 'Black Week' in the second week of December. The British Army was soundly beaten – Lord Methuen at the Battle of Magersfontein, Brigadier Gatacre at Stormberg and General Buller at Colenso.

The international press poured scorn on the British effort, which was remembered for many years afterwards. As Ian Hay wrote:

Many of us are old enough to remember the anxiety and humiliation of the first six months of the Great Boer War, during which the British Army, in one blind and ill-directed onslaught after another, failed to make the slightest impression upon an enemy force composed of invisible sharpshooters.[8]

The British Government and public were not impressed and Field Marshal Lord Roberts of Kandahar, who lost his son fighting at Colenso, and his chief of staff, Lieutenant General Lord Kitchener of Khartoum, colloquially known as 'Bobs' and 'K', were called upon to save the situation. A German report commented, 'The presence of both of these men restored confidence in the leadership and in the luck of the army, and renewed the eagerness of the troops to be up and doing.'[9]

What about Major Monro? He was in England when war began, as one of the commander of 6th Division's key staff officers. He knew the commander well, as he had been his adjutant in the 1st Battalion the Queen's (Royal West Surrey) Regiment seven years before. This was Lieutenant General Thomas Kelly-Kenny, described in the *Times History of the War* as 'a shrewd, drily humorous Irishman of long and varied experience of military administration'.[10]

Major Monro was one of the 6th Division's two deputy assistant adjutant generals (DAAGs) working for Colonel A. Goldsmid, the assistant adjutant general to the divisional commander. The other DAAG was Major J. Caunter of the Lancashire Fusiliers.[11] Major Caunter became professor of tactics at the Royal Military College after his 6th Division service and wrote a useful paper entitled, *The Campaign in the Free State and its Lessons*.

The 6th Division received its orders to move on 2nd December and it embarked over the last two weeks of that month. With his responsibilities for administration and logistics in the division, this was a busy period for Major Monro, placing the right unit at the right time with its equipment, ready for embarkation. Once deployed in South Africa, the 6th Division was to be made up of the following elements:[12]

13th Brigade (Commander – Major General C. E. Knox)
2nd Battalion Royal East Kent Regiment (the Buffs)
2nd Battalion Gloucestershire Regiment
1st Battalion West Riding Regiment
1st Battalion Oxfordshire Light Infantry
7 Bearer Company
Field Hospital
Detachment Army Service Corps

Field Marshal Lord Roberts. (Author's collection)

Major General Kelly-Kenny. (Author's collection)

Major General Lord Kitchener of Khartoum.
(Author's collection)

Major General French. (Author's collection)

18th Brigade (Commander – Major General T. E. Stephenson)
  2nd Battalion Royal Warwickshire Regiment
  1st Battalion Yorkshire Regiment
  1st Battalion Essex Regiment
  1st Battalion Welsh Regiment
  Bearer Company from 6th Division Field Hospital
  3 Section Cape Field Hospital
  Detachment Army Service Corps

6th Division Divisional Troops
  Royal Navy 12-pounder guns (2)
  76th, 81st, 82nd Batteries Royal Field Artillery
  Ammunition Column
  Number 38 Field Company Royal Engineers
  Field Hospital
  Detachment Army Service Corps

The 6th Division headquarters, including the commander and Major Monro, sailed on SS *Dunnottar Castle* alongside Lord Roberts, Lord Kitchener and their staff.[13] General Buller met this varied group on their arrival and commented, 'I found Roberts sitting in one building with his Hindu staff, Kitchener in another with his Egyptian staff, and Kelly-Kenny in a third with an English staff, all pulling against each other.'[14]

These disparate 'rings' of staff did not bode well for future efficient command and control. Lieutenant General Kelly-Kenny had served with Lord Roberts in the Abyssinian Expedition of 1867–68 and they knew each other. Certainly, Lord Roberts had made his mind up already about the character of the commander of 6th Division. Unfortunately, it was not that complimentary – on 29 January 1900, he wrote to Lord Lansdowne about his subordinates, 'At present it is difficult for me to decide what commanders I can rely on for work in the front. Kelly-Kenny seems to be nervous and over cautious.'[15] This is an interesting early assessment, in light of Kelly-Kenny's clash a month later with Lord Kitchener at Paardeberg.

Formations of units and staff hurriedly pulled together from various sources, who had not trained with each other before, was not an efficient way to start a war. Meanwhile, in transit, Major Monro wrote on 9 January 1900:

> Tomorrow our journey is over and I suppose we shall get final instructions as to our destination. Everyone is in an advanced excitement for news. Our company has been very distinguished, Lord Roberts with a big staff, Lord Kitchener, General Pretyman and a lot of aides-de-camp, all members of

A Boer trench. (Imperial War Museum. Q101768)

the aristocracy. Also about twenty young fellows who have given up their businesses with a view to joining some corps in South Africa … After the succession of reverses one does not know what to expect, and I rather dread the time when we shall hear the last news from the front. I wonder where the use of our schools, staff colleges, etc, come in if a body of half-civilised farmers are able to achieve so much against us …[16]

These are thoughtful comments on the old-fashioned establishment of the British Army, alongside the probably naïve optimism of the volunteers and the effect of 'Black Week' on the way ahead. In another letter of 22 January he wrote:

I was put to work very soon after arrival. We got here at 10 a.m. and at 2 p.m. I was sent off with a patrol to make a reconnaissance. I was out for four days and found it a bit hard after board-ship life. We were in the saddle all day and the sun was hot enough. My escort were a few colonial mounted infantry, splendid chaps and full of cunning comparisons are odious so I confine myself to saying they were very good. It will give Miss Saward great pain to learn that the doctors are very apprehensive of my complexion. It received a very rude shock during my tour of patrol and I am afraid it will never recover its former beauty …[17]

He was busy. In the meantime, General Buller had received further setbacks at Spion Kop in January and Vaal Krantz in February.

However, Lord Roberts was frantically reorganising the army and establishing new mounted infantry units from both the infantry and cavalry; the latter replacing their lances with rifles and carbines. He was about to launch his first action to relieve the Boer siege of Kimberley, concentrating his force, with Bloemfontein, capital of the Orange Free State, as his objective. This 'great flank march' was an ambitious but clear plan as he advanced with about 18,000 infantry and 8,000 cavalry. The pace of the advance was illustrated by the loss of 500 horses from exhaustion or death within the first forty-eight hours.

Lieutenant General John French, later a field marshal, commanding the Cavalry Division, relieved Kimberley on 15 February after four months of siege. He had been ordered by Lord Roberts to move quickly, whilst he outflanked Boer Assistant Commandant General Piet Cronjé. The seizure was a symbolic success and the first significant British victory of the war – there were 48,000 people within this centre of the diamond fields, including Cecil Rhodes. The momentum of the advance was slowed, however, because of the difficulty crossing the River Riet. As a result, a third of the transport wagons for the infantry were abandoned, unprotected, and attacked by Chief Commandant Christiaan de Wet, one of the most aggressive and successful Boer leaders. The effect was a loss of enormous amounts of rations and cattle as well as nearly sixty men.

With such a fragile logistic tail, Lord Roberts considered halting his advance but instead put the remaining troops on half rations and determinedly pressed on. This had the desired effect as General Cronjé was completely surprised by the speed and direction of movement and the unexpected British gunfire that was starting to fall on Magersfontein. Consequently, he abandoned that position and moved east with a huge wagon train and families. British cavalry were to the north at Kimberley and the rest of Lord Roberts' force was at the River Modder to the east. He believed that he could sneak past them to Bloemfontein, but this was going to be a challenge with his slow-moving oxen.

On 15 February his 5,000 men assembled in moonlight, alongside women and children and 400 ox wagons. They abandoned their earthworks at Magersfontein and set off in a 5-mile long train, passing only 3 miles in front of the British positions at Klip Drift. This was a frustrating moment for both Lieutenant General Kelly-Kenny and Major Monro; it was the 6th Division which the train slipped past, undetected. The division was probably exhausted, having just travelled 27 miles in twenty-three hours 'when the intense heat of the sun by day, the drenching rain storms by night, the suffocating sand,

and the heavy going are considered'.[18] Kelly-Kenny recorded on 14 February, 'This day was a trying one ... The men deserved a night's rest.'[19]

Major General Knox's 13th Brigade, the 81st Field Battery and mounted infantry were ordered to pursue. Kelly-Kenny recorded that his brigade 'was engaged all day from dawn to dusk in attacking General Cronjé's rearguard ... He did a considerable amount of damage, both to the convoys and laagers.'[20] The following morning, dust clouds were seen by Captain Chester Master of Rimington's Guides, local colonial troops known as 'Tigers' because of their leopard-skin scarves, and Colonel Ormelie Hannay gave chase with his mounted infantry. They had discovered Cronjé's column and helped slow it down, though the troops were beaten off by a Boer rearguard. That evening, Lord Roberts ordered Lieutenant General French to cut off General Cronjé. Consequently, in the early hours of the following day he led 1,500 men with a battery of guns the 30 miles towards his fugitive's force.

Paardeberg (18–27 February 1900)

General Cronjé arrived at Paardeberg Drift on 17 February, ready to cross the River Modder. Very soon after adopting a defensive but relaxed position as an attack was not expected, the Boers came under artillery fire from Lieutenant General French's twelve guns. Though French was outnumbered by four to one, he had surprised the enemy and then managed to 'fix' him in the position, giving other British troops, including men of Lieutenant General Kelly-Kenny's 6th Division, time to surround the Boers by early next day. The key British forces on the perimeter were the 6th Division and General Sir Henry Colvile's 9th Division.

It was at this point that Major Monro witnessed an important command and control and personality clash. The British gathered, Lord Roberts fell sick and Kelly-Kenny, as the next senior officer present, should have taken command. However, Lord Roberts had said that Lord Kitchener's instructions should be 'as an order from Roberts', so 'K' took command. He was the chief of staff, rather than the commander, so Kelly-Kenny was not a happy man. He had already been hassled by Kitchener, with whom he had little in common prior to this action, 'in fact, he found his fussiness and interference intensely irritating'.[21] He felt that he was not being trusted and when it was confirmed to him who was in command, he stated, 'This is not the time to enter into personal matters. Till this phase of the operation is completed, I will submit to even humiliation rather than raise any matter connected with my command.'[22]

One historian has commented, 'then he sulked, and did not pull his weight'.[23] The 4,000 Boers were surrounded by Lieutenant General French's force and the two brigades, but they were also in good defensive positions, with trenches which were quickly improved by General Cronjé. There were two choices – to isolate the enemy and bombard them into surrender at minimum loss of Allied life, which was the Kelly-Kenny plan, or to attack the increasingly protected defensive position with the inevitable greater casualties. Lord Kitchener preferred the latter option and 'threw caution overboard (as well as the lessons learnt thus far in the war)'.[24] It is not known whether Lord Roberts had shared his previous thoughts about the cautious character of Lieutenant General Kelly-Kenny with his chief of staff. However, as he was his closest confidante, it is likely that Lord Roberts would have had that thought in mind when confidently 'fronting-up' to Commander 6th Division.

It is worth making a few comments about Lord Kitchener's character at this point. He was not a popular person amongst many of his peers and, as Lord Roberts' chief of staff, he was quick to recommend officers to be removed from post. He has been quoted as saying, '… people here do not seem to look upon the war sufficiently seriously. It is considered too much like a game of polo with intervals for afternoon tea.'[25] He had no time for socialites and had an extremely aggressive spirit, but 'got things done', including the expansion of mounted infantry so quickly after his arrival in South Africa, though in his enthusiasm he had also severely tampered with the transport system.

In this incident with Kelly-Kenny, his aggression only led to a greater loss of British lives than there would have been if Commander 6th Division had been listened to. The Battle of Paardeberg has been called 'the most controversial episode in Kitchener's career', as he appeared to favour tactics more suited to fighting tribesmen in the Sudan, which was the only theatre of war he had previously experienced.[26] He ordered an attack on the Boer defensive position, 'Gentlemen! It is now six-thirty. By ten-thirty we shall be in possession of that laager; and I shall then load up French and push him on to Bloemfontein with the cavalry!'[27]

The British attack on 18 February was poorly co-ordinated by Lord Kitchener, who had only two staff officers and a few aides-de-camp helping him to command a force of nearly 20,000 men, spread widely. There was poor co-operation between artillery and infantry and there was inadequate communication between the different infantry formations on the battlefield. It followed an ineffective reconnaissance of the enemy positions. One biography comments, 'He had no members of the HQ Staff, signalling personnel, gallopers, or orderlies, and with this meagre staff was to conduct his first battle against a white enemy equipped with modern arms. Lord Roberts knew and believed in him …'[28]

He wanted to deal with the situation quickly with a simple plan, ensuring that General Cronjé did not escape the trap. However, he did not believe in writing orders, so clear instructions were not issued and confusion reigned. Lieutenant General Kelly-Kenny commented, 'No written orders of any sort. Kitchener only sends verbal messages – takes my staff and my troops on no order or system.'[29]

The artillery fired and the assaults from different directions were launched. The 6th Division led with a frontal assault 'over 2,000 to 3,000 yards of open veldt, studded here and there by occasional ant heaps' to fix the enemy from the south, whilst left and right hooks were planned with Colvile's 9th Division attacking on the left upstream, the Highland Brigade on the south side of the River Modder and Major General Smith-Dorrien's 19th Brigade would cross the river from the north.[30] On the right of the 6th Division, their 18th Brigade would attack downstream from the north bank. The initial result is best summed up by Conan Doyle:

> Everywhere there was a terrible monotony about the experiences of the various regiments which learned once again the grim lessons of Colenso and Modder River. We surely did not need to prove once more what had already been so amply proved – that bravery can be of no avail against concealed riflemen well entrenched, and that the more hardy is the attack the heavier must be the repulse.[31]

In both of these other battles, the British had charged against rapid firing and extremely accurate Boer rifles, firing smokeless ammunition, from dug-in positions, and the result had been disastrous with many casualties. Pakenham comments, 'Of the revolution in tactics – of the new, invisible war of the rifle-plus-trench he showed himself supremely unaware.'[32] Major General Colvile, commanding 9th Division, recorded that the attack 'was delivered with extraordinary courage and determination, but was, I regret to say, unsuccessful and resulted in the death of Colonel Aldsworth and the loss of a considerable number of officers, non-commissioned officers and men'.[33]

Major General Smith-Dorrien, who received great praise from Colvile after the battle, commanded one of the attacking brigades, the 19th, within 9th Division, and later wrote, 'It was a gallant charge, gallantly led, but the fact that not one of them got within 300 yards of the enemy is sufficient proof of its futility.'[34]

There were 1,300 British casualties on this day, compared with seventy Boers, as brave battalions attempted to secure the enemy position. The

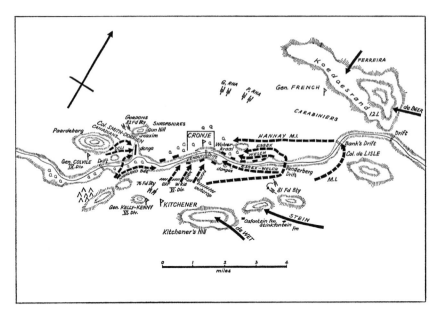

Battle of Paardeberg. (Selby)

number of British dead and wounded at Paardeberg was a greater total than any other battle in the war. The Boers 'had dug out bomb-proof shelters in the steep banks of the river' and their holes 'could not be reached by flat trajectory field guns' – only one howitzer battery, with a higher trajectory, was available.[35] It was difficult to locate the Boers amongst the scrub and although the friendly artillery appeared to be destroying wagons little other damage was being done to soften up their positions. An Austro-Hungarian officer, who was military attaché with the British, mentioned that the artillery shrapnel fire at the battle had little effect on the well-protected enemy.[36]

The 1st Battalion Welsh Regiment and 1st Battalion Essex Regiment were the first to suffer, with four more 6th Division battalions following. The commanding officer of the 1st Battalion Yorkshire Regiment was killed as the troops discovered the river was flooded and impassable and the commander of the 13th Brigade was wounded.

Lord Kitchener would not have been impressed by Lieutenant General Kelly-Kenny's reaction to all of this, which was to issue a message to not attempt to cross the river and storm the laager, 'I resisted assault in front, as troops were exhausted and I could not get the Brigade together.'[37] Also, he wrote in a despatch, 'the enemy held such a strong position on the northern bank and the River in flood, I decided not to assault in front'.[38] This meant that Kitchener could not renew the frontal attack from the south. The left-hook attack was also delayed as various commanders recognised the futility of what was happening.

Meanwhile, the Highland Brigade was seen to launch their frontal attack and suffer the consequences, pinned down on their stomachs in front of the enemy position, just as they were at the previous battle at Magersfontein. Colvile wrote, 'I never hope to see or read of anything grander than the advance of that thin line across the coverless plain, under a hail of lead from their invisible enemy in the river banks.'[39] The Highland Brigade's commander was also wounded.

Men were lying under the hot sun as casualties were sustained for no gain. One attack on day two of the battle was by the 2nd Battalion Gloucester Regiment, part of 13th Brigade, 6th Division, as described by Lieutenant Gardner, 'The Glosters advanced in grand style and were soon under a very heavy fire at 800 yards from the position; we had to advance over a plain without any scrap of cover.'[40] A Press Association report stated:

> Last Monday night (19th) a brilliant piece of work was performed by the Gloucesters. During the afternoon they approached within a short distance of a Boer kopje and contained the enemy until nightfall, when 120 men charged the kopje with bayonets and drove off the Boers with loss, bayoneting several.[41]

In fact, it was 6th Division battalions from 18th Brigade that included the only two awards of the Victoria Cross from Paardeberg – Lieutenant Francis Parsons of 1st Battalion Essex Regiment and Sergeant Alfred Atkinson of 1st Battalion Yorkshire Regiment. Major Monro processed their citations through Lieutenant General Kelly-Kenny. Twenty-four-year-old Lieutenant Parsons assisted Private Ferguson, who was wounded, dressed his wounds, fetched water for him to drink and recovered him from the battlefield, all whilst under heavy enemy fire. Unfortunately, he was to die at Driefontein on 10 March 1900. Sergeant Atkinson, 26, carried water to the wounded seven times, whilst under fire, until he was shot in the head and died from his wounds three days later.[42]

The 1st Battalion Welsh Regiment also fought hard for 18th Brigade and 6th Division. Lieutenant General Kelly-Kenny praised his formation thus:

> I will take an opportunity of bringing to notice the special acts of devotion to duty on the part of the individuals; I confine myself at present to representing the fine spirit and gallantry of all the troops engaged; I feel bound, however, to bring to your lordship's notice now the very gallant conduct of the 1st Battalion Welsh Regiment, who were on our right flank: a portion of the Battalion charged right up to the Boer laager with the bayonet in the finest possible manner, losing heavily in their gallant attempt to capture it.[43]

On the right flank, there were brave, but totally uncoordinated attacks from units, including the Royal Canadian Regiment, facing action for the first time:

> The hours dragged by under a hot, pitiless sun. The men had not rested or eaten since the previous day. Exposed movement could be fatal. Scanning the enemy trenches through his binoculars, Captain Arnold, Officer Commanding A Company, was shot through the head. Two stretcher-bearers going to his aid were shot down.[44]

They were part of 19th Brigade, who had waded across the river. Their commander, Major General Horace Smith-Dorrien, claimed that throughout the day he was 'left in a complete fog, and knew nothing of the situation either of our own troops, or of the Boers, beyond what I could see, or infer, myself'.[45] However, he has been criticised for failing to use his initiative, despite the failings of Kitchener's orders. As night fell, Colonel Hannay was told by Kitchener to link up with the 18th Brigade and launch one more attack, as a right hook – no link up occurred, instead only fifty mounted infantry attacked and their leader, Colonel Hannay, was killed.

In the late afternoon, the situation was not helped by a surprise attack by the Boer General de Wet in the rear of the British position, taking 'Kitchener's Kopje [Hill]', a piece of ground that had been used by the

Battle of Paardeberg. (Postcard. Price's)

commander at the beginning of the battle and had been identified by Lieutenant General Kelly-Kenny as key terrain, but not defended effectively. The Boers then proceeded to launch a surprise bombardment into the rear of the British lines, though the scene of their fellow burghers was not good, as General de Wet recorded, 'All round the laager were the guns of the English, belching forth death and destruction, while from within it at every moment, as each successful shell tore up the ground, there rose a cloud – a dark cloud of dust.'[46]

General de Wet had taken sixty prisoners and managed to stay on the position for two and a half days. Lord Roberts, hearing of the high cost of the first day, rose from his sickbed and reached the battlefield on day two to take over command. Kelly-Kenny sent one despatch to Lord Roberts on 20 February 1900, which hinted at his frustration with the chain of command arrangements, 'In accordance with instructions conveyed to me in your note of the 17th, I recognised his [Kitchener's] suggestions as conveying to me your Lordship's orders and acted thereon.'[47] This is unusual wording.

Meanwhile, Lord Kitchener was champing at the bit to continue the assaults. However, Lord Roberts was convinced that more infantry attacks would just result in unnecessary loss of life. He wrote in a despatch, 'The troops in camp were too much exhausted by the marching and fighting of the two previous days to attempt a second assault of the laager, the defences of which had been materially strengthened.'[48]

He effectively agreed with Lieutenant General Kelly-Kenny's original plan of bombarding the Boers into surrender and Kitchener was despatched elsewhere to sort out the lines of communication. Lord Kitchener's handling of the battle received mixed criticism immediately after the event with different histories either blaming him or supporting his decisions. A more recent one comments, 'Kitchener was heavily and justly criticised (except by Roberts) for his tactics and handling of the Battle of Paardeberg, but his instinct was sound.'[49] Another historian calls Kitchener 'a relentless martinet, quite indifferent to the personal considerations of the troops he commanded'. He goes on to state that:

Both Roberts and French had some consideration for the lives of the men they led in battle. Not so Kitchener; having determined a line of strategy he pursued it ruthlessly, at whatever sacrifice of human life he believed necessary for success. What he effected on the eighteenth of February 1900, at the foot of the Paardeberg, was but a puny foretaste of the great chances of human slaughter he was to exploit on the field of Flanders fifteen years later.[50]

However, an older biography is supportive, 'the notion that in war he held human life cheap was as false as it was foolish'.[51] The reader must make his own judgement. Interestingly, when writing to Sir Ian Hamilton three years later, 'K' denied the difference of opinion with the other commanders, writing, 'I believe that every general on the ground agreed with me that, under the circumstances, an attack on Cronjé's force was the right action to take; certainly not one of them suggested any other course.'[52]

Lord Roberts did not hold the Paardeberg experience against Kitchener and both Kelly-Kenny and Kitchener were recognised for their service in South Africa in a despatch from Lord Roberts in March 1900; the same despatch also recognised the services of Major Monro.[53] Six months later, he provided an assessment of the senior officers to Lord Lansdowne, Secretary of State for War:

> I cannot describe what an assistance he has been to me … I can only say that I have never been served more loyally or more efficiently than by Kitchener, and on no single occasion has there been the slightest friction between us, or anything but the most complete harmony … He is untiring in the performance of his duty, and the services rendered during the war have been most exceptional and distinguished. It has been a real pleasure and of the greatest advantage to me personally to have had him with me during the anxieties of the Campaign.[54]

It is not surprising that the conduct of the battle remains controversial. There were even some accusations that Lord Kitchener did not care for the wounded.[55] Major Baden-Powell made his view very clear in a 1903 analysis of the South Africa campaign, when he wrote that the British 'received a very severe lesson as to the uselessness of attacking. The assault resulted in the most disastrous battle of the whole war, and did us no good whatever.'[56] Later military text books used the battle as an illustration of how not to conduct an action 'owing to the interference with the normal chain of command, the lack of co-ordination of attacks and the complete lack of objectives for units'.[57]

The bombardment of the Boer position continued over the next days, along with some minor British night attacks. 'Each day the laager was bombarded from the surrounding heights, and the space occupied by the doomed army encroached on by means of sapping.'[58] General de Wet was eventually driven off Kitchener's Kopje. De Wet had tried to persuade Cronjé to attempt to break out using one intrepid Boer, Danie Theron, as a messenger. He crawled in and out of General Cronjé's laager, amazingly undetected, but to no avail. Meanwhile, Cronjé asked for an armistice, but this was refused and unconditional surrender demanded. The effect of fifty guns, including more howitzers, firing continually at his position for nine days was recorded:

> There is hardly any food … The stench of the decomposed oxen and horses is awful. The water of the river is putrid with carrion … The sufferings of the wounded are heartrending. Little children huddled together in bomb-proof excavations are restless, hungry and crying. The women adding their sobs to the plaintive exhortations of the wounded.[59]

General Cronjé surrendered his 4,000 men and five artillery pieces on 27 February 1900, the nineteenth anniversary of the British disaster at the hands of the Boers at Majuba in the First Boer War. This was a considerable victory in the war, albeit a costly one for the British. The Boers were realising that they could not beat their enemy using conventional tactics and many of them withdrew to protect their homes.

General de Wet, who was subsequently appointed C-in-C, wrote that the surrender 'forms one of the most important chapters in the history of the two Republics'.[60] He goes on to say that General Cronjé did not appreciate the effect of his capture. 'If the famous Cronjé were captured, how could any ordinary burgher be expected to continue his resistance' and 'the effects of this blow, it is not too much to say, made themselves apparent to the very end of the war'.[61] President Kruger commented, 'The English have taken our Majuba Day away from us.'[62]

The British heralded the victory, but those on the ground were shocked by the carnage delivered in the laager and the presence of women and children. Meanwhile, on 1 March, the British troops heard of another victory elsewhere in South Africa – General Buller's relief of Ladysmith.

Major Monro witnessed the Battle of Paardeberg, which became known as 'Bloody Sunday', as a loyal key staff officer to Lieutenant General Kelly-Kenny. He saw the needless loss of lives and the controversial clashes between commanders about the tactics used. He had this to say after the battle:

> From a text book point of view the position of the Boers combined every disadvantage possible, yet it was tremendously strong. I visited their laager and found their trenches about five feet deep and most ingeniously arranged, giving them perfect cover. Our shell and howitzer fire really did them very little damage. Times have been very hard, in the first place bivouacking in the rain is not as comfortable as Gardener's Hotel (in Guernsey) and we have been living on rations which have not been sumptuous. Biscuit and the captured cattle (Boer bull is not a tender beast!) and Modder River water, flavoured by the body of an occasional dead Boer.[63]

He avoids controversial comment, which was one of his traits, but the lessons learned about tactics, command and control and clear orders would help equip him in his next key appointment.

Meanwhile, Monro received a special mention from his divisional commander following his actions at Paardeberg, appearing first in a list of 'recognised' officers:

Major C. C. Monro. The Queen's. DAAG.
On every occasion this officer devoted himself with ability and energy to his duty. I hope your Lordship will recommend him for advancements in the Army and for some mark of Her Majesty's favour.[64]

His war was not over yet, however, as he was to be present with the 6th Division at Poplar Grove and Driefontein.

Poplar Grove (7 March 1900)

The British objective remained Bloemfontein, the capital of the Orange Free State. However, General de Wet had established a defensive position in small hills around the River Modder, at Poplar Grove (Modderrivierpoort), 15 miles east of Paardeberg, 10 miles east of the surrender and 50 miles west of the capital. He intended 'to stop Robert's advance at all costs, and to get together every available man for the purpose'.[65]

Lord Roberts' bold plan of attack for 7 March 1900 was to envelope the enemy position of 8,000 men with two divisions from the south and south-west, including 6th Division, whilst isolating the Boer force and cutting their lines of communication to the rear by a swift 15-mile outflanking move by Lieutenant General French's cavalry. There were no written orders but Roberts' verbal address, referring to the enemy's southern 'seven kopjes' position, told his audience, 'General Kelly-Kenny will not, I think, have much difficulty in driving the enemy off these kopjes.'[66]

Unfortunately, French's cavalry were not in good order, with tired horses and without adequate food, so their move was not as swift as it should be. By the time the 6th Division reached their final objective they were only left with a small rearguard action, as General de Wet's burghers were fleeing east. The Boer general could not stop them:

A panic had seized my men. Before the English had even got near enough to shell our positions to any purpose, the wild flight began. Soon every position was evacuated. There was not even an attempt to hold them, though some of them would have been impregnable. It was a flight such as I had never seen before, and shall never see again.[67]

This could have been a very different engagement if the cavalry had cut off his retreat, the advancing divisions had arrived earlier and the Boers had stood and fought. There was some comment after the battle that the 6th Division could have moved more quickly than it did and should have engaged the enemy sooner. Indeed, Lord Roberts' despatch of 15 March stated that the 6th Division had 'made too wide a detour to the south, result being that before it approached the seven kopjes the enemy had been dislodged by the Horse Artillery fire in reverse, coupled with the well-aimed shell-fire of the 4.7 inch naval guns in front'.[68]

One key historian, Amery, blamed Lieutenant General Kelly-Kenny for being overcautious, like many of the commanders, for 'had Kelly-Kenny attacked with promptitude, he would either have engaged the attention of the Boers, or else have converted their retreat into a real flight; in either case French would have felt himself freer to act with boldness'.[69]

However, the recent successes by the British on the conventional battlefield had had a significant psychological effect, so the Boers did not stay put and there were only limited firefights. Large amounts of Boer resources may have been captured if they had stayed, or if the British advance had been more rapid and timely. This could have included the capture of two key personalities – President Kruger of the Transvaal and President Steyn of the Orange Free State, who had attempted to rouse this Boer force. Perhaps a British victory at Poplar Grove may have ended the war. More positively, important ground blocking the route to Bloemfontein had been captured by the British with the relatively small loss of about fifty cavalry.

Lord Roberts was not happy with both lieutenant generals French and Kelly-Kenny, though he is reported to have said at the end of the day, 'In war you can't expect everything to come out right.'[70] However, he accused French of not being focussed enough and failing to look after his horses, whilst Kelly-Kenny was told that he should have been quicker into action and caught the Boers in their trenches. Both generals complained about the poor supply system for men and horses, though Lieutenant General Kelly-Kenny admitted that he might have attacked earlier if he had known of the demoralised state of the enemy.

Lord Roberts said at the Elgin Commission, 'The Poplar Grove Day, however, was a most disappointing one for me, as I had quite calculated on cutting the enemy off from the Bloemfontein road, and forcing him to get entangled in the difficult drifts of the Modder ...'[71]

An opportunity had been lost and, according to Pakenham, 'the effects of the Battle of Poplar Grove were disastrous and long-lasting for the British'.[72] This was because the Boers' actions were misinterpreted as marking the end of the war, when in fact this was just the end of the conventional phase prior to the long drawn-out guerrilla period of the campaign.

Major Monro wrote of the event:

> We were occupied all day in keeping out of the light of those confounded kopjes, but as we worked to our right, they moved to their left and at night-fall we had to get them out because they had the commanding ground and because of water. We were handicapped by our Royal Artillery being unable to move out of a walk; their big horses had been on half rations for some time and were completely done. The infantry were splendid; they really went at the Boer with grand dash. They [the Boers] tried the white flag trick and suffered for it. The Buffs bayoneted those who did it up to the hilt. Our troubles were increased at night time trying to get the wounded in. We were fighting till dark, there was no moon and it was bitterly cold, and the difficulty in finding the poor chaps amongst the kopjes was very great. I am afraid there was a lot of suffering among them, but the doctors worked grandly. In fact all through this war you hear nothing but praise of their work.[73]

Driefontein (10 March 1900)

General de Wet occupied another defensive position 15 miles away, three days later, at Driefontein/Abraham's Kraal. This was to be the final Boer stand before the British capture of Bloemfontein. About 5,000 Boers and twelve guns dug in, whilst General de Wet identified another potential fall-back position nearer to Bloemfontein.

In the early hours of 10 March 1900, British reconnaissance cavalry and mounted infantry made contact with the enemy and began to identify their positions and some of the advanced artillery began shelling Boer positions. Lieutenant General Charles Tucker's 7th Division had been sent far right to envelop the enemy position.

Meanwhile, Lieutenant General French commanded the left wing, which included Lieutenant General Kelly-Kenny's 6th Division, the 1st Cavalry Brigade and Alderson's mounted infantry. The 6th Division was ordered to move forward to support the cavalry and mounted infantry at 1000 hours and, just over two hours later, was given the impression by Lieutenant General French that the enemy were low in number and withdrawing from their position, though the 7th Division had not yet completed their envelopment. Thus a line of his infantry in 18th Brigade (from left to right: 1st Battalions of the Essex, Welsh and Yorkshire regiments) moved against the Driefontein kopjes, followed by the Buffs and Gloucesters of 13th Brigade. The other battalions were to the rear when Commander 6th Division came under fire and realised that the enemy position was not lightly held after all. 'They were passing over the open when the crash of Mauser fire burst out in front of them, and the bullets hissed and thudded amongst the ranks. The ordeal was a very severe one.'[74]

Lieutenant General Kelly-Kenny's 6th Division was, therefore, committed to an assault that they would not have chosen. Friendly casualties were sustained, but:

> The advance, nevertheless, was continued slowly but steadily until the line was sufficiently close to rush the enemy when, led by the Essex, who made a magnificent charge, Welshmen and Men of Kent rushed cheering forward into the Boer position. The majority of the enemy had not waited for the bayonet ...[75]

This battle lasted from 1030 hours to 1720 hours. Unusually, Boer casualties were heavier than the British – 100 of the enemy killed and possibly 200 wounded, compared with sixty-eight killed and 360 wounded from the four battalions. However, there had been over three hours of bitter fighting and Lieutenant Parsons of the Essex, who had won his Victoria Cross at Paardeberg, fell mortally wounded.

General de Wet wrote about the Boer withdrawal, 'But with the setting of the sun a change came over them. Once more panic seized them; leaving their positions, they retreated in haste towards Bloemfontein.'[76] From the British perspective, this was an example of a successful encounter battle, where there was little information about opposing forces and reactions had to be quick to succeed. The Boers, however, were proud that 1,500 of their men had held off 10,000 of the enemy for a day, General de Wet writing, 'They had offered a magnificent resistance.'[77]

The British intelligence was poor and the cavalry had limited value, as they failed to pursue the enemy, but 6th Division's attack was a well-delivered one that brought victory – the road was open to Bloemfontein, which was occupied by the British on 13 March 1900 'without a shot being fired'.[78] A biased observer commented:

> On Wednesday morning the 6th Division marched through the town. It was a fine sight. The physique of the men and their gallant bearing as they

tramped proudly through the enemy's capital made a great impression upon all who were present.[79]

The British strategy appeared to have succeeded, despite the struggle of winning the Battle of Paardeberg. The capital of the Orange Free State was in friendly hands, Ladysmith had been relieved and other smaller scale actions had ended favourably. Lord Roberts was treated like a hero for so many successes in one month but, as his army recuperated, he was too optimistic about the future, believing that the war was almost over. His optimism and positive reporting on the recent victories in the war was reflected on the Home Front. The October 1900 'Khaki Election' was won by the Conservative Government off the back of the recent successes and before major public concerns arose about the conduct of the guerrilla war.

Guerrilla War Begins

The British believed that it was only a matter of a short time before the Boers surrendered. Consequently, Lord Salisbury, the prime minister, made it clear that the British Government was not prepared to recognise Boer independence, demanding unconditional surrender from the two presidents, who had offered peace proposals. In fact, there was to be another two years of guerrilla warfare, the establishment of concentration camps and many atrocities by both sides before peace occurred. General Buller predicted a guerrilla war and, to no avail, advised Lord Roberts to destroy the enemy forces rather than rely on capturing their capitals.

Lines of communication were vulnerable to sporadic attacks, logistic support was weak and matters were not helped by outbreaks of typhoid amongst British troops – of the 30,000 troops in the capital, over 7,000 were hospitalised. It was spread by contaminated drinking water and was a disease not unknown in Great Britain, a number of outbreaks occurring over the previous few years. The British soldiers were tired, they had used contaminated sources and drinking water discipline, such as boiling before drinking, was not as good as it should have been – problems were referred to as 'a dose of the Modders'. Nearly 1,000 died within a month of entering the capital 'and they died miserably, they really did. Feverish, dehydrated, diarrhoea, haemorrhaging, a dry foul mouth, delirious, extreme headache, it was not pleasant, it is not a kind disease.'[80]

The medical support did not match the requirement and comparisons with the Crimean War were made, as more soldiers died. As the medical staff did their best and commanders were asked for additional support, Lord Kitchener reportedly said, 'You want pills and I want bullets, and bullets come first,' though Lord Roberts later placed the blame firmly on the doctors:[81]

> Doctors, with scarcely an exception are a very inefficient lot and have given me more trouble than I can describe. I have had to do their work for them throughout the Campaign and the department must be thoroughly reorganised. They are insufferably conceited and are inefficient as surgeons, as physicians and as administrators.[82]

Lord Roberts remained in Bloemfontein for six weeks. The 6th Division had completed its main experience of the war and its 13th Brigade became the main garrison in the capital, which was annexed and renamed the Orange River Colony on 28 May.

Lieutenant General Kelly-Kenny was made responsible for keeping control of the new colony, his division being reorganised – 18th Brigade was moved to join the Guards Brigade within a newly formed 11th Division elsewhere, and 12th Brigade, under Major General R. Clements, joined him. Meanwhile, Mafeking was relieved in mid-May and Lord Roberts entered Johannesburg on 31 May, then Pretoria, capital of the Transvaal, on 5 June. Many burghers had handed themselves in to the British authorities and President Kruger even suggested surrender. However, President Steyn responded that the war should be fought 'to the bitter end'.

Major Monro and his commander's last six months in South Africa included just the beginning of the guerrilla warfare. At a council of war, the Boers realised that they had to leave their wagons behind and adopt 'hit and run' tactics. The aim was to wear the British down and encourage other countries and even the British public to help negotiate peace. They enforced the need for their fighters to stay on duty rather than disappear when they liked on leave and placed a younger leadership in command: Louis Botha in the Transvaal and Christiaan de Wet and Assistant Commandant General Jacobus de la Rey for Free State forces. Successful strikes were made at Sannah's post, cutting off the water supply to the sick garrison of Bloemfontein and numerous other locations, particularly the vulnerable railway lines. Within ten days, the Free State Boers had inflicted 1,500 British casualties, inspiring the Transvaalers to fight on.

From the middle of June 1900, anyone illegally carrying weapons was declared a 'rebel' by the British – homes could be burned to the ground and property confiscated. By the end of the war 30,000 farms were destroyed as part of a common pacification measure, which the British had also employed in the North-West Frontier of India, as described in Chapter 2. This only hardened attitudes within the Boer community. Meanwhile, increasingly numerous British forces attempted to hunt down the rebels and adopted a 'scorched earth' policy, ensuring that the Boers were starved of food and supplies in the countryside. Lieutenant General Kelly-Kenny clarified the definition of 'lay waste to':

> ... gather all food and wagons, Cape carts, sheep, oxen, goats, calves, cows, horse, mares, foals, forage, poultry, destroy what you cannot eat ... burn all farmhouses – explain reason [for so doing] as they have harboured enemy and not reported to British authorities as required. Give no receipts, search for hidden stores of ammunition and destroy what you find ... The question of how to treat women and children and what amount of food and transport will arise, as regards to the first part they have forfeited all right to consideration and must now suffer for their persistency ignoring warnings against harbouring and assisting our enemy – as regards the second give them the bare amount to reach Winburg and then confiscate all transport. The object is to destroy or remove everything which may help the enemy or his horses or oxen to move. Definition ends.[83]

In today's environment, this does not make pleasant reading. Similar to the North-West Frontier experience, British power and destruction of the enemy were all-important, rather than an attempt to foster the 'hearts and minds' of the population. Looting and burning were commonplace, innocent civilians were caught up in shooting incidents and crimes were committed. Interestingly, General Buller did not allow his separate army to burn Boer farms; he did not believe the policy worthwhile, wanting to defeat the enemy in the field, and achieving some successes, but he left South Africa in October 1900.

Boer groups of fifty to 200 Boers were to continually harass lines of communication, particularly the railways, and launch sporadic and unpredictable ambushes. The British controlled the towns and, for most of the time, the routes to and from them, but were unable to totally control the countryside. Most of the 200,000 British troops were fixed in static positions, such as the blockhouses, whilst about 22,000 of them were formed in mobile columns, normally of between 1,000 and 2,000 troops, attempting to hunt the Boer forces that only ever managed to field 25,000 men. They failed to hunt down General de Wet and other Boer leaders and their commandos as, consistently, accurate intelligence on the enemy and communications failed.

However, on 1 October 1900, Transvaal was also declared a British colony. At that stage, the next long guerrilla period of the war and its effect was not anticipated and Lord Roberts could return home to a hero's welcome. He praised Lieutenant General Kelly-Kenny for his performance:

> He did good service by the judicious way in which he commanded in the Orange River Colony after we crossed the Vaal, and by the steady front he showed at a time when the line of communication behind the main army was cut, and affairs looked somewhat serious.[84]

The omens were not good, however, as summed up by an officer in late October:

> Bloemfontein is practically in a state of siege. The Boers have held up the mail train, and I presume, collared and destroyed our letters. They have been playing about all round us for two months in parties and small commandos, all well-mounted and equipped. They pass their time sniping at us, cutting the railway and telegraph lines, shooting at sentries, capturing small detached posts and unprotected convoys.[85]

Major Monro. (British Library. Mss Eur D783/7)

Lieutenant General Kelly-Kenny and his immediate staff, including Major Monro, accompanied Lord Roberts on his return home to England in December 1900, as Lord Kitchener was left in command – 'left to get on with the dirty work'. [86]

The war was entering its pure guerrilla phase, when Lord Kitchener would instigate the setting up of forty-six 'concentration camps' to isolate the Boer fighters from their families, with all the suffering that entailed. As further peace negotiations failed, he established the first of 8,000 blockhouses across the country, linked by 3,700 miles of barbed wire and interlocking fire, again to isolate the enemy and protect the lines of communication. The Boers were gradually worn down and many atrocities occurred on both sides, but this final period of the war did not affect either Lieutenant General Kelly-Kenny or Major Monro, as they were elsewhere. Final peace did not come until May 1902.

It is worth summarising the main effects of the whole war. Nearly 450,000 British troops were deployed to combat 87,000 Boers, including 2,000 foreign fighters. The British lost 6,000 killed in action and 16,000 deaths from wounds or disease; 7,000 Boers died, including 2,000 foreigners, though somewhere between 18,000 and 28,000 died in concentration camps. Thousands of farms were burned and cattle killed, and official statistics record that over 400,000 British horses, mules and donkeys died. The figures of black Africans killed are not recorded, though there are estimates of perhaps 7,000–12,000.

Financially, this had been an expensive campaign, costing the British tax-payer over £200 million. Politically, Milner did not achieve his objective of having a South Africa dominated by the British, as not enough immigration occurred, so the Boer still outnumbered his white counterpart. In addition, the Liberal Government of 1906 endorsed the Treaty of Vereeniging, which gave the two Boer states self-governing colony status and led to the establishment of the Union of South Africa in 1910. Despite a further failed rebellion by de Wet in 1914, its generous terms meant that, in the longer term, the Boers assisted the British in both the First and Second World Wars.

Lord Roberts made a final assessment of Kelly-Kenny, which still hinted at his cautiousness but acknowledged what had been achieved by his 6th Division:

On the whole he has done very well. He had very responsible work to carry out both at Paardeberg and on the engagement of the 10th March. He is careful, painstaking, and showed coolness, steadiness, and resource, when our line of railway was cut early in June. He looks after his men and his sick and wounded, and knows all that is going on in his command. He is probably not a brilliant commander, but can, I believe, be trusted to carry out whatever he is told to do.[87]

Lord Roberts was very frank with these reports. Whilst General Ian Hamilton, of later Gallipoli prominence, was described as 'quite the most brilliant Commander I have serving under me', Lieutenant General Tucker of the 7th Division was 'not a man I would trust' and Lieutenant General Sir Leslie Rundle, with the unfortunate nickname of Sir 'Leisurely Trundle', commanding 8th Division, 'failed twice in this country as a divisional commander'. Also, the cavalry Brigadier Broadwood 'is undoubtedly good, and he would be better still if he were more intelligent'.[88] Many of the British commanders would surface again prominently in the First World War. Allenby, Birdwood, French, Haig and Robertson would all later become field marshals.

South Africa and the Second Boer War was a significant experience for Major Monro. His 6th Division had played a prominent part in Lord Roberts' successes and he had played a key staff officer's role for its commander. He became known for his thoroughness and was thought of as being cautious in attitude and hated doing anything without preparation, both at work and in personal matters. His decisions were always carefully considered and he was not an adventurer taking risks. At the same time, he hated British amateurism. These particular traits of character appear very similar to Lieutenant General Kelly-Kenny's approach to business. Having spent some key formative periods with this man, both as his adjutant and divisional staff officer, this should come as no surprise.

Professionally, he now knew how a division operated in war and how the three combat arms of artillery, cavalry and infantry could be orchestrated to achieve best effect, but he had also had to learn the challenges of achieving good administration and logistics to make success happen. He had witnessed significant command and control issues and the effect of attacking well-defended dug-in positions. He had also seen the early challenges of guerrilla warfare. He was able to learn from the successes and failures of the British Army in South Africa and, in his next appointment, was in an influential position to improve its performance.

ARMY REFORM

The army had to change as a result of the Boer War experience and Charles Monro was to play a key part, helping to shape the future of rifle shooting or 'musketry', develop more realistic training and influence the adoption of effective 'fire and movement' tactics.

The army's poor performance in the war was summed up by many writers, including L. S. Amery in his book *The Problem of the Army*, published in 1903. He identified the following key weaknesses:

Poor intelligence on the Boers and their environment.
Failure to adopt the best methods to beat them.
Poor structures and strategic dispositions.
Inadequate training, particularly when dealing with long-range rifles and smokeless ammunition.
Lack of mobility and initiative.[1]

Meanwhile, Charles Monro's fellow DAAG in the 6th Division, Major Caunter, was posted to the Royal Military College and was identifying lower-level tactical lessons to be learned and corrected. He was not the only critic of the British Army's performance in the war. Whilst acknowledging that South Africa had been a unique environment, he noted that there were many areas needing improvement, including the requirement to improve individual initiative, reconnaissance skills and, in particular, the co-operation between artillery and infantry in the assault. He warned against long bombardments before the infantry attack, as surprise was lost:

We learned this lesson, then, for our future guidance, that the artillery preparation and the infantry advance should be very nearly simultaneous; that the infantry, pushing on at widely-extended intervals and in several lines, must force the defenders to expose themselves to meet the attack, and thus offer the artillery the opportunity and target necessary to effective practice.[2]

Linking competent shooting skills with tactical acumen was recognised as the key to success on the battlefield. Another critic, Lieutenant Colonel E. May, wrote that troops must adjust to the ground and not just rely on 'blundering courage'. He added that:

> An attack should go forward in echelons, and that one echelon should cover the advance of the other … We should teach men to shoot at such targets and under such conditions as would confront them on active service. Not at squares of white with black patches in the centre; but at indistinct, indefinite objects at unknown ranges which the rifleman must gauge himself.[3]

German criticism of British tactics in South Africa was translated and also published. A series of articles by Major Balck of the German General Staff made comments such as:

> The want of success of the English attacks was to be traced to defective arms and inadequate training in shooting under battle conditions, and more especially to the unsatisfactory tactical training of the superior officers, whose lack of initiative and fear of taking responsibility became a by-word, while the younger officers did very much better. The troops themselves were brave enough, but not prepared for such duties as fell upon them in South Africa.

And:

> The knowledge also that infantry and artillery must work together in order to establish fire superiority was not general in the Army. Artillery preparation in advance and infantry attack were two things sharply separated from each other.[4]

Winston Churchill agreed, writing, 'On frequent occasions there was a failure of the artillery to co-operate with the infantry attack.'[5] Measures were needed 'to solve the problems of British military weakness', as tactics, training and equipment all needed review.[6]

A great deal of army reform was to occur over the next few years, from the strategic to the tactical level, in order to improve the situation and prepare the

School of Musketry badge.
(Author's collection)

army for the next significant conflict, the First World War. However, despite a great deal of debate there were many conflicting views about the correct way ahead on most issues, as there were conflicting lessons learned from the Boer and Russo-Japanese wars.

Lieutenant Colonel Charles Monro, now 40 years old, had served in the army for twenty-one years and in two very different wars. He had passed Staff College and held some important appointments, but was still little known. Indeed, his original biographer stated, 'To the majority of his comrades he was just a sound, sensible infantry officer, devoted to his Regiment, loyal to his chiefs, thorough in his work, the best of good fellows, whose hall-mark was little above mediocrity.'[7]

All this would change. His latent talents were discovered, amidst significant changes in the army dominating the years between the Boer War and First World War. He was to flourish and spend the next six years as first the chief instructor, then the commandant as a full colonel of the School of Musketry at Hythe in Kent, though initially he thought that he did not have the capacity for such a job. This was an unusually long period in one establishment, but the continuity and his expertise were to drive change in low-level tactics and the use of the rifle, which laid the foundations of the army's professional performance in the early months of the Great War.

Hythe is a likeable small town on the south coast of Kent and one of the original Cinque ports, known to many, even in 1903, for 'old houses, old plate and old people'.[8] Napoleonic defences dominated the landscape, including the Royal Military Canal and the distinctive round Martello towers. There had been ranges there for many years, but in 1853 the School of Musketry was established, just as the army was starting to switch from the smooth-bore Brown Bess musket to the Minié rifle. 'Shooting – formerly almost as lethal to the firer as the fired upon – now became science. Problems of windage, elevation and ballistics arose.'[9] A small-arms wing remained at Hythe until 1969 before being moved to the School of Infantry, Warminster. However, both Hythe and the nearby Lydd Ranges are still critical British

Army training assets; the author has spent many hours on the pebble-covered ranges, in all weathers, preparing for operational tours.

The staff at the school, known as the Corps of Instructors, experimented with new weapons, improved drills and techniques, wrote training manuals and were the origin of the specialist unit, the Small Arms School Corps. The instruction in the past had not always been relevant. The future Field Marshal William Robertson had completed a course there as a sergeant in 1881, recording:

> I was sent to the school of musketry at Hythe to qualify as assistant instructor of musketry. The curriculum was then about as unpractical and wearisome as it could well be, the greater part of the time – two months – being devoted to acquiring efficiency in repeating, parrot like, the instructions laid down in the drill book. Little or no attention was paid to the art of shooting in the field, and the total amount of ball ammunition expended was restricted to the orthodox forty rounds per man. It was not till some years later, under such commandants as Ian Hamilton and Monro, that a more intelligent system, better suited to modern requirements was introduced, and Hythe began to be a really useful institution.[10]

The syllabus had to be changed, and this work was accelerated between 1898 and 1900 by Colonel (later General) Sir Ian Hamilton, who was to be relieved by Charles Monro at Gallipoli in 1915. He increased the amount of training and ammunition available for shooting, started courses for the militia and volunteers and tightened up officer musketry skills requirements. Further improvements had to be made, particularly after the bitter lessons learned from the importance of applied accurate firepower from the Boer War. Charles Monro and his successors led further change, as their staff trained regimental instructors on courses, before returning them, qualified, to their parent units – they were 'training the trainer'.

The variety and change of emphasis of instruction was detailed in a 1903 article:

> The 'courses' alternate between Regular and Militia, which occupy six weeks, and Yeomanry and Volunteers, lasting only three. In addition, there is an occasional fourteen-day course for officers qualifying for the post of district inspector of musketry or regimental adjutant.[11]

The students learned the detail of weapons first, construction and care, then fired on the normal ranges on the beach, facing the English Channel. They then learned how to run ranges and mastered more technical information

THE SCHOOL OF MUSKETRY.

Hythe School of Musketry, 1903. (Author's collection)

before conducting field firing, which involved live-firing weapons in conditions as similar to those on operations as possible; not dissimilar to the framework of small-arms training conducted today.

Charles Monro earned his reputation and future promotion to higher command from these six years at Hythe, first working as chief instructor for the commandant, Colonel R. Pennington. Initially, they became familiar with and visited continental musketry schools, as they realised that the British system was antiquated and not fit for purpose on the modern battlefield – soldiers were of no use unless properly trained. Then, as commandant from 1903, he was aided by the new chief instructor, Major William Bird, a veteran of the Boer War, who was also an officer in the Queen's (Royal West Surrey) Regiment. Major Bird helped his leader shape future low-level tactics and contributed to the Infantry Fire Tactics debate in the *Royal United Service Institution Journal* in 1905:

> As there can be no effective fire without sound tactics, so tactics cannot be successful without efficient fire, for with the exception of the final assault, every manoeuvre, every movement, undertaken by Infantry in war, has but one aim and object, viz., Fire Action.

'Fire and movement' were critical for success – the ability of different elements of the attacking force to support each other with covering fire from static positions making best use of cover, whilst the other part moves forward ready to do the same for them. He recommended that fire superiority was attained with:

Superiority of numbers.
Better leadership.
More modern armament.
Greater accuracy of fire, and if accuracy is not sacrificed, rapidity of fire.
More skilful use of cover.
Surprise.
Establishment of moral superiority. And judicious employment of covering fire is, for the assailant, an essential condition for success.[12]

Major Bird was followed by Major Norman McMahon, the 'musketry maniac'.[13] McMahon went on to command a Royal Fusiliers battalion in the BEF in 1914 and his personal efforts were recorded by Corporal W. Holbrook who wrote about McMahon:

He was responsible for improving the firepower of the British Army. Wonderful man he was. Before he came to us he was in charge of the School of Musketry at Hythe and he was musketry mad! He started the fifteen rounds a minute.[14] When I first joined the Army you fired at a bulls-eye that was your target. He ended all that. You fired at moving figures – khaki, doubling – so from about five rounds a minute you went to about fifteen. You had to lie in the box, unloaded, with three rounds in clips of five in the pouches. When the whistle went you'd have to load your rifle and fire, tip the case out, *fire, fire, fire* … and get it all into the minute. His one craze was musketry.[15]

McMahon was a machine gun enthusiast and an influential officer who had given an important lecture on the subject of firepower to the Aldershot Military Society in 1907. Although less effective in South Africa, their worth had been proven in the Russo-Japanese War. As a result, Field Service Regulations were rewritten to include his teachings.

However, though the School of Musketry had recommended in 1909 that each infantry battalion should have six machine guns instead of two, the suggestion was denied because of financial reasons and infantry battalions were still only equipped with two at the start of the First World War. In addition, there had been mixed messages about their performance in the Boer and Russo-Japanese wars; some British observers believed them unreliable, costly in ammunition expenditure and too vulnerable as targets. Therefore, every effort had to be made to make best use of the rifle and the British soldier's weakness was his ability to provide accurate fire at close range up to 400 yards. At the same time, a higher rate of fire was needed, at the expense of accuracy, in order to hit the mass of advancing enemy –'What was required was the "browning" of a mass, rather than careful snap shooting at the glimpse of a head behind a rock.'[16]

Charles Monro's teachings became known as the 'Monro Doctrine'. It was through the efforts of him and his staff at Hythe and their successors, that shooting and effective fire and movement became so critical and successful for the professional British Army of 1914. Volley firing and tight infantry tactical formations were abandoned in favour of high standards of realistic marksmanship, better use of the ground and encouragement of initiative amongst lower ranks. The result was that, in the initial clashes on the Western Front around Mons, the Germans thought that they were facing machine guns because of the accuracy and volume of British fire. The effect was described in 1914 at Mons by Corporal John Lucy of the Royal Irish Rifles:

> Our rapid fire was appalling, even to us, and the worst marksman could not miss, as he had only to fire into the 'brown' of the masses of the unfortunate enemy who on the front of our two companies were continuously and uselessly reinforced at the short range of 300 yards … It was all too easy.[17]

The Monro Doctrine was widely recognised as a significant contribution to an expeditionary force that was described by the *Official History of the Great War* as 'incomparably the best trained, best organised and best equipped British Army which ever went forth to war'.[18] Lessons had been learned from poor performances during the Boer War and observations from the later Russo-Japanese War. His efforts were part of a wider army reform, which transformed a traditional policing 'amateur' approach to warfare to a more professional one, albeit still not perfect. This period marked the most significant period of reform since Cardwell's.

His years at Hythe were during a changing political landscape in Europe, dominated by the rising threat of Germany and the end of 'splendid isolation'. An alliance was made by Great Britain with Japan in 1902 and the *entente cordiale* was signed with France in 1904 to counter the German threat – the Continent was being focussed on for the first time since the Napoleonic Wars. Britain needed strong allies. However, once the Boer War was over, the public were more interested in changing social issues than the military. A major social reform programme was begun, constitutional changes occurred, there were significant industrial disputes and the challenge of Home Rule in Ireland. In addition, the Royal Navy secured the most defence funding and attention as major technical advances resulted in the

Colonel Monro, 1903. (Surrey History
Centre. QRWS 1-16-7-19)

new Dreadnoughts and the naval arms race with Germany – the army was,
as usual, in competition with higher political priorities.

In 1888, the Minister for War, Edward Stanhope, had had to deal with the
clash of interests and priorities between Eurocentric and Indocentric strategists. He issued his little-known memorandum, not seen by the public until
1901, which provided thoughts on a future role for the army:

> To find men for India, for garrisons, for fortresses and coaling stations, and
> for home defence … But it will be distinctly understood that the prob-
> ability of the employment of an Army Corps in the field in any European
> war is sufficiently improbable to make it the primary duty of the military
> authorities to organise our forces efficiently for the defence of this country.[19]

It would be a few years, however, before a continental role was to be seriously
considered.

Strategic Reform

The Boer War had seen the deployment of a large British Army, denuding
the United Kingdom of any reserve to defend the homeland or conduct any

other task. The Royal Navy had provided a defensive shield, but the war had alienated much of Europe and helped encourage Germany's Navy Bill of 1900 which doubled its naval building programme, setting the course for an arms race and later clash.

As Secretary of State for War in 1901, St John Broderick began a programme of ambitious reform, similar to German thinking, which was to result in the establishment of an expeditionary force. He stated:

> I propose to reorganise the Army on a new system of which the bedrock will be that the whole country will be divided into six Army Corps by districts, that each district in times of peace will have the same relative proportions to the various arms that are necessary to make up the corps, and that they will be under the commanders who will lead them in time of war.[20]

In his vision, three of the army corps would be supported by sixty battalions of militia and volunteers with specific extra training requirements. He wanted to expand the yeomanry and abolish the militia reserve. He wanted better training for officers and expected over half of the Regular Army to be based in its homeland.

Laudable though his aspirations were, including better integration of regulars and auxiliaries, he was trying to reform the army at a time when it was embroiled in a major war in South Africa, so he made only limited progress. Many observers, including L. S. Amery who had written the *Times' History of the War in South Africa* and later *The Problem of the Army*, criticised his plans as being too inflexible and impracticable.[21] Lieutenant General Kelly-Kenny described the army corps system as 'not applicable', as an organisation based on smaller and more manageable divisional building blocks was preferred.[22] However, soldiers' pay and barracks were to be substantially improved, standards raised within the Royal Army Medical Corps and a working uniform was to be introduced that was to be the same as that worn on active service – khaki service dress.[23] He also succeeded in decentralising command and control of the army and creating an expanded key training area on Salisbury Plain and the Tidworth Garrison in Wiltshire.

Broderick's greatest success was providing the basis of the Committee of Imperial Defence (CID), to improve imperial security by co-ordinating defence issues at the strategic level. This would consist of 'the Prime Minister, the Lord President, the War Minister, the C-in-C, the First Sea Lord and the heads of naval and military intelligence'.[24] This strategic-level committee provided the basis for effective decision making in both world wars.

In addition, during Broderick's tenure, many of the weapons used by the British Army in the First World War were ordered. This included better, quick-firing 18- and 13-pounder artillery and the Short Magazine Lee–Enfield rifle for both cavalry and infantry. The new rifle was easier to handle than its predecessor, could be fast-loaded by charger and the breech mechanism could be operated quickly to allow rapid fire – ideal for executing the Monro Doctrine.

These were important measures that reinforced an ex-Boer leader's views, expressed in a *Royal United Service Institution Journal* of 1902: 'The British soldier is a brave man and a good fighter and, were he armed with the latest and best arms, would be a dangerous foe to even the mighty armies of Germany and Russia.'[25]

Broderick was replaced as Secretary of State for War by Arnold-Forster in 1903. He had new ideas for reform and declared in 1904 that he wanted two new armies – a general service army and a home service army. These ideas were impracticable and were not executed. The idea was that the general service army would serve home and abroad at times of peace or war and service would be for nine years with the colours, followed by three with the reserve. There would be a 'striking force' based at Aldershot and large training depots instead of Cardwell's linked battalion system.

Meanwhile, the Home Service Army would be based at home and serve abroad only in time of war. The commitment for a recruit would be shorter, with two years with the colours and six with the reserve. This latter army would be territorially recruited. It was acknowledged that some change was inevitable, the Secretary of State saying, in July 1904:

> It is absolutely necessary to make a change in the organisation, composition and distribution of the Army. The late war and the Commission on the War which had recently reported, have made it abundantly clear that the Army in its present form is not suited to the requirements of the country or adapted for war.[26]

To help influence organisational change at this time, five reports were available. Clinton Dawkins' report analysed the War Office, whilst the Elgin Royal Commission reported on the Boer War in 1903. In addition, in 1903 Akers-Douglas reported on officers' education. Subsequently, Lord Esher's *War Office (Reconstitution) Committee* and the Duke of Norfolk's *Royal Commission on the Militia and Volunteers* were published in 1904. There was even a debate about the need for conscription, as continental practices were taken into consideration. Never before had there been, in such a short space of time, so much analysis affecting the future of the army.

Mr Clinton Dawkins criticised the lack of co-ordination between military and civilian personnel and the centralised control of administration. The idea was to 'bring the work of the War Office more into harmony with that of large business undertakings'.[27] Lord Elgin's report, which has been mentioned before, analysed the poor performance of the army. It criticised leadership, equipment and training, efficiency, and failure to take heed of intelligence assessments.

Norfolk had similar comments to make on the poor state of the militia, yeomanry and volunteers in the home defence role. His commission included the comment, 'the Militia in its existing condition is unfit to take the field for the defence of this country'.[28] Lord Esher, who had also been a member of the Elgin Commission, joined Admiral Sir John Fisher and Colonel Sir George Sydenham Clarke in recommending a major reorganisation of the War Office, the end of total control by the C-in-C and a new appointment – Chief of the General Staff (CGS) – and an Army Council and General Staff to support it. In addition, responsibilities should be divided logically, by function.

Rather than just tinkering with lower structures, as previous secretaries of state had done, Lord Esher recommended changes to the critical command node at the top. However, this activity was not welcomed by all elements of the army. Most senior officers realised that significant change was required, but the views of the more conservative ones were probably reflected in a mid-1904 note sent from the king to the prime minister: 'The King is strongly of the opinion that what the army, especially the officers throughout the army, requires at the present time, is a period free from disturbance and constant change.'[29]

Fortunately, the prime minister, Lord Balfour, quickly established both the new CID and the Army Council, and Lord Roberts was removed as the old C-in-C, as that post folded. Henceforth, control of the army was decentralised, rather than leaving the power in one senior officer's hands – it would be impossible in the future for any professional head of the army to counter the ultimate control of military administration by the Secretary of War.

The new Army Council consisted of appointments broadly recognisable today: Chief of the General Staff (CGS) (from 1909 known as the Chief of Imperial General Staff, or CIGS), Adjutant General to the Forces, Quartermaster General to the Forces and Master General of the Ordnance. It was led by the Secretary of State for War and had two other civil members, the Parliamentary Secretary of State and the Financial Secretary. A new post of Inspector General of the Forces reported to the council on efficiency. The General Staff had their responsibilities divided between the Director of Military Operations (DMO), Director of Staff Duties and Director of

Military Training. It was to take time before the new structure worked, however, as the CGS, Lieutenant General Sir Neville Gerald Lyttelton, was not that enthusiastic about all the reform measures being suggested.

The years between 1900 and 1905 came to be known as the 'period of attempted reforms', but many things *had* actually changed. Training area, barrack facilities and officers' education were improving; administrative districts were being formed and the army's centre of gravity had moved to Aldershot, where Lieutenant General Sir John French's Army Corps was located. It consisted of a cavalry brigade and two divisions (the 1st and 2nd), each of two brigades of four battalions. The 5th Division had two brigades at Shorncliffe and Dover. These formations were the most capable, though still limited in logistic capabilities. The other five divisions had substantial reinforcement and mobilisation requirements if they were to deploy on operations. In addition, twelve battalions were still required to garrison South Africa.

New rifles were being issued, the new drab uniform was being worn and new doctrine was being developed. With the orders of new guns, regular artillery units were being modernised, but progress to improve the militia and volunteers was slow – there was still a lack of integration with the Regular Army. This would change under the direction of the new Liberal Secretary of State for War, R. B. Haldane, in 1906.

Sir Douglas Haig, who was to be instrumental in preparing the British Army for a European war and held the War Office appointments of Director of Military Training in 1906, then Director of Staff Duties in 1907, described Haldane as 'the greatest Secretary of War England has ever had'.[30] He was also an ally of Lord Esher, appreciating the work that he had done to help reform the army, writing, 'Now thanks to your energy, things seem on the right road to efficiency.'[31] The feeling was mutual; Esher writing to the king about Haig, 'In him your Majesty possesses a very fine type of officer, practical, firm and thoughtful, thoroughly experienced not only in war, but in military history.'[32]

Haig does not feature positively in the *Blackadder* view of the First World War, however the Haldane and Haig team helped substantially in improving efficiency and professionalising the British Army in time for 1914. As Sheffield writes, 'As Director of Military Training, Haig sought to inculcate the precepts of uniformity, efficiency, and preparedness by organising staff tours, formulating mobilisation plans, devising training schemes, and testing embarkation and disembarkation procedures.'[33]

During this period, Charles Monro had both the support of Lord Roberts when he was C-in-C and then the War Council and Haig as he pushed on with his own reforms at Hythe's School of Musketry. Lord Roberts was a keen supporter of shooting and had helped drive the army's renewed interest in musketry and tactics. His approach was illustrated by an extract of his speech at Bisley Ranges in July 1902:

> However brave our men may be, however well drilled, well set up, and disciplined they may be, however capable they may be of enduring great fatigue, and however well they may be able to ride over most difficult country … they will be valueless as soldiers unless they are expert in the use of the rifle … It is on the perfect shooting of our men that the efficiency of the British Army will mainly depend.[34]

Haig had a wide range of responsibilities as Director of Military Training, which included the requisitioning of training areas and ranges and production of training manuals, so he was supporting Charles Monro's efforts.

The new Secretary of State, Haldane, was to hold his new post for six and a half years, implementing the Esher Report and adding value to it in his reforms. He believed that 'economy and efficiency were not incompatible' as he cut costs and reduced the size of the Regular Army, but set the conditions for a more efficient and capable organisation.[35] He succeeded in providing the country with its first expeditionary force in peacetime, a Territorial Force and a General Staff, as he balanced the British defence interests of defending overseas possessions and the British Isles whilst maintaining a contingency force potentially bound for Europe.

He was intelligent and determined to learn before encouraging change, taking advice from various experts and reading the work of military experts such as the Prussian Clausewitz and German Von der Goltz. His military private secretary was Colonel G. Ellison, who had acted as secretary to the Esher Committee. He believed that home defence was best protected by the Royal Navy, which put him at odds with Lord Roberts. However, the First Sea Lord maintained that if the navy was kept up to strength then 'an invasion on even the moderate scale of 70,000 men is practically impossible'.[36]

Concurrent to these various reforms, a key advocate of developing an efficient continental commitment was the future Field Marshal Sir Henry Wilson. As a colonel, he had lobbied for a British General Staff in support of Arnold-Forster, but he wielded more influence as commandant of the Staff College from 1907 to 1910, than as DMO.[37] In the former role, he created new links with General Foch and the French Staff College and, in the 1908 map, exercised a deployment of an expeditionary force to France with a scenario based on an invasion of Belgium by Germany.

In the War Office, as DMO, he drew up detailed plans for an expeditionary force, deploying to the left flank of the French Army if war occurred. This 'WF' (With France) scheme significantly improved Anglo-French military co-operation and Wilson's attitude was described by Colonel Hankey, secretary to the CID, as 'a perfect obsession for military operations on the continent'.[38]

Probably his greatest achievement was on 23 August 1911 when, following his detailed briefing to the CID, the French commitment was accepted as British strategy; a critical moment in the preparation of British forces for war.

Haldane's priority was to establish an expeditionary force. On first examination, it was confirmed that it would take the country two months to mobilise a force of 80,000 to France; by 1912, the plans were to deploy 160,000 across the English Channel in just one week. To begin with, only the Aldershot-based formations were really capable of deployment, but after reorganisation, six infantry divisions and a cavalry division were poised to deploy. However, this would mean cutting the budget by £2 million and reducing army strength by 20,000; not a popular move for many soldiers, especially as it involved the reduction of some artillery and infantry units, including two Guards battalions.[39] The new force would have integrated reserves, dedicated staff and lines of communication troops.

Whilst reserves were prepared to complement the Regular Army as individuals, Haldane decided to form a Territorial Force to provide home defence and form the basis of expansion to the Regular Army. In addition, he identified schools and universities as training opportunities for an increase in officers if war was declared.

A new Territorial Force was to be established from the old yeomanry and volunteers. It was to be formed into fourteen cavalry brigades and fourteen infantry divisions and be an integrated force with its own artillery, engineers and specialist support, despite the reluctance of Lord Roberts and Major General Henry Wilson, then commandant of the Staff College. Though there was no liability for overseas service, it was accepted that with six months of post-mobilised training, the force could be deployed abroad and that individuals would volunteer to do so. It was to be administered, but not commanded, by county associations chaired by lord lieutenants. Meanwhile, the militia were to become the Special Reserve, after some resistance from the militia colonels, supplementing the Army Reserve in war, providing additional valuable reinforcements to the Regular Army.

Seventy-four battalions were formed in 1908, one battalion per line regiment, to form the 3rd (Special Reserve) Battalions to the line regiments. Another twenty-seven battalions became 'Extra Reserve'. There were nearly 68,000 Special Reservists by the end of 1908 and they suffered heavy casualties in the early months of the First World War, reinforcing the Regular Army, yet they are relatively unknown to the public who tended to think that the army only consisted of the Regulars and the Territorials.[40]

At the same time, following the Ward Committee recommendations, the Officers' Training Corps was introduced, with senior divisions in universities and junior divisions in schools. This initially involved nineteen universities and 152 public schools.

There was a lot of opposition from traditionalists to these changes, which in hindsight were vital to the army's performance and expansion at the beginning of the First World War. Haldane worked closely with Haig to develop the General Staff, who soon began to make a difference and the Staff College was revitalised. As the esteemed historian Correlli Barnett has commented, 'Not since the days of the Commonwealth had the British Army been so generally gripped with a sense of professional purpose in peacetime.'[41]

Doctrine, Training and Tactics

The British Army's view on doctrine – 'what is taught' – has varied in history, as many commanders have feared dogma and a lack of flexibility in thought. The less than professional Victorian army was not committed to any formal written doctrine and before the establishment of the Army Council there was no top-down mechanism to enforce any doctrine. There had been few large exercises and the lack of any doctrine meant that different units performed in different ways depending on the experiences of individual officers in command, so there were no documented best practices to adopt and little cohesion or mutual understanding between units and their headquarters when they deployed on operations.

Some doctrine was published for the first time, prior to the First World War, though it can be strongly argued that it was not enough. Detailed staff responsibilities were shown in two key documents, driven by Haig in his role as Director of Staff Duties: *Field Service Regulations Part I – Operations – 1909* and *Part II – Organisation and Administration – 1909*. Part I provided the requirements for training for war, whilst Part II provided guidance to the adjutant general's and quartermaster general's branches. System and uniformity were being introduced, providing 'a basic war organisation and method, both of which the army had so seriously lacked in all previous conflicts'.[42] These documents would take time to assimilate in an army dominated by experience not theory, but they were significant milestones towards greater professionalism at an important time. Note this comment in Part I about avoiding frontal attacks:

A decisive attack against some portion of the enemy's front offers a possibility of breaking his army in two and may give great and far-reaching results.

The long range, accuracy, and rapidity of fire of modern weapons reduce, however, the chances of success of such an attack, while failure may result in the attacking force being enveloped and destroyed. It will usually, therefore, be wiser to direct the decisive effort against one of the enemy's flanks.[43]

Clearly, lessons from failures in the Boer War were being learned, though trying to achieve successful flanking attacks in the First World War on the Western Front's trench-locked battlefield was going to be nigh impossible.

At lower levels, old drill books were being replaced by tactical manuals and Charles Monro and the School of Musketry had a part to play in their production. *Combined Training 1902* was the first significant product and a greater emphasis was placed on the need for initiative than in the past. In the foreword, Lord Roberts wrote:

Success in war, cannot be expected unless all ranks have been trained in peace to use their wits. General and Commanding Officers are, therefore, not only to encourage their subordinates in so doing by affording them constant opportunities of acting on their own responsibility, but they will also check all practices which interfere with the free exercise of the judge-ment, and will break down, by every means in their power, the paralyzing habit of an unreasoning and mechanical adherence to the letter of orders and to routine, when acting under service conditions.[44]

These aspirations were partially achieved by the beginning of the First World War. The Boer War had shown that advancing in close-order formations against a dug-in, well-armed enemy was suicidal, as witnessed by Charles Monro at the Battle of Paardeberg. More dispersed formations were required and they could not be controlled in detail by individual officers on their own; initiative amongst all ranks was key. A number of books on low-level tactics were written in this period by different officers, who attempted to influ-ence change. They extolled the virtues of the need for initiative in all ranks and advised the schools of musketry to teach more than just basic shooting, making their exercises as realistic as possible – music to Charles Monro's ears. For example:

Greater stress than at present should be laid on shooting with time limit, in order to encourage quick aiming, so as to make it a habit. The power of the quick aiming is of the utmost importance in war in both snap-shooting and in firing at vanishing objects. The higher part of the company train-ing will be the field practices over varied ground and unknown ranges, in connection with some sound tactical idea, which should be varied for each practice. The men should also be dressed in the same kit as they would wear in war time, so as to accustom them to firing, moving and taking cover with all the impediment that a fully weighted equipment causes.[45]

And another author:

The man may be a good shot on the rifle range, he may be able to patter off by heart the rules of aiming, his weapon may be the best that art can devise or science produce, and yet if he cannot intelligently use it in the field its tactical utility will be lost or the results obtained as exiguous as if he were armed with a Snider or even a Brown Bess.[46]

However, the value of advice varied on some subjects. Whilst the well-respected tactician and author, Colonel Charles Callwell, supported the essence of the Monro Doctrine of Fire and Movement and the importance of company level tactics and training, he also wrote, astonishingly, 'it does not appear probable that machine guns will ever play a very great part in battle'.[47]

Other new lower-level tactics manuals appeared: *Cavalry Training* in 1904; *Infantry Training* in 1905; the *Manual of Engineering* in 1905 and *Field Artillery Training* in 1907. In addition, the handy *First Field Service Pocket Book* was published in 1906. Forewords made it clear that they dealt with elementary training 'and with the general principles which are to govern the further training in peace and the employment in war of that arm'.[48] The efficient linkage of realistic training and war was being made formally, for the first time. Initiative was again encouraged, as illustrated in the *Infantry Training Manual* rewrite of 1911:

The difficulties of command are much increased by the fact that the leader can no longer personally control and direct all ranks by word of mouth … In view of the paramount importance of decentralisation of command, it is essential that superior officers, including battalion commanders, should never trespass on the proper sphere of action of their subordinates.[49]

Artillerymen argued about the balance required between direct and indirect fire, as new, heavier and longer-range guns came into service, whilst there was mixed reporting from the Russo-Japanese War, with one observer writing, 'The great impression made on my mind by all I saw is that artillery is now the decisive arm and that all other arms are auxiliary to it.'[50] The Royal Artillery concentrated on long-range accurate shooting and not enough on artillery–infantry co-operation.

Meanwhile, the cavalry had to repair its damaged reputation after the Boer War and shake off the dominance of mounted infantry in that conflict. As part of professionalisation, as well as new manuals, the Cavalry School was established at Netheravon in 1904 and a year later the *Cavalry Journal* was published. The lance was abolished and then there was a debate about whether the sword or rifle was the cavalryman's most important weapon.

The hierarchy was still convinced that the cavalry had a very important mobile role on the battlefield and that hunting and riding skills were important. However, there was no full agreement on the required balance of skills: reconnaissance, shock and fire tactics. By the time the manual *Cavalry Training 1912* was published, a hybrid compromise solution was in place, resulting in 'a flexible and well-considered approach to delivering shock action, emphasising surprise and fire support as prerequisites for anything other than small-scale actions'.[51] One significant positive change was that the cavalry had to reach the same standards of musketry as the infantry. Even provincial newspapers were reporting this reform:

> The spirit of reform has recently been busy in the Army Bureau that deals with musketry. It has now been laid down as an axiom that musketry is the drill of paramount importance in the training of a soldier. Orders have been given that the cavalryman shall use the time he is said to have wasted on sword exercise in learning to shoot better, not with the carbine of the pre-war days, but with the Lee–Enfield rifle.[52]

Formal regulations were produced for exercises and new 'Exercises on the Ground without Troops'[53] and Staff Rides. The Staff Ride of 1909 included mobilisation training and highlighted a lack of co-ordination and problems in 'disembarking, moving, accommodating, and concentrating of troops'; all valuable lessons for the future.[54] Again, initiative was emphasised: 'Criticism by senior officers should be kindly, helpful and constructive. Criticism of a fault finding or discouraging nature tends to create an unwillingness to face responsibility and display initiative and originality.'[55] This last comment looks incredibly modern and is a challenging aspiration even today.

Musketry regulations manuals were published, driven by Charles Monro and the Hythe School, along with more populist and readable pocket pamphlets such as *The Musketry Teacher* and *How to Use a Rifle and Pistol*. Colonel (later Major General) Pennington, who was Charles Monro's commandant when he was chief instructor at Hythe wrote of his efforts:

> I wrote no page of the new musketry regulations which he did not review, and his criticism and suggestions on that and all other matters were always

invaluable ... His Staff College training, staff experience and general first-rate knowledge of his profession qualified him especially for the varied work he had to undertake. His tact, geniality and unfailing good temper contributed greatly to the smooth introduction of the many changes which were being affected. The credit for the complete revision of the courses of training was almost his entirely ... I consider that he raised the standard of instruction and increased the value and interest of the courses at least a hundred per cent.[56]

Rifle shooting was being practised more than before and the volley firing used by closely packed ranks of the past became obsolete. New field firing ranges were being built, but Charles Monro, whilst improving shooting standards, was critically preaching the importance of 'Fire and Movement'. That meant that an infantry attack must be assisted with its own fire as well as that of the artillery, right up to the moment of assault. This also encouraged initiative, resourcefulness and the attitude of seizing fleeting opportunities. As Barrow wrote:

It gave to the 'Other Ranks' an interest in training which had been absent from the former methods of linear tactics and volley firing by word of command. It remedied the defects which are contained in Lord Roberts' strictures after the South African War, when he said: 'Our soldiers have no initiative; they are not clever at making use of the ground, and although good target shots, are not trained to battle shooting.'[57]

Fortunately, the School of Musketry and its leaders had the patronage of Lord Roberts and then the Army Council, otherwise many of these important changes would never have occurred before the First World War. The National Rifle Association was totally against the greater concentration on rapid fire and movement, snap shooting and moving targets; 'match shooting' was preferred to 'battle shooting'. However, the association could not operate without War Office supplies, so it was forced to come into line with the new procedures.

The British Army's improving professionalism and shooting skills were noticed by the German von Lobell's reports for 1904:

In their manoeuvres the British Infantry showed great skill in the use of ground. Their thin khaki-clad skirmishers were scarcely visible. No detachment was ever seen in close order within three thousand yards. Frontal attacks were entirely avoided. No attack on entrenched positions was adjudged successful unless with a numerical superiority of six to one.

> The excessive extension allowed militated against really powerful attack. The machine guns were too exposed. Volley firing is abolished. Slow fire and rapid fire – the latter not exceeding fifteen rounds a minute – being used alone.[58]

However, it can be argued that whilst effective tactical improvements were being made, as eventually proved in 1914, the higher-level doctrine had still not made a huge impact on the British Army, as argued well by Spencer-Jones. He comments, 'Although *Field Service Regulations* was an important advance in British military thinking, it did not represent the creation of a formal written doctrine, and it continued the trend of rejecting the concept.'[59]

Despite the preaching of the importance of inter-arm co-operation, there were few coherent approaches to formation or inter-arm training, though some improvements were made in artillery and infantry co-operation. There were also shortages of personnel for training, as under-strength units turned up for training exercises, having provided reinforcements for other tasks and garrisons throughout the Empire. A 1912 inspection identified disparate methods of attack in different army divisions, though junior officers and men were performing well.[60] There was also some lack of communication between the newly formed General Staff and lower levels of the army, the Duke of Connaught commenting in 1907, 'The General Staff did not provide leadership that filtered down, arguing that the body was "out of touch" with the army as a whole and in danger of being viewed as "just another War Office organisation".'[61]

In the same year, the Inspector General wrote, 'We are in danger of having a different school of thought in each command, resulting in an absence of uniformity which is much regretted.'[62] There was also an underlying concern about the availability of blank ammunition to train with and the proficiency of umpires on training exercises. However, some key personalities, such as General John French commanding at Aldershot, did insist on high training standards and arguably 'did more than any other British officer to prepare the army for the continental war'.[63]

Tactical achievements were being made, but there was still a lack of doctrine put into practice at higher levels. Whilst the British Army was undoubtedly very effective at lower levels at the beginning of the First World War, many historians point out that it also had many weaknesses, with 'its lack of trained staff, its inability to sustain large-scale operations over a prolonged period, and the lack of experience at commanding large numbers of men'.[64] However, it was a more efficient army than fifteen years before, Colonel Dunlop concluding his analysis of army reform by writing, 'The South African War was a lesson, a bitter one, but to the credit of the entire nation the lesson was learnt and not ignored.'[65] Without the contribution of key secretaries of state, particularly Haldane, putting in place critical structural changes and procurement of new equipment, combined with important doctrinal, training and tactical reform, the performance of the British Army in 1914 and its ability to expand would have been disastrous.

For all of his hard work at the School of Musketry, Colonel Charles Monro was to receive the first of his many awards in 1906 – Companion or Ordinary Member of the Military Division of the Third Class to the Most Honourable Order of the Bath (the CB).[66]

He was still writing about tactical issues as a major general in 1911, so it is obvious that he kept a keen interest in the subject as he progressed up the highest ranks in the army and was about to take command of a division. His article in *The Army Review* of July 1911 was again about the importance of 'Fire and Movement'. Its aim was to advise on procedures so that:

> … rifle fire may be applied in the most effective manner to meet tactical requirements, and to lay stress on the necessity of rifle fire being invariably regarded as the chief means by which progress can be denied to an enemy or rendered feasible in the case of attack.[67]

He provided practical guidance to both battalion and company commanders, extolling them to work closely with neighbouring units and highlighted the importance of concealment, observation and intercommunication. Many of his thoughts were incorporated in the latest *Infantry Training Manual* of the time, again illustrating his professional influence.

Whilst the British Army may not have learned all the lessons they might have from both the Boer and Russo-Japanese wars, it is hard not to agree with the assessment that by 1914 'the infantry, in fact, attained a peak in individual and company training never before achieved in the British Army and unequalled among the contemporary armies in Europe'.[68]

Colonel Monro had done his bit to achieve this. A soldier is rarely rewarded financially; his rewards are mainly based on awards, posting locations and promotion. Along with the CB, he was now posted to Ireland as a newly promoted brigadier general commanding a brigade, and it would not be long before he commanded at the divisional level. He was extremely well thought of, as he had achieved formation command from his performance at Hythe, having not even led a regular battalion – extremely unusual.

Before the War

Ireland and Brigade Command

Brigade command at 46 years old was pretty good. Here was an officer who was going places as a result of his outstanding performance at Hythe and his competence during the Boer War, yet he had not commanded an infantry battalion and had no recent operational experience. This was a highly professional, sometimes too serious, officer who had earned his rewards through hard work. For the next three and a half years, he was the brigade commander of 13th Infantry Brigade, based in Dublin, Ireland, which he led with 'conspicuous success from 1907 to 1911', though little is recorded of this period of his service.[1]

The Irish Command was one of the four Home Army Commands established by a Special Army Order of January 1907, which reorganised the army as part of the Haldane Reforms. The other commands were: Aldershot (1st Cavalry Brigade, the 1st and 2nd Divisions and Army Troops); Southern Command (3rd Division) and Eastern Command (2nd and 4th Cavalry Brigades and the 4th Division). This was the foundation of the future BEF of 1914.

The C-in-C in Ireland for most of Charles Monro's command was General the Right Honourable Sir Neville Lyttelton, the former CGS, who many years before had helped defeat Fenian raids in Canada and commanded a battalion of his regiment, the Rifle Brigade, in Ireland. Irish Command comprised the 3rd Cavalry Brigade at the Curragh and the 5th and 6th Divisions.

The 5th Division, commanded by Major General Herbert Plumer, comprised:

13th Infantry Brigade (Dublin) – Brigadier General Monro's command.
14th Infantry Brigade (Curragh).

15th Infantry Brigade (Belfast).
Three Field Artillery Brigades (headquarters at Newbridge).
One Field Artillery (Howitzer) Brigade (Athlone).
Two Field Companies Royal Engineers (Curragh).

A brigade was made up of around 3,000–4,000 officers and men, and 13th Brigade was based on three infantry battalions, who for most of this period were: 2nd Battalion the Royal Scots Fusiliers, 2nd Battalion the Royal Inniskilling Fusiliers and 2nd Battalion the Wiltshire Regiment. His right-hand man was the brigade major, or chief of staff, Major T. Shoubridge, Distinguished Service Order (DSO), of the Northumberland Fusiliers.[2]

Major General Plumer was Charles Monro's senior commander for his first eighteen months. Only three years older than Monro, Plumer, whom General Douglas Haig disliked, went on to command V Corps on the Western Front in April 1915 at the Second Battle of Ypres and then led the 2nd Army from May 1915, culminating in a victory against the Germans at the Battle of Messines in 1917. He has been described as 'a meticulous planner, cautious and impossible to fluster'; similar traits to Charles Monro, who

ARRAH! FOR AULD IRELAND!

Sons of the Empire (7)   *Copyright*

'Arrah! For Auld Ireland!' postcard.
(Author's collection)

would have been keen to learn some of his command skills.[3] Interestingly, it is Plumer, as a retired field marshal and outliving Charles Monro, who wrote the foreword to the original Monro biography in 1931. There must have been a great deal of mutual respect between the two men and Plumer lists amongst Monro's attributes his high sense of duty, earnestness, thoroughness and ability to give sound judgements.[4] Both Plumer and Lyttelton were counted as Monro's friends.

Ireland was a popular posting for Charles Monro, especially now that he had new and increased responsibilities. He knew the country well, having spent six years there with his own regiment in the 1880s in Dublin and Tralee and he was fond of country life. His first month in Dublin coincided with the city's Irish International Exhibition, which ran for six months and attracted 2.75 million people, whilst in July 1907 the state visit of King Edward VII and Queen Alexandra to Ireland began.

Ireland was relatively quiet during this period and the Liberals returned to power after the 1906 general election with a big enough parliamentary majority not to have to worry about the need to placate the Irish Nationalists. However, all was not totally peaceful on the political front, as Sir Edward Carson's Protestant Ulster Unionist Council had only been set up two years before, in the same year as Arthur Griffith's Sinn Féin ('we ourselves') Republican Party. The latter organisation was demonstrating outside the Mansion House, Dublin, in September 1907 and in the North Leitrim by-election, held in 1908, Sinn Féin managed to secure 27 per cent of the vote, though the party's support in Ireland dropped afterwards. Most Nationalists supported the mainstream and more moderate Irish Parliamentary Party, led by the conciliatory John Redmond, fighting peaceably for Home Rule. Redmond's party was to increase its influence on British politics after the two general elections of 1910, when their eighty-three Members of Parliament held the balance of power at Westminster and made the Liberal Party support the 3rd Home Rule Bill in 1912.

Meanwhile, at the end of July 1907, part of the army was deployed on the streets, when a non-sectarian dockers' and carters' strike of 10,000 workers occurred in Belfast over a three-month period. The police refused to break the picket lines and the army was brought in to help. Unfortunately, two civilians were shot dead in one riot in August on the Falls Road.

Brigadier General Monro's 13th Brigade was lucky to be in Dublin, as part of a large British garrison, the largest barracks being in the Curragh, near Kildare, in the centre of the country. The Irish Command was seen by most of the locals as a force of occupation with its mixture of English, Scottish and Welsh soldiers. Ironically, some of the British Army's greatest officers and soldiers were Irish and there were many Irish cavalry and infantry regiments.

This included Brigadier General Monro's Royal Inniskilling Fusiliers, who were well known for their excellent performance in the Peninsular War of the early 1800s and whose heritage went back to loyal service to the Crown against enemy Roman Catholic forces in Ireland during 1689. At Waterloo, the Duke of Wellington commented on the 'Skins', 'That is the Regiment that saved the centre of my line.'[5]

The British Army was to clarify its political position during the so-called 'Curragh Mutiny' in March 1914, when cavalry officers refused to take possible action against the Protestant Loyalists, the Ulster Volunteers, if they rebelled against Home Rule. The political and religious divide between Loyalists and Roman Catholic Nationalists was growing. At this time, General Sir Henry Wilson, DMO in London, supplied the Conservative leader, Bonar Law, and the Unionist Sir Edward Carson with advice and military intelligence. That incident was after Charles Monro's period of command, but the fragile political and social scene was being set with this high-profile incident, the massive rally of the Ulster Unionist Council in Belfast in 1912, the formation of the Irish Nationalist Volunteers in 1913 and the later violent clashes, such as the Easter Rising in Dublin during April 1916.

But this was 1907 and an opportunity for Charles Monro to put into practice his own doctrine and training methods within 13th Brigade. He made his mark quickly as his brigade developed excellent fire and movement tactical skills and its 'field firing was stimulating and progressive'.[6] He got on with his professional duties, never complaining. His divisional commander was impressed by his judgement and professionalism as he improved the fighting standards of his command and demonstrated 13th Brigade's prowess at the manoeuvres in Carlow during 1910.

Ireland was a great place for country sports for the middle and upper classes, especially hunting, which Charles Monro enjoyed, although he had a continuous problem controlling his weight which sometimes slowed his riding expertise down. Whilst in Gibraltar he had hunted with the Calpe hounds, in Ireland he enjoyed joining the Meath and Ward hounds and was recorded as saying that hunting was 'a quite admirable nerve-tonic'.[7] He would join his commander, Major General Plumer, at the Kildare Hunt.

The country was also a good place for socialising and the brigadier general mixed with the Irish upper classes and Dublin society, including the Lord Chancellor of Ireland. At the time, he lived with and was supported socially by his sister, Amy. She had played a similar role when he was in Gibraltar in 1898. They both organised popular gatherings at their home.

Charles Monro also took on some extra-curricular duties within the committees running the Royal Hibernian Military School and the Drummond Institute. The school had been established in Dublin during 1769 and was set up to educate children of deceased members of Great Britain's armed forces in Ireland. It had also catered for children of soldiers who were deployed overseas on operations. It moved to Shorncliffe in the 1920s, after Ireland's partition, and then merged with the current Duke of York's Royal Military School at Dover. The Drummond Institute was another educational establishment in Dublin. Both of these commitments demonstrate Charles Monro's altruism and it was written that 'his kindness to the officials of these institutions was unvarying'.[8]

Although Charles Monro had only been able to demonstrate his proficiency in training his brigade, rather than on operations, during his five years he earned the respect of his superiors and was promoted to major general in 1911 and given command of the 2nd London Territorial Division in 1912. He is reported to have enjoyed a little 'gardening leave' between commands, but managed to continue hunting in the Midlands with his fellow regimental colleague, Hubert Hamilton, who was to be the best man at his forthcoming wedding.

Mary O'Hagan

Charles Monro was not a soft or fragile character, as can be seen from his portraits. Intelligent and professional as he was with his 'bluff directness', he was also shy. In fact he was not very open and could easily have become a recluse. However, he had fallen in love with Mary O'Hagan and his fondness for her was revealed in a letter during the First World War, when he wrote, 'Fourteen months are now over and each succeeding month makes me long all the more eagerly to be back with her again and share the most sacred life that was ever given to living man.'[9]

Aged 33, the Honourable Mary Caroline Towneley O'Hagan was nineteen years his junior.[10] Marrying a 52-year-old major general could have been a challenge for her, yet they were very happy together. They had first met in Gibraltar during 1898, when she was only 19. Her late father was Thomas 1st Baron O'Hagan, Lord Chancellor of Ireland for two periods in the late nineteenth century. He had been a lawyer and a Liberal, and was the first Roman Catholic to hold the chancellorship, the highest judicial office in the country, since the reign of King James II. Her mother was the Dowager Lady Alice Mary O'Hagan, who was also the heiress of Towneley, near Burnley in Lancashire, though she lived at Pyrgo Park, Havering-atte-Bower in Essex.[11] The original house at Pyrgo Park had been the place where Henry VIII had dined with his daughters Elizabeth and Mary in 1542 and decided to reinstate them in the royal line of succession. Lady Alice had bought the house at the end of the nineteenth century.

Tragically, Mary's brother, Thomas, the 2nd Baron, was killed on active service in South Africa, so her brother Maurice had succeeded to 3rd Baron. He was first a Liberal, then a Conservative politician who had been the lord-in-waiting, government whip in the House of Lords, a few years prior to the wedding.

The O'Hagans' local *Essex Newsman* newspaper of 3 August 1912 proudly announced the engagement of the couple on its front page. Charles Monro had certainly married into the aristocracy, reflected by the location and array of guests at their wedding in Westminster Abbey on 1 October 1912. This was a society wedding, announced in both national and regional newspapers. Archdeacon Wilberforce of Westminster officiated, whilst Mary's brother Maurice gave her away.

Master Sandy Monro, nephew of the bridegroom, was the sole page, dressed in Highland dress and wearing the Monro tartan. There were eight child bridesmaids: 'Misses Elizabeth and Marguerite de Beaumont-Klein, nieces of the bride, Miss Troutbeck, Miss Janet Monro, niece of the bridegroom, the Misses Aline and Viola Birk, Miss Vivian Guenod and Miss Hermione Carmichael.'[12] Military guests at the wedding included ex-CGS and C-in-C Ireland, General Lyttelton; Charles Monro's ex-divisional commander in Ireland, General Plumer; his old boss at both battalion and divisional level, General Kelly-Kenny; and generals Charles Fergusson, who was to command the 5th Division in 1914, and Alfred Codrington, general officer command-ing (GOC) London District and major general commanding the Brigade of Guards. Notable civilian guests included the Maharaja of Jhalawar, Edith Countess of Hardwicke and twenty lords and ladies. The Dowager Lady O'Hagan held the reception at 2 Upper Belgrave Street.

Wedding gifts included a china tea set from the Duchess of Albany, a bracelet watch set in pearls from the Bhawani Singh of Jhalawar and a grand piano from Lord and Lady O'Hagan. General Kelly-Kenny and the officers of the 6th Division South African Staff presented a silver tray, whilst the staff of the School of Musketry gave a silver ink stand.[13] This was a very high-profile society event, well reported in national and provincial newspapers of the time.[14]

The nave of Westminster Abbey was lined by a guard of honour from Charles Monro's own regiment, the Queen's (Royal West Surrey) Regiment. 'Later in the day Major General and the Honourable Mrs Monro left for their honeymoon, which will be spent on the continent.'[15] However, one notable incident at their wedding concerned the presence of 'Turk', the Dowager Lady O'Hagan's wire-haired terrier. The *New York Times* reported the incident as the bride creating 'a mild sensation by bringing to the church her favourite terrier'.[16] Turk wanted to go to the abbey! The *Essex County Chronicle* made a little more of the event, commenting:

> As the procession of motor cars left Upper Belgrave Street for the church he suddenly jumped onto one of the seats beside a chauffeur, and all efforts to remove him were futile. When the bride alighted from her car she saw Turk on his seat, and the dog whined with pleasure when she came over and caressed him. With the train of her beautiful wedding dress over her arm, the bride patted Turk and talked to him, and the dog raised his head forward, as though saying 'Goodbye'.[17]

It is not known what her husband thought of the fuss.

Charles Monro's best man was his old regimental friend, Major General Hubert 'Hammy' Ion Wetherall Hamilton. He was only one year younger than Charles, but had been commissioned into the 2nd Battalion of the Queen's (2nd) Royal Regiment in 1880, rather than Charles' 1st Battalion. Their careers had run in parallel. As a subaltern Hubert Hamilton had served on operations in Burma, whilst Charles Monro was in a quiet Ireland. Then he was on the Nile Expedition in the Sudan, when his friend was in action in the North-West Frontier region of India. Both were adjutants of their respective battalions at the same time and they shared the same dates in the ranks of major and lieutenant colonel.[18]

Hamilton had also served Major General Kelly-Kenny as his aide-de-camp and was awarded the DSO in 1898, following the battles of Atbara and Khartoum. They had served together on the staff during the Boer War in the same period and Hamilton had also been a DAAG, but additionally the assistant adjutant general (AAG). They were both at the Battle of Paardeberg. During his time in South Africa, Hubert Hamilton was picked out to be military secretary to the GOC, Lord Kitchener, and he was mentioned in despatches three times.[19] Following the war, he received promotion and the appointment of aide-de-camp to the king.

Though Hubert Hamilton seemed to be edging ahead in their parallel careers, the major generals were both commanding Territorial divisions from 1911 to 1914 and they were both honoured with regular divisional command in the original BEF of 1914. Whilst Charles Monro was to command the 2nd Division, Hubert Hamilton led the 3rd Division. Unfortunately, Hamilton was to earn the unenviable distinction of being the first British divisional commander to be killed in action during the First World War, when he was hit by artillery fire and died on 14 October 1914, the anniversary of the date that their regiment had been raised in 1661.

A Taste of Divisional Command

Major General Charles Monro commanded the 2nd London Division Territorial Force for two years from 1912 to 1914, continuing to impress the army with his professionalism. He had been promoted whilst still commanding 13th Brigade, occupying the few months in between his commands with a little 'gardening leave'. Haldane's new Territorial Force was only four years old when he took command. 'He proved a sympathetic and successful chief' with this new responsibility.[20] Once again, Charles Monro was able to put into practice the musketry and fire and movement skills that he had taught at Hythe and directed previously as a brigade commander, though this time on a larger scale.

His command consisted of the 4th, 5th and 6th London Brigades, supported by London artillery and engineer units. His twelve battalions of the London Regiment reflected their territorial roots, including some affiliated to his own regiment, the Queen's Royal West Surreys. They were:

4th Brigade:
    13th (Kensingtons).
    14th (London Scottish).
    15th (Prince of Wales's Own, Civil Service Rifles).
    16th (Queen's Westminster Rifles).

5th Brigade:
    17th (Poplar and Stepney Rifles).
    18th (London Irish Rifles).
    19th (St Pancras).
    20th (Blackheath and Woolwich).

6th Brigade:
    21st (First Surrey Rifles).
    22nd (Queen's).
    23rd.
    24th (Queen's).

He insisted that his new formation, roughly three times bigger than his previous responsibility, was trained effectively in a practical and thorough manner despite being made up of part-time Territorials. His evident enthusiasm earned him the nickname of 'Old Squad Drill'. He recognised the strengths and weaknesses of his officers and soldiers, who were intelligent and keen to learn, though limited in time for training. Concentrating on the basics, he set an example to others of how to command a Territorial Force formation. He 'set his division a standard which was not beyond its powers to attain'.[21] 'His genial and sympathetic personality, his obvious professional ability won the affection as well as the respect of all ranks.'[22]

It was during the 1913 manoeuvres that his division provided the 'enemy' against Regular Army units. According to one account, 'his men took cover, cut off convoys, destroyed communications, and generally made things distinctly unpleasant for their opponents; and at the end of it all it was hard to say who was the proudest, the Territorials of their commander, or he of them'.[23]

He was a popular and competent leader who delivered results as a 'progressive moderniser'.[24] During the manoeuvres, he built on the relatively successful performance of the Territorial Force on a similar exercise the previous year.[25] There is no doubt that his hard work helped forge this division prior to its deployment to France in the First World War, when it became the 47th (2nd London) Division.

Twenty-three battalions of Territorial infantry were deployed to France in 1914. Eventually, there were to be twenty-six Territorial divisions in the First World War. Initially, the Territorials were mainly deployed overseas to release regular units for the Western Front, or placed on guard duty. Meanwhile, the Secretary of State for War, Field Marshal Earl Kitchener of Khartoum, raised new armies, whilst 'the Territorials found themselves neglected and put in the shade'.[26] Lord Kitchener distrusted the Territorial Force and the civilian-run county associations set up by Haldane, describing them as being 'administered by mayors in their parlours'.[27] However, Viscount French believed that the Territorial Force should have been treated better than they were and more appreciated, especially by Lord Kitchener, writing at the beginning of the Great War:

> I say without the slightest hesitation that without the assistance which the Territorials afforded between October 1914, and June 1915, it would have been impossible to hold the line in France and Belgium, or to prevent the enemy from reaching his goal, the Channel seaboard.[28]

Viscount French understood that the Territorial was different from both the Regular soldier and the New Army, as did Charles Monro, who succeeded in making the most of their talents in his two years in command. French realised that:

> They were quite different to professional soldiers, who are kept and paid through years of peace for this particular purpose of war; who spend their

lives practising their profession and gaining promotion and distinction; and who, on being confronted by the enemy, fulfil the great ambition of their lives.[29]

Charles Monro's Territorial division was to become one of the first two Territorial divisions to fight in France, though he would not be commanding it – that honour went to Major General St Leger Barter, who was able to take advantage of Charles Monro's high standards of training in preparation for the war.

Commanding a Territorial division was not an easy task when so many senior officers had differing views about the value of the force itself. In addition, Lord Roberts' National Service League was highly critical, still calling for conscription as the most efficient way to man the army, encouraged that recruiting figures were declining in the Territorial Force – during Charles Monro's first year in command, the Territorial Force's strength dropped from 263,994 to 248,340.[30] The league was publicly accused of discouraging enlistment in the organisation. Another pressure group supporting conscription

Major General Monro. (Wills)

at this time, the National Defence Association, criticised the lack of government preparation for war, and sent a memorandum to the prime minister in 1913: 'The Association emphasised the inadequacy of the training of the Territorials, the poor attendance for the full duration of the annual camp, and the inability of the Force to protect the country against attack.'[31]

Even the Haldane-established county associations were criticising the inability of the volunteer system to produce the right number of soldiers and were advocating conscription. Incentives were introduced to encourage service, including a separation allowance for married men to attend annual camp in 1912, some assistance with national insurance contributions the following year and a £1 bounty for attending fifteen days of camp in 1914. These measures were only achieved after a great deal of lobbying and without consistent army support; the director general of the Territorial Force was concerned that the new bounty might attract soldiers who were not of the 'right class'.

With an annual manpower wastage of 12.5 per cent, retention was another important concern; 80 per cent had less than four years' service. The result was that Territorial Force soldiers were relatively young and by 1913, nearly 40,000 Territorials were under the age of 19. In 1913, this 'excessive number of the physically immature' failed to impress both a correspondent in *The Times* and the Inspector General of Home Forces.[32]

Meanwhile, the training commitment was seen by many civilians as being too much as this was higher than previous Volunteer requirements. In addition, civilian employers, national and regional, were not all supportive to the new commitment though many were helpful:

> Employers in Birmingham, such as BSA, the Dunlop Rubber Company and Mitchell & Butler, actively supported the Territorials. W. D. & H. O. Wills in Bristol promised Territorials in their employ a full twenty-one days' annual leave on full pay to attend camp and fulfil other obligations, while Colman's of Norwich also promised support, albeit for no more than one hundred of their employees.[33]

The Trades' Union Congress was not keen on the force and the ongoing public debate did nothing to boost the confidence of the Regular Army. It is interesting to note that similar challenges, concerning numbers able to be recruited, employer support and confidence of effect, exist as this book is written and the British Army relies more heavily on reserves' capabilities.

There was always an overall officer shortage of 20 per cent and whilst they were generally praised for their enthusiasm and intelligence, they 'were unable to spend sufficient time studying the details of the military profession or attending specialised courses'.[34] Particular criticism was aimed at the artillery units; as far as most regulars were concerned, the Territorial would never be able to master the technical challenges in that arm. In general, standards of training were never going to be as high as those in the Regular Army unless an intense training programme was established, but the aim was to allow time for that extra training if the Territorial Force was required for war – a fact not always recognised by vocal critical observers.

The issue that turned many against the Territorial Force was the lack of foreign service obligation. Unlike today, a reservist was not obliged to be deployed overseas in time of war, as the priority was home defence. A voluntary call for overseas deployment was only taken up by about 10 per cent of the force. 'In 1913 out of a total strength of 251,000, only 1,152 officers and 18,903 NCOs and men had taken the imperial service obligation.'[35] However, these numbers rapidly increased as war came closer and whole units volunteered for foreign service.[36]

Amongst these mixed perspectives of the Territorial Force, Lord Kitchener was not impressed by the 'Town Clerk's Army' and had never agreed to its inception in the first place. In 1906, he had written to Lady Salisbury:

> I suppose the militia and volunteers will demand greater expenditure, and probably get it. Then whatever is given, plus all the economies in the budget, will have to come out of the Regular Army, which we shall be told we can do without. That sort of thing is all very well until the bullets begin to fly.[37]

As far as he was concerned, it was poorly manned and trained, whilst unreliable, and 'well-meaning amateurs could never replace fully-trained soldiers'.[38] This perception was not helped by the fact that they had not been equipped with the latest weapons and equipment. And yet, as illustrated already, they were critical in the first two years of the First World War and formed the basis of further expansion of the army.

It may have been easier and more efficient to have generated more soldiers through the existing establishments than creating Kitchener's New Armies of fresh volunteers from scratch. In the first week of August 1914, he called for 100,000 volunteers, who were administered through the Adjutant General's Department with the highest priority, whilst the county associations continued to administer the Territorial Force. In the first eighteen months of the Great War 1,741,000 joined the New Armies, whilst 726,000 joined the Territorials.[39] Inevitably, however, as war began it was easier to deploy Territorial battalions to France whilst the New Armies were still being prepared.

The first Territorial Victoria Cross was won in April 1915, despite the various criticisms. The Territorial Force was an important portion of the British Army of 1914, as can be seen by this balance of manpower:

Regular Army	247,432
Army Reserve	145,347
Special Reserve	63,933
Territorial Force	268,777

Major General Charles Monro had done his bit in preparing his division as best he could for action, despite the plethora of public, political and army criticism of the Territorial Force. His renamed 47th (2nd London) Division was one of the first two Territorial divisions to be deployed to France in March 1915, where it acquitted itself well. 'The Territorial Force stood in 1915 between the dead Regular Army and the living Kitchener Armies that fought the Battle of the Somme and enabled the war to be ultimately won.'[40]

However, in August 1914, he was posted away from the division he had trained and was moved to take command of the Regular 2nd Division. Despite the fact that his operational experience of command had last been as a meagre major at company level in the North-West Frontier of India during the 1890s, he was about to command one of the few infantry divisions to be deployed, initially, to France as the British Expeditionary Force.

1914

War

Only six British infantry divisions and one cavalry division went to war in 1914 and Charles Monro was selected to command one of them. He would lead the Regular Army's 2nd Division from August through to December, during a critical period of the First World War when the German advance on France was stopped, but at a very high cost in lives. As his original biographer wrote, 'In 1901 he was an unknown major in an infantry regiment; in 1914 he was a major general commanding a war division.'[1]

Britain's initial contribution to the war was small compared with other nations; France and Germany had much larger armies based on conscription, with France's force of sixty-two infantry and ten cavalry divisions pit against Germany's eighty-seven infantry and eleven cavalry.[2] The British Army was well trained at the tactical level and could shoot well, but it did not expect the attrition and massive loss of casualties it was about to suffer. Unfortunately, in 1914 it was not going to be possible for the British to emulate Wellington's tactic of preserving his small army, as he did during the Peninsular War of the 1800s.

The British Expeditionary Force (BEF) was commanded by the 62-year-old cavalryman, Field Marshal Sir John French, who had resigned as CIGS in April 1914 as a result of fallout from the Curragh incident mentioned in Chapter 5. He was popular with the troops, with a sound reputation from the South African War and command in Aldershot; he was very confident in his ability and brave. However, he also had deep mood changes, could be very bad tempered, indecisive and harboured grudges. Like his subordinate generals, he had no experience of commanding large formations in the conditions they were about to experience and he was a 'fighting soldier' rather than a staff officer.

Douglas Haig was very critical of Sir John French. Prior to the Boer War, he had worked for him as his brigade major (chief of staff) and had even lent him money. One of Haig's confidential discussions was later reported by Captain (later Brigadier) John Charteris, his assistant military secretary:

> He thinks French quite unfit for command in time of crisis. He says French's military ideas are not sound; that he has never studied war; that he is obstinate, and will not keep with him men who point out even obvious errors. He gives him credit for good tactical powers, great courage and determination.[3]

He also passed similar comments to the king. In addition, he believed that French's key staff officers in General Headquarters (GHQ), Major General Archibald Murray and Major General Henry Wilson, were respectively weak and untrustworthy. His views were largely supported in the first few months of the war. In the early retreat Murray, whom Haig described as an 'old woman', collapsed under the pressure, whilst opinion on Wilson's performance was divided. The GHQ had not been effectively exercised in the army manoeuvres of 1913 and one modern historian has written, 'Taken as a whole, the performance of GHQ during 1914 might be judged barely adequate.'[4] This may be a little harsh, though, when one considers the unfamiliar situation in which the BEF was about to be placed.

Haig was much happier with the standard of brigades and battalions, the cavalry and artillery, though he was concerned about the relatively small scale of the BEF and the danger of it being committed in action before it had time to absorb the reservists. However, Haig himself did not always make the right decisions. One officer compared the personalities of French and Haig, 'French was a man who loved life, laughter and women, whereas Haig was the dullest dog I ever had the happiness to meet.' He also stated that Haig owed everything to French.[5] Interestingly, Winston Churchill also compared the two personalities:

> French was a natural soldier. Although he had not the intellectual capacity of Haig, nor perhaps his underlying endurance, he had a deeper military insight. He was not equal to Haig in precision of detail; but he had more imagination and he would never have run the British Army into the same long drawn-out slaughters.[6]

Both of the key commanders above Charles Monro were strong, though controversial, characters who attracted mixed criticism. It is to his credit that he earned the respect of the very critical Haig and, eventually, his trust. However, he was never to be one of his favourites.

Lord Kitchener's instructions to the BEF commander included these words:

> The special motive of the Force under your control is to support and coop-
> erate with the French Army ... in preventing and repelling the invasion
> by Germany of French and Belgian territory and eventually to restore the
> neutrality of Belgium ... It must be recognised from the outset that the
> numerical strength of the British Force and its contingent reinforcement
> is strictly limited, and with this consideration kept steadily in view it will
> be obvious that the greatest care must be exercised towards a minimum
> of losses and wastage ... every effort must be made to coincide most
> sympathetically with the plans and wishes of our Ally ... I wish you dis-
> tinctly to understand that your command is an entirely independent one,
> and that you will in no case come in any sense under the orders of any
> Allied general.[7]

Sir John French had some challenges in this intent, which would play out once battle commenced; working with the French armies as they repelled invasion, yet preserving his force and its independence.

He had two corps in the BEF, along with Major General Edmund Allenby's Cavalry Division: I Corps, commanded by Lieutenant General Sir Douglas Haig and II Corps under Lieutenant General Sir James Grierson, who died of a heart attack on 17 August and was replaced by Lieutenant General Sir Horace Smith-Dorrien.[8]

Douglas Haig, who was Charles Monro's commander, had the advantage in his I Corps of having the core staff posts already filled pre-war, so at least most of his immediate team were used to working together. The other division in I Corps, the 1st Division, was led by Major General Samuel Lomax. At 59, Lomax was five years older than Monro and had not had any operational experience since fighting the Zulus as a young officer in 1878, thirty-six years before. He had been about to retire, due to his lack of war experience, but was highly respected and had commanded 1st Division since 1910, so there was some continuity in his leadership. One senior officer wrote, 'He took his division to France and, until mortally wounded in the Salient, he was perhaps the best Divisional General of those early days of the War.'[9] Samuel Lomax had the higher profile of I Corps' two divisional commanders and he was trusted by Douglas Haig from the beginning of the war.

Charles Monro was a hurried choice for the 2nd Division, because the incumbent leader, Major General Archibald Murray, had been posted as Sir John French's CGS in GHQ.[10] Douglas Haig was never shy in criticising people in his diary, as he compared his two key subordinate commanders:

> I have a first rate Staff and my troops are throughout well commanded. Major General Lomax commands the 1st Division. He is an experienced and practical leader, much beloved by the men, most loyal to me, and I have a thorough trust in his ability to command his division well, even in the worst of difficulties. The 2nd Division has just been given to a new Commander, viz. Major General Monro in the place of Major General Archibald Murray … Monro proved himself to be a good regimental officer and an excellent Commandant of the Hythe School of Musketry, but some years with Territorials has resulted in his becoming rather fat. There is, however, no doubt about his military ability, although he lacks the practical experience in commanding a division.[11]

Samuel Lomax was obviously the favoured man and would initially be given greater critical responsibility than Charles Monro. Monro's competence was recognised, though he seems to be tainted by both his stature and association with the Territorial Force. Haig would discover that Monro was more than just a safe pair of hands and a divisional commander that he could trust; Monro would be fighting with his division within eighteen days of taking command.

It was quite a responsibility he was taking on. A BEF division consisted of just over 18,000 men and 5,500 horses, twenty-four machine guns split into two machine guns for each infantry battalion, seventy-six guns in four artillery brigades, two field companies of Royal Engineers, a cavalry squadron, a signal company and integrated medical and logistic support. This was an all-arms formation that could operate independently in the field. The backbone of the 2nd Division was its three brigades, each with four infantry battalions:

4th (Guards) Brigade (Commander – Brigadier General R. Scott-Kerr, wounded 1 September 1914; Colonel P.T. Fielding (acting), then Brigadier General F. R. Earl of Cavan):

    2nd Battalion Grenadier Guards.
    2nd Battalion Coldstream Guards.
    3rd Battalion Coldstream Guards.
    1st Battalion Irish Guards.

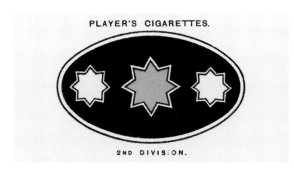

2nd Division badge.
(Player's)

5th Brigade (Commander – Brigadier General R. C. B. Haking, wounded 16 September 1914, then Colonel C. B. Westmacott (acting) until Haking reassumed command on 20 November 1914):
> 2nd Battalion Oxfordshire and Buckinghamshire Light Infantry.
> 2nd Battalion Worcester Regiment.
> 2nd Battalion Highland Light Infantry.
> 2nd Battalion Connaught Rangers (amalgamated with the 1st Battalion in November 1914 and replaced by the 9th Highland Light Infantry).

6th Brigade (Commander – Brigadier General R. H. Davies, then Brigadier General R. Fanshawe from 23 September 1914):
> 1st Battalion King's (Liverpool) Regiment.
> 2nd Battalion South Staffordshire Regiment.
> 1st Battalion Royal Berkshire Regiment.
> 1st Battalion King's Royal Rifle Corps.[12]

Charles Monro was to command from August until 26 December 1914, assisted in his headquarters by fifteen officers and sixty-seven other ranks, five motorcycles and fifty-four horses for riding and pulling various wagons. His key staff in 2nd Division were:

General Staff Officer 1 (GSO 1) [chief of staff (COS) in modern parlance] – Colonel the Honourable F. Gordon; from 5 September 1914, Lieutenant Colonel A. J. B. Percival; from 18 September 1914, Colonel R. Whigham. This critical officer led the planning on operations, administration and intelligence.

Assistant Adjutant and Quartermaster General (AA and QMG) [deputy chief of staff (DCOS) in modern parlance] – Lieutenant Colonel G. Conway-Gordon. This key officer arranged transport and supplies.

Brigadier General Royal Artillery (BG RA) – Brigadier General E. M. Perceval. He co-ordinated all the four artillery brigades, heavy artillery battery and ammunition columns.

Commander Royal Engineer (CRE) – Lieutenant Colonel R. H. H. Boys (wounded 31 October 1914); Major C. N. North (killed 1 November 1914); Captain A. J. Darlington; from 9 November 1914, Major A. H. Tyler (killed 11 November 1914); Major G. H. Foulkes; from 12 November 1914, Lieutenant Colonel G. P. Schofield. He co-ordinated the two field companies, a signal company and all engineering tasks.[13]

Many history books, official records and academic documents list the assets in a British First World War division, but few mention its all-arms grouping, command and control and effectiveness. Most focus on the strategic and operational levels and then on the lower tactical level, with stories of units' actions and individual accounts of bravery. This is mainly because that is where most of the information is. The centenary commemoration in 2014 has spawned two magnificent tomes on the way to war and 1914, but scant mention is made of the individual divisions, as limited information is available.[14]

Reporting on personalities at the divisional level is also patchy. Inevitably, the higher commanders and those who were the most flamboyant receive the limelight. There are more than enough treatises on Sir John French and Douglas Haig, but little on the first four divisional commanders in the BEF: major generals Lomax, Monro, Hamilton and Fergusson, who were simply doing their jobs as efficiently as they could.

Corps command has been analysed, particularly by Andy Simpson, who identifies that this level of command was not effectively organised before the war, but at least Haig's I Corps had a core staff before the war began and seemed to operate the most efficiently in 1914.[15] Whilst corps headquarters were needed to co-ordinate the divisions, it was just as important that brigades were co-ordinated by divisional headquarters, but accounts of 1914 tend to only describe the story of the two corps. The divisional headquarters was a vital conduit for orders down the chain of command and co-ordination of vital tactical inter-brigade activity, though by 1915 some of its responsibilities had been watered down; control of artillery was one of these.

The passage of orders and information down and up the chain of command was a huge challenge in 1914, particularly during the period of co-ordinated manoeuvre prior to trench warfare. Communication was by wire (telephone or telegraph) or runner/person; radios or wirelesses were too bulky and inefficient for tactical use. Both of these means of communication meant that it took a long time to pass a message and they could easily be stopped

Lieutenant General Haig, Major General Monro, Brigadier General Gough and Colonel Perceval, 1914. (Imperial War Museum. Q54992)

by effective enemy artillery fire either cutting wires, disrupting communication routes and killing or wounding the runner. It is no surprise that orders often just did not get through to the recipients, even when a headquarters' staff were efficient.

Despite the lack of experience of all commanders, the BEF mobilised with great efficiency and speed in 1914, following the German advance into 'Gallant Little Belgium' and the declaration of war. The 4th (Guards) Brigade prepared in Windsor and London, whilst the rest of 2nd Division mobilised from their barracks in Aldershot, as the Regular Reservists and Special Reservists rapidly filled nearly 60 per cent of the Regular Army's ranks.

Charles Monro expressed his own feelings about the war in a letter to his wife, Mary, dated 14 August 1914:

> Am off early tomorrow morning for the 'Continong', hardly a holiday trip this time. I am absolutely certain that our cause is just and that when we meet the Germans we shall lick them, even with the numerical odds heavily against us. I went up to London to say goodbye to them all and came back early this morning. So here it is to our next merry meeting. I wonder if I shall ever cut thistles at Auchenbowie again. I cannot grumble. I have had two years of happiness such as has never been given to a mortal man.[16]

The 2nd Division sailed for France from 12 August 1914 and formed up in the Wassigny area, located just south-east of Cambrai in northern France, near the Belgian border and Mons. The troops felt welcome in France, Rudyard Kipling writing that the Irish Guards, part of Monro's 4th Brigade, 'received an enthusiastic welcome from the French, and were first largely introduced to the wines of the country, for many maidens lined the steep road and offered bowls of drinks to the wearied'.[17]

On 20 August, whilst the Divisional War Diary recorded, 'Weather good. Infantry marched well', Charles Monro issued the First Divisional Operation Order, 'The Division would move on the morrow towards its allotted place in the line of battle.'[18]

Mons (23 August 1914)

The BEF was to be positioned on the left of the French line to the west and south of Mons, in Belgium, with Belgian forces to their left. II Corps was on the far left from Condé to Mons inclusive, with Douglas Haig's I Corps on the right from Mons exclusive to Binche. Within I Corps, Samuel Lomax's 1st Division was on the right, critically ensuring that Mons was protected and could not be outflanked to the east, with Charles Monro's 2nd Division on I Corps' left. To the right of the 1st Division was the French 18th Corps, part of their 5th Army, which was commanded by General Lanrezac.

Co-operation between the two main Allied armies was going to be a challenge. Apart from the historical tensions, the initial meeting on 17 August between Sir John French and General Lanrezac did not go well. French reports that 'his personality did not convey to me the idea of a great leader. He was a big man with a loud voice, and his manner did not strike me as being courteous.'[19] Lanrezac was not impressed with French either. Both men had little command of each other's language and interpreters were not present.

This combination of factors and the lack of accurate and shared intelligence on enemy dispositions and intent did not bode well for Allied co-operation in the fluid battles of 1914; both armies had enough difficulties controlling their own assets efficiently, let alone working closely with neighbouring foreign armies. Besides, the French expected the main German attack further south of the border area and did not consider the 'small' BEF of just under 100,000 men as a particularly significant player at the beginning of the war. To them, co-operation did not seem to be that critical. At least French-speaking Charles Monro could liaise with his neighbouring French formations.

By the morning of 22 August, Great Britain's two corps, the Cavalry Division and the 5th Cavalry Brigade, were mostly all in their designated locations, making best use of various water ditches and the natural obstacle of the Mons-Condé Canal, running from east to west for just over 16 miles. It was 64ft wide, with a depth of 7ft. However, fields of fire were limited in this coal-mining area because of ditches, slag heaps and buildings. The British Army dug in and awaited action, confident that they would acquit themselves well.

The German advance and the Battle of the Frontiers had begun, as its seven armies executed the Schlieffen Plan. As French pressure further south – part of their Plan XVII counter-attack – was absorbed by the Germans, the bulk of the German force in the north concentrated their efforts and swung rapidly through northern France and Belgium. The German main effort was on their right wing, to outflank the French fortress system and march on Paris. General von Kluck's 1st Army was heading towards the British and on 19 August, the Kaiser issued a famous order:

> It is my Royal and Imperial command that you concentrate your energies for the immediate present upon one single purpose, and that is, that you address all your skill and all the valour of my soldiers to exterminate the treacherous English and walk over General French's contemptible little Army.[20]

The Belgians bravely helped stem the German tide for a few days, but old established fortresses, including Liège, fell and Brussels was occupied on 20 August. Meanwhile, General Lanrezac's 5th Army on the British right flank received heavy casualties in its first battle against the German 1st and 2nd Armies on 22 August, being forced to fall back on 23 August.

The British Army's first battle of the First World War was at Mons. It was General Smith-Dorrien's II Corps that would feel the brunt of the German assault on 23 August 1914; six German divisions were pitched against the two British divisions on the canal. It was here, as already mentioned, that the Germans thought that they were under machine-gun fire, when in fact the volume and accuracy of rifle fire had been developed by Charles Monro and others at the School of Musketry in the years prior to the war.

Lieutenant Colonel McMahon, ex-chief instructor at Hythe, commanded 4th Battalion of the Royal Fusiliers on the Condé Canal and watched the effective results of modern musketry teaching in practice, along with his orderly, Corporal Holbrook:

> They kept retreating, and then coming forward, and then retreating again … but we kept flinging them back. You don't have to think much. You don't even feel nervous – you've got other fellows with you, you see. I don't know how many times we saw them off. They didn't get anywhere near us with this rapid fire.[21]

Two soldiers from the battalion's machine-gun section earned Victoria Crosses. Unfortunately, the sheer weight of German numbers and the withdrawal of the French 5th Army necessitated a British pull back and adjustment of the line south of Mons. There had been 1,600 British casualties, mainly in II Corps, compared to 5,000 Germans. Many British soldiers felt that they had won the Battle of Mons and could not understand why they were retreating, indeed, one German officer wrote on Mons, 'A bad defeat, there could

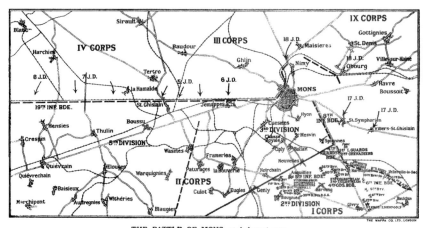

THE BATTLE OF MONS, 23rd August 1914.
Position of 2nd Division (1st Corps) and Approximate Positions of other Divisions of the British Army ; and of the First German Army.

Battle of Mons. (Wyrall)

be no gainsaying it; in our first battle we had been badly beaten, and by the English – by the English we had so laughed at a few hours before.'[22] German forces had been held up and the Allies had not been outflanked. The BEF was also able to disengage itself without being vigorously pursued by the enemy.

Haig's I Corps had not been seriously engaged with the enemy on 23 August, only suffering forty casualties. Charles Monro's 2nd Division Mounted Troops, B Squadron of the 15th Hussars and the 2nd Cyclist Company had skirmished with the Germans, losing three dead, and as positions were adjusted enemy artillery fire caused five casualties amongst the 1st Battalion Irish Guards. This was a historical moment as it was the first time that this new regiment had been in contact with an enemy.

Major General Hamilton's 3rd Division, positioned on Monro's left flank, requested reinforcements for Hill 93 from their corps commander. Consequently, for a short time Monro detached Lieutenant Colonel Corry, with 2nd Battalion Grenadier Guards in support, alongside another unit. The 'fog of war' and lack of clarity of responsibilities within boundaries led to both Hamilton and Monro failing to include the Guards battalion and the other unit in their subsequent withdrawal orders and when Corry realised the line was pulling back, he used his initiative and withdrew. Unfortunately, this led to the wrath of his 4th (Guards) Brigade commander, Brigadier General Scott-Kerr, and although it could be argued that Corry did no harm, he was relieved of command two weeks later.

Elsewhere in the 2nd Division further casualties were sustained from artillery fire, but the day was frustrating for most of the troops who could hear the firing, were tired digging trenches and then had to move without knowing what was going on – the classic 'fog of war'. The comments of Lieutenant Crosse of 2nd Battalion Oxfordshire & Buckinghamshire Light Infantry, 5th Brigade, were typical:

At five pm we marched out of Genly towards Bougnies where we found other troops of the 2nd Division were already digging hard. We had just received our task and settled down to dig, when yet another order arrived. This time it was to close up and follow the Worcesters and the Highland Light Infantry north-westward to Frameries to fill a gap …[23]

Retreat from Mons (24 August–5 September 1914)

The 2nd Division extracted itself from positions on 24 August at 0445 hours, following a personal visit from Haig, and began what became known as the

Retreat from Mons. (Murland)

'retreat from Mons', leapfrogging backwards in concert with its neighbouring 1st Division, alongside II Corps on the left. The 2nd Division War Diary recorded, 'Cramped country with winding roads making issue of orders a great difficulty.'[24]

'Retreat' is not a comfortable word for any army as it suggests that an operation is out of control, which it was not, though there were critical periods when the operation was in doubt. The preferred military definition is a 'retirement' or 'withdrawal'. A retirement can be described as a movement away from the enemy by a force out of contact with the enemy, whilst:

> A withdrawal occurs when a force disengages from an enemy force in accordance with the will of its commander. It seeks to break contact with the enemy. This does not necessarily imply that reconnaissance and/or guard elements do not maintain surveillance over the enemy.[25]

Command and control is particularly difficult in this type of operation, especially at night. In the early hours of the morning, I Corps artillery fired on the enemy positions as the 4th (Guards) Brigade covered the withdrawal. British battalions suffered more casualties from enemy shell fire and the troops were tired, 'the infantry are done up after trying days without regular food and with little sleep'.[26] Again, II Corps suffered the most as some orders to retire never made it through to front-line units, and 1st Battalion Cheshire Regiment was overwhelmed. At least more friendly troops were arriving to reinforce II Corps, as the BEF's newly despatched 4th Division were brought into play, though they were, at this stage, without their supporting engineers, medical support or transport.

The march continued southwards towards a temporary position at Maubeuge, then ideally Le Cateau. I Corps' commander, Douglas Haig, had decided to form a rearguard which was skilfully handled by his senior artillery officer, Brigadier General Horne, of 5th Cavalry Brigade, two battalions of infantry and two brigades of artillery, as both of his divisions retired. He was putting into practice some of the procedures he had helped write in the manuals of *Field Service Regulations 1909*, as mentioned in Chapter 4.

It was not only the troops who were tired at this time. Haig recalls issuing this order to Charles Monro, 'Having given Monro orders in above sense, I marked his map, as he and his Staff officer (Colonel Gordon) were very sleepy.'[27] However, Sir John French was impressed with the way that I Corps and its two divisions were performing, later writing, 'The steadfast attitude and skilful retreat of our right wing at Mons had much to do with the success of our withdrawal. And the short time I spent with the I Corps that morning inspired me with great confidence.'[28]

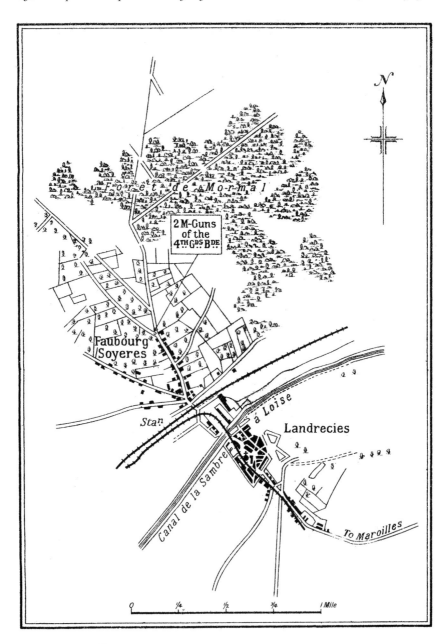

Landrecies. (Wyrall)

Concurrently, some key decisions were being made that would shape activity over the next few weeks. Sir John French was suggesting a retreat to the coast to preserve the BEF, but was directed to withdraw to the River Seine. The French formed a new powerful 6th Army to secure the Allies' left flank, whilst the Germans were complacent about their successful advance, underestimating the BEF and the French Army and removing some important formations from the front line, thus weakening their original Schlieffen Plan.

On 25 August, 2nd Division had its first significant contact with the enemy. At this stage, the two corps were dangerously split by the 6-mile wide Mormal Forest, with I Corps to the east and II Corps to the west. The plan to bring the two corps together again at Le Cateau was never achieved and there was a gap of eight days and 90 miles of withdrawal before they would rendezvous again. The 4th (Guards) Brigade reached the small town of Landrecies, guarding a bridge over the River Sambre on the southern tip of the forest, after a hot and tiring march. Haig's I Corps headquarters was also located there and enemy action was unexpected; civilians were still in the town and cafes were open. Outposts to act as early warning were not posted as the corps believed that there were no routes through the forest. The British were not aware that 5th German Division was setting up camp there for the night and was exploring the rides.

Just as the British troops were settling down there was a rumour that Germans were moving through the forest from the north-west and there were rumours that the Germans had taken the town. They came from the north-west, and first contact between the Coldstreamers and Uhlan Cavalry occurred at 1900 hours. A short time later the enemy, who were not expecting to come across the British and had been marching through the forest singing 'La Marseillaise', managed to surprise and overwhelm a Coldstream machine-gun position and the gunner, Guardsman Arthur Robson, was bayonetted whilst the company commander, Captain the Honourable Charles Monck, was knocked down. The Germans had 'replied in French when challenged'.[29]

Captain Robert Whitbread, one of the company commanders, takes up the story:

> We lay down in the road in readiness for a rush, we next heard some words of command in German and dimly saw a mass approaching, apparently slowly and without noise. When this mass was about fifty yards off we let them have five rounds rapid and a burst of machine gun fire … the same thing was repeated several times, each rush being stopped by our fire.[30]

Douglas Haig, who seems to have always been critical of others, commented in his diary that the Guards did 'not seem to have been very alert'.[31] However, many historians have accused Haig of uncharacteristically panicking at this point by ordering the destruction of secret documents, telling GHQ that he was under heavy attack, demanding reinforcement from II Corps and claiming that it was his own personal intervention that meant that the town was successfully defended.

Charles Monro was also reported as being confused and excited at this time. Major 'Ma' Jeffreys of 2nd Battalion Grenadier Guards recorded seeing the major general on the edge of the forest, shouting at him to react to enemy cavalry he had just seen exit the forest:

> General Monro said, 'They've got their cavalry round! Quick! Get these men to change front and open fire!' I was almost certain they were British but I ordered the platoon to change front, but not to open fire, and got my glasses on to them and at once saw the grey horses of the Scots Greys. I said, 'But it's the Scots Greys, Sir.' To which the General said, 'Thank God!' I think he was tired and overwrought.[32]

All the senior British commanders were under pressure that day, even Sir John French's headquarters moved amidst the panic.

Smith-Dorrien's exhausted II Corps, which was still moving south on the western side of the forest, was unable to help. Fortunately, 3rd Battalion Coldstream Guards 'now attacked their assailants with great vigour and drove them back with considerable loss into the shadows of the forest', supported by elements of the 2nd Battalion and the Grenadiers, as the Irish Guards defended the town, barricaded the buildings and loopholed their walls.[33] This was in the face of a German field gun firing at the guardsmen over open sights. Major General Monro witnessed the German attacks up the streets being beaten back, aided by some accurate British artillery fire, though at a high cost to the 3rd Coldstreams – fourteen dead, 107 wounded and seven missing.

One account from the Irish Guards states, 'The Germans shelled us very heavily. It did not seem as if there was much chance of getting away, but no one was despondent.'[34] More emotionally, one history of the same regiment records, 'That night was the first they heard wounded men scream.'[35]

There were 200 friendly casualties overall and, unfortunately, two sections of 4th Field Ambulance were captured by the enemy. However, to the brigade's and 2nd Division's credit, the attack had been beaten off, allowing a divisional disengagement and a further withdrawal southwards. The divisional War Diary acknowledged the action, recording, '800 dead Germans are said to have been counted after their attack was repulsed.'[36]

One guardsman's actions at Landrecies contributed to his Victoria Cross (VC) and three others won Distinguished Conduct (DC) medals. The VC went to 27-year-old Lance Corporal George Wyatt of 3rd Battalion Coldstream Guards. Enemy gunfire had set light to straw stacks in a farmyard, but because of his bravery in dashing out twice under heavy enemy fire to extinguish the flames, his battalion was able to hang on to its position. He continued fighting despite blood streaming from his face and being told by the medical officer to go to the rear.[37]

All three brigades of 2nd Division were withdrawing as best they could, co-ordinated by Charles Monro and his staff. Sir John French was impressed with their performance again, later commenting, 'the retirement of I Corps was continued in excellent order and with complete efficiency'.[38] However, at the time this did not prevent concerns about the ability of the British troops to hold their positions and Douglas Haig encouraged the thought, picked up by both Sir John French and General Lanrezac through Colonel Huguet, the head of the French mission to the BEF, that there was a worrying crisis on the British right flank.

Meanwhile in 6th Brigade, defending Maroilles Bridge over the River Sambre, east of Landrecies, 1st Battalion Royal Berkshire Regiment and a detachment of the 2nd Division's cavalry, 15th Hussars, skirmished with the enemy. Despite conducting another effective rearguard action, the Germans held the bridge.

The next significant contact with the enemy was by 2nd Battalion Connaught Rangers of 5th Brigade. They were the brigade and the division's rearguard, but had lost communication and were, like much of the 2nd Division, bumping into French forces, logistic convoys and refugees as they withdrew. As they approached the village of Le Grand Fayt (which they wrongly thought the 5th Brigade was holding) they came under very heavy enemy fire from the German 2nd Army, resulting in nearly 300 officers and men 'missing'. Douglas Haig blamed these casualties on Charles Monro, because of a misunderstanding of verbal orders issued by him to the divisional commander at Landrecies.

However, Haig's verbal skills were often at fault. 'Given Haig's lack of verbal facility, one wonders if the fault was all on one side.'[39] Also, the various accounts of this action illustrate a certain amount of misunderstanding and poor co-ordination within the battalion, not helped by difficult terrain of hedges and orchards providing poor visibility between the rifle companies and approaching darkness. The fog of war again came into play. The 5th Brigade had lost communication with one of its battalions in a very confusing environment and had withdrawn, unbeknown to the stranded Connaught Rangers.

It is not clear what part of the chain of command, from unit, through brigade, to division, was at fault. The commanding officer was never able to give his version of events as he died in captivity in November 1915. The battalion was to be amalgamated with its 1st Battalion in December 1914; the only permanent arrangement of this type for two regular battalions in the war.

Douglas Haig's I Corps was not engaged in the Battle of Le Cateau on 26 August, a bigger affair than Mons and a critical day in the retreat from Mons when the two corps were split, making the BEF particularly vulnerable. Horace Smith-Dorrien had hoped for support from his brother corps' commander, as he fought a successful, though bloody action, but I Corps, between 8 and 30 miles away and delayed by the rearguard actions already mentioned, continued its withdrawal; German forces appearing on his right instead. Sir John French had not wanted II Corps to stop, but Smith-Dorrien decided to check the enemy with a substantive delaying action before allowing his exhausted troops a smoother retirement. He achieved what he wanted with the assistance of a slightly less tired 4th Division and bought time for French forces to reorganise elsewhere, but 7,812 men and thirty-eight guns were lost, some British battalions were destroyed and, initially, the French thought that the British had lost the battle.

Most modern historians believe that Smith-Dorrien made the right decision to stand, breaking the momentum of the German advance and buying time for other Allied formations to withdraw or recover. Sir John French initially castigated his subordinate for his action at Le Cateau, though confusedly, he expressed his gratitude in his first despatch on 7 September 1914:

> I say without hesitation that the saving of the left wing of the Army under my command on the morning of the 26th August could never have been accomplished unless a commander [Smith-Dorrien] of rare and unusual coolness, intrepidity, and determination had been present to personally conduct the operation.[40]

A bitter debate between French and Smith-Dorrien about the value of the Battle of Le Cateau would rage for years after the event and Smith-Dorrien described French's comments in his book, *1914*, as 'mostly a work of fiction and a foolish one too'.[41]

Von Kluck's 1st Army failed to pursue II Corps south and instead moved south-west towards the new French 6th Army, creating a gap with Bulow's 2nd Army to his east. This created an opportunity for the French to further blunt the German advance by hitting their exposed 2nd Army flank in the Guise-St Quentin area.

Von Kluck had lost contact with the British, who were still withdrawing in good, though tired, order with General Allenby's effective cavalry screen behind them. 'For nine days the men had been marching and countermarching, covering in that time a distance of 143 miles.'[42] Straggling and falling out had occurred everywhere, and on the I Corps route in particular much confusion had occurred amongst the French logistic supply routes.

But at last, after all that marching on sore feet, with little food and water, the British Army was able to rest briefly on 29 August, having crossed the River Somme. Some further sacrifices had occurred en route, and on 27 August, Major General Lomax's 1st Division had to fight a rearguard action at Etreux and 2nd Battalion Royal Munster Fusiliers was destroyed as, again, an order to retire had not reached a unit in time.

On 28 August Douglas Haig realised that his I Corps could assist the French in their attack against the exposed German flank and offered his support to General Lanrezac. Here was an opportunity to launch what could have been a decisive British attack with the stronger I Corps, but Sir John French would not give his support, much to the chagrin of Haig, who responded to his allies that his position covered their flank and he could not do more. Again the British withdrew whilst Lanrezac launched his attack, breaking the German momentum. The Battle of Guise was a critical, though bloody, French success which could have been supported by I Corps, yet Haig wrote to his wife on 3 September, 'The French are most unreliable. One cannot believe a word they say as a rule!'[43]

The British withdrawal had continued. Drummer Slaytor of 3rd Battalion Coldstream Guards, 4th (Guards) Brigade said, 'The marching was hard. The sun always seemed to be beating fiercely down – no doubt a very lovely summer on a sandy beach but most exhausting to the plodding infantryman in retreat.'[44]

Lieutenant Colonel Davies, 2nd Battalion Oxfordshire & Buckinghamshire Light Infantry, 5th Brigade, reported:

> Whenever there was a halt, men dropped down and slept on the road, and one had to allow extra time at each halt to wake them up before we could get on the move again. Sometimes a company commander going down his company to wake the men would find at the end that some of the men he had awakened first had dropped asleep again … We had marched 59 miles in the last 64 hours, beginning the march in the middle of an entirely sleepless night, and getting no more than eight hours' sleep altogether during the other two nights. Many men could hardly put one leg before another, yet they all came into Servais singing.[45]

The 2nd Division War Diary recorded, 'The day was hot and the infantry felt it. Though the casualties were not heavy, the Division has had a very trying time, marching 143 miles in nine days.'[46]

By the night of 31 August I Corps was south-west of Soissons, though short of its intended destination. The previous day, a new British III Corps had been formed under General Pulteney, comprising 4th Division and

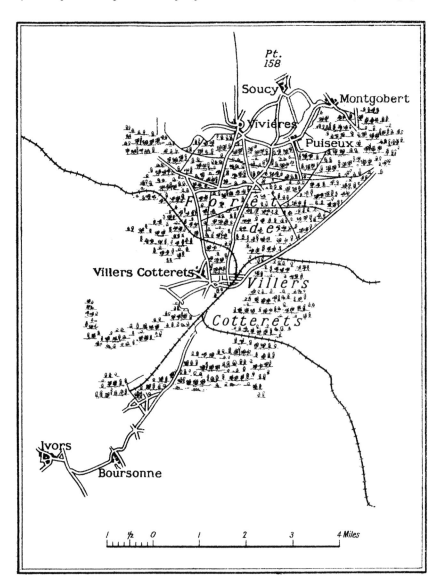

Villers-Cotterêts. (Wyrall)

19th Brigade. However, with further French withdrawals it appeared that Paris was under threat, and there was shock in London from both the British Government and Lord Kitchener when Sir John French sent a message stating that he would be withdrawing his troops even further south beyond the River Seine. The result was a personal visit to Paris by a concerned Lord Kitchener, who wanted to ensure that any plans were in concert with the Allies. There was a difficult discussion with Sir John, which resulted in him reversing the BEF commander's original intent.

Two effective rearguard actions in each of the two corps' areas were undertaken on 1 September. Whilst the artillery and cavalry fought successfully at Nery, Charles Monro's 2nd Division fought their next rearguard action, again by the 4th (Guards) Brigade, at Villers-Cotterêts Forest, following four days without contact with the enemy. The brigade had been ordered to 'arrest and delay the advance of the enemy with the greatest energy and stubbornness'.[47] Its commander, Brigadier General Scott-Kerr, also had command of the divisional cavalry and 41st Brigade Royal Field Artillery. The 2nd Battalion Grenadier Guards, 3rd Battalion Coldstream Guards and a battery of guns were to the front, north, of the forest with the 1st Battalion Irish Guards and 2nd Battalion Coldstream Guards to their rear.

In the morning there were a couple of skirmishes and there then followed a leapfrogging of battalions and companies, as the 4th (Guards) Brigade withdrew 1 mile south through part of the forest to a main ride. The Irish Guards and 2nd Coldstreamers were in the front, when the main attack began, 'The Germans were very cautious at first, because of our fire discipline, as we fell back, gave them the impression that the forest was filled with machine guns instead of mere trained men firing together sustainedly.'[48]

The environment in the dark woodland was confused, as the enemy suddenly appeared at close quarters and men from different battalions became mixed up. Orders were difficult to convey, officers and NCOs did their best to muster diverse groups of soldiers and 'when a man dropped in the bracken and bramble, he disappeared'.[49] The Irish Guards' commanding officer, Lieutenant Colonel the Honourable G. Morris, paid the ultimate sacrifice and seven other officers went missing in the regiment's first ever serious action. Number 4 Company of the 2nd Grenadiers launched a successful counter-attack with the bayonet, but the regiment's last two platoons were surrounded and fought to the last man. It had been a painful day for 4th (Guards) Brigade; success for the price of twenty officers and 471 other ranks killed, wounded and missing. Even the brigade commander had been wounded, but once again quick action had been taken that had saved the 2nd Division. So far, Major General Monro had successfully co-ordinated the movement of his three brigades.

Meanwhile, the Guards pulled back through 6th Brigade and 1st Battalion Royal Berkshires took the brunt of the enemy attack, helping to save six guns, though twenty-five men were lost. The brigade lost another 140 men that day, mainly from German artillery.

The withdrawal continued in suffocating heat with 2nd Division crossing the River Marne at Meaux on 3 September, destroying bridges and boats behind them. The Germans still had Paris as their goal, but they were also exhausted, one officer recording:

> Our men are done up. For four days they have been marching twenty-four miles a day … The men stagger forward, their faces coated with dust, their uniforms in rags, they look like living scarecrows. They march with their eyes closed, singing in chorus so they shall not fall asleep on the march.[50]

The British retreat was coming to an end, having covered over 200 miles in thirteen days since the Battle of Mons. The BEF had lost, officially, 15,000 killed, wounded and missing, yet morale was still remarkably high and the new fresh 6th Division had just arrived to bolster numbers. Nearly two-thirds of the casualties were from Smith-Dorrien's II Corps. The French C-in-C, General Joffre, prepared to give orders for an Allied counter-attack.

The Miracle of the Marne (6–9 September 1914)

The Marne proved to be the turning point in the first year of the war. It was predominantly a French battle but the BEF had an important role on the right flank of General Maunoury's 6th Army. A few days earlier, the French 6th Army had successfully struck at the exposed German western flank. At the River Marne, activity was mainly manoeuvre rather than technically a battle, as the overextended and exhausted Germans withdrew. They had failed to fully execute the Schlieffen Plan, yet had almost reached Paris. They also had a significant concurrent pressure on the Eastern Front with Russia.

General Lanrezac had now been replaced as the commander of the French 5th Army by the aggressive and successful General Louis-Felix Franchet d'Espèrey, known to British troops as 'Desperate Franky', and his army was to be on the BEF's right. The British liaison officer with General Joffre, Lieutenant Spears, observed the meeting between generals Joffre and French to discuss the imminent assault:

> The time for retreating was over. Those who could not advance were to die where they stood. No man was to give away even as much as a foot … His plan depends entirely upon British cooperation, its success on their action.[51]

Charles Monro's 2nd Division had had enough of withdrawing, as recounted in the Divisional History:

> The longing to turn about and fall upon the enemy was intense, and no commander ever made a greater mistake than von Kluck, who having accomplished what he deemed as a series of wonderful successes, appears

to have imagined he had completely overthrown and disorganised Sir John French's little Army![52]

Von Kluck had underestimated the strength left in the Allied armies when he changed his axis from south-west to south-east and exposed his flank. The BEF was ordered to march east, between the two French armies, with 2nd Division holding the northern, left flank of I Corps, with 1st Division to its south. As the division faced east, ready to attack, Sir John French's Order of the Day included the words:

> ... the British force stands today formed in line with their French comrades ready to attack the enemy ... They are exposing their right flank and their line of communications to an attack from the combined 6th French Army and the British forces. I call upon the British Army in France now to show the enemy its power, and to push on vigorously to the attack beside the 6th French Army ... They will fall on the enemy's flank with all their strength, and in unison with their Allies drive them back.[53]

Douglas Haig was more optimistic of the offensive opportunities than Sir John French, telling both major generals Lomax and Monro of 'the necessity for quick and immediate action' and to press forward vigorously.[54] However, the BEF had a relatively quiet start to the Battle of the Marne on 6 September 1914. Artillery and cavalry were engaged and 4th (Guards) Brigade received a few casualties from the enemy guns as they advanced, but most action was with the French who were seizing ground. It was during this period that the Paris defender, General Gallieni, famously seized the initiative and used taxis and other vehicles to reinforce General Maunoury's 6th Army.

Remarkably, 2nd Battalion Coldstream Guards, as part of the 2nd Division's Advance Guard, received their first casualties of the war at an enemy road block at Moinerie, early in the morning of 7 September. That day, 2nd Division continued its move forward on the left of the corps, gaining ground, having the occasional firefight with German Uhlan cavalry and even taking some German prisoners, which was a boost for morale. The Germans gave ground for two days, but were then ordered to stop and delay the BEF on the River Petit-Morin.

The passage of the Petit-Morin took place on 8 September. On the right of I Corps, the 1st (Guards) Brigade of 1st Division led the assault. On the left, in 2nd Division, 4th (Guards) Brigade were again in the lead. The Irish Guards and 3rd Battalion Coldstream Guards took the brunt of the enemy artillery and machine-gun fire as they attempted the river crossing in the area of the villages of Tretoire and Boitron. Again, there was the challenge of fighting in woodland, 'The wood was very thick, and companies got somewhat disorganised, consequently platoons had to act on their own initiative' and 'the machine guns were so well placed that, whenever our infantry came into action, they were met by a heavy fire from these guns'.[55] The Irish Guards were particularly pleased with their attack:

> Here the Battalion re-formed and pressed forward in a heavy rainstorm, through a flank attack of machine-guns from woods on the left. These they charged, while a battery of our field guns fired point-black into the thickets, and captured a German machine-gun company of six guns, three officers and ninety rank and file.[56]

There is still some dispute about which Guards battalion actually achieved this success. Two bridges were seized by the Worcesters and Grenadier Guards, allowing the progress of the 2nd Division across the river and the Royal Artillery proved its expertise as they forced enemy guns to withdraw. Meanwhile, 5th Brigade supported the Guards, but also the neighbouring 3rd Division, whilst 6th Brigade had had a quiet day. Divisional casualties for the day were about 180 men. Sir John French was pleased with the BEF's performance, writing, 'The British troops fought all along the line with splendid spirit, energy and determination, and they were skilfully handled and led.'[57] However, he also issued orders telling his army to make better use of its artillery in the front line and to avoid bunching the infantry, thus reducing their vulnerability to enemy fire.

Douglas Haig receives some criticism from a number of eminent historians, including Liddell Hart, for the handling of his I Corps with its two divisions during the Marne battle. He is accused of being too timid, moving forward too slowly and failing to inflict a significant blow to the Germans, despite the order to his divisional commanders to be aggressive. Haig's chief of staff later wrote, 'No attempt was made by General Headquarters to explain to the Corps and Divisional commanders the extraordinary opportunity now available for a decisive blow at the enemy.'[58] However, despite his effective use of cavalry and aircraft for reconnaissance, there was still some concern about his flanks and uncertainty about French successes. With that in mind, it is hardly surprising that he was avoiding unnecessary risks.

I Corps reached the River Marne on 9 September, prepared to advance in the gap that had developed between the German 1st and 2nd Armies. The new III Corps was left, II Corps in the centre and Haig's I Corps on the right. The river was crossed unopposed, with 2nd Division's 6th Brigade leading the crossing at Charly. Lieutenant Scott-Tucker of 1st Battalion King's (Liverpool) Regiment recorded, 'And so we crossed absolutely unopposed;

we learnt from the inhabitants that the enemy had got everything ready for defending the bridge, and had then got hopelessly drunk.'[59]

However 6th Brigade, as the advanced guard, had a tough fight on 10 September. Whilst Major General Monro ordered 5th Brigade to guard the northern flank and had 4th (Guards) Brigade in Reserve, 1st Battalion King's Royal Rifles launched a battalion attack on behalf of 6th Brigade against enemy infantry near the village of Hautevesnes. As artillery on both sides engaged, two more battalions in 6th Brigade joined the fray; Royal Berkshires on the right and South Staffords on the left. Two hours of hard fighting led to a German withdrawal and 350 prisoners were taken at the cost of 109 casualties.

On 11 September the BEF was ordered to 'wheel towards the right'. Douglas Haig was not happy with this order as he believed that his corps could have pursued the enemy more aggressively and taken more prisoners. By the end of 12 September the BEF was on the line of the River Vesle, a tributary of the Aisne.

The Marne battle had lasted for four days, with the brunt of the fighting between French and German troops. However, the BEF's activity had helped persuade the Germans to withdraw. Haig's I Corps had been most engaged, with 779 casualties out of the British total of 1,700. The Germans had been successfully driven back 65 miles to the River Marne and lost vast amounts of men and materiel, but they were far from defeated. They had withdrawn their forces with great skill to the River Aisne, where they had consolidated, dug in and were preparing their defences as a new form of trench warfare was about to begin.

The Aisne (13–26 September 1914)

'The offensive movement will, therefore, be continued along the whole front in a general north-north-east direction.' This was a key part of the order issued by the French GHQ on 10 September.[60] The German situation was uncertain as intelligence was poor, but GHQ ordered the River Aisne to be crossed as soon as possible and the heights beyond captured. Douglas Haig is criticised for being too cautious and delaying his I Corps move, which gave the enemy more time to regroup and prepare for the British assault as the enemy rapidly closed the gap between their 1st and 2nd Armies. The German 13th Reserve Division was positioned to thwart I Corps' advance, with just two hours to spare. It is argued that if I Corps had moved more quickly before the German reserve division had arrived, then there may have been the opportunity to outflank the enemy at Chavonne and achieve a victory at the River Aisne, but as always, this is easy to say in hindsight.

The River Aisne was deep and wide and the banks were high on the enemy northern side, including the Chemin des Dames Ridge. This ground, which ran for 25 miles between the River Aisne and the northern River Ailette was ideal for defending. Visibility for German artillery observers was much better than for the Allies and the British and French troops would have a steep assault against dug-in positions that would be difficult to see, particularly because of the woodland. The River Aisne was a significant 50–60ft-wide obstacle, which was too deep to ford, so bridging was required in order to cross.

The BEF was ordered to advance on the morning of 13 September 1914. On the left was III Corps, then II Corps, then I Corps. The 6th French Army was on the left with their 5th Army on the far right. First to reach the river were III Corps. Within I Corps, 1st Division was on the right, with an axis towards Bourg-et-Comin, with Charles Monro's 2nd Division on the left, moving towards Pont-Arcy.

By the end of the day, 2nd Division had secured two of the corps' three crossings over the River Aisne, at Chavonne and Pont-Arcy – a significant achievement. The latter crossing site had been seized without opposition by 5th Brigade and an effective pontoon bridge had been built by the Royal Engineers, who were critical, maintaining the lines of communication across the river during this battle. Two and a half miles west, at Chavonne, 4th (Guards) Brigade were again in action. Enemy artillery and machine-gun fire was heavy, but the 2nd Battalion Coldstream Guards managed to secure the crossing, thanks to the accurate supporting fire from friendly guns, though they suffered twenty-three casualties and had to withdraw temporarily across the river. During the day, the field companies of the Royal Engineers successfully built further bridges across the river.

By 14 September, crossings were seized, but as the troops advanced it became obvious that the Germans were well prepared on the high ground north of the River Aisne. Douglas Haig's I Corps bore the brunt of the fighting and he commented on his neighbouring II Corps, 'It was impossible to rely on some of the regiments in the 3rd Division which had been so severely handled at Mons and Le Cateau.'[61] Meanwhile, his 1st Division came up against well dug-in Germans on the Chemin des Dames Ridge and experienced enemy soldiers raising their hands, attempting to surrender whilst their comrades in further depth positions opened fire so that extra friendly casualties were taken. This 'unfair' action by the enemy hardened the attitude of the British troops when subsequent groups of Germans appeared to be surrendering.

Some progress was made, partly because of the thick fog reducing visibility for enemy artillery. In the 2nd Division, each of Charles Monro's brigades advanced steadily beyond the river after a slow two-hour crossing, with 4th (Guards) Brigade left and 6th Brigade right, in the lead, but soon ran into heavy opposition from well-concealed positions on the high ground. However, 2nd Division had seized part of the ridge by mid-afternoon, despite enemy counter-attacks, though with significant casualties. Douglas Haig commented in the I Corps War Diary:

> The 4th (Guards) Brigade found itself pinned down by a counter attack against the exposed left, and again the danger on this flank checked a great part of the line. The 1st Division on the right gained some ground, but could not maintain itself in the face of the opposition countered. Only in the Centre, the 5th Brigade moving along the eastern slopes of the Beaulne ridges, was able to get forward and continue its advance until it reached the ridge about Tilleul de Courton. In the dark General Haking failed to get in touch with the 1st Division, but his patrols found German outposts on both flanks. He consequently drew back his troops under cover of darkness to the neighbourhood of Verneuil.[62]

Private George Wilson of 2nd Battalion Highland Light Infantry, 5th Brigade, was to win the VC on 14 September, near Verneuil, during a series of attacks and counter-attacks. He had identified a German machine gun holding up the advance:

> Alone, he dashed towards it, and jumped into a hollow where he found a group of eight Germans with two British prisoners. He shouted: 'Come on, men, charge!' as if his regiment was with him. The Germans instantly surrendered. Once they were secured, he continued his attack on the machine-gun, shooting six of the enemy, bayonetting the officer and cap-turing the gun.[63]

Most of 2nd Division's battalions were engaged with the enemy that day and suffered terribly both in the assault and resisting counter-attacks; Charles Monro was particularly concerned about his increasingly exposed left flank, where 3rd Division had lost ground. Matters were not helped by the effectiveness of German heavy artillery; once the fog had cleared it was able to wreak havoc amongst the British troops and artillery. The Divisional History explains, 'The Germans fired from a higher altitude, which hid their guns, whereas the British guns were easily discovered as they lay or moved about the valley of the Aisne.'[64] The Royal Artillery was also being outranged, reducing the effectiveness of their supporting fire to the deployed units.

Near La Cour de Soupir Farm, 3rd Battalion Coldstream Guards and the Irish Guards suffered casualties in enemy attacks. Both battalions experienced bogus German use of the white flag:

> Lieutenant J. S. Fitzgerald with No. 8 Platoon and a party of Coldstream under Lieutenant Cotterel-Dormer found some hundred and fifty Germans sitting round haystacks and waving white flags. They went forward to take their surrender and were met by a heavy fire at thirty yards range, which forced them to fall back.[65]

Attitudes to potential surrenders were rapidly changing and casualties to 2nd Division on crossing the Aisne stood at over 100 killed, 550 wounded and 515 missing by the end of 14 September. In the first two days, I Corps had lost 160 officers and 3,500 soldiers as casualties. Despite hard work by the engineers, bridges rarely stayed intact, though two pontoon bridges were kept in operation and there was a ½-mile gap between 2nd Division and the neighbouring 3rd Division on the left. Parts of the Chemin des Dames had been captured, but it was becoming obvious that an Allied frontal assault was unlikely to be successful. Sir John French commented that Haig, with his two divisions, had 'made an excellent advance considering the strong opposition which confronted him' and he commended the progress of his corps to Lord Kitchener.[66] Late on 14 September, the two corps commanders were ordered by French to entrench where they stood.

The next day, heavy gunfire from the German heavy artillery, known to the BEF as the 'Black Marias', fell on 2nd Division and enemy snipers were at work as the division improved its defences. Barbed wire started to be used by the Germans and planking was procured to strengthen 'dug-outs'. 'Thus began the terrible system of living in trenches, which, until the close of the Great War, was to be the New Warfare.'[67] There would now be a series of attacks and counter-attacks, but not much ground gained by either side, despite individual heroic acts. The 2nd Division had fought hard and was congratulated by the I Corps commander on 15 September. He concluded with, 'I heartily congratulate Generals Lomax (1st Division) and Monro (2nd Division) and their gallant Divisions upon their splendid behaviour.'[68]

On 16 September, Brigadier General Haking, commanding 5th Brigade, was wounded and one shell landed on a building housing the King's Royal Rifles, killing twelve and wounding fifteen. Two determined enemy attacks were driven back on the 19th and 20th, but with high casualties. In one particular counter-attack by the Worcesters and Highland Light Infantry, all the officers involved were either killed or wounded. The pressure on I Corps was so great that the newly arrived 6th Division was provided as an additional reserve. Meanwhile the weather deteriorated, making conditions in the trenches even worse. Sir John French visited the two divisional commanders and some of their brigadiers on 20 September and realised that I Corps needed a rest. The first British heavy artillery went into action on 23 September.

From 20 September, the front became quieter, though the French Army on the left attempted to turn the German flank. 'Sapping' began between the two lines of opposing trenches and the Germans experimented with grenades and early trench mortars. Both sides began to use their snipers and aircraft in more sophisticated ways, improving the gathering of intelligence, whilst packing the lines with reinforcements. The French began to bear the brunt of the fighting. Two more VCs were earned by 2nd Division – Captain Harry Ranken of the Royal Army Medical Corps and Private Frederick Dobson of 2nd Battalion Coldstream Guards. Despite having most of a leg blown off, Captain Ranken continued to treat other casualties before dying from his own wounds. Private Dobson retrieved a wounded soldier under enemy fire. Between 16 September and 14 October, 2nd Division had lost 167 men killed, 676 wounded and 1,000 missing.

At this time, Major General Monro tried to tone down some of the enthusiasm of individual soldiers' brave actions in assisting with the wounded, for the wider safety and effectiveness of his division. On 22 September, he issued the order:

> It has come to the notice of the General Officer Commanding 2nd Division that it is not uncommon for men to leave the firing line to succour the wounded and even to assist them to the rear. Major General Monro desires brigade commanders to impress on the troops that this practice must cease. The care of the wounded is the business of the Regimental stretcher-bearers and the personnel of the Royal Army Medical Corps and the sole object of the attention of the fighting troops must be the enemy.[69]

This is a difficult order for any commander to sign and seems to stifle some initiative and bravery. However, in general war, the handling of the wounded can limit the momentum of an operation and the actions of some individuals can place the safety of others in jeopardy. Even today, it can sometimes be a challenge to balance the needs of the individual wounded compared to the needs of the group's mission.

Meanwhile, both adversaries were now concerned about their western flank, which was still open, and the Allies were becoming increasingly worried about losing contact with the Belgian Army or losing key Channel ports and the French coalfields. What became known as the Race to the Sea was about to begin as each side attempted to outflank the other. The BEF was to be moved to the left flank of the French again and began to be relieved on the line of the Aisne by French forces on 2 October, though I Corps and 2nd Division were to be the last formations to move. The last brigade was relieved on 14 October and the 2nd Division moved by train to the Hazebrouck area. As a key divisional commander, Charles Monro had now commanded his formation in a withdrawal, the attack, in defence and now a relief in place with the French Army. He had also seen the beginnings of trench warfare. Sir John French issued a Special Order of the Day on 16 October, thanking the BEF for their performance on the Aisne. This included the words:

> Throughout the whole of these twenty-five days a most powerful and continuous fire of artillery, from guns of a calibre never used before in field operations, covered and supported desperate infantry attacks made in the greatest strength and directed at all hours of the day and night on your positions. Although you were thus denied adequate rest and suffered great losses, in no case did the enemy attain the slightest success, but was invariably thrown back with immense loss.[70]

The die had also been cast for trench warfare. As Murland summarises in his excellent detailed book on the battle, 'The trench system which came to characterise and then symbolise the Western Front for generations to come was created by the weeks of flanking attacks which were forced upon both sides by the stultifying stalemate on the Aisne.'[71]

Whilst the Allied line to the coast was being secured and the BEF moved into Flanders, Charles Monro was told on 19 October that Lomax's 1st Division was to move to Poperinghe, whilst his 2nd Division was to close on Ypres. Douglas Haig's I Corps was not involved in the Race to the Sea, but was going to be in a critical position on the extreme left, north-west of the British line at Ypres. To its right was the newly formed IV Corps under Lieutenant General Sir Henry Rawlinson. The First Battle of Ypres had already begun.

Ypres (20 October–11 November 1914)

At Ypres, by the third week in October, I Corps had been allocated the critical offensive role in the BEF, highlighting the performance of Douglas Haig and his commanders and reflecting the depleted state of II Corps. The

First Battle of Ypres actually lasted from 10 October to 22 November 1914 and was to be the first of the four major engagements there during the First World War. As I Corps moved into position, the BEF and its other corps were already in action at La Bassée, Armentières and Messines and this was also a significant battle for the French Army, as French and British troops intermingled. The town was a vital centre of communications and if it fell to the Germans would make the defence of the key channel ports extremely difficult. The Menin Road was particularly valuable and the modest Flanders Ridge, needed for observation, featured heavily in the coming battle, along with the rest of the salient east of Ypres.

Haig's I Corps had arrived just in time to relieve elements of 7th Division, IV Corps, who were weary after three days of fighting. It had an initial ambitious and unrealistic goal of advancing and capturing Bruges and Ghent. However, the corps became involved in an encounter battle 7 miles northeast of Ypres, near Passchendaele, as the German 4th Army was moving in the opposite direction. On the left was 1st Division, with 2nd Division right and 7th Division further right.

Charles Monro's 2nd Division's 5th Brigade was left in the attack with 4th (Guards) Brigade right, as the Battle of Langemarck developed. Ground was gained, but at high cost. Within 5th Brigade, the Oxfordshire & Buckinghamshire Light Infantry lost 200 men, including five officers killed and another five officers wounded within a few minutes in one contact with the enemy. That day, 2nd Division had 600 casualties as it faced new reserve elements of the German 4th Army.

Douglas Haig described 2nd Division's advance, 'Fighting was hard and came to bayonet work' as 1st Division's advance was delayed.[72] He ordered I Corps to go onto the defensive on 21 October in the face of such strong opposition, as Sir John French also ordered IV Corps to stop and hold the ground gained. This marked an important halt of forward movement on the British front. Passchendaele would remain in German hands for the next three years.

Meanwhile, 2nd Division dug in and formed a reserve from three battalions and a battery of artillery. At this stage of the battle, the BEF were forced to be more flexible with groupings of units, making sure that gaps were filled as quickly as possible with locally available troops – 'The work of divisional and brigade commanders resembled that of men trying to repair a dam which is undermined by continuous flood.'[73]

This was a soldier's battle at the lowest level as a series of confusing attacks and counter-attacks developed amongst a mixture of units, often split from their parent formations across the whole battlefield. The effect of the enemy artillery was described:

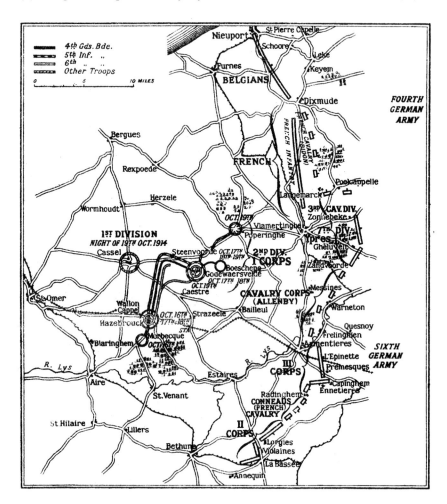

Ypres, 1914. (Wyrall)

> The German fire was so severe that it was reckoned that 120 shells an hour into or around a trench was a not uncommon rate of fall … So great was the concussion and the nervous strain that many of the men exposed to it got completely dazed or even became delirious.[74]

A major German assault was made on 22 October in waves of 'grey lines' forming easy targets for the division and on the following day a counter-attack occurred. Some 500 prisoners were taken, though in just a few hours nearly fifty men of the Staffords were casualties. All of the three brigades came under heavy shell fire on 23 October and 5th Brigade successfully held their line against another assault. That evening, the 2nd Division had a slight break as they were relieved in the line by the French 17th Division. They had successfully held the line and the following day they were ordered to relieve part of 7th Division on the right flank, then launch another attack.

The 5th Brigade succeeded in driving the Germans out of Polygon Wood 'at the point of the bayonet'. The Worcesters had the hardest fight; the commanding officer died of his wounds, four officers were wounded and seventy-five soldiers killed. That evening the badly bruised battalion dug in next to the wood alongside the other three battalions of the brigade and the Warwick's and Queen's from 21st Brigade of 7th Division. Meanwhile, 6th Brigade advanced along the other side of the wood in conjunction with a French division, the Berkshires and King's leading the way. There were further casualties and the commanding officer of the 1st King's (Liverpool) Regiment, 6th Brigade, also died in action, but ground had been gained.

The following afternoon, it was 4th (Guards) Brigade's turn to lead the advance and positions were seized, serious contacts being made with the enemy into 26 October. The Irish Guards suffered more casualties. Further assaults were launched by 6th Brigade; there was another bogus white flag incident with the enemy and the Royal Engineers Field Company in support proved its worth around Reutel village. The King's Regiment lost all their officers in two of their companies amongst the confused fighting. British losses were high and it was decided to break up IV Corps and allocate 7th Division to I Corps.

The First Battle of Ypres had now reached a critical stage as the Allies attempted to stem the German attacks. The period from 27–31 October was acknowledged by Sir John French to be 'more momentous and fateful than any others which I directed during my period as Commander-in-Chief in the field'.[75]

On the night of 27 October, 2nd Division's positions ran from west of Reutel village to near the Moorslede–Zonnebeke road. Further assaults were halted as it was reported that a major German attack was going to take place at Gheluvelt. A German Army corps was preparing to attack at the join between 1st Division and 7th Division, to the left of the 2nd Division positions and Polygon Wood. Charles Monro quickly engaged the enemy with his artillery and established a 2nd Division reserve in preparation, under Brigadier General the Earl of Cavan, from two battalions each from 5th Brigade and 4th (Guards) Brigade.

The Battle of Gheluvelt lasted for three days, beginning on 29 October – Gheluvelt was on the main Ypres–Menin road and the key to I Corps' position. The 2nd Division assisted the other neighbouring formations as best they could, with both its reserve and artillery, whilst massive German assaults were launched at them. At one stage they were outnumbered by eight to one, yet doggedly held on to their positions, the Divisional History commenting, 'In all the history of the nation there is nothing more grand or noble than the stand of the British soldier during the Battle of Ypres, 1914.'[76] On the morning of 30 October, two enemy attacks were successfully repulsed by 6th Brigade. The troops held, though the poor weather and mud was now adversely affecting their weapons, as there was little rifle oil available to keep weapons clean.

A most critical day was 31 October, as thousands of Germans prepared to assault across the front of the BEF and I Corps, inspired by the presence of their kaiser. The Germans were backed by 260 heavy guns compared to the British fifty-four, which were short of ammunition. Sir John French wrote:

> October 31 and November 1 will remain forever memorable in the history of our country, for, during those two days, no more than one thin and straggling line of tired out British soldiers stood between the Empire and its practical ruin as an independent first-class power.[77]

The previous night 2nd Division had been ordered to hold their positions the following day, no matter how high their losses were, and there were no reinforcements available. At 0800 hours the two-hour-long German barrage began. Attacks and counter-attacks took place mainly in front of 1st Division and 7th Division. The 1st Division was broken, Gheluvelt taken by the Germans and one British battalion, the Royal Scots Fusiliers, was surrounded and cut off. The position was extremely fragile. Lomax and Monro had agreed to mutually support each other and, fortunately, Charles Monro had placed 2nd Battalion Worcestershire Regiment in support of 1st Division at 1015 hours and warned his reserve of a potential requirement for further supporting counter-attacks. These were sound anticipatory arrangements, as events proved.

There was now a command and control crisis at this critical moment. There is a populist *Blackadder* view of the First World War, encouraged by some of the war's poets, the musical *Oh! What a Lovely War* and Alan Clark's book entitled *The Donkeys*, published in 1961. Whilst there may be 'no smoke without fire' and Field Marshal Bernard Montgomery had strong views about generals in the First World War being out of touch with their troops, generals were often placed in danger and were not always just pushing paper in large chateaux! Many British generals were killed from enemy fire during the First World War. Major General Hubert Hamilton's death at Le Couture on 14 October 1914 has already been mentioned in the previous chapter. He was 3rd Division's highly respected commander within Smith-Dorrien's II Corps:

> Hammy is dead, and we lose a splendid soldier and I a very good friend … He had gone to see personally why our left was hung up. They were dismounted and standing on the road, when a salvo of shrapnel burst right

over them. One bullet hit him in the forehead, and he died almost immediately. He never spoke or opened his eyes.[78]

These words could easily have been written by Charles Monro, his regimental friend for so many years, rather than his aide-de-camp. Losing his 'best
man', close friend and fellow divisional commander was a major blow to him
and only two weeks later he almost suffered a similar fate. This occurred on
31 October 1914, ironically in a chateau.

Recently promoted in the field, Lieutenant General Samuel Lomax
(1st Division) met with Major General Charles Monro (2nd Division) at
their headquarters at Hooge Chateau at 1245 hours on 31 October to help
deal with the ongoing crisis around Gheluvelt. He told his fellow divisional
commander, 'my Line is broken'. Their immediate staff were with them. The
chateau was an exposed target, only 2 miles behind the front line with a row
of staff cars parked outside, and earlier it had been flown over by an enemy
aircraft. Suddenly, at 1250 hours two enemy 'high explosive shells struck the
outside of the building in which the staffs were assembled'.[79]

Charles Monro was lucky enough to have moved to an adjoining room on
the edge of the building with his key staff officer, Colonel Robert Whigham,
as the second incoming round wrought disaster. Samuel Lomax was mortally
wounded from another shell, dying of his wounds in England six months
later.[80] Charles Monro lost Lieutenant Colonel Arthur Perceval, his GSO 2,
Captain Rupert Ommaney, GSO 3, and Captain Francis Chevenix Trench,
his brigade major Royal Artillery. Two other key staff officers were mortally
wounded and two more had serious injuries. So 1st Division had lost its
commander, but also its GSO 1 and the general's ADC. Charles Monro and
Whigham were both dazed, not unconscious as mentioned in some descrip-
tions of the event, but not for long.

Charles Monro 'walked to the window directly after the catastrophe had
occurred, passing over the bodies of some of the officers who had been
killed'.[81] He had a quick rest and took some brandy from Douglas Haig's
flask, as he recovered from the incident. The 2nd Division headquarters was
quickly moved to a small farm 2 miles away and Charles Monro was in
conference there with a French divisional general, using his fluent French,
into the early hours of the next morning; once again he demonstrated his
professionalism and determination in adversity. Losing the brains of the two
divisions at this stage, when the 1st Division's line was breaking, could have
been a total disaster and Sir John French wrote, 'To me, indeed, it seemed as
though our line at last was broken.'[82]

Amidst this crisis, Douglas Haig issued an order at 1330 hours to withdraw
to the first of the two reserve lines of trenches, about 1,000–2,000 yards

behind current positions. The I Corps War Diary states, 'these orders were taken to divisional headquarters'.[83] The news of a worrying potential withdrawal had certainly reached the French commanders, but both 1st and 2nd Divisions' diaries do not indicate whether the order arrived and it is not clear how many troops retired because of it. Charles Monro is reported to have read the order at 1540 hours when the situation had changed for the better and they were no longer relevant.[84] In the Official History, Edmonds writes, 'Haig was actually suffering from a "scare" similar to that at Landrecies', though Sir John French and other evidence recorded that Haig was 'cool and alert' on 31 October, 'the only noticeable sign of unusual anxiety being a constant pulling of his moustache'.[85]

Fortunately, the 1st Division rallied east of the Menin Road and the 2nd Division's Worcesters, led by Major Edward Hankey and supported by 41st Brigade Royal Field Artillery, were to save the day by driving the enemy back out of the trenches previously held by two other British battalions with the bayonet, at the expense of 120 casualties. Private Cole wrote, 'They fled in a solid mass and we watched the boys winkling them out. Remorseless. It was slaughter.'[86] Local leadership on the ground had been inspired by Brigadier General Fitzclarence, VC, the commander of 1st (Guards) Brigade; despite being in the neighbouring 1st Division, he improvised the successful counter-attack.

Douglas Haig was about to order a significant withdrawal, but then he heard of the Worcesters' success. The effect was enormous in breaking the German momentum and allowing 1st Division to regroup. In addition, French troops were brought in to help plug the gaps. The enemy had been halted, but the line was still fragile. One composite group of five under-strength British battalions had beaten off thirteen times their number. Douglas Haig wrote:

> We have had terribly hard fighting during the last week, but we have held
> our ground and the Germans seem to be almost more tired than we are …
> Our men are very tired: they fight hard by day and then during the night
> dig all they can to strengthen their position so they get very little sleep. We
> ought to have more men.[87]

His thoughts were reinforced over the next week as his commanders started to report less motivation amongst the tired troops. There were also increased concerns about the availability of ammunition, particularly for the artillery, which was increasingly being outgunned by the Germans. Charles Monro maintained his cool throughout this difficult period. One observer was told by Monro that things were not as bad as they looked and commented, 'I know that his steady level-headed courage that day put me to shame, and it was based on a better knowledge of the actual situation in the front line than even I had got.'[88]

Individuals in 2nd Division continued to inspire others. One example was Lieutenant Arthur Leake VC, Royal Army Medical Corps. He earned the extremely rare distinction of winning a bar to his Victoria Cross by rescuing a large number of wounded men under enemy fire at Zonnebeke.

The period of 1–10 November consisted of a confusing series of attacks and counter-attacks across the front, as 2nd Division's battalions were attached and detached from various brigades, sometimes even outside I Corps. Charles Monro also had to co-ordinate support for the neighbouring French units, led by General Foch, as they attacked. The battalions continued to suffer heavily from casualties, as the old Regular Army's numbers disintegrated. There were also some disasters – on 2 November, 1st Battalion King's Royal Rifle Corps of 6th Brigade lost all officers and 437 men as prisoners to the enemy.

An example of remaining battalion strengths, which in August 1914 were established at about 1,000 men a piece, were as follows: 1st Coldstream – 180; 1st Irish Guards – 296; and 1st King's Royal Rifle Corps – 180.[89] Charles Monro's own parent regiment, 1st Battalion Queen's (Royal West Surrey Regiment), which had been serving in 3rd Brigade of the 1st Division in Haig's I Corps, finished the Battle of Gheluvelt commanded by Lieutenant John Boyd and consisted of only thirty-two men. The 1st and 2nd Battalions had fought side by side and both commanding officers lost their lives. The 3rd Brigade's brigade major, Charles Grant, wrote to Boyd, as the remnants of that unit were removed from his organisation:

> How miserable I am at the Battalion leaving the Brigade for such a reason … I can honestly say that your Battalion, officers and men, has impressed me enormously, and I often thought yours was the best battalion I had ever seen, or certainly (as a Guardsman you will forgive me saying it) equal to the very best in the Brigade of Guards in every way. I can hardly bear to think of its unhappy fate.[90]

Another 2nd Division VC was awarded in a hand-to-hand fight with the enemy in the trenches of 2nd Battalion Highland Light Infantry of 5th Brigade on 7 November. The Germans had approached in the mist from their trenches only a few yards away, when the fight began in the Scottish trench. Fifty-four of the intruders were taken prisoner and eighty killed or wounded, for the price of one officer wounded and forty-four casualties. In this action, 29-year-old Lieutenant Walter Brodie 'led a gallant bayonet charge and cleared the enemy out of the trenches' earning his VC.[91] He personally killed four Germans, shot four or five and mounted and fired a machine gun to help drive them out.

The Germans made one more big attempt to break through at Ypres with the Battle of Nonne Bosschen on 11 November 1914 and I Corps received the main onslaught. Six and a half enemy corps were launched at the British and French from the line Messines to Zonnebeke, including the Prussian Guard Division – 'At 0730 a.m. the enemy's artillery opened with a roar!'[92] The BEF had never experienced such a deadly enemy barrage before and it is fortunate that Douglas Haig, his chief engineer and commanders had organised strong points in depth and the best use of scarce manpower as reserves. Casualties were high and some British and French battalions were forced back to the extremities of both Polygon and Nonne Bosschen Woods, whilst 2nd Division's 5th Brigade and 4th (Guards) Brigade helped fill the gaps and counter-attacked. Corporal Letyford of 5th Field Company, Royal Engineers, wrote:

> At nine we suddenly have to take up arms. The enemy has broken through! We man an old trench in the rear of the wood. The enemy approach and we begin to bowl them over. After a while we charge and drive them nearly back to their original position. Only about 110 of us in the charge against some hundreds of Prussian Guard. We suffered rather severely.[93]

One death outside I Corps was the commanding officer of the 4th Royal Fusiliers, Colonel McMahon who, like Charles Monro, had made such a difference at the Hythe School of Musketry before the war and had gallantly led his battalion in action since Mons. One of the heroes from a few days before, on 31 October, Brigadier General Fitzclarence, VC, was also killed, on 11 November.

The British line held – just – over the next two days and there was relief when orders were received on 14 November instructing I Corps that it was going to be relieved by the French on the night of 15–16 November. Douglas Haig was recommended by Sir John French for immediate promotion to full general for his performance as I Corps commander and Haig replied, stating, 'Whatever success the I Corps has gained is mainly due to untiring zeal of my Staff and to the fine soldiery spirit fostered by Commanders of Divisions, Brigades and Battalions in their units during peace.'[94]

The German attacks against the salient died down from 18 November. Once 2nd Division had been relieved in the line, Charles Monro, who had already pushed for leave for his men, wrote at the end of the month:

Every day without exception, the Germans have attacked us – fresh corps, one after another – and we have had no relief by any troops, so there has been very little time to do anything. Our troops have recently been relieved and sent back to an area of rest. The men want sleep, food and rest very badly now.[95]

These are not the words and deeds of a chateau-bound general only interested in himself. They reinforce his known considerateness and acceptance of responsibility and duty; he thought of his men, alongside his very traditional sense of discipline. In one month, from 21 October to 21 November, his 2nd Division had suffered casualties of 227 officers and 5,542 other ranks. The conditions had been terrible. Soldiers had stood in trenches with water above their knees for three weeks, 'Seas of mud covered the dead and drowned the wounded as they fell.'[96]

The Germans called First Ypres '*Der Kindermord von Ypern*' (the Massacre of the Innocents at Ypres). Ypres can be said to have marked the end of the first chapter of Britain's First World War. First Ypres had nearly been a disaster, it was the closest that the BEF got to defeat in 1914. The German advance into Belgium and France had been stopped, but at the expense of the old Regular Army. The Territorial Force would now have to take the lead, along with forces from the Empire.

Since August 1914, Major General Charles Monro had successfully commanded the 2nd Division in a time of great crises. Operations had included withdrawal, attack, relief in place, the passage of lines and defence. He had co-ordinated the actions of his three brigades and divisional resources admirably and had also worked closely with neighbouring French formations, making best use of his grasp of the French language, in the new combined arms environment.

Co-ordinating his three brigade commanders had been challenging as personalities changed over. Since the wounding of Brigadier General Scott-Kerr, 4th (Guards) Brigade, in September, that brigade had been commanded by two different personalities. In 5th Brigade, Haking had also been wounded in September and, whilst he was recovering, Colonel Westmacott held command. Meanwhile, Monro had to relieve the New Zealander, Davies, of 6th Brigade in September, because of his physical and mental state. All this disruption in command and control occurred as 2nd Division became more involved in the action and Monro consistently demonstrated his ability in high command when under intense pressure. He was successfully earning his spurs and gaining respect for his professionalism in front of his subordinates, fellow divisional commanders, Douglas Haig and Sir John French. The historian, Bourne, sums up his performance, 'Monro remained self-possessed

GRANT THEM O LORD
ETERNAL REST

Memorial to the 2nd Division,
Aldershot. (Author's collection)

and confident amid the supreme confusion and violence of modern war … Monro had passed the test of battle. He could command.'[97]

Within I Corps, there is no doubt that Douglas Haig had trusted and favoured the unfortunate Samuel Lomax from the beginning of the campaign, as reflected by his key responsibilities and promotion in the field to lieutenant general. Sir John French also approved of Lomax, stating that 'his services were invaluable' and that he commanded 1st Division 'with consummate skill and dash'.[98] The BEF had lost two very capable divisional commanders in both Lomax and Hamilton and it is quite possible that these senior officers could have been given more responsibility before Charles Monro. Of the four remaining initial BEF divisional commanders, another had been injured from a horse fall, whilst one had been sent home.

However, the very experienced 2nd Division commander now received reward for his performance, in competition with other major generals – promotion to lieutenant general and command of I Corps, to replace Douglas Haig, who had enhanced his reputation at First Ypres and been appointed commander of the new British 1st Army. Charles Monro relinquished command of 2nd Division on 26 December 1914. One obituary, published immediately after his death in 1929, stated, 'His division, moreover, was so far inspired by his martial ardour that it became noted for its fierce determination in battle.'[99]

Major General Monro. (Wyrall)

A Summary of 2nd Division's Key Operations in 1914

Date	Activity
1–22 August	Arrived in France, moving to Mons
23–24 August	Battle of Mons
24 August–5 September	Retreat from Mons
25 August	Landrecies
1 September	Villers-Cotterêts
1–5 September	Across the rivers Marne and Grand Morin
6–9 September	Battle of the Marne
13–26 September	Battle of the Aisne
19 October–20 November	Battle of Ypres
20–24 October	Battle of Langemarck
29–31 October	Battle of Gheluvelt
11 November	Battle of Nonne Bosschen

DEADLOCK

Corps Command

For Lieutenant General Charles Monro, 1915 marked his time as corps and army commander but also saw him in a high-profile and controversial role in Gallipoli. It has been described as the 'stalemate' or 'deadlock' year of the First World War, as all sides grappled with the dominance of seemingly immoveable static trench warfare on the Western Front. The so-called 1914 'War of Manoeuvre' was over.

Liddell Hart described the attempts to break the deadlock as both tactical and strategic; on the Western Front attempts were made to find ways to break through the trenches using new machines, tactics and weapons, whilst elsewhere attempts were made 'to go round the trench barrier'.[1] The former led to the first use of gas in 1915 and the tank in 1916, whilst strategic ideas produced the 'easterners' who favoured striking the enemy in other parts of the world, including in the Balkans, Dardanelles and the Middle East. Charles Monro was fully engaged in all of these developments.

The French priority was simply to drive the Germans from their occupied homeland, supported by the British, who debated the relative merits of whether the decisive blow should be in the west or east. The Germans, however, decided to hold onto their gains in the west, whilst concentrating on defeating Russia in the east. Germany alone can claim some achievements in 1915, driving Russia out of Galicia and Poland and conquering Serbia. Meanwhile, Turkey entered the war on the side of Germany and the Austro-Hungarian Empire, whilst Italy joined the Allies by declaring war on Austria–Hungary. Allied spring and autumn offensives took place on the Western Front, but even the Official History concludes that they 'resulted in heavy losses, without any compensating gain'.[2] Also, in the Dardanelles, the Allies failed to make headway.

1st Battalion the Queen's (Royal West Surrey) Regiment, Bordon, 1914, on mobilisation. By November 1914, this battalion was reduced to thirty-two men. (Surrey History Centre. QRWS 2-13-7-38)

The British Army had to recover from the decimation of the old Regular Army. A few Regular units returned from overseas, Territorial Force divisions began to occupy the trenches and the British Empire did its duty as Indian and Canadian troops made significant contributions. It was this mixture of forces that had to learn the lessons of trench warfare during 1915, whilst Kitchener's New Armies prepared themselves for action. The Official History describes 1915 as 'a period of education and instruction' for the leaders of all ranks. 'Neuve Chapelle, Aubers, Festubert and Loos were most valuable lessons in the staging of the offensive and in the comprehension of the enemy's methods.'[3] This was a period, however, when there was a shortage of personnel and a lack of equipment, heavy artillery, shells and efficient fuses. As the Official History commented:

> The awful slaughter and pitiably small results of the battles of 1915 were the inevitable consequences of using inexperienced and partly trained officers and men to do the work of soldiers, and to do it with wholly insufficient material and technical equipment.[4]

The BEF was expanding to eleven infantry divisions and five cavalry divisions and was reorganised into two armies, each led by the original two corps commanders – the 1st Army by Douglas Haig and 2nd Army by Horace Smith-Dorrien. Charles Monro, who was now a very experienced and trusted senior commander, led Haig's old I Corps from 26 December 1914 to 12 July 1915. His I Corps stood beside Lieutenant General Henry

Rawlinson's IV Corps, which had the higher profile, and Lieutenant General James Willcocks' Indian Corps, within Haig's 1st Army. He had the 1st and 2nd Divisions under his command and his two principal subordinates were major generals Richard Haking (1st Division) and Henry Horne (his old 2nd Division).

Richard Haking was an infantryman who had been commissioned into the 67th Foot, later the Hampshire Regiment, in 1881 and went on to become a full general. Like Charles Monro, he eventually became the colonel of his own regiment, holding that position for twenty years. In the First World War, he went on to command IX Corps and after the conflict became GOC in Egypt. Again, similar to Monro, there are virtually no existing personal papers, but in his case there is no known family or schooling information. One excellent recent book has analysed his performance and character in depth and it is clear that he was often a difficult person to command.[5]

His intellect is proven by his two books, *Staff Rides and Regimental Tours* (1908) and *Company Training* (1914), and his selection as professor at the Staff College. In addition, his regiment's history states, 'His bluff, hearty manner and his great personal interest in the British soldier as an individual endeared him to all.'[6] Nevertheless, the Australians nicknamed him 'Butcher Haking' for his fondness of the attack at Fromelles in 1916 and one of his future subordinate divisional commanders described him as 'a bully' and 'a madman'.[7] There is no doubt he had always espoused the attack; his *Company Training* book finished with the comment, 'However good the commanders, and their staff may be, no one can win the battle except the infantry soldier, and he cannot win except by attack' – he was committed to the 'cult of the offensive'.[8]

Whilst both Charles Monro and Douglas Haig had recommended him for command of the 1st Army in 1916 and put him in temporary command, the CIGS rejected the request, appointing Henry Horne instead, and in 1918 the Liberal War Committee recommended his dismissal for incompetence. Some other observers were more complimentary about Haking. Confusingly, his fellow divisional commander, Henry Horne, described him as 'dull and unimaginative', yet also 'always good company'.[9]

As for Horne, whose career has also been analysed, 'He shunned publicity. He was a quiet, retiring, competent Gunner.'[10] He had proved his competence as an effective rearguard commander in the retreat from Mons, was highly respected by Douglas Haig and succeeded Charles Monro in both divisional and army command, yet was not their first choice for the latter. Like Monro, he was generally seen as being professional, reliable and competent, though Liddell Hart later stated that Horne was incompetent and 'should have been sacked at the Battle of the Somme'.[11] However, he was thought of as the model of integrity and loved his family, the army, sport and religion. He

Lieutenant General Monro with I Corps Staff, 1915. (Surrey History Centre. QRWS 1-16-11-28)

believed that God was on the Allied side in the war and wrote, 'No men fight better than those who fight for their religion and the more we can foster the spirit of the Covenanters the better will our men fight and the more rapid will be our success.'[12] Horne was one of only seven war generals made a peer and one of ten awarded a sum of money by a grateful Parliament. He also effectively commanded an army on operations for two years.

There is no doubt that both of Charles Monro's major generals were determined, competent and intelligent divisional commanders with different styles. It was his and his staff's job to co-ordinate both of these groupings plus additional corps level troops, particularly artillery – a force of over 40,000 men. His key staff officers were Brigadier General Robert Whigham, the CGS, who as a colonel had been Monro's right-hand man in 2nd Division, and Brigadier General R. Montgomery, who was his Brigadier General Royal Artillery.

On 1 January 1915, he wrote from his headquarters at Hinges Chateau:

I have been translated from the 2nd Division to the 1st Corps. They say this new billet gives more emoluments, so one ought to be pleased, yet my thoughts are centred in a different channel, you know well what they are, so any satisfaction is tempered to a great degree.[13]

The harsh weather in the deadlocked trench systems was the initial challenge for the new I Corps commander and his troops, as senior officers tried to work out how they could break the impasse with limited manpower and technology, prior to the arrival of Kitchener's New Armies. On 14 February he commented:

> Since Christmas time we have been kept busy by the Bosches, as the French call them … We have been having the most miserable winter, constant rain and fog, although the inhabitants say that it has been a most favourable one. The fact is that this part of France is a horrible and filthy part of the world, offering no attractions of any kind. I try to get as many people away as I can, especially the regimental officers.[14]

The welfare of his men was always a critical issue for him, particularly in the difficult conditions in the trenches where:

> Those gallant men who stood for days in water reaching half-way up their benumbed bodies, suffering intense agonies from cold and exposure, to say nothing of the constant shelling which by day and night went on almost without ceasing … It is tedious anxious work for the officers and men and when the country gets drier we may be able to do something.[15]

Haig's 1st Army occupied the right of the British line between Cuinchy and Bois Grenier with the French on its right. The relative peace over the Christmas period was broken by a German attack on Haking's 1st Division, near Cuinchy and Givenchy on 25 January 1915; some of the forward British trenches were taken and then partly recaptured following counter-attacks. Horne wrote, as a result of this experience, 'We cannot fight nowadays without casualties on a large scale.'[16]

The CGS was not impressed by the loss of the trenches, writing to Haig on 31 January, 'As you are aware, there is no part of the Line held to which greater importance can be attached than that on the right of the 1st Army.'[17]

The line was eventually restored by Horne's 2nd Division counter-attack on 4–6 February and his fellow divisional commander's performance was reported. 'Special credit is due to Major General Haking commanding 1st Division for the prompt manner in which he arranged this counter-attack and for the general plan of action, which was crowned with success.'[18]

A subsequent successful reinforcement of the line by Horne a few days later was also acknowledged. I Corps was being efficient and Monro was seen to be co-ordinating his formations effectively. Monro was not afraid to apportion blame for the loss of ground at Cuinchy. This is illustrated by his damning of one of Haking's brigade commanders:

> Brigadier-General Lowther's report is so wanting and incomplete that it is not possible to learn therefrom the steps which he took to carry out the spirit of the instructions given him by his divisional commander … It appears to me clear that the Brigadier had little grasp of his brigade or of the situation.[19]

In modern parlance, he was 'gripping' the situation. He was also very much involved in low-level tactical debates on the use of weapons, making best use of his experience from Hythe School of Musketry. He collated reports on the use of machine guns, including the need for reliable Vickers models, rather than the older Maxims, and the requirement to obtain shields for protecting machine guns. He wanted better training in trench warfare, concealment and maintenance of defensive positions and he was helping to develop the use of trench mortars, hand grenades and rifle grenades.[20]

Field Marshal Sir John French visited his headquarters on 13 February and congratulated Monro and his divisional commanders 'on the success of the recent minor operations'. On 9 March 1915, Monro reported to Haig that 'his corps was in splendid condition',[21] and his performance in the war so far was recognised in the same month when he was appointed a knight commander of the Order of the Bath. He had a sound reputation.

I Corps badge. (Player's)

Neuve Chapelle (10–13 March 1915)

The first significant set-piece British offensive of the First World War against a dug-in enemy was at Neuve Chapelle and it was conducted by Haig's 1st Army. There was pressure on the C-in-C, Sir John French, to achieve some form of breakthrough and Kitchener had stated that unless there was success the government would have to switch their attention elsewhere. In addition, there was French pressure on the British to demonstrate a credible offensive spirit and capability.

Originally, the assault was to be a joint British and French effort, but it became an independent British operation that began on 10 March 1915. The main assault was by IV Corps, under the command of Lieutenant General Henry Rawlinson. It was also the first significant engagement of the Indian Corps, which was on IV Corps' right.

Neuve Chapelle was a German salient protruding into the British line – it provided a constant threat of enfilade fire into British positions. Apart from tidying up the Allied front, the area was above the waterlogged British trenches and included the drier ground of the relatively insignificant Aubers Ridge. This overlooked Allied positions and would be an ideal location to dominate an advance on the industrial town of Lille, just 12 miles east. The odds on paper appeared good – two German divisions faced the six divisions of 1st Army on a 13-mile front.

Haig had grand ambitions for the attack, as illustrated in a 1st Army conference note of 5 March 1915, 'Sir Douglas Haig wishes it to be made clear that all staff officers and battalion commanders realise that the forthcoming operations are a deliberate attempt to break the enemy's line on a large scale.'[22] It was also stated, 'Very likely an operation of considerable magnitude may result.'[23]

However, Rawlinson appeared to have limited objectives. Rawlinson realised the importance of artillery planning and preparation for the assault, though he only had ten days to prepare, compared to the months of preparation in later battles:

> An undertaking such as that which is under consideration depends for its success almost entirely on the correct and efficient employment of the artillery. It is primarily an artillery operation and if the artillery cannot crush and demoralise the enemy's infantry by their fire effect the enterprise will not succeed.[24]

This lesson was to be learned time and time again on the Western Front, but at this stage the British Army was still trying to work out whether short and sharp bombardments or days of preparation were the most effective way to employ artillery.

A great deal of thought went into the consideration of different options, whilst the troops rehearsed for the attack. Eventually, four phases were executed: just ten minutes of wire cutting, thirty-five minutes fire on enemy trenches, a curtain of fire east of Neuve Chapelle to discourage German reinforcements and once the trenches had been taken, twenty-five minutes of bombardment on the village. In all, 340 guns were concentrated for the assault and one was to be deployed for every 6 yards of German trench; this sort of concentration had never been achieved before.

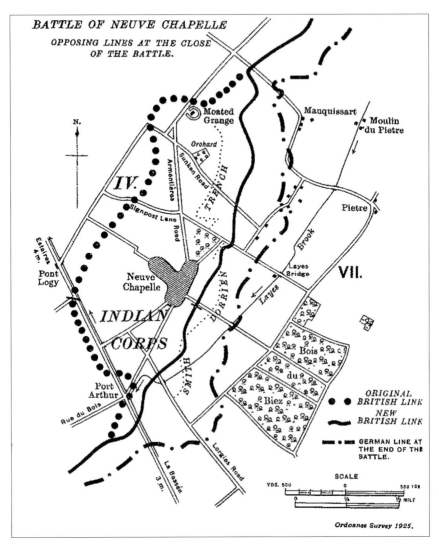

Neuve Chapelle, March 1915. (Edmonds)

Surprise was achieved on day one, and when the attack began at 0730 hours on 10 March there was some success as parts of the enemy front line were captured within the hour. Unfortunately, on other parts of the front the bombardment had little effect on the enemy wire and the 2nd Battalions of the Scottish Rifles and the Middlesex Regiment were cut down by German machine guns which had not been neutralised by the bombardment. Sergeant Davis of the 2nd Middlesex provided a graphic account of the assault, including:

A whistle sounds, and over the parapet we go. Go on, Die-Hards! Don't forget Mons! The sight that met our eyes almost staggered us – our poor first and second line lying in all positions. Then we saw red; we reached the barbed wire, trampled on it, cut and hacked it, the barbs cutting us all in places. We were beaten back.[25]

However, they had also taken the closest enemy trenches by 1120 hours. The advance was to continue against the Aubers Ridge and Neuve Chapelle village. The diverse actions and mixed success across the battlefield demonstrated the difficulty for a corps commander like Rawlinson or Monro to co-ordinate and influence the situation. To the frustration of Haig, a breakthrough was not achieved. Communications were poor and it was impossible to respond quickly to the changing environment.

What of Monro's I Corps? This was to the right of the 1st Army line, whilst the Canadian Division was to the north. Both formations were to provide 'fire and demonstration' initially and then were to exploit any enemy weaknesses by 'vigorous offensive'. For Monro's corps, this would be towards Violaines. The hope was that if IV Corps was successful, there could be a general advance across the front.

In I Corps, subsidiary attacks were launched with 2nd Division on the left and 1st Division on the right. Horne's 2nd Division orders had an optimistic series of attack stages: the artillery bombardment, followed by the critical assault and then 'the consolidation of ground gained either for incorporation in our line, or as a jumping off place for a forward bound'.[26]

He attacked at 'zero hour' near Givenchy on a 700-yard front, but all battalions were stopped by heavy machine-gun fire and the failure of the bombardment to clear the wire or to silence the enemy. The accuracy of friendly artillery fire was not helped by the mist and the leading men of 1st Battalion King's Regiment, 6th Brigade, 'were killed on the wire itself in their endeavour to break through it'.[27] A second assault also failed. The corps War Diary recorded, 'The second assault had failed, the enemy being in considerable strength in his trenches and having disclosed additional machine guns. The wire had not been destroyed by the artillery bombardment.'[28]

Monro forbade a planned third attempt in the dark, showing some compassion after the day's casualties and effectively ending his corps' involvement in the battle. Earlier, Haking's 1st Division had not participated in the assault because of the boggy ground in its area, so it only provided supporting artillery and small-arms fire to 2nd Division's efforts. The attacks of I Corps were unsuccessful, but it did divert the enemy from their defence of Neuve Chapelle, which was taken by IV Corps. Nevertheless, this achievement cost 2nd Division 600 casualties.

The battle raged for three days, Neuve Chapelle was taken and the line straightened, though at a high cost of 11,652 casualties. Lessons were learned, including the difficulty of command and control and the need to have more artillery shells available for assaults. Rawlinson had proved to be an effective commander, but was criticised for not exploiting some of the initial successes and being too timid. He did suggest that future attacks should 'bite and hold' ground gained, rather than be too ambitious. Haig was not impressed by that attitude as he strived for a breakthrough, and whilst Haig criticised Rawlinson, Rawlinson initially blamed one of his divisional commanders for the failure to exploit early success in the battle.

Monro had not been able to significantly affect the battle, though he had had his first experience at corps level of translating army intent into co-ordinated divisional action. Analysis of I Corps' actions after Neuve Chapelle has deduced 'that corps were still acting only as a medium of communication between GHQ, army and divisions, rather than taking a more active role in operations'.[29] However, direction from *Field Service Regulations* and the practical experience of the battle were being blended together and many historians comment that the actions of the British Army at Neuve Chapelle proved to both the Germans and French that the BEF was a fighting force to be reckoned with. A note by the CIGS, Robertson, of January 1916 commented, 'The attack at Neuve Chapelle was carried out in order to raise the offensive spirit of our troops, who had passed through a long period of inactivity.'[30]

For the 1st Army, the next two months were spent surviving in the trenches as various new small trench weapons were introduced, including catapults, mortars and Bangalore torpedoes, whilst new sapping tactics were developed. In addition, improvised respirators were issued for the first time following the first use of gas against the British 2nd Army by the Germans in April during the Second Battle of Ypres, further north of the Allied line. Horne's reaction to German use of gas was that it was 'a barbarous thing. They are extraordinary, inhuman brutes, and grow more and more so. I think England is perhaps at last beginning to realise that it is time to take the war seriously.'[31]

The Second Battle of Ypres lasted from 22 April to 25 May and the hope was that an attack by the 1st Army further south might relieve the pressure on Smith-Dorrien's 2nd Army. At this point, it is worth mentioning the Territorial Force again, which at this stage of the war had become a critical part of the British Army. Monro, of course, was well-versed in their strengths and weaknesses from just before the conflict began. Apart from some isolated operational circumstances, up until this point in the war, most Territorials had been posted overseas to relieve Regular units for the Western Front or had been involved in drill and duties in France and Belgium. That had to change as they took on front-line responsibilities, but there were still some concerns about their capabilities. Horne expressed his worries about two of his units in a confidential note to Monro:

The officers are keen and the material seems quite satisfactory. They lack confidence in themselves and experience in the art of command, but this will improve with responsibility. Their hearts are in their work … Bearing in mind that these two battalions have been embodied for seven months, the standard of training is very disappointing.[32]

All commanders had to come to terms with the demise of the Regular forces and the subsequent reinforcement by Territorials and troops from elsewhere in the Empire. Monro echoed these concerns to GHQ, writing, 'The British Army in the Field must suffer', but had to make the most of the material he was given and train them as best he could.[33]

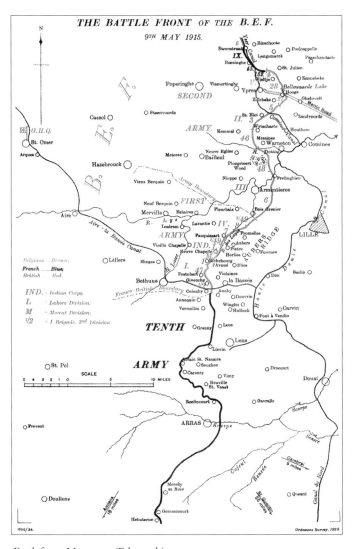

Battlefront, May 1915. (Edmonds)

Aubers (9 May 1915)

The first big Allied assault of 1915 began on 9 May as the French attacked Vimy Ridge as part of the Second Battle of Artois. Haig's 1st Army was the BEF's contribution to this action, which was known as the Battle of Aubers Ridge. The ridge, 20 miles south of Ypres, was only minor, though it dominated the area.

Haig was determined to put into effect the lessons learned from Neuve Chapelle and IV Corps was to be on the left with Monro's I Corps working closely with the Indian Corps to their right on a front of 2,400 yards. As well as supporting the French 'big push', it was hoped that the attack would take some pressure off the 2nd Army at Ypres. The objective of the operation was to break 'the German line on a broad front and drive them eastward'.[34]

For this battle, Monro worked closely with another division as well as the 1st and 2nd – the 47th (London) Territorial Division under Major General Charles St L. Barter. The 47th was actually the renamed 2nd London Division, which had been commanded by Monro before he took command of 2nd Division in August 1914. Therefore, he had the advantage in his I Corps of commanding divisions that he knew very well and whose leaders at different levels also knew him. There were also two Territorial battalions of his own regiment in one of the 47th Division's brigades: 1/22 Londons and 1/24 Londons of the Queen's Royal West Surreys. In addition, most of 1st Battalion the Queen's (Royal West Surrey) Regiment was attached (Monro's original battalion) as part of his corps troops. This mutual understanding helped the passage and understanding of orders from I Corps headquarters, though the command and control frustrations common to all the senior commanders on the Western Front continued.

Douglas Haig briefed all corps and divisional commanders, including Monro, on 27 April and 6 May. He wanted a 'decisive battle, not a local success'.[35] This was going to be a simultaneous two-pronged attack by the three corps in conjunction with the French 10th Army to the south, on the British 1st Army's right. The French, under General d'Urbal, would aim to capture Vimy Ridge, amongst other objectives, on its 4-mile front. Haig's orders were issued on 4 May, including the words, 'The 1st Army will take the offensive on 8th May. Its mission is to break through the enemy's line on its front and gain La Bassée–Lille road between La Bassée and Fournes.'[36]

A great emphasis was placed on improving communication. Commanders were to 'be kept in close touch with the situation … This is of first importance. And all commanders will give this matter their close attention.'[37] This indicates the continual effort to learn from previous assaults during 1915 and to improve operational methods.

The British thought that they had learned some vital lessons from Neuve Chapelle and were overly optimistic and confident of success. Two staff papers were produced by the 1st Army: *General Instructions for the Attack* and *General Principles for the Attack*. A vigorous offensive was required, along with reserves well forward to exploit success. In addition, the critical role and timetable of artillery fire was reinforced. This included the need for a short bombardment of plenty of artillery to gain surprise, and a British memorandum had stated that the outstanding lesson was 'by means of careful preparation as regards details and thorough previous registration of the enemy's trenches by our artillery, it appears that a sector of the enemy's front line defence can be captured with comparatively little loss'.[38]

The British planned a forty-minute bombardment and also brought into play trench mortars in intimate support and wireless-equipped aircraft to help direct accurate timely artillery fire. Unfortunately, there was going to be less density of British artillery fire at Aubers Ridge, so there were not enough guns to destroy the enemy trenches and wire. At Neuve Chapelle, there was one gun to every 6 yards, at Aubers Ridge the same number of guns covered 8 yards.

The firepower directed at the German front line was also less, because the plan was to provide a greater proportion of fire against the depth of enemy strongpoints, so in fact the initial supporting fire density was even less and the weight of shell to fall was about one-fifth of the Neuve Chapelle total. The weather and terrain were also unhelpful, as the mist across the flat battlefield and numerous trees made the accurate registration of fire extremely difficult. Prior and Wilson sum up the artillery situation well:

> The British had done only one thing well at Neuve Chapelle. They had fired a crushing artillery bombardment, which had facilitated an initial advance by their infantry. At Aubers Ridge, the artillery bombardment was certain to be a good deal less than crushing.[39]

There was another critical factor at Aubers Ridge – the Germans had also learned from their experience at Neuve Chapelle and were well prepared for the British attack. The three enemy divisions facing the 1st Army had spent two months improving their defences and they were more concentrated than at Neuve Chapelle, which the Germans regarded as 'almost disastrous' because the BEF had been close to breaking through their lines.[40] Sandbagged emplacements with well-protected and camouflaged machine-gun positions were sighted in enfilade positions, bunkers reinforced, thick wire laid and artillery accurately registered to prepare to engage the British infantry in no-man's-land.

Charles Monro had a second lucky escape from death in early May, as a shell landed on his bedroom at the corps headquarters at Bethune, just after he had left it. Meanwhile, I Corps staff issued his operational order for Aubers Ridge on 7 May 1915. The War Diary recorded:

> The task allocated to the 1st Corps was to break the enemy's line between Festubert and Orchard Redoubt and holding Cuinchy and Givenchy as pivot to gain the line Festubert, Logies, and thence move on Illies, while the Indian Corps on the left move on Ligny Le Grand to La Cliquetue Farm.[41]

The key extracts were:

I CORPS OPERATION ORDER No 79

1   The First Army will advance tomorrow morning with the object of breaking through the enemy's line and gaining the La Bassée–Lille Road between La Bassée and Fournes.

Two cavalry corps and three divisions are being held in readiness as a general reserve under the orders of the Field Marshal Commanding-in-Chief to exploit any success.

2   The I Corps is to attack from the Rue do Bois and advance on Rue du Marais-Illies, maintaining its right at Givenchy and Cuinchy.

3   The Indian Corps is to attack on the left of the I Corps and is to capture the Distillery and the Ferme du Biez. Its subsequent attack will be directed on the Ligny le Grand-La Cliquetue Farm.

4   The 1st Division will attack from its breastworks in front of the Rue du Bois. Its first objectives are:

Hostile trenches P.8–P.10, the road junction P.15, and the road thence to La Tourelle.

Its subsequent advance will be directed on Rue du Marais-Lorgies, a defensive flank being organised from P.4 by La Quinque Rue to Rue du Marais.

Touch will be made with the Indian Corps throughout.

5   The infantry under GOC [general officer commanding] London Division holding the defensive line north of Festubert will be prepared to relieve the infantry of the 1st Division at PO.4, La Quinque Rue, and Rue du Marais, when those points have been secured, and to take advantage of any weakening of the enemy about the Rue d'Ouvert to occupy that locality.

6   The 2nd Division (less 4th Guards Brigade), with Motor Machine Gun Battery attached, will be in Corps Reserve in the area Loisne-Le

Touret-Le Hamel in readiness to continue the advance. The troops of 1st Division must be clear of above area by 3.30 A.M.

7   The 5th London Brigade will be in First Army Reserve, about Essars and Les Choquaix, from 5 A.M.

8   The 1st Battalion Queen's Regiment (less two companies) will be under the direct orders of the Corps Commander north of Bethune.

9   The artillery will complete such registration as may be necessary by 5 A.M. at which hour the preliminary bombardment will begin in accordance with special instructions already issued as to times and objectives. GOC London Division will arrange for wire-cutting batteries and machine guns to open fire on enemy's wire opposite Festubert and Cuinchy at 4.45 A.M.

10   At 5.40 A.M. the infantry of the 1st Division will assault. The troops under GOC London Division will at the same time open a vigorous fire attack along their entire front.

The French assault began with a five-day artillery bombardment of 1,200 guns on a 4-mile front followed by an infantry advance at 1000 hours on 9 May 1915. Their battle would last until mid-June and involve some initial successes and gain of ground, but at the expense of 100,000 casualties, including over 42,000 dead.

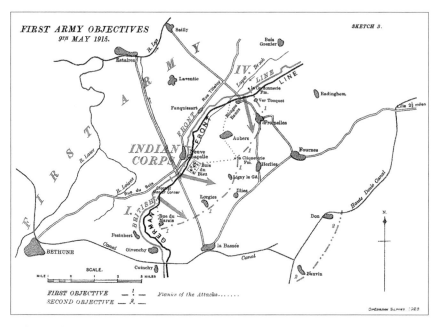

Aubers Ridge, May 1915. (Edmonds)

Preceded by the successful laying of sixty-four bridges placed over 12ft gaps in no-man's-land by the Royal Engineers, 600 British guns began their bombardment just before 0500 hours on 9 May. Wire cutting commenced, but unlike at Neuve Chapelle surprise had been lost. For Monro's I Corps, Haking's 1st Division led the assault with Horne's 2nd Division in reserve, 3 miles behind the line. At 0540 hours, the fire lifted to 600 yards ahead and the infantry advanced.

Haking's 2nd and 3rd Brigades led the way within his 1st Division, but it was soon clear that the barbed wire was still intact and the Germans were firing on them as soon as they moved forward. The Official History recorded, 'Many men fell dead on the ladders and on the parapet.'[42] The enemy machine guns decimated the advancing troops and by 0600 hours there had been 2,135 casualties – 60 per cent of the six infantry battalions engaged – for no gain.

Some men from the 1st Battalion Northamptonshire Regiment and the 2nd Battalion Royal Munster Fusiliers made it into the enemy trenches, but were never heard of again. The 1st Northamptonshires lost over half of their officers and men on 9 May. Meanwhile, the Meerut Division of the neighbouring Indian Corps fared no better. A second attempt was made by Haking shortly after 0700 hours after another bombardment aimed at cutting the German wire, but many British troops were cut down by friendly fire for no gain.

Haking attributed the failure to 'hostile machine-gun fire from low loop-holes at the foot of the parapet, and the small effect of High Explosive shell on the soft ground'.[43] He wanted to try again and relayed to his commanders that he would be able to attack if the wire was cut and more enemy machine guns destroyed. Subsequently, he telephoned Charles Monro at 0720 hours stating that his second attack had failed, but he could deploy his reserve, the 1st (Guards) Brigade, and assault again. Charles Monro would not allow it, demonstrating his humanity and realism, instead he ordered Haking to just hold the line with the Guards Brigade.

Despite the failure of the attack, another assault was ordered by Douglas Haig when he heard the lack of progress. Initially, he wanted Monro's I Corps and IV Corps to advance at 1200 hours, but this kept being postponed as Haig realised the developing poor situation. Haig visited Monro at I Corps headquarters and promised support from all available 18-pounder guns with high-explosive shells, even though the 18-pounders had seemed to have little effect on the enemy positions so far. As Neillands points out, 'At this point General Haig's actions must be queried.'[44]

Despite the casualties so far and further lack of surprise, a southern prong attack was launched after another forty-minute bombardment at 1600 hours.

This time, the 1st Battalions of the Black Watch and Cameronians, both in the 1st (Guards) Brigade of Haking's 1st Division, took the brunt of enemy fire. The Black Watch bravely advanced with their pipes playing, but lost 475 casualties in this one failed assault and then Haking ordered another attempt at 1645 hours after a ten-minute bombardment. Fortunately, this did not occur, Haking being told by both his lead brigade commanders 'that it was mere waste of life to send men forward'.[45] Bristow comments that Monro 'distrusted Haking's handling of his troops in battle but he knew that Haig approved of Haking's zeal for attack'.[46]

One moment of glory was achieved by fifty men of the Black Watch on the right flank of their assault, where they reached the German support trench. Forty-seven-year-old Corporal John Ripley led his men and was the first to reach the enemy positions. He earned the VC for his brave leadership, holding the position until the point when the rest of his section had been killed or wounded. The battalion was visited a few days later by Charles Monro, accompanied by His Royal Highness the Prince of Wales. Monro, their corps commander, addressed the troops and congratulated them on their 'fine behaviour'.[47]

Overall, however, Haking commented, 'Both Brigadiers reported that the attack had failed and so I ordered them to withdraw under cover of artillery fire and re-occupy our original line.'[48] Haking's performance and keenness to attack did not endear him to his soldiers, Robert Graves writing, 'He came over this morning and shook hands with the survivors. There were tears in his eyes. Sgt Smith swore half aloud: "Bloody lot of use that is … busts up his bloody division and then weeps over what is left"'.[49]

At 1900 hours, Monro ordered Horne's 2nd Division to take over from the 1st and a further assault was planned by Haig for the evening, but was abandoned due to the strong arguments made by his corps commanders, including Monro. There had been a failure to seize ground, a huge volume of wounded to deal with in the forward trenches and a lack of artillery shells. The Indian and IV Corps had fared no better than I Corps and, in fact, IV Corps had suffered most. No ground had been gained and the British losses in just one short day were 11,619; 4,000 of those were in Haking's 1st Division.

Further attacks were formally cancelled in the afternoon of 10 May following two conferences led by Haig, including Charles Monro and the other corps commanders. A night assault was considered along with a further day attack following another barrage, but the extent of casualties and lack of effective artillery ammunition became apparent. The situation for Haig was particularly frustrating as the neighbouring French assault had started off so successfully. Later analysis showed that the short artillery barrage was simply not enough to destroy the enemy defences and that 'Fire and Movement' tactics were not used effectively.[50] The shortage of artillery ammunition was highlighted in *The Times* newspaper on 14 May and the politically charged 'Shell Scandal', which lasted months, ensued. The BEF's capability was still not sufficient to break the German line, however, another attack was planned for a few days later at Festubert.

Festubert (15–25 May 1915)

It was Horne's 2nd Division, within Monro's I Corps, that was to lead the fight for the assault at Festubert. The element of surprise was partially dropped as the short and intense bombardments used so far by the BEF were replaced by a three-day artillery barrage over the period 13–15 May 1915, designed to destroy the enemy wire entanglements and strongpoints. Haig recorded one of his key lessons from Neuve Chapelle, which resulted in this change of tactic:

> The defences in our front are so carefully and so strongly made, and mutual support with machine guns is so complete, that in order to demolish them a long methodical bombardment will be necessary by heavy artillery (guns and howitzers) before infantry are sent forward to attack.[51]

This time the corps commander, Charles Monro, would set the exact time for assault based on the effectiveness of the friendly artillery fire, 'A more deliberate approach to battle was beginning to emerge, and with it a more important role for corps command.'[52] Another change, to achieve some surprise, was the plan to launch 2nd Division in a night attack.

There was another reorganisation of I Corps for Festubert. This time, Monro commanded Horne's 2nd Division again and from 10 May 1915, Gough's 7th Division. Haking's 1st Division and the 47th Division were grouped under the latter's leader, Major General Barter and known as 'Barter's Force'. Meanwhile, the Canadian Division formed a reserve for I Corps.

Major General Hubert Gough was yet another character for Monro to deal with.[53] A favourite of Haig, he shot up through the senior ranks during the war and would end up taking over command of Monro's I Corps in July 1915. He later led the Reserve (or 5th) Army from 1916 to 1918, though he lost that appointment after the failure to resist the German Spring Offensive in 1918. He was a cavalryman, though like Monro he had served in the Tirah Expedition and the Boer War. He commanded his own regiment, the

16th (Queen's) Lancers, and had been the youngest lieutenant colonel in the British Army. He had also commanded a cavalry brigade at the Curragh, Ireland, before the war and earned attention for his refusal to intervene against the Unionists, if ordered to do so. He took his brigade to war in 1914 and later had his command expanded before taking over 7th Division in mid-April 1915.

This was a controversial and impatient character with 'energy, drive and ruthlessness', and a close relationship with Douglas Haig.[54] Views have varied about his competence, from both academics and the military. The Australian Official History castigated him as 'the very worst exhibition of army command-ship that occurred during the whole campaign', and he was known to some observers for being a bully, who ordered poorly prepared attacks with a weak supporting staff.[55] On the other hand, Liddell Hart, well known for his later criticisms of many generals, was supportive and wrote, 'World War One cramped his dynamism and acute sense of mobility.'[56]

Gough was certainly critical of his new corps commander, though it is not clear what Monro thought of him. Monro had told Gough to choose his own objectives, within boundaries, for the Festubert attack, providing he kept the Germans facing him occupied. His response to this included:

> I cannot say that I approved the idea of leaving this matter to me; inasmuch as the attack of my division was part and parcel of an attack by a whole corps, the locality of its attack and its immediate objectives were hardly matters which should have been left to the decision of the divisional commander. Moreover, I was in entire ignorance of the ground, and had never been in the neighbourhood before.[57]

Monro's flexible approach had given Gough some freedom to use his own initiative with a very narrow divisional front and obviously fitted with the corps plan. Gough quickly sorted the issue out by conferring with other officers who knew the ground. He did respect Monro, writing later, 'If the I Corps had allowed an unwise amount of initiative to its Divisional Commanders as regards choosing localities and hours for the assault, once the battle opened there was no lack of energy and grip in Monro.'[58]

On the Festubert battlefield, the I Corps' 3-mile front ran from Festubert to Neuve Chapelle. The Indian Corps was on the left with Barter's force to the right. Within the corps, Horne's 2nd Division was left and Gough's 7th Division right. The main aim was to help the concurrent French offensive by providing a diversion with very limited objectives of only up to 1,000 yards. There was again going to be a two-pronged assault, but the two thrusts would be much closer than at Aubers Ridge, being only 600 yards apart. The ground to be covered was easier going than before and was deemed to be less well defended.

It was decided that it was not practical for Gough's division to assault at night as they were unfamiliar with the ground. The odds against the German VII Corps troops seemed reasonable, Sir John French pointing out to Haig, 'The strength of your Army is far superior to the hostile forces in front of you. The enemy has suffered heavy losses in the fighting near Arras, and he has few or no reserves, other than local, which he can bring up.'[59]

Of course, having superior numbers was not the only battle-winning factor required. The enemy were well dug in and protected and British stocks of artillery ammunition were still limited, though more guns were brought to bear than in the previous attacks.

The French were not happy that it had taken the British so long to launch this assault after the Aubers Ridge experience, which had come to a halt after only one day of battle. They felt that the BEF was not pulling its weight as their armies continued to take high levels of casualties and were to sustain over 202,000 casualties during the Second Battle of Artois for little ground gained.

The British artillery bombardment began on the morning of 13 May in a far more accurate and methodical manner than at Aubers Ridge with a demonstrably improved effect on the enemy wire. However, the Meerut Division of the Indian Corps on I Corps' left were not content with the initial effect and there was also concern about boggy ground, so the main attack was delayed for a further twenty-four hours. This meant that the bombardment lasted for sixty hours rather than the originally planned thirty-six. A number of feints occurred, using different rates of artillery fire and even shouting from the trenches, to try and disguise the future timing of the British assault.

Charles Monro's orders were issued on 14 May and after the delay, zero hour for Horne's 2nd Division was 2330 hours on 15 May. In all, 10,000 troops were to launch this first deliberate British night attack of the war, with Horne's 5th and 6th Brigades forward and the 4th (Guards) Brigade in support, and the Meerut Division on the left.

On the right, 6th Brigade moved out of their trenches, crossed a 4ft-deep water obstacle using ladders, lay low for a while in no-man's-land closer to the enemy, then advanced quietly and steadily with bayonets fixed, achieving complete surprise over the enemy. The German second line of trenches was in their hands, for minimum loss, by 0130 hours on 16 May.

Unfortunately 5th Brigade's advance, along with their neighbouring Indian division, did not achieve surprise, because another Indian division provided what they thought was supporting and diversionary fire, which only alerted the Germans to their front. The moment the advance took place, illumination turned the battlefield into day, making easy targets for both German machine guns and artillery, particularly as the troops attempted to cross the water obstacle to their front.

On 5th Brigade's right, some success was achieved by 2nd Battalion Inniskilling Fusiliers as they occupied German trenches, but only at the cost of 649 men. Despite the effects of a further British short artillery bombardment, the Germans had three hours to reorganise their defences so the subsequent planned dawn attack of 2nd Division and Indian Meerut Division, which was due to coincide with Gough's 7th Division dawn attack, did not happen. In the end 6th Brigade was told to hold its positions, whilst a further Indian division was made ready to reinforce them.

Gough's attack began at 0315 hours on 16 May, following half an hour's barrage led by 20th and 22nd Brigades, supported by 24th Brigade. Two innovations were made: firstly, the final supporting bombardment included German trenches further north and south of the assaulting area, making reinforcement by them less easy; secondly, six field guns were brought into the lines in very close support to the advancing infantry, providing high-explosive, close-range, accurate supporting fire which 'at a range of less than 200 yards blew holes in the enemy's parapet during the thirty minutes preceding the actual advance of the infantry'.[60] These seemed prudent measures, but the advancing infantry were instantly engaged by the enemy.

It was 2nd Battalion the Queen's (Royal West Surrey) Regiment who were attacking within 22nd Brigade:

> As soon, however, as the heads of the attackers showed above their parapets, the enemy, apparently in no way affected by the intense British bombardment, opened a sustained rifle fire; none the less, the second line of A Company followed, and then the first of C Company, but the enemy fire seemed to gather volume rather than to lessen, so the British guns opened again with lyddite on the opposing trenches and the rest of "C" and "D", pushing on, forced the Germans out of their lines.[61]

Their commanding officer was killed and there was a total of 454 casualties (60 per cent) in the battalion from this single day's action. The 1st Battalion Royal Welch Fusiliers had also lost their commanding officer and a total of nineteen of their twenty-four officers in the assault and were also to lose heavily from hand-to-hand combat in the enemy trenches. Gough described both battalions' actions as 'a fine and most gallant performance'.[62]

Across Monro's I Corps' front by 0900 hours on 16 May, Gough's 7th Division on the right had reached the enemy trenches and pushed forward about 600–1,000 yards in some cases. On the left, Horne's 2nd Division's 6th

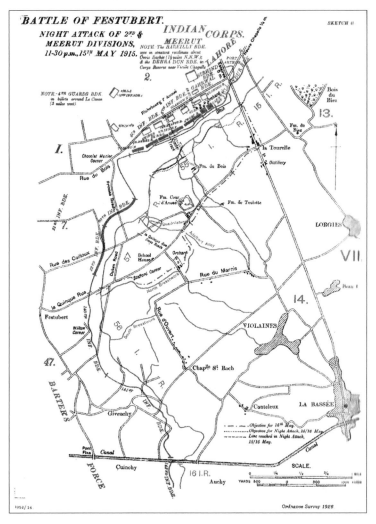

Festubert, May 1915. (Edmonds)

Brigade was in enemy lines, along with one battalion of 5th Brigade, but the majority of 5th Brigade and the Indian Garhwal Brigade had gone nowhere. Therefore, the plan to link both of his divisions had failed. He visited both of his divisions' headquarters and ordered another attempt to link up, which began at 1000 hours but had petered out by mid-afternoon.

Haig and Monro had decided that it was in Gough's 7th Division area, where there was less enemy resistance, that any further attack might be launched. Sir John French was most concerned about keeping the pressure on the Germans to aid the French and made the attrition requirement clear to Haig. The Official History recorded, 'The main object to aim at for the present is to continue relentlessly to wear down the enemy by exhaustion and prevent him from detaching troops to oppose the French.'[63] Monro's I Corps was now the sole attacking element of the new plan to close the gap between the two divisions and hold the line, with slightly altered objectives.

There was little time for preparation but there was some solace as, after an early morning intense bombardment on 17 May, there was a sudden increase in the numbers of German soldiers surrendering. After some changes of zero-hour timings, the next attack was planned for 0930 hours, by which time more rain had worsened the mud, making any progress extremely difficult. The gap was gradually being closed between the divisions, however, partly caused by Germans surrendering or withdrawing from that area, but this was still at a high price of casualties. The small success did inspire Haig to write, 'There are signs of enemy resistance breaking down.'[64] He encouraged the brigade commanders to use their initiative to advance.

Again, there was no significant progress by the two divisions or the now supporting Canadian Division, despite his optimism. On 18 May, the Canadian Division and 4th (Guards) Brigade were particularly heavily engaged after they tried to advance again after another bombardment, but with little progress. The Germans had operational fields of fire, were well protected and had altered their front lines so that they were not effectively engaged by British artillery fire. In addition, there were further significant water obstacles in depth.

The divisions were ordered to dig in and hold their positions and Monro stated that there would not be an attack on the 19th. Over the next few days, I Corps' two divisions were relieved in the line, though the Battle of Festubert did not officially end until 27 May 1915. Monro's command was again reconstituted to 1st, 2nd, 6th and 47th Divisions.

The British had 16,648 casualties at Festubert, gaining an average depth of just 600 yards of ground but relieving some of the enemy pressure from the French assault and in front of the British 2nd Army at Ypres. Total casualties in just three days included 2nd Division, 5,445, and 7th Division, 4,123. Horne wrote, 'Casualties very heavy. One must not allow oneself to think of them, but must accept that it is for God and country.'[65] He acknowledged the loss of friends, but his comment does reflect a different attitude to casualties than exists today. Charles Monro visited the depleted 2nd Battalion the Queen's (Royal West Surrey) Regiment on 31 May, stating:

> How pleased he was to see that the 2nd Battalion was more than main-
> taining the exceptionally high standard of the Regiment. He knew
> how well they had done in the recent fighting and had the greatest
> confidence in their behaviour in the future. As a former officer of
> the Regiment he was more than gratified with their successes and he

wished them always to remember the great and glorious traditions of the Regiment.[66]

Although again there was perhaps little emotion, this was how senior officers of the time praised their troops and that is what the officers and men expected. In fact, Monro had a reputation for being able to relate to his troops and is said to have delivered very memorable talks, which 'always struck the right note'.[67]

One regimental story from the battle, related by Gough, refers to Private Thomas Hardy of the Queen's. Despite being severely wounded, he dangerously exposed himself and continually threw grenades at the enemy before being shot dead. He might have been decorated, but it was then discovered that he was actually Captain Smart of the 53rd Sikhs, Indian Army, who had been reported as a deserter. Home on leave and destined to return to India, he enlisted as a private soldier in the Queen's in order to fight. Gough arranged for the desertion notification to be expunged, because of his 'gallant and ardent spirit'.[68]

The Germans lost 5,000 men, 785 prisoners and ten machine guns and British infantry had seized objectives at a high cost, but Aubers Ridge was still not taken. Experimentation in the attack had occurred and some important lessons were learned, including the future need to co-ordinate maximum artillery firepower at corps headquarters rather than at lower levels. Monro wrote a joint report to 1st Army HQ in June stating, 'success rested upon finding targets for the heavies and the factor of surprise'.[69]

Were Haig, Monro, Gough, Horne, Haking and other senior generals all 'donkeys' leading 'lions' in the three battles of Neuve Chapelle, Aubers Ridge and Festubert? Little was gained for very high casualties, but these were not stupid leaders and the plans had been quickly altered as lessons were learned. They were battling a new war environment which heavily favoured the defence over offence, whilst attempting to control large numbers of troops in a very confusing situation, with extremely poor communications and only limited resources.

Monro was doing his best in the circumstances. His performance is best summed up by Neillands' comments about Haig, 'He had a limited number of cards but he appeared to be playing them well.'[70] It was difficult for him to flourish in a corps command, which in 1915 tended to be a 'post-box' headquarters between army and divisions. The role of the corps would become more important as it gained more control of artillery and had stronger co-ordinating powers over inexperienced divisional staff.

The 3rd Army

Monro took command of the newly formed 3rd Army on 15 July 1915, following his promotion to 'temporary' general two days earlier. The appointment demonstrated the hierarchy's faith in his ability to command at the highest levels in the war. Five officers were considered for the post, but it was Douglas Haig who pushed for Monro's appointment.[71]

This was not without some controversy, as Monro was given command rather than the more senior General Henry Rawlinson, who was not a favourite of Sir John French. Rawlinson commented:

> Monro passes over my head to get III Army. I don't think with Sir John at the head of affairs they would select me … suppose I cannot expect fair treatment with Sir John & old Robertson against me. I must await my time & be patient.[72]

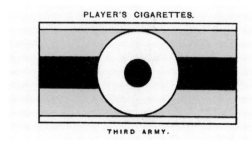

3rd Army badge. (Player's)

This is a small glimpse into the politics of military high command during the First World War, as various 'schools' of officers attempted to promote their own interests. The ultimate official appointer of these senior officers was the king himself. There is no evidence that Charles Monro was within this web of intrigue, rather he gained his appointment through his own proven competence. He had the honour of being one of only three army commanders, the two others being Haig (1st Army) and Plumer (2nd Army), though he was the most junior and had the least responsibility, as his formation took over a quiet part of the French line.

His new 3rd Army, headquartered first at St Omer then Chateau Val Vion near Beauquesne, occupied a 16-mile sector of that line and consisted of VII Corps (4th, 37th and 48th Divisions, commanded by Lieutenant General Sir T. D'O. Snow) and X Corps (5th, 18th and 51st Divisions, commanded by Lieutenant General Sir T. L. N. Morland). The Indian Cavalry Corps were also initially under his command. His key staff were:

Major General Arthur Lynden-Bell, senior staff officer.
Major General Walter Campbell, deputy assistant and quartermaster general.
Lieutenant Colonel Lord Herbert Scott, military secretary.
Major Bridges, staff surgeon.

Lord Herbert Scott was to be with him during command of both the 3rd and 1st Armies and at Gallipoli. Bridges accompanied Monro throughout his time in France, India and Gibraltar.

Within one year Charles Monro was experiencing command at divisional, corps and army level, though he only held 3rd Army command during a relatively quiet period until October 1915. Allenby, Byng and Rawlinson trod similar paths of promotion, but are far better known. His area of responsibility was later part of the Somme battlefield, but in the summer of 1915 it was relatively peaceful. General Joffre had pressurised Kitchener to relieve one of his armies with a British one back in May 1915, so this had been a political move, which was to have greater consequences in 1916, when the Battle of the Somme ensued.

Monro's first action was to liaise with the French and relieve part of their line. In addition, he had to contend with the challenge that many of his 3rd Army were inexperienced at this stage – not ideal for any offensive action. His initial appreciation of the situation included a request for an additional two divisions to hold the line.[73] His period in this command was dominated by the emphasis on defence in this sector of the front and important liaison with the neighbouring 10th French Army. Another first task was to move the Indian Cavalry Corps on the right of his line, neighbouring with the French 'owing to objectives on the part of the French'.[74] Remarkably, by today's attitudes, Foch had written to GHQ as he did not want 'coloured troops at the point of junction of the French and English formations'.[75]

In August 1915 there was a recorded example of Monro's traditional and disciplined approach to routine in the trenches. This comes from records of a 3rd Army conference on 4 August 1915. Divisional commanders were told that 'Order and regularity in trenches must be of the nature we are accustomed to in barracks. Elaborate orders must be drawn up to provide for everything and "go as you please" methods must be suppressed.' Also:

It must be properly explained to them why we are fighting and the great part they are playing in the welfare of the Empire. The strictest attention must be paid to turn out, guards, saluting etc. in order to keep off slackness which is common to trench warfare.[76]

Travers calls this a 'fear of soldiers' individuality', but this is an incorrect assessment. Long periods in the trenches required tight discipline, and team needs and cohesion were greater than individual freedoms. His comments ignore Monro's well-known concern for his soldiers, though this was not necessarily a popular directive.

Even in recent years, when the British Army has been in Afghanistan, modern generals have from time to time issued similar direction, which is usually necessary but receives bad reports in the media. Also, Travers picks on only a few paragraphs from a much longer document recording the actions to be taken following the 4 August 3rd Army conference.

Monro's conferences do provide some useful insight into his approach to command. The main purpose of this, his first conference, was to provide guidance to his commanders about the defence of their sector of the line. It is recorded that 'once we have made our lines thoroughly secure, we must give the Germans no peace, but pester them night and day by every means at our disposal, using every form of ingenuity that we can devise'.[77]

The document then goes on to mention German attack methods, the importance of counter-attacks and defence in depth. It also describes the need for loyalty to commanders and the training of 'bombers' before mentioning Travers' discipline extracts.[78] Monro's comments included:

> Every man must be involved in the idea of not giving ground to the enemy … Self-respect must be stimulated in every way possible … The bearing of staff officers has an important effect on the morale of those with whom they are in contact. Cheerfulness and reticence must be cultivated. There must be no long faces. A despondent staff officer is not likely to be of much use.

These are the words of a professional, tough commander who realised the challenges of maintaining morale in a defensive position. In a subsequent army conference of 1 September he had to deal with further aspects of discipline, including sentries sleeping, crime and drunkenness on duty. These aspects of misbehaviour are rarely mentioned in the war histories, but were prevalent in quieter areas of the line. Discipline was key, and Monro knew that and reacted extremely effectively.

General Pétain visited 3rd Army headquarters at Beauquesne one day and asked Monro whether his young officers amused themselves with the French ladies of Amiens. 'Oh,' Sir Charles said. 'My young officers do not confide their love affairs in me.'

'That's true,' said General Pétain. 'When we are young we are all discretion, but when we come to your and my age, dear General, we boast of any conquest from the rooftops!'[79] No additional comment is recorded from Monro. The French did recognise his performance at that time by appointing him a *grand officier* of the French Legion of Honour in September.

Another unusual story involving a meeting with Monro as 3rd Army commander is identified by Charles Messenger. Dorothy Lawrence was a determined lady who tried to get to France as a war correspondent. Failing this, she disguised herself as a soldier, reached the front and was arrested by the 51st Highland Division. Allowed to leave, she disguised herself as a sapper for ten days and worked in the trenches with them, but was discovered, re-arrested and briefly considered a spy. Eventually, she appeared in front of Monro and he ensured that an officer took responsibility for her as she was returned home, on the same boat as the suffragette Mrs Pankhurst. She commented, 'At this moment, when Allied forces were hoping that a great victory might result from the first battle of Loos, I, a foolishly unimportant English girl, occupied the undivided attention of six famous generals.'[80] She appears oblivious of the trouble she had caused, though the incident must have provided an unusual source of amusement to Monro and the chain of command.

The next significant offensives were not until September 1915 when the Battle of Loos took place along with French offensives in Champagne and Artois. There were still 300 British casualties a day in this 'quiet' period, as trench warfare became more sophisticated. Mines, machine guns and snipers became increasingly deadly, whilst new grenades and trench mortars were developed and tested. Gas also remained a real threat. In this period, the 1st Army saw action near Givenchy and the 2nd Army fought at Hooge.

The Battle of Loos, which began on 25 September 1915, involved the 1st Army assault of six British divisions of Gough's I Corps and Rawlinson's IV Corps over ground described by both Haig and Rawlinson as 'unfavourable'. The 2nd Army were to provide subsidiary attacks to aid deception, whilst Monro's 3rd Army, now joined by XII Corps, provided artillery support to the attack and was to be prepared to commit its nine divisions to assist the French Army if the enemy withdrew. However, this did not occur and Monro's artillery was the only supporting element in action, so the battle is not described here.

Before leaving Monro's time commanding the 3rd Army it is important to mention his influence on improving training for the BEF. Standards of training and tactical skills were low after the decimation of the Regular Army in 1914 and the situation was becoming worse as Kitchener's New Armies deployed, often commanded by ex-retired officers who were out of date with modern tactics. They had been trained with the minimum of integration with either Regular or Territorial Force expertise, despite the potential opportunity to do so, as Kitchener said they 'would ruin it'. Skills were particularly weak amongst junior commanders:

> General Rawlinson calculated in 1915 that owing to casualties the 'officers were at least fifty per cent less efficient than they were last Autumn and our troop leading is correspondingly less good'; and this was having 'a marked effect on our fighting efficiency'.[81]

There was also a concern that too much time was spent on defences and fatigues rather than tactics. One author has commented, 'The British Army was unable to employ the flexible tactics developed by the Germans, since these tactics demanded a very high standard of low-level initiative, a virtue possible only if based on thorough training.'[82]

The same author highlights the lack of experience and low standard of training in the New Armies, though he fails to appreciate the changes made over the next three years that led the British Army to victory at the end of the war. To help deal with this critical training issue, Charles Monro set up the first 'army school' in the 3rd Army and his example was eventually copied by other formation commanders from army down to divisional level. This initiative was his, without any assistance or lead from GHQ, and at one stage Haig tried to remove corps schools in favour of divisional ones, as he was not convinced of the value of the new school network.

The 3rd Army School, run by Brigadier General R. J. Kentish, instructed fifty officers and fifty non-commissioned officers on a month's course 'training the trainer', and later doubled its throughput. The success was recorded as 'due to the individual effort' of Monro 'who first originated the idea'.[83] Monro understood the need to train both at home and on operations, making the most of his previous experience at the Hythe School of Musketry and his subsequent command at different levels of operations.

Over the next two years, other commanders set up training schools, many specialising in sniping, artillery techniques, trench mortaring, bombing, signalling, machine guns and bayonet fighting. Monro began a critical legacy that by 1918 helped provide the basis of a series of war-winning battles. These skills took time to develop and there were still only seventeen schools for twenty corps in September 1917, but British tactical skills were improved.

One of Monro's enthusiastic supporters was Major Vernon Hesketh-Prichard, who as a big game hunter used his shooting skills to improve sniper training. The sniper's effectiveness was not fully appreciated at the beginning of the war, but that situation changed as it took only three seconds of exposure above a trench before being shot by an enemy sniper. Hesketh-Prichard wrote, 'In early 1915 we lost eighteen men in a single day to enemy snipers', in his determination to improve British sniping capability.[84]

Charles Monro and Lynden-Bell encouraged him to serve with the 3rd Army as a sniping expert and he went around units showing their snipers how to zero their weapons properly and how to engage the enemy more effectively. At one stage, he introduced a heavy game-hunting rifle to the trenches as it could penetrate German metal plate armour, however, it had such a distinct firing sound that it encouraged a flurry of enemy grenades and trench mortar rounds to the firing point, so was not always popular! Hesketh-Prichard quotes one of Monro's supportive comments, 'It is not only that a good shot strengthens his unit, but he adds to its morale – he raises the morale of his comrades – it raises the morale of the whole unit to know that it contains several first-class shots.'[85]

Monro had not forgotten the importance of accurate shooting on the battlefield, despite his now exalted rank and the fact that even in 1916 there were still some senior officers who were not convinced about a sniper's importance. Hesketh-Prichard records that the 3rd Army was the best sniping army in France and when Monro returned from Gallipoli to command the 1st Army, Hesketh-Prichard continued his good work with him there.

Charles Monro had only commanded the 3rd Army for three months and had not been called upon to lead his men in action, but he had enhanced his reputation as an extremely competent commander and had influenced improved training in the BEF for the future. Meanwhile, in October 1915 Charles Monro reported to the War Office in London to be told that he was to take over command of the Gallipoli operation from General Sir Ian Hamilton. This experience was to significantly raise his profile.

8

GALLIPOLI

The Context

General Charles Monro's arrival at Imbros on 28 October 1915 to take command of the Mediterranean Expeditionary Force (MEF) was not welcomed by many of the existing Gallipoli commanders and the campaign's political supporters. This led to Winston Churchill's later description of Monro's actions, 'He came, he saw, he capitulated.'[1] Though Monro had established an excellent professional reputation and was described by Moorehead as 'a methodical and authoritative man, one of the kind who accepts the rules and excels in them', who displayed great calmness and 'an aura of responsibility', he was also identified as a 'westerner' who was unlikely to support the Gallipoli effort.[2]

Gallipoli campaign histories vary in their coverage of Monro. Although he only arrived towards the end, 'he played a dominant part in that scene', so it is surprising that some of the analysis is so sketchy.[3] Unsurprisingly, he is praised most by Australians, who recognised that by his sound judgement and advice to evacuate further unnecessary casualties were avoided on the peninsula. This chapter will concentrate on the part Monro played, rather than the detail of the campaign.

By the time Monro arrived, the Allied troops – British, French, Australians and New Zealanders (Anzacs) – had been on the ground at Gallipoli for over six months with little to show for it. The over-ambitious campaign had been instigated by the Russian Tsar's request in January 1915 for an Allied demonstration to relieve pressure on the Russian front, but the landings had become more than a demonstration. In an attempt to help knock Turkey out of the war, threaten the German flank and support Russia's war efforts there had been unsuccessful Allied naval bombardments between February and March, then landings at Kum Kale by the French and Anzac Bay and Cape Helles by the British on 25 April. Unfortunately, these assaults achieved no surprise and, as in Mesopotamia, the Turkish capability and reaction were underestimated.

After various attacks and counter-attacks by both sides, the Allies launched a second wave of landings in order to break the deadlock, by outflanking the Turkish lines at Suvla Bay in August, simultaneous with further assaults. However, hopes following initial success were short-lived. By then, seven British divisions had been committed to the campaign – 410,000 troops from the British Empire were involved, sustaining just under 200,000 casualties; the French lost nearly 50,000 killed and wounded out of 79,000; and the Turks had around 195,000 casualties, of which 87,000 were killed.[4]

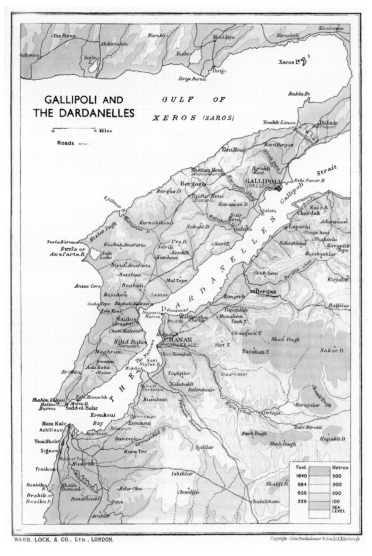

Gallipoli. (Birdwood)

Sixty-two-year-old General Sir Ian Hamilton had been the C-in-C since March 1915, supported by the brave and confident naval commander, Admiral John de Robeck. Hamilton was a highly respected and extremely experienced infantry officer who was very charismatic and popular with both officers and men, despite some disloyalty within his Gallipoli head-quarters, making Monro's position as his successor even more difficult, even though Hamilton had failed to break the deadlock on the peninsula. Initially, Hamilton had had only forty days to prepare and improvise the Gallipoli landings with one, untrained, regular division – the 29th Division. Without the vital element of surprise, the Allies had failed to reach 3 miles inland because of excellent Turkish leadership and the combination of enemy wire, machine guns and well-prepared dug-in positions.

As Correlli Barnett put it, the Allied force 'was neither large enough, nor well-enough equipped, trained and organised to fulfil the ambitious strategic vision'.[5] Liddell Hart also blames the execution, rather than the concept, writing, 'If the British had used at the outset even a fair proportion of the forces they ultimately expended in driblets, it is clear from Turkish accounts that victory would have crowned their undertaking.'[6] Hamilton wanted more troops and was reported as saying, 'It was as hard to get troops out of him [Lord Kitchener] as to get butter out of a dog's mouth.'[7]

Hankey's Dardanelles Commission of 1916 analysed the campaign, finding faults in its execution, though Asquith claimed that the operation had saved Russia in the Caucasus, delayed Bulgaria's entry into the war, fixed Turkish troops in one position and 'annihilated a *corps d'élite*, a whole flower of the Turkish Army'.[8] After 100 years, controversy still surrounds the pros and cons of the Gallipoli campaign, so one can imagine the pressures on Charles Monro when he took command and had to make a decision on whether or not to recommend evacuation.

The concept of the campaign had been pushed by the First Lord of the Admiralty, Winston Churchill, who mentioned the Dardanelles at the first meeting of Prime Minister Herbert Asquith's War Council. He declared that it was the only place in the Ottoman Empire where a decisive action could be fought and had been encouraging naval bombardments on the Turkish forts. Asquith opposed significant commitment, though the war secretary, Lord Kitchener, asked Churchill if any naval action might assist the Russians by forcing Turkey to divert some of its forces from the Caucasus.

A naval plan was devised and supported by Chancellor of the Exchequer David Lloyd George, ex-Prime Minister Arthur Balfour, Secretary of State for Foreign Affairs Edward Grey and Kitchener. Kitchener was, however, reluctant to commit troops, though it was eventually agreed to move 29th Division and Anzac troops closer to the Dardanelles area.

Meanwhile, Churchill had the support of both France and Russia, despite First Sea Lord 'Jackie' Fisher threatening resignation because he found Churchill far too dominating a personality to work with. He was against a naval attack and was convinced that troops would be needed on the ground to make the plan a success. Mission creep then ensued, the naval attacks failed, a French division and the Royal Navy division were placed on standby and a series of landings occurred.

By June, the Dardanelles Committee was established and further New Army and Territorial Force divisions were deployed to support the operation. This strategic perspective illustrates the powerful political 'buy-in' that the Gallipoli campaign had at the beginning, as the politicians listened to a persuasive Churchill, determined to break the deadlock on the Western Front.

Changing Factors

The optimism following the initial Allied success soon turned to pessimism as the deadlock experienced on the Western Front started to affect operations on the Gallipoli Peninsula, despite various attempts to outflank the Turkish enemy. The high level of casualties and deteriorating health of the troops led to a change of heart amongst many soldiers and politicians, who needed a judgement on the future of the operation to be made by October 1915.

One influencing factor surrounded the sacking and changeover of a number of generals. Lieutenant General Sir Frederick Stopford, commanding IX Corps at the Suvla Bay landing in August, was accused of advancing too cautiously, allowing the Turkish commander to effectively block and contain his advance. Further problems 'were lack of orders, poor maps, ineffective leadership, inadequate staff work, and, especially, water shortages'.[9] Stopford defended himself by blaming the lack of success on the minimal artillery support, but both he and Major General F. Hammersley, commanding his 11th Division at Suvla Bay (who added that there had been a heavy loss of officers and that the troops were exhausted), were removed from command and sent home.

The Official History records that early in the Suvla landing Hammersley 'had been feeling the climate severely, was by that time rather exhausted', implying that his decision making was not sound.[10] Their orders were not clear and the same history commented that misfortune was caused by 'the absence of resolute leadership, not only on shore but at corps headquarters and even at GHQ. Lack of leadership on the 7th August had jeopardised the whole plan. And now on the 8th it brought the operations to ruin.'[11]

The Turks later commented, 'Had this sound plan been executed with resolution and energy it would have effected very far-reaching results.'[12] Hamilton accused Stopford and Hammersley of having no heart for the operation at Suvla Bay and not being fit to command, and after gaining the support of Kitchener the two officers were replaced. Hamilton did not want Stopford as a key commander in Gallipoli in the first place as his professional reputation was so poor.

Another divisional commander resigned and one other brigade commander was sacked. Hamilton may have been justified in making these changes, but they were certainly unusual and controversial and partially reflected his style of command. The disgruntled Stopford returned home and immediately sent the War Office his own account of the Suvla Bay issue, blaming poor intelligence and orders from the GHQ for his performance. He believed that the handling of Hamilton's subordinate generals was unmerited. The result was that four generals were appointed by Kitchener to analyse the Suvla Bay action and subsequently Kitchener informed the government that it 'had resulted in considerable criticism of Sir Ian Hamilton's leadership'.[13] Hamilton's future was now in doubt.

The next influencing factor was the critical reporting by two journalists, Ellis Ashmead-Bartlett and Keith Murdoch. Initially, the *Daily Telegraph's* Ashmead-Bartlett was appointed as one of only two war correspondents, though they were unable to send criticism home and their reports were not allowed to arrive before the official despatches. As the campaign developed, Ashmead-Bartlett made himself unpopular with the GHQ on Imbros as he became increasingly critical about what was happening and was judged to be 'glum and despondent'.[14] Hamilton's nephew wrote in his uncle's biography, 'It seems curious that when the Cabinet required information from someone on the spot they should have listened to such an irresponsible person.'[15]

Yet he was an experienced and professional correspondent, popular with the troops, who regularly visited the front line and had the ear of some key personalities back home. His despatches praised the bravery of the soldiers but became increasingly critical of the leadership and the futile sacrifices being made. On a trip to England in May he briefed some politicians of his views, but things came to a head in August after the Suvla Bay landings.

Ashmead-Bartlett wrote a letter to the British prime minister on 8 September 1915 and persuaded a recently arrived Australian journalist, Keith Murdoch (father of the future newspaper magnate Rupert Murdoch), to take it to England with him. Murdoch, who was anti-British, had quickly assessed for himself that things were not going well at Gallipoli, though he was not aware of the complete picture, and agreed that the 'true' uncensored situation needed to be communicated back to their home countries.

Unfortunately, the French police and British officials were tipped off about Ashmead-Bartlett's letter and it was confiscated when Murdoch arrived in Marseilles. The document included the following phrases:

> ... the most ghastly and costly fiasco in our history since the Battle of Banockburn ... they threw away their lives against positions which should never have been attacked ... The staff seem to have carefully searched for the most difficult points and then threw away thousands of lives in trying to take them by frontal attacks ... bad staff work ... no adequate steps were taken to keep the troops supplied by water ... The Army is in fact in a deplorable condition ... The muddles and mismanagement beat anything that has ever occurred in our Military History ... The confidence in the troops can only be restored by an immediate change in the supreme command.[16]

Incensed, Murdoch reported to his own Australian prime minister, Andrew Fisher, using the same themes of Ashmead-Bartlett's original letter and composing 8,000 words of his own, highlighting that 'it is undoubtedly one of the most terrible chapters in our history'. One of his comments was:

> The conceit and self-complacency of the red feather men are equalled only by their incapacity. Along the line of communications, especially at Moudros, are countless high officers and conceited young cubs who are plainly only playing at war ... appointments to the general staff are made from motives of friendship and social influence.[17]

Asquith, Lloyd George and the Cabinet saw the letter, and the newspaper baron, Lord Northcliffe, who thought evacuation the best course of action, arranged for some of the content to be published. There were some inaccuracies in the journalists' letters and Murdoch was described as being 'completely ignorant of military affairs and his facts and figures were generally inaccurate', but neither Hamilton nor Kitchener were asked to comment – instead Murdoch's letter was made available to the Dardanelles Committee and the CID.[18]

Later, and too late to alter his removal from command, Hamilton was back in England and saw the letter. He wrote a nine-page commentary to the committee castigating Murdoch for his inaccuracies, biased comments and 'sweeping generalities and charges ... ignorance of staff-work as well as the staff'. He concluded by stating, 'No chance was vouchsafed me of proving the malignancy of these attacks.'[19]

Murdoch's letter became another important contributory factor to Hamilton's downfall and the deployment of Monro. Ashmead-Bartlett returned to England in October, in his own words, 'To press for the with-drawal of the Expedition before it was too late, being firmly convinced that we would be risking a disaster unparalleled in English history if we remained at Anzac and Suvla during the winter months.'[20]

Meanwhile, one of GHQ's key staff officers, Captain Guy Payan Dawnay, had been sent by Hamilton to London to discuss the campaign's future. He was disloyal to Hamilton by stating that little success could be gained at Gallipoli even with all available supplies and reinforcement. His trip included an audience with the king. Dawnay now favoured evacuation and there were other members of GHQ, including Orlo Williams, the cipher officer, and Lieutenant Colonel Pollen, who were showing disloyalty and questioning the capability of their commander.

Historian and journalist Charles Bean wrote of Hamilton in his diary on 17 October 1915:

> He has no strength to command his staff – they command him: especially Braithwaite his Chief of Staff…Braithwaite is a snob – only a snob could support this lazy GHQ and so far as I know he has only been to Anzac once. He is certainly utterly disloyal to his chief. If Hamilton had had a loyal, agreeable, capable Chief of Staff his success might have been different; but he is not capable of standing up to any of them.[21]

Unsurprisingly, Travers has commented that Hamilton had become 'something of a figure head, a commander-in-chief who did not really command'.[22] This was a disconcerting time for the commanders at Gallipoli, who wondered what the future of the operation was. Major General Stanley Maude, a replacement for one of the sacked generals and then in charge of 13th Division, vented his frustration in his diary, 'always a policy of drift … Why cannot the policy be definitely shaped, either to go on with this or give it up?'[23]

Many senior military officers and politicians believed that scarce resources should be diverted to Salonika and the Balkans to support Serbia and to deal with a new enemy, Bulgaria, rather than reinforce failure in Gallipoli. Lloyd George reflected these concerns in his memoirs, commenting on a letter sent to him on 16 October 1915 by Charles Beresford, ex-senior naval officer and Member of Parliament. Two of Hamilton's divisions were redirected and Cecil Aspinall-Oglander, one of his staff officers, believed that this sounded the death knell of the Dardanelles campaign:

> This letter reflects the rising and spreading dubiety amongst men who were watching the course of events with some accumulated knowledge and experience. As yet the general public were still trustful though a little

mystified. Their faith in Kitchener and their invincible belief in British luck had not yet been shaken.[24]

There was also pressure from France, which appeared to be losing interest in the campaign despite a recent announcement that the country was going to reinforce Gallipoli, and the Allies had to prepare for the next autumn offensives on the Western Front, including the Battle of Loos and the French push in Champagne in late September. General Robertson had been recalled from France to provide advice and wrote, 'I recommended cutting our losses, and said that although evacuation must necessarily be attended with difficulty and risk it ought nevertheless to be a feasible operation provided that careful arrangements were made, especially with respect to secrecy.'[25]

Hamilton was warned of the gist of some of these factors, commenting in his diary, 'A "flow of unofficial reports from Gallipoli", as Kitchener cables to me, is pouring into the War Office' and Kitchener suggested replacing his chief of staff, Major General Braithwaite, as a scapegoat.[26] However, following a worrying comment from Hamilton that any evacuation would involve 50 per cent casualties, the Dardanelles Committee met on 14 October 1915 and decided to bring the commander back to England and replace him. The same day, Lord Milner and Lord Ribblesdale argued for evacuation in the House of Lords. Hamilton's replacement in this difficult military and political environment was Charles Monro.

The New Commander

Monro's original biographer remarked, 'It was decided to recall Ian Hamilton and replace him by a general who, coming with a fresh and unbiased mind, would be better able to advise on this question of evacuation.'[27]

Unsurprisingly, a different view is offered by Ian Hamilton's nephew, also Ian Hamilton. He acknowledged Monro's ability and reputation, but described him as 'a large stolid man, a blameless, sealed-pattern type of general, without much imagination or initiative, but genial and popular with his staff'. He also wrote, 'He was deeply imbued with the principles of the western strategy and could scarcely be regarded as impartial.'[28] This is unfair; there is no doubt that Monro was a 'westerner', and he believed that the critical place for success in the war was the Western Front, but he always delivered intelligent, logical and impartial views.

Though Aspinall-Oglander seemed to have a mixed opinion of Monro, in the Official History, 'A shrewd, hard-headed and capable soldier, he had

Portrait of General Charles Monro.
(Imperial War Museum. Q68187)

a ripe judgement, a facility for making up his mind and sticking to it, and a most determined and independent will.'[29]

Lord Kitchener had given Monro some very clear instructions on 20 October 1915, as he took over the Mediterranean Expeditionary Force. This included:

> General Monro's first duty will be to report **fully and frankly** to the Government on the military situation: (1) on the Gallipoli Peninsula; (2) in the Near East generally. With regard to (1) he will consider the best means of removing the existing deadlock on the Peninsula, and he will report as soon as he is in a position to do so (a) whether in his opinion on purely military grounds it is better to evacuate Gallipoli or to make another attempt to carry it; (b) what is his estimate of the loss which would be incurred in evacuation. This estimate should be made jointly with Admiral de Robeck, or an independent estimate should be obtained from the Admiral; (c) how many troops, in his opinion, would be required (i) to carry the Peninsula? (ii) Would it be possible with that number to keep the straits open? (iii) to take Constantinople?[30]

Monro was also given wider strategic reporting responsibilities concerning operations in Salonika and Egypt, so allowing Lieutenant General William Birdwood to command the MEF in Monro's absence from the headquarters.

Another factor concerning the future of the Dardanelles expedition, was de Robeck's chief of staff, Commodore Roger Keyes' attempts for a further naval assault, however, he was told by Balfour that, 'There was nothing to be done for a few days until Monro's report had been considered.'[31]

The new commander of the MEF arrived in London on 20 October, along with his chief of staff, Major General Arthur Lynden-Bell, and his military secretary, Lieutenant Colonel Lord Herbert Scott. He spent two days with Kitchener and the General Staff in order to familiarise himself with the situation. Lieutenant Colonel Maurice Hankey, secretary to the War Council, described Charles Monro unflatteringly 'as having the strange habit of slapping his listener on the arm while shouting the word "Ja"'.[32] He added, 'Rather a sound old bird, I thought, but not very quick' – a comment totally out of step with every other reference seen by the author that describes Monro's character.[33]

However, in his normal professional manner, Monro was made aware of the various 'unofficial' reports which had been received by Kitchener and the government and he had four briefings with the war secretary, who reminded him that a swift judgement on the best course to take in the Dardanelles was required and that substantial reinforcements would be made available if another assault was recommended. Kitchener was not in favour of evacuation, particularly after Hamilton's prediction of likely casualties if that course was followed. Monro was also provided a note from the DMO, General Sir Charles Callwell, which included the comment:

> Ian Hamilton's failure was to my mind to a large extent due to his disinclination to tell Lord Kitchener unpleasant things and I think he was backed up in this by Braithwaite. They did not insist on having what they wanted and invariably communicated in an unduly optimistic strain. I do not suggest that your Chief and yourself will adopt the same line, but I would urge you not to hesitate before telling unpleasant truths in your wires to K.[34]

Concurrently, Kitchener received negative information from Lieutenant General Birdwood, commanding the Australian and New Zealand Army Corps on the peninsula. Writing on 21 October, Birdwood stated:

> We have everywhere in front of us continuous front of Turkish trenches, the flanks of which cannot be turned, and which, therefore can only be taken by assault. This precludes the possibility of an advance being made with any element of surprise, which is the only method by which rapid progress can be hoped for.[35]

Birdwood goes on to say that he had 'wastage' of personnel of 20 per cent per month, there was a lack of officers and 'indifferent company leadership', and a shortage of ammunition and health issues meaning that the troops were not 'capable of great physical exertion'. He said he needed two new divisions in order to gain any success and a few days later he commented that the new division was 'only fit for trench warfare'.[36]

The night before the new command team's departure from England, Lord Herbert Scott was invited by Lord Northcliffe to report to his *Times* newspaper office to receive a briefing on what the newspaper magnate knew about Gallipoli from all of his gathered intelligence, on both friend and foe. This information proved accurate, but remarkably was not briefed to Monro prior to the evacuation. It reinforced the decision that he eventually made corroborating the various factors that he would have to take into account when he reached Gallipoli. Barrow, Monro's first biographer, was confused as to why this information was not passed to Monro earlier – so is this author.

Just before departing London, another bizarre incident occurred. This time it was the unlikely appearance on a Charing Cross railway platform early in the morning, of Winston Churchill, who had been removed from the Admiralty in May. He was determined to pass a message to the team:

> Everyone felt a bit under the weather at 6 am and we were not cheered up by the appalling smell of beer exhaled by our servants who had spent the night 'celebrating'. Just as the train was about to start Winston Churchill rushed along the platform, threw a bundle of papers into our carriage and shouted, 'Don't forget, if you evacuate it will be the biggest disaster since Corunna!'[37]

Churchill does not recount this story later, probably because this was not a realistic comparison of two campaigns – Corunna bought time for later Allied victories in the Iberian Peninsula; Gallipoli was an isolated failure. However Churchill who, as prime minister in the Second World War, always had tight control over his favoured generals, developed strong views about Monro, who ultimately disagreed with his Dardanelles adventure. He had his own perception about Monro's attitude:

> Anything that killed Germans was right. Anything that did not kill Germans was useless, even if it made other people kill them, and kill more of them, or terminated their power to kill us. To such minds the capture of Constantinople was an idle trophy, and the destruction of Turkey as a military factor, or the rallying of the Balkan States to the allies, mere politics, which every military man should hold in proper scorn.[38]

Churchill always believed that strategically the Dardanelles campaign was the right thing to have done, but to succeed it needed greater support and resources than it ever received. To him, it was not an exclusively military issue.

General Sir Charles Monro arrived at Mudros on 27 October 1915 and spent three days carrying out Lord Kitchener's directions, thoroughly examining the situation. His team did not get a good first impression of the existing staff at Imbros, Lynden-Bell commenting, 'As we passed through the line of them Sir Charles said to me, "Did you ever meet such a down and out lot of fellows in your life?" ... They were not a united Staff ... They were not on speaking terms.'[39]

Yet the new commander seemed to gain the support of many of Hamilton's old staff quickly. Dawnay wrote to his wife, saying that Monro:

> ... is a fine fellow. I am getting a great admiration for him. A perfectly delightful man, genial, great sense of humour, a wonderful sound judgement of men and affairs, and one who sees down to the root of things – sweeping irrelevancies aside! I see nothing better than to be allowed to go on soldiering on his staff![40]

Resentment was put aside as, once again, Monro displayed his professionalism and meticulousness.

Monro's Report

Monro's report was wired to Kitchener on 31 October. This was all too quick for his critics, unaware of the detailed instructions he had received prior to his embarkation and a reminder from Kitchener twenty-four hours after his arrival in theatre that he wanted an answer quickly. Churchill cynically called him 'an officer of swift decision' who had already made up his mind to recommend evacuation.[41] He goes on to comment that Monro only reached the peninsula on 30 October, did not go beyond the beaches and spent only six hours familiarising himself with the 15-mile front. He accused Monro of not interrogating the existing commanders effectively and notes that Lynden-Bell did not even set foot on the peninsula.

His views are partly corroborated by Major General Sir Alexander Godley, commanding the Anzac troops, who wrote of meeting Monro, 'He had obviously made up his mind that the Peninsula would be untenable for the winter; his conversation was chiefly about hunting in Meath and our many mutual friends.'[42] However, Godley was one of the Gallipoli commanders who always believed that victory was possible if only the right resources were available. Further criticism came from 13th Division's commander, Major General Maude, who wrote in his diary, on 30 October:

> Monro saw each divisional commander separately and talked to me for
> about half an hour. He was too much on the defensive tack as everyone
> seems to be in my mind ... We are a weak kneed nation. Why not push
> through and finish the business? It would not be so difficult, given men,
> ammunition and guns.[43]

Maude just wanted a decision to be made, 'It is this dreadful policy of doing
nothing that is fatal.'[44] In addition, Hamilton's nephew was not impressed
that Monro had not visited the troops or trenches on 30 October, missing
the point about Monro's strategic perspective and requirements. Views about
what the future should be were split.

In his defence, Monro had been studying the situation for ten days before
he travelled to Helles, Anzac and Suvla on 30 October. In each location he
spoke to the corps and divisional commanders to gain their views on the
campaign. He wanted to know whether they would be able to launch a
sustained offensive and if they would be able to resist Turkish attacks in the
winter. The consensus was that only very short twenty-four-hour offensives
would be possible and that there was no guarantee of success against well-
supplied Turkish winter assaults.

Concurrent to this visit, and not mentioned by Churchill, was a memorandum that had been prepared by Hamilton's staff prior to and anticipating
Monro's arrival. Sir Charles examined it on his first evening at Mudros.
It concluded that an advance was needed on both sides of the straits to
achieve success and 250,000 fresh troops were required with a great deal
more ammunition. Preparations would have to start immediately. There was
also some doubt that the Suvla position could survive a determined Turkish
assault without securing the ridges around it with two more divisions. It also
stated, 'The evacuation of the Peninsula was also a feasible operation ... if
undertaken voluntarily' – 50 per cent casualties might occur, but that would
be better than trying to withdraw under Turkish pressure.[45] Monro told the
memorandum's author that he accepted the conclusions, though they did not
recommend a clear option for the way ahead. Lynden-Bell told the author
that he hoped that he had recommended evacuation.

The following day, 28 October, Monro sent a short and vague message
back to Kitchener, though it did not hint of any evacuation decision. It may
even have encouraged false hope as he remarked that he had met the corps
commanders and been impressed by the 'military bearing of an Australian
Brigade'.[46] 'K' replied curtly that he wanted an answer on the main issue
as soon as possible – 'leaving or staying'. Monro was not happy about the
pressure he was under to make a decision and spoke to his military secretary
that evening:

The Cabinet have asked me for a definite decision on a difficult and vital point on the policy and future destiny of the War within a few hours of my arrival at the scene of action, which is hardly fair and reasonable. I have done my best to gather information first hand from the Navy and Army, to understand the position by my personal inspection, and, in addition, I have carefully studied the weather forecast of the coming weeks and months, and the amount of sickness on the Peninsula, which is increasing at an alarming rate.[47]

His chief of staff had sprained his knee the night before, so Monro was accompanied by Aspinall-Oglander on the quick 'tour' of 30 October. He witnessed the confusion at the beaches and the haphazard logistic arrangements within enemy shell-fire distance, commenting to Aspinall-Oglander, 'It's just like "Alice in Wonderland", curiouser and curiouser.'[48]

The comments made by the three corps commanders and their divisional subordinates have already been mentioned and his mind was quickly made up to evacuate. He sent the key telegram on 31 October and arranged for a joint naval and army committee to start working out a plan the following day. His conclusions were critical:

The troops on the Peninsula – with the exception of the Australian and New Zealand Corps – are not equal to a sustained effort owing to the inexperience of the officers, the want of training of the men, and the depleted condition of many of the units.

We merely hold the fringe of the shore, and are confronted by the Turks in very formidable entrenchments with all the advantages of position and power of observation of our movements. The beaches are exposed to observed artillery fire, and in the restricted areas all stores are equally exposed. We can no longer count upon any action by surprise as the Turks are in considerably stronger force than they were, and have had ample time to provide against surprise landings.

Since the flanks of the Turks cannot be attacked, only a frontal attack is possible, and no room is afforded on any of the beaches for the distribution of additional divisions should they be sent, nor is there sufficient space for the deployment of an adequate force of artillery, the action of which would be impaired by poverty of observation and good positions for searching or counter battery effects. Naval guns could only assist to a partial degree.

In fact an attack could only be prosecuted under the disadvantages of serious lack of depth, and of absence of power of surprise, seeing that our line is throughout dominated by the Turk's position. The uncertainty of the weather might also seriously hinder the landing of reinforcements and regularity in providing the artillery ammunition to the amount which would be required.

It is therefore my opinion that another attempt to carry the Turkish lines would not offer any hope of success; the Turkish positions are being actively strengthened daily. Our information leads to the belief that heavy guns and ammunition are being sent to the Peninsula from Constantinople. Consequently by the time fresh divisions, if available, could arrive, the task of breaking the Turkish line would be considerably more formidable than it is at present.

On purely military grounds, therefore, in consequence of the grave daily wastage of officers and men which occurs, and owing to the lack of prospect of being able to draw the Turks from their entrenched positions, **I recommend the evacuation of the Peninsula**.

I have endeavoured in the expression of my opinion to give full weight to the effect which will be created in the East by our evacuation, and I consider that the force now in the peninsula, or such portion of it as we may be able to evacuate, would be more favourably placed in Egypt. This force stands in need of rest, re-organisation, and especially of training, before it could be usefully employed. The Corps and Divisional commanders have done splendid work in the peninsula, but they do not possess the opportunity of time, as they now stand, to create the force into a reliable fighting machine. Hence I think loss of prestige caused by withdrawal would be compensated for in few months by increased efficiency.[49]

Very high sick rates affected his decision, the Dardanelles Commission recording that diarrhoea and skin sores were particularly debilitating and that 1,000 troops were often evacuated from the beaches daily because of health issues. In 1920, one of Monro's staff officers, Orlo Williams, the chief cipher officer who had been on Hamilton's staff, wrote his views about this important message:

Very few people knew the context of that telegram. To those who did it gave the first ray of hope for the future – a hope that wise and definite decisions would be made at once, that a waste of energy and lives on useless ends would cease, and that the force would not long remain the lame, uncared for thing, looking out doggedly but dully on a grey future, that it now was.

Much of the staff knew that the situation was hopeless.

The Impact

Kitchener was not happy with this report. Churchill commented, dramatically, that 'Monro's telegram of "Evacuation" fell like a thunderbolt on Kitchener'.[50] He could not believe that a responsible officer could deliver such a drastic decision, though the Australian Official History records his judgement as 'courageously stated'.[51] Monro had been asked to report 'fully and frankly' and that he had done. Kitchener was under increasing political pressure; he was losing support and he was fired up by Commodore Keyes' naval suggestions to break the deadlock at Gallipoli.

At this stage of the First World War, the political knives were out for Kitchener, who was being blamed by Lloyd George and others for mishandling the Western Front and the shells crisis, the Balkans and the Dardanelles. However, the new War Committee was briefed on 3 November but could not be persuaded of the need for evacuation until Kitchener had examined the situation in Gallipoli for himself. At the time, the naval option looked appealing, though it proved a nuisance to Lynden-Bell and Monro:

> The Navy are giving us a great deal of trouble – I say the Navy but it is really Roger Keyes – by continually trying to urge us to help them in putting forward their pet scheme of forcing the narrows. This we absolutely decline to do as we cannot see how the operation could possibly succeed, and if it did succeed it would not help the military situation at all. This has been pointed out frequently to the Vice-Admiral and to Keyes, but they still persist, and their last effort has been to wire to the Admiralty and urge that we should make a land attack on Achi Baba. To this we have replied that the operation is quite beyond our powers and would require at least 100,000 men.[52]

This option, described by Lynden-Bell as 'the swansong of the lunatics', was discussed at various levels for over a month until the impracticalities were identified and the idea quashed by the First Sea Lord. But Keyes had always believed in it, writing in his memoirs, 'A successful naval attack would ensure the defeat of the Turkish Army.'[53]

Meanwhile, Kitchener quickly tasked Monro to confirm with the corps commanders whether they also favoured withdrawal. Lieutenant generals Sir Francis Davies (VIII Corps at Helles), Honourable Sir Julian Byng (IX Corps at Suvla) and Sir William Birdwood, Australian and New Zealand Army Corps (ANZAC), were asked by Monro to 'give their opinions without paying any heed to his' – a gesture that demonstrated Monro's equanimity and fairness. Byng and Davies agreed with the need for evacuation, whilst

Birdwood acknowledged Monro's concerns, but did not favour withdrawal and was very concerned about the effect on Allied morale and the impact on attitudes in the East and Turkey about the Allies' perceived defeat, 'I feared the repercussions of such a move throughout the Muhammadan world.'[54]

Separately, similar concerns were expressed to Kitchener by General Sir John Maxwell, C-in-C Egypt. In his second telegram of 2 November, Monro reiterated to Kitchener the need for evacuation and informed him that the forces on the peninsula, less the Anzacs, 'Should be rested, and will not be fit for offensive operations until officers and men have been further trained, and deficiencies in staff and regimental officers have been made good.'[55] He also expected losses during the evacuation of between 30 and 40 per cent.

The Official History provided a balanced view of Monro's decision. It commented that there was 'no fault to be found with Monro's bold recommendation' and it was 'a matter of relief and thankfulness'.[56] However, on the down side, it acknowledged that Monro could have been more positive when asking the generals questions by acknowledging the potential reinforcements available in men and materiel, whilst emphasising the vital strategic importance of the operation. This could have resulted in 'a new spirit of hope and confidence'.[57] However, Monro knew what the decision had to be as he saw the state of the Allies on the ground. There were no fresh troops or ships to carry them, whilst increased pressure came from the French to reinforce the Western Front and Salonika. Interestingly, the French did not want the peninsula evacuated as they wanted pressure on the Turks to remain.

Monro travelled to Egypt on 3 November, aboard HMS *Chatham*, to discuss the effect of evacuation with the doubtful Maxwell. As he left, he sent clear direction to GHQ at Imbros to continue the planning for withdrawal. The previous day Kitchener had seen Commodore Keyes in London to discuss the new offensive, in the light of information received in Monro's telegrams.

Kitchener had an ally in Birdwood at Gallipoli and was still clutching to Keyes' naval initiative, so he sent a 'Very Secret' message to Birdwood, rather than Monro, on 3 November. Kitchener said that he was about to set off for the Dardanelles and that Birdwood should prepare for a new landing whilst the reinforced navy forced the straits. He did not want to evacuate the peninsula and he concluded his message by saying, 'I absolutely refuse to sign orders for evacuation, which I think would be the gravest disaster and would condemn a large percentage of our men to death or imprisonment. Monro will be appointed to the command of the Salonika Force.'[58]

At this stage, his views were on very close hold as he attempted to move Monro out of the way. A War Office signal duly appointed Birdwood to command the MEF, whilst Monro was shifted to Salonika. Meanwhile, the

Royal Navy nominated four more battleships and four extra destroyers for the Dardanelles. However, on the evening of 3 November it was clear that key politicians were split over further action at Gallipoli and that the new naval and army plan could be unworkable and might not even be approved. This resulted in yet another signal from Kitchener to Birdwood on 4 November in which he stated, 'The more I look at the problem the less I see my way through, so you had better very quietly and secretly work out any scheme for getting the troops off the peninsula.'[59]

Birdwood, meanwhile, had told Kitchener that the proposed new offensive was impracticable, that Monro should retain command and that Kitchener should not make a decision about the way ahead until he had at least seen the ground for himself. Birdwood respected Monro and was loyal to his new commander, writing, 'Monro, who had only given his honest opinion, should remain in command and not be superseded, for I know how loyally he would carry out any orders that the Government might see fit to issue.'[60] Meanwhile, Birdwood kept the order for Monro's change of command quiet. In due course, but not known at that stage, Monro was to continue to lead both the MEF, with Birdwood commanding the Dardanelles Army, and Mahon's force at Salonika.

Monro was now in Egypt and was entertained by Maxwell at the Shepheard's Hotel in Alexandria on the evening of 4 November. After a jovial and hearty meal, Monro was informed by Maxwell that Kitchener disagreed with his recommendations and that he was to be relieved of his new command. This was an extremely low point for Monro, who had been withdrawn from his army on the Western Front, selected by Kitchener to conduct this important mission and had then given his honest and well-considered opinion. Barrow later recorded his emotions, 'Shortly after receiving this mortifying intelligence Sir Charles went out on to the veranda, where later a member of his staff found him greatly perturbed.'[61] Orlo Williams commented that after the staff had had a night out in Cairo, they 'woke up next morning to find a deep depression instead of the cheerfulness of the night before'.[62] He awaited Kitchener's arrival.

The senior officers converged at Mudros on 9 November. On board HMS *Lord Nelson* that evening Kitchener appeared confused and indecisive about the correct course of action in the Dardanelles. He remained under intense political pressure from home, where senior politicians were plotting behind his back to remove him from power. Fortunately, he was not aware that Asquith had informed Bonar Law 'that he personally now favoured evacuation, whatever Kitchener might report'.[63] That evening he was joined, amongst others, by Monro, Maxwell, Birdwood, de Robeck and Sir Henry MacMahon, the high commissioner in Egypt. One friendly face, from

Monro's perspective, was General Horne, who had been one of his divisional commanders in I Corps and who had accompanied Kitchener on his journey as the chief military adviser. On the way from Egypt to Mudros, Monro had taken the opportunity to assuage Maxwell and MacMahon of their concerns about the adverse effects of an evacuation, so they were far more favourable than before, but at that first gathering of thoughts and ideas Monro was under intense pressure. Orlo Williams described Monro, 'with his warrior's face set hard as rock'.[64] The conference continued on the 10th and 11th.

On the morning of the 11th, Monro was about to be taken by boat on rough seas to the conference when he had a nasty accident. As he stepped into the boat, a wave swelled and the deck smashed into his foot, severely damaging his ankle. He was taken to the yacht *Liberty* and examined by the naval director of medical services. There was then a slight panic as the *Liberty* flew a Red Cross, so legally Monro could not command from there. Despite being in some pain, he was transferred to HMS *Aragon*, his headquarters, and continued to work hard over the next few weeks. It is recorded that 'the injury left a permanent mark and Sir Charles was never able afterwards to walk any distance or over rough ground in comfort'.[65]

Meanwhile, the conference debate included agreement between Monro, Maxwell, MacMahon and Horne that evacuation could take place providing a landing at Ayas Bay, near Alexandretta in Syria, occurred. This would involve holding a position astride the Turkish railway, providing the route for reinforcements for the Egyptian and Mesopotamia fronts and minimising the political effect of evacuating Gallipoli. However, Birdwood then accepted evacuation without the Ayas Bay landing and Admiral de Robeck was happy to evacuate Anzac and Suvla, but wanted to retain Helles in order to continue to block the straits.

Whilst Kitchener was favouring the Ayas Bay option, Asquith and the War Office at home took against the idea when informed on 11 November. Kitchener's 10 November report recommended evacuation, but only if it included the Ayas Bay option, which may have helped the situation in Mesopotamia but would have meant committing considerable numbers of troops to the new operation. The War Office thought that Kitchener was not being logical and were not prepared to commit the manpower and the amount of troops that would have to be tied down indefinitely to defend the position. Meanwhile, the French, whose government had fallen on 28 October, wanted Gallipoli held whilst reinforcing Salonika, otherwise they believed a defeat could trigger a rising in their North Africa colonies.

At home, Lieutenant General Robertson made his strategic priorities clear in a memorandum dated 8 November 1915 on the *Conduct of the War*, in which he clarified the importance of the Western Front:

General Monro conversing with Lord Kitchener at Mudros, 11 November 1915. (Imperial War Museum. Q13585)

> Obviously, the most effective method of attaining the end we desire is to defeat decisively the main German army, which are still on the Western Front … We are only justified in not concentrating our full resources on the Western Front if we find an easier road to success in a subsidiary theatre … The force in the Peninsula has no longer any prospect of contributing directly or indirectly to the defeat of Germany.[66]

Meanwhile, Kitchener undertook a reconnaissance of the Dardanelles positions – Helles on 12 November, Anzac on 13th and Suvla on 14 November. He was warmly welcomed by the troops on the ground and as he observed their positions close to the front line he was even cheered by the Anzac troops, 'It was purely a soldier's welcome.'[67] He told the troops that the king was grateful for their work and he congratulated them on their fortitude but, like Monro, he was shocked by what he saw. He said to Birdwood, 'Thank God Birdie, I came to see this for myself. You were quite right. I had no idea of the difficulties you were up against. I think you have all done wonders.'[68] He provided an update for home which included the words, 'Careful and secret preparations for the evacuation of the peninsula are being made', acknowledging the work that Monro had put in train.[69]

Kitchener also travelled to Greece, where he acquired some security for Allied troops who were struggling to locate the Serbs in Bulgaria. In Salonika, with Monro he identified that Allied reinforcement was required, but at the expense of Gallipoli. Ultimately, however, 'influenced by Monro's able and unhesitating arguments, he decided on evacuation'.[70] This was despite further Australian observations that the Turks were weakening and that the enemy were unlikely to drive the Allies off the peninsula without German support.

Kitchener sent an important note to the prime minister on 15 November. This included the words:

> To gain what we hold has been a most remarkable feat of arms … The landings are precarious and often impossible through rough sea and want of harbours, and the enemy's positions are peculiarly suitable for making our communications more dangerous and difficult.[71]

He went on to say that the positions could be held, but that this would be a challenge if German troops were used in the attack. He still supported the Ayas Bay scheme and stated that the Allies' position in Gallipoli was not as critical as it had been. He reported that evacuation was being planned and that if it occurred there would be fewer losses than originally envisaged. His telegram was agreed by Monro, Birdwood and de Robeck. Another telegram from Kitchener, dated 17 November, included the words, 'the evacuation of Suvla and Anzac should be proceeded with'.[72] These views and subsequent decisions triggered the resignation of Winston Churchill, in disappointment, from the government.

The Alexandretta option was quashed by London on 19 November, and on 22 November CIGS Lieutenant General Archibald Murray provided a conclusion to an important document entitled 'Recommendation of the General Staff on the Question of the Action to be taken at Gallipoli'. This included the key telegrams sent between commanders and London in the period between 21 October and 22 November 1915 and summarised the arguments for and against the complete or partial evacuation of the peninsula. The arguments against withdrawal were:

> A drop in Allied morale and reduced indirect support to Russian war efforts.
> The negative reaction of Arab and Mohammedan in the region.
> The ability to contain a large force of Turks in Gallipoli.
> The level of casualties if evacuation took place.
> Allied naval value.

Murray concluded the analysis with the words:

> The arguments in favour of retaining our positions on Gallipoli are based mainly on conjectures as to the effect on the East of withdrawal, and on questions of Imperial and military sentiment. The arguments on the other side are based on cold calculations of military strategy. From a military point of view, withdrawal is likely to prove ultimately more advantageous than resolution of our positions.[73]

Charles Monro's original assessment was being endorsed. The War Committee decided that evacuation should occur on 23–24 November. However, the British Cabinet continued to prevaricate, the final decision being made on 7 December to evacuate Anzac and Suvla. The decision to evacuate Cape Helles was not made until 23 December after further pressure from Charles Monro. Ashmead-Bartlett observed, 'For five months the Army was left to rot in the trenches.'[74] Barrow aptly described the delays thus, 'It was an exhibition of vacillation and hesitation almost without parallel in military history.'[75]

Charles Monro had admirably persisted in trying to obtain an early decision throughout this period and his frustrations were reflected in London by Callwell, who wrote to Robertson on 1 December 1915:

> This delay in deciding as to the Dardanelles is terrible and the Cabinet have incurred a very grave responsibility in not accepting Monro's decision … Monro reported on the 3rd, the War Council on the 24th and here we are still with no final orders.[76]

As Kitchener departed for London on 24 November, he had appointed Charles Monro as C-in-C Mediterranean, with subordinates Birdwood in command of the evacuation of Gallipoli and Mahon at Salonika. The Official History records that Kitchener was 'powerfully attracted by Monro's unbending steadfastness of purpose' and he 'was trusting more and more to his judgement'.[77] Moorehead observes, 'It was to Monro and not Kitchener that they were turning for the last word.'[78]

Kitchener had endorsed Monro's views after weeks of prevaricating, though he was more accurate than Monro when he predicted that, despite the challenges of evacuation, 'It could be completed with less loss than had hitherto been feared.'[79] Barrow wrote that Kitchener's attitude towards Monro 'was slighting to a degree' and that 'K' 'ignored him as much as possible'.[80] Charles Monro declined a 'private' rather than 'official' invitation to dinner at Gallipoli on one occasion. However, Barrow remarked that when the two men met later in France, it was obvious that 'K' again respected Monro having misjudged him a few months before.

Monro had his new command and issued orders, whilst Birdwood was made responsible for the execution of the evacuation:

HMS *Dartmouth* 23rd November 1915
General Sir C Monro,
You will be in command of the forces in the Eastern Mediterranean outside Egypt. General Sir W Birdwood will command at Gallipoli, where the evacuation of the peninsula will be proceeded with on the plans arranged

for in cooperation with the Navy ... In order to avoid unnecessary delay General Birdwood ... will continue to communicate with the War Office, reporting direct on important active operations and matters of extreme urgency, sending you copies of all such correspondence.

Kitchener[81]

Monro's GHQ, responsible for both Gallipoli and Salonika, was located at Mudros with Lynden-Bell as his CGS.

It is worth briefly dwelling on Monro's other command, in Salonika (today Thessalonika) – perhaps one of the most forgotten campaigns from the First World War, described by Horne as 'absurd and unsustainable'.[82] Lieutenant General Mahon's 10th (Irish) Division had been sent there from Suvla in October 1915, as part of a Franco-British force invited into the country by the Greek prime minister. The aim was to help the Serbs fight the Bulgarians, but the Serbs had already lost when the force arrived. It was decided to keep Allied troops there to help stability in the region, despite a great deal of Greek internal opposition and pressure from Kitchener as late as 2 December 1915 to consider transferring four divisions to Gallipoli.

Monro quickly identified the challenges of supporting a losing Serbian Army and ordered a withdrawal to more favourable defensive positions. The 10th Division was attacked by Bulgarians over arduous terrain for three days in early December, whilst it provided cover for the French force to withdrawal. Monro ordered Mahon to reinforce the positions as more Allied troops were disembarked. Though Monro's decisions in this theatre were limited during his time in command and Mahon was the effective commander on the ground, they were sound operational orders that had the desired effect. The Salonika commitment would continue throughout the war.

Meanwhile, forces on the Gallipoli Peninsula were retitled the Dardanelles Army. Mother Nature created additional challenges over the next few days as torrential rain and strong gales hit the peninsula and swept away some of the Allied piers vital for evacuation. As the army awaited orders, many soldiers were drowned in their trenches or died from exposure. At Suvla Bay alone 2,000 men drowned and there were 5,000 cases of frostbite. Unsurprisingly, these harsh conditions hit both sides; hostilities were paused and there were more calls for withdrawal though Commodore Keyes and Vice Admiral Wemyss, who had taken over from de Robeck, were still canvassing the generals for further action.

They were supported at home by Lord Curzon, who said that the decision to evacuate was not just a military one and claimed that Monro 'had made his recommendation after an extremely cursory glance at the Peninsula'.[83] Roger Keyes' *Naval Memoirs* consistently castigate Monro and other generals, including Horne, for the decision to evacuate, calling them 'defeatist counsels'.[84] Keyes saw Monro on the *Aragon* shortly after Monro's accident with his foot. He recorded:

> I let myself go and delivered a fiery attack on his policy. I told him the whole story from beginning to end and begged him to help; but he raised every kind of difficulty, and even catechised me on the naval side … If they did not want to share in the glory, some other soldiers would … Sir Charles said, 'Look out Lynden-Bell, the Commodore is going to attack us; I can't get up'… It was quite obvious that I would get no support from Monro and that he had come out absolutely determined to put an end to the Gallipoli campaign, and nothing would deviate him from his intention.[85]

On a later occasion, Keyes asked about Monro's foot, to which Monro is reported to have retorted, 'It will be well enough soon to get up and kick somebody's ---stern!'[86] Keyes and Wemyss continued to try and influence other army commanders about the virtues of another assault and this led to Monro banning any meetings between them and his subordinates unless they had obtained permission from him. This naval enthusiasm to continue the campaign was only quashed by London on 10 December, though only the week before the final decision had still been in doubt.

Monro had remained under pressure from home, Kitchener warning him that because of General Townshend's difficulties in Mesopotamia and retirement to the town of Kut it was even more important that Turkey was not seen 'to claim a success from the Peninsula'.[87]

Whilst Monro waited for decisions to be made in London, planning for evacuation continued at Gallipoli. He ordered Birdwood to base a plan on three stages:

> One. All troops, animals and supplies not required for a long campaign should be withdrawn.
>
> Two. To comprise the evacuation of all men, guns, animals and stores not required for defence during a period when the conditions of weather might retard the evacuation, or in fact seriously alter the programme contemplated.
>
> Three. In which the troops on shore should be embarked with all possible speed, leaving behind such guns, animals and stores needed for military reasons at this period.[88]

The evacuation involved the withdrawal of a large army across beaches within effective enemy artillery range from front-line positions, which in some areas

Guns leaving Suvla. (Imperial War Museum. Q13637)

were only a few yards from Turkish trenches. Monro decided that it would be better to avoid conducting a feint; instead he would rely on maintaining normal routine so that the Turks were not alerted to any change. Speed was essential, as were good weather conditions. Monro was still concerned about casualties and had requested fifty-six hospital ships on hand and 12,000 hospital beds available in Egypt and Malta. It was a significant challenge to evacuate an army of 134,000 men, 14,000 animals and almost 400 guns in secrecy.

The British Cabinet's decision to evacuate, made on 7 December, thirty-seven days after Monro's first report, meant that Birdwood would receive Monro's direction on 8 December and, in due course, the night of 19–20 December was confirmed for the evacuation of Anzac and Suvla. The Cape Helles extraction was to eventually take place on 8 January 1916. Monro stated that Birdwood 'proceeded on receipt of his orders with the skill and promptitude which is characteristic of all that he undertakes'.[89] The troops were gradually thinned out from Anzac and Suvla, though front lines were manned to the end, trying to maintain normal routine and avoiding Turkish suspicion.

The weather on the night of 19–20 December was perfect for the Allies. The sea was calm and there was a haze veiling the full moon. The last man left the Anzac beaches at 0530 hours leaving some destroyed guns and some mules. At Suvla, all had been evacuated bar a few burned stores. To complete all this undetected was a remarkable feat.

French troop numbers at Helles were reduced and steps were in hand to extract the British from the third beaches, and as the good news was received from London on 7 December to continue with that evacuation, final orders arrived with Monro on 28 December 1915. Meanwhile, the Turks had concentrated their artillery on the remaining beaches after the initial evacuations and were conducting more aggressive patrols and reconnaissance activities, but that did not significantly affect the next Allied moves at Helles.

Planning and gradual withdrawal continued as Monro and his immediate staff moved to Cairo, where the new GHQ was established. The French infantry were removed from Helles on the night of 1–2 January 1916, though there was a concern that the weather was turning for the worse. On land, an aggressive spirit was maintained by the Allies to deceive the enemy as front lines were again held till the last, though there was considerable concern on 7 January due to intense Turkish gunfire and the false perception that an enemy attack was imminent. Fortunately, as the last of the troops were withdrawn from Helles on the night of 8–9 January 1916, the weather was relatively calm again, though one connecting pier was washed away. The evacuation was complete by 0330 hours and two large stores of ammunition were blown up on the beaches shortly afterwards. It was only then that the Turks realised that something had occurred.

The evacuation of Gallipoli without any friendly casualties was remarkable and the most positive effect to come out of the campaign. Monro's overall influence, direction and leadership had been critical since he had arrived in the area in October. However, characteristically, he put the final success down to 'good luck and skilled disciplined organisation' combined with outstanding detailed orders, co-operation between Birdwood, his corps commanders and the Royal Navy and efficient lines of communication. He also praised his staff who 'showed themselves without exception, to be officers with whom it was a privilege to be associated; their competence, zeal and devotion to duty were uniform and unbroken'.[90]

Charles Monro's performance was recognised by Field Marshal William Robertson, who had taken over as CIGS in December 1915. He wrote in *The Times*:

Credit for the successful evacuation of the Gallipoli Peninsula was due to all who took part in it as Sir Charles himself was the first to declare, but to him alone, almost, was due the credit for evacuation taking place when it did … Had not Sir Charles stood firm and declined to water down his expressed opinion that evacuation was imperative it might have been deferred until too late to be carried out at all, and at the best great hardships and additional loss of life would have been suffered by the troops for no useful purpose.[91]

The nation recognised his success; Charles Monro was made a Knight Grand Cross of the Order of Saint Michael and Saint George. He then began his return to the Western Front, at one stage under submarine threat and this time as commander of the 1st Army.

Meanwhile, during her husband's time in Gallipoli, Mary Monro had been busy at home. She wrote from her home at the time (24a, Hill Street, Knightsbridge) to various newspapers as part of her 'Lady Monro's Appeal' for the Comforts Fund for the Forces in the Mediterranean and the Balkans:

> I wish to make an earnest appeal for comforts for the Forces in the Mediterranean and Balkans now under my husband, General Sir Charles Monro's command. Winter with all its hardships and terrible suffering, is now upon us. The cold is bitter and the storms have been very bad. Nothing can be obtained locally, and our men depend entirely for any comforts upon what we can send from home.[92]

She went on to say that she had the support of both Queen Alexandra and Lord Kitchener and hoped for a generous response to the appeal. 'We want warm clothing, tobacco, cigarettes, pipes etc. and money to spend on the comforts not supplied by the War Office.'[93] As usual, the British public responded well. The Monros were, not for the first or last time, working as a team during this difficult period.

Hamilton's Bitterness

The author has not seen any comment about Hamilton's bitterness against Monro in any history of the campaign on Gallipoli. However, there is documentary evidence that he was bitter. The first observation can be seen in Hamilton's personal scrapbook, where a picture of Monro is shown next to a caption stating that he was to be awarded the Order of St Michael and St George; by this, Hamilton had scribbled, 'Heroes of Gallipoli rewarded = Tis not what man does which exalts him [Browning], but what the P[rime] M[inister] decides.'[94]

Also, Hamilton received a letter from his friend 'Nellie' (Eleanor C. Sellar):

Sir Charles Monro's despatch makes me furious. He never alludes to the irresistible good that was done by holding up the best fighting force of Turkey for 7 months! Of course it is the despatch of a man who went out with a *parti pris*.[95]

Hamilton responded by quoting a note that was sent to him from Lord Haldane.[96] Haldane reputedly wrote, 'Monro's despatch is beastly. You must just receive it in silence, your time will come.' Hamilton then goes on to say, 'Monro was bound to try and justify the advice he gave, advice which came so pat that he must either be the lucky possessor of a Napoleonic eye or else, as you shrewdly suggest, must have embarked with a *parti pris*.'[97]

Even more bitter comment is made in a letter from Hamilton to an unknown recipient in 1919 in which he describes a dinner party where Brigadier General Cecil Aspinall-Oglander, former CGS to General Sir William Birdwood, recounts various staff meetings on the peninsula in autumn 1915. Monro's key staff officer, Lynden-Bell, is criticised heavily for a bias against the Gallipoli situation even before he had heard the options for and against evacuation and is accused of drafting a cable insisting on immediate evacuation before Monro had returned from his reconnaissance. He then comments on Monro, 'Although constitutionally, he was a courageous man, he had been blown up at Ypres and his nerves had not yet recovered from the shock!'[98] He goes on to claim that Monro and Lynden-Bell had nothing to do with the orders for the evacuation, as Birdwood did all the work, yet Monro was praised and decorated, whilst Birdwood received nothing. However, none of these views were reflected in Birdwood's 1941 autobiography.

The last evidence of Hamilton's bitterness is illustrated in a letter he wrote to *The Times* newspaper in 1931, though it was never published as the paper replied that there was no room. His letter is in response to Barrow's 1931 biography of Monro. Hamilton, who had served at the School of Musketry at Hythe before Monro, claimed that Lord Roberts should have all the praise for improved marksmanship and tactics during that period as Monro was only obeying Robert's orders rather than using any initiative.[99] From the evidence that the author has seen, it was Hamilton who was still in shock and very bitter, having never recovered from Gallipoli.

Previously, in July 1915 the Gallipoli Fund had been set up by Lady Jean Hamilton, wife of General Ian Hamilton and a keen member of the Red Cross organisation. Lady Jean had invited Lady Monro to join the committee despite the fact that her husband had lost his appointment and been replaced by Charles Monro.[100] Jean Hamilton was one of those observers of the Gallipoli situation who always believed that the campaign could have been won by her husband if he had been allocated the appropriate resources, later writing in her diary:

> The fatal mistake there was sending Monro, nothing could be done after that, as he went with evacuation in his pocket and was only two hours on Gallipoli himself. Before that, with proper reinforcements, Ian could have taken the Peninsula at any time, gained Constantinople, and ended the war.[101]

This is unfair and ill-informed comment. Charles Monro had effectively done his duty, saving thousands of lives. The last words in this chapter go to General Sir Charles Monro, extracted from his Special Order of the Day, issued after the evacuation:

> The arrangements made for withdrawal and for keeping the enemy in ignorance of the operation, which was taking place, could not have been improved. The General Officer Commanding the Dardanelles Army and the General Officers Commanding the Australian and New Zealand and IX Army Corps, may pride themselves on an achievement without parallel in the annals of war … Regimental officers, non-commissioned officers and men carried out, without a hitch, the most trying operation which soldiers can be called upon to undertake – a withdrawal in the face of the enemy – in a manner reflecting the highest credit on discipline and soldierly qualities of the troops. It is no exaggeration to call this achievement one without parallel … There is only one consideration – what is best for the furtherance of the common cause. In that spirit the withdrawal was carried out, and in that spirit the Australian and New Zealand and the IX Army Corps have proved, and will continue to prove, themselves second to none as soldiers of the Empire.[102]

All of Charles Monro's despatches and reports were persuasive, supportive to the officers and men he commanded and almost self-deprecating. The Dardanelles Commission endorsed Monro's decision making at Gallipoli, calling it 'wise and courageous'. It also commented on his many commendations of other people, rightly adding, 'The name of Sir Charles Monro himself should be added.'[103]

THE 1ST ARMY AND THE
NEW BEF

Charles Monro returned to the Western Front in early 1916. By this time the BEF had been reorganised and in July 1916 it consisted of nearly 1.5 million men. Led by Sir Douglas Haig, who had replaced Sir John French as the C-in-C, it eventually became divided into five armies:

1st Army, General Sir Charles Monro.
2nd Army, General Sir Herbert Plumer.
3rd Army, General Sir Edmund Allenby.
4th Army, General Sir Henry Rawlinson.
Reserve (later 5th) Army, General Sir Hubert Gough.

The BEF had expanded from the original two corps of four divisions to eighteen corps containing fifty-eight divisions, and 1916 was the year that

PLAYER'S CIGARETTES.

FIRST ARMY.

Kitchener's New Army divisions were to be tested in battle. According to Correlli Barnett, this expeditionary force was 'the largest, most complicated and most comprehensive single organisation ever evolved by the British nation'.[1] Once the French 10th Army had been relieved by the British in March 1916, four armies ran from north to south – 2nd, 1st (Monro's), 3rd, and 4th – positioned between the Belgians to their left and the French on the right. Although the period between mid-December 1915 and 1 July 1916 was relatively quiet for the British, there were still over 125,000 casualties.

1st Army badge. (Player's)

Most of the weaponry was similar to that used in the previous year, but there was considerably more artillery. Specialist troops had been developed and increased in numbers, headquarters staff and logistic organisations were expanded and more machine guns were available. The British also brought the steel helmet into service.

As a past advocate of the machine gun at the Hythe School of Musketry, Monro could at last see them being deployed more intelligently. Battalions had their complement doubled from two to four in February 1915 and four additional Lewis machine guns were added four months later. A specialist Machine Gun Corps (MGC) was established in October with an MGC company attached to each brigade, manning sixteen Vickers or Maxim guns. By then, there were eight machine guns per battalion – either Lewis or Hotchkiss. A machine gun training centre was set up at Grantham, and by the beginning of the Somme battles of 1 July 1916 each battalion had sixteen machine guns.

Command

Charles Monro was one of a select group of generals who had commanded divisions in France in 1914 and were now commanding one of the five armies, although until the Gallipoli issue he had been relatively unknown. Of this group, Rawlinson and Gough had the most recent experience of commanding large formations in battle at Loos in September 1915, the first large-scale British attack. It was their two armies who were to bear the brunt of the most significant action of 1916 – the Somme.

The army commanders were Haig's peers, with the same rank and, as Sheffield has written, 'Haig had to build a relationship with his subordinates' at this stage of the war.[2] Whilst Rawlinson and Gough were his favourites, it was Plumer, commander of the 2nd Army, who he was most concerned about and this subordinate was nearly sacked for inefficiency in February 1916. Haig was not impressed with his defences and thought that he was too slack when dealing with his corps commanders. Plumer even offered his resignation, and one staff officer commented in early 1916, 'Poor old Plum was in deadly fear of Haig at that time. Haig twice had him on the carpet threatening to send him home.'[3] Yet this was the general whom Haig had tasked to examine options for British assaults on the Western Front in early 1916. Plumer's suggested options of a Messines area of assault potentially coupled with an attack along the coast were later commented on in the Official History, favourably compared against the attrition battles of the Somme.[4]

General Monro in London.
(Author's collection)

There is mixed comment about Haig's style of command; whether he encouraged successful commanders and rewarded efficient performance or was simply a feared bully. One of Monro's subordinate commanders, Henry Wilson, wrote that Monro was also afraid of Haig, stating, 'He is terrified of Haig and thinks if we don't constantly raid that Haig will be angry.'[5] This fear is not mentioned in Barrow's 1931 biography, though he does say in his autobiography:

> It struck me as odd that Haig, himself a singularly inarticulate man, should turn a readier ear to the opinions of the vocal commanders of the Fourth and Fifth Armies than to those of the more reticent, but by no means less capable commanders of the First and Third Armies. But Haig often erred in his judgement of men.[6]

Monro took over his new appointment from Rawlinson on 4 February 1916 and was back at a headquarters location from the year before – Hinges. Shortly afterwards, this moved to Chateau Jumelles at Aire, then Chocques (called 'Chokes' by the troops), near Bethune and later to Chateau Philomel at Lillers. However, Haig had wanted Rawlinson, whom he knew well and trusted implicitly, to stay in command of the 1st Army, not Monro, but Kitchener had not endorsed his preference.

Monro eventually had under his command, at slightly different times, the following corps and lieutenant generals:

I Corps (Hubert Gough; then from April 1916, Charles Kavanagh).
III Corps (William Pulteney).
IV Corps (Henry Wilson).
XI Corps (Richard Haking).
In due course, the Canadian Corps (Julian Byng).

His core staff were:

Major General George Barrow (his original biographer).
Lieutenant Colonel Lord Herbert Scott, assistant military secretary.
Captain Orr and Lieutenant Troutbeck (his nephew), aides-de-camp.
Major General 'Freddie' Mercer, commander Royal Artillery.
Major General R. Heath, commander Royal Engineers.
Colonel 'Sammy' Wilson, General Staff Officer grade 1.

As part of organisational changes his headquarters then commanded 'army troops' as well as his formations. These included heavy guns and anti-aircraft artillery, Royal Engineer mining and camouflage companies, Royal Flying Corps squadrons, balloons, and signal and logistic units. He also had 4A Special Battalion (Gas) which could deploy the new, more efficient chemical mix of 50 per cent phosgene and 50 per cent chlorine – the new 'White Star' gas. The nature of war was changing and he had the task of co-ordinating and concentrating these assets at the critical points of his battlefield.

There were many visitors to 1st Army HQ, including Lord Kitchener and Joffre. Monro described Joffre:

Old Joffre came to lunch with us. Such a fine old boy, a very quiet taciturn old gentlemen very unlike our estimate of a Frenchman. Unfortunately, he does not speak a word of English and my French conversation is a very stunted vehicle so intercourse was not very easy.[7]

Georges Clémenceau, the French prime minister, also visited, as did the Archbishop of Canterbury. Barrow recounted, 'The old Arch himself is a very amusing old bean and very human. He regaled us with lots of amus-ing stories.'[8]

The pattern of Allied offensive operations had been set at the end of 1915. The Allied War Council had agreed that actions in 1916 'should be founded on the plan of a general, simultaneous offensive in the main theatre of the War'.[9] This envisaged simultaneous offensives by France, Great Britain, Russia and Italy, with greater co-operation between the French and British on the Western Front – 'A vigorous and simultaneous stroke' which would relieve the pressure on the Russian front.[10]

Joffre pushed for two British preparatory offensives in April and May with a main attack occurring north and south of the Somme in July 1916. The 1 July offensive was agreed by Joffre and Haig in mid-February and endorsed by the military and political hierarchy at home. However, the German assault on Verdun began only a week later, severely reducing the French contribution, though twenty divisions were still promised. It was thought that the Somme offensive would relieve the pain being inflicted on the French at Verdun. Meanwhile, the two British preparatory attacks were reduced to one attack, ten to fifteen days before the main assault.

The year 1916 was to be dominated by the British offensive, further south of the line on the Somme from July to November, and the German assaults at Verdun, which began in February 1916 in order to 'bleed France white'. In March 1916, Monro commented on the big issue – Verdun:

> The main point of interest of course has been the Verdun fighting, which has been terrific, according to what we hear. The heavy artillery bombardment was simply terrific, quite beyond anything that has ever been experienced. The net result has been that the French have got their tails up and are in high spirits, while the Germans have lost a host of men. They attacked in the old way and with great determination, but when their columns get under fire of the French guns, which is a very deadly weapon, the consequences are inevitable and some of their corps have been decimated. What a tribute the whole business is to the humanity of the world and Christianity.[11]

These words seem strange from the modern perspective, but illustrate the attitude at the time. Both French and Germans suffered terribly from the battles around Verdun from February to December 1916, casualties eventually reaching over 300,000 each. Monro stood by his traditional Christian convictions; he attended services as often as he could and the 1st Army was the first to establish schools for chaplains.

Other notable events in 1916 were Major General Townshend's disastrous surrender at Kut, Mesopotamia, the Easter Rising in Dublin and the naval Battle of Jutland. In addition, it was the first year of British Army conscription as the British Army needed even greater numbers than previous volunteers could provide; the Regular Army had been decimated in 1914, then the Territorial Force in 1915, whilst 1916 was to be the testing ground for the volunteers of Kitchener's New Armies.

Haig was concerned about the standard of training within his command, describing the army in France as not really an army 'but a collection of divisions untrained for the field'.[12] He did not want to commit the new divisions to battle until they were prepared and he placed his own preferred generals, Rawlinson and Gough, in command of the Somme front, which was his decisive point of action. Allenby was to conduct a secondary attacking role on the Gommecourt salient, whilst Monro's 1st Army was to have its ill-fated subsidiary assault at Fromelles on 19 July 1916.

However, in early 1916 Monro's sector of command was relatively quiet and seen as less critical by the C-in-C. The British outline Plan of Campaign had identified that an attack should be delayed 'until the time arrives when all the allies can assume the offensive'. It also stated, 'that the country between the Somme and Ficheux is the most suitable place for the main attack'.[13]

Monro's area of responsibility has been called 'some of the least desirable real estate in the world'.[14] Haking, XI Corps commander, described his position:

> The greater part of the front held by my Corps is in a bog, and every shower of rain or period of frost or wet, causes great damage throughout the defences with the result that work is endless and that there is always a greater demand for labour than can be supplied.[15]

The 1st Army was positioned there, not because of any great tactical value, but because that was where they were left after the battles around Loos in the autumn of 1915. The result of this was that Monro did not have the opportunity to distinguish himself during the period of his command of the 1st Army. Much smaller offensives than the Somme did take place – at the Hohenzollern Redoubt in March and, controversially, at Fromelles in July. In addition, the 1st Army had to resist German attacks north of Loos in April and May. However, these actions were not always successful. Notably, Monro's 1931 biography provides no detail of these smaller offensive and defensive operations, yet the author, George Barrow, was Monro's 1st Army chief of staff.

Raids

Apart from preparing for the big offensive, Haig had issued guidelines for action as he took command. In essence, he demanded 'winter sports' or raids to capture enemy trenches at favourable points, 'wearing out fights' and 'decisive attacks on several points, object to break through'.[16] There was no intention, as Richard Holmes so eloquently described, to allow 'comfortable fraternisation of live and let live' between the British and German lines.[17]

The value of trench raids, or 'stunts' as some critical soldiers called them, has been much debated. On the one hand, it was believed that they were essential to maintain British morale and the offensive spirit, they kept the Germans wondering what their enemy was going to do next and they provided valuable intelligence about the enemy positions. On the other hand, it was argued that lives were needlessly wasted for spurious reasons. Wilson's comment on Monro's concern about Haig's attitude to the subject has already been mentioned. Interestingly, Barrow also mentioned this subject, somewhat defensively, illustrating that there must have been a difference of opinion between the two generals concerning the value of raids:

> In France he [Monro] favoured raids on the enemy trenches for the purpose of obtaining important identifications, to wipe out some annoying machine-gun post, to hold the enemy in his front and keep them from transferring troops to some other part of the line. Raids for the sake of raiding, in order 'to kill Germans,' which often meant the killing of greater numbers of British; the periodical raids which some commanders persisted in ordering with the mistaken notion that they maintained a moral superiority over the enemy – these were abhorrent to him.[18]

Yet one regimental history states, 'Sir Charles Monro, commander of the 1st Army, was an enthusiastic supporter of the raiding policy, and stressed to all corps and divisional commanders the importance of fostering the offensive spirit … whatever the cost.'[19]

It is also difficult to square Barrow's comments with an order he personally distributed to Monro's corps commanders on 30 July 1916:

> The enemy has shown a considerable amount of activity along the front during the past few days. The Army commander [Monro] hopes that you will continue your measures of annoyance and carry out as many raids as you can manage.[20]

What is clear is that Monro did show compassion and was prepared to stand by his views to his superior commander, despite his intense loyalty to the chain of command. Haig had made it clear to his subordinates that he favoured raids with 'vigour', as they aided training and improved a unit's fighting capabilities. French had also provided clear orders to the 1st Army just before Monro arrived. He had ordered small frequent operations, whilst the defensive positions were held to 'wear out and exhaust the enemy's troops, to foster and enhance the offensive spirit of our own troops and to encourage them to feel superior to the enemy in every respect … Pressure on the enemy should be relentless.'[21]

Monro sanctioned raids when he thought them essential. He had to cope, however, with aggressive and enthusiastic subordinate commanders such as Richard Haking, commanding XI Corps. They knew each other well. Only a year before, Haking had been one of Monro's brigade commanders within 2nd Division, then later one of his divisional commanders within I Corps.

It was in this period of 1916 that Haking earned his nickname of 'Butcher'. No senior general seemed more enthusiastic than him to launch raids and assaults. Haking was continually encouraging his divisional commanders to be on the offensive and was asking Monro for enough ammunition to launch a series of assaults in March 1916 to 'improve their fighting spirit'.[22] In one of his February conferences, he stated the need for raids to kill Germans, lower their morale and raise that of his troops.

On 29 February, Monro made his position clear on raids:

> All minor enterprise of the kind referred to were useful not only bringing infantry and artillery into closer touch, but also in encouraging the offensive spirit and initiative in all ranks. The GOC hoped that Corps Commanders would continue and even increase their efforts to arrange for the carrying out of such enterprises.[23]

Therefore, he followed the party line, but with reservations. Across the British front, during the months December 1915 to May 1916, there were officially sixty-three raids involving ten to 200 soldiers, of which forty-seven were recorded as successful. Monro's 1st Army averaged four raids a week in 1916 – not a considerable number, even with Haking's enthusiasm. The Germans launched thirty-three raids across the British front, twenty successful, in the same period.[24]

Hohenzollern Redoubt (2 March 1916)

The Hohenzollern Redoubt had been fought over in the autumn of 1915, leaving just the western half in British hands. German mining had been successful; large craters had been created overlooking British lines and the British had lost the trench line known as 'the Chord', lying across the higher ground. The sector was held by the 12th (Eastern Division) of Gough's I Corps from February 1916.

Mining had become an increasingly important part of trench warfare tactics for both sides, as they attempted to break through each other's lines using new techniques and technology. Shafts were dug for 'listening' or for offensive mining, being eventually 'blown'. Haig acknowledged the increasing role of mining in his spring 1916 despatch, 'Their importance in the present phase of warfare is very great.'[25]

In December 1915, an inspector of mines was appointed as a specialist adviser at GHQ, whilst each army, including Monro's 1st, was provided with a controller of mines (Lieutenant Colonel G. Williams[26] in his case), with an additional staff officer. Williams directed work on mining operations throughout the 1st Army. Knowing Monro's enthusiasm for training, it is not surprising that his army was the first to set up a mining school on the Western Front.

At Hohenzollern, 170th Tunnelling Company Royal Engineers had succeeded, over four months, in digging three mines under the German lines.[27] Gough decided after much debate to blow the mines and seize the Chord back. It was decided that 36th Brigade were to lead the assault, supported by artillery and mortars that would only start firing once the mines were blown to gain maximum surprise.

The attack occurred at 0545 hours on 2 March 1916. The effect of the three explosions was to create craters 30ft away from the objective, ideal for the assault.[28] One of the two lead battalions, the 9th Royal Fusiliers, quickly took the enemy trenches of the 23rd Bavarian Regiment and captured eighty prisoners. Its neighbour, the 8th Fusiliers were not so lucky, as the Germans there had time to man their parapets. Most of the objectives had been taken but there was a series of German counter-attacks over the next four days, capturing some of the lost ground and involving some bloody hand-to-hand fighting over craters. Within forty-eight hours, 36th Brigade had nearly 1,000 casualties as a result of intense German counter-attacks and 'under terrible conditions of snow, rain and intense cold'.[29]

After a few days of lull, the Germans blew five mines, launching a significant counter-attack on 18 March employing accurate new trench mortars (*minenwerfers*) for the first time. They regained some lost ground,

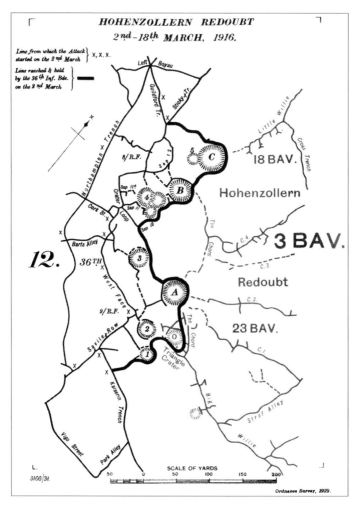

Hohenzollern Redoubt, March 1916. (Edmonds)

though they did not remain in the craters because they were so exposed. There were no more British attacks to seize the Chord. The British view was:

> The holding of the interior of a crater was costly in men, as it only formed a target into which every kind of gun and mortar lobbed shells, from the effect of which in a confined space – the bottom of a morass of liquid, chalk and black mud – there was no protection.[30]

The horror of fighting in that environment is obvious and four New Army battalions from the south-east of England bore the brunt of the final German assault, including some of Monro's own parent regiment, 6th (Service) Battalion the Queen's Royal West Surreys.

Incredible bravery was displayed during those few days. The most notable-act of bravery recorded was from the same brigade, the 37th. William Cotter was a corporal serving with the 6th (Service) Battalion of the Buffs (East Kent Regiment). He earned a posthumous VC on 6–7 March 1916 whilst attacking the 'Triangle Crater'. His citation read:

> For most conspicuous bravery and devotion to duty. When his right leg had been blown off at the knee, and he had also been wounded in both arms, he made his way unaided for fifty yards to a crater, steadied the men who were holding it, controlled their fire, issued orders, and altered the dispositions of his men to meet a fresh counter-attack by the enemy.
>
> For two hours he held his position, and only allowed his wounds to be roughly dressed when the attack had quieted down.
>
> He could not be moved back for fourteen hours, and during all this time had a cheery word for all who passed him. There is no doubt that his magnificent courage helped greatly to save a critical situation.[31]

This 'Battle of the Craters' was a relatively small area of engagement over sixteen days in March 1916, on Monro's front – but not so for the troops involved, who had to fight hard for their lives. It had little strategic value in the big scheme of things, as stalemate was the result and casualties were sustained for no overall gain. It is hard to understand what both Gough and Monro were trying to achieve, though commanders were all under pressure to produce local successes. Monro's area was predicted to remain relatively quiet, as reflected by a letter to Monro near the end of March 1916, in which General Kiggell said, 'so far as we are capable of judging, nothing on any considerable scale is threatened on your front'.[32] Yet this was a bloody engagement for the soldiers involved and Monro appreciated the attacking troops' efforts, as reflected in his message to the 12th (Eastern Division):

> The Army Commander will be glad if you will convey to Brigadier-Generals Boyd-Moss and Cator, and the troops who have been engaged in the recent operations at the Hohenzollern Redoubt, his appreciation of the determined and gallant spirit in which they have held to the craters under exceptionally arduous conditions.[33]

Sir Douglas Haig also acknowledged the division's efforts, stating, 'the results gained justify the undertaking', though little was achieved for the sacrifices made. Strategically, the event was of little importance and the 'bigger picture' was explained by Haig in his spring 1916 despatch, which described this period on the Western Front:

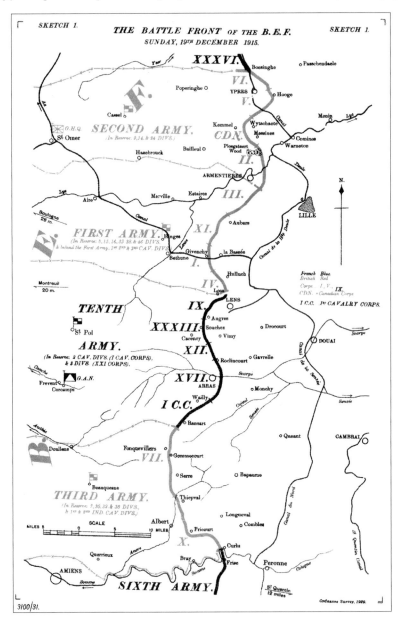

Battlefront, 1916. (Edmonds)

In short, although there has been no great incident of historic importance to record on the British front during the period under review, a steady and continuous fight has gone on, day and night, above ground and below it.[34]

The next significant action in the 1st Army's area was in late April against I Corps, then commanded by Lieutenant General Charles Kavanagh.

German Gas Attack at Hulluch (27–29 April 1916)

> There they lay, scores of them (we lost eight hundred, nearly all from gas)
> in the bottom of the trench, in every conceivable posture of human agony;
> the clothes torn off their bodies in a vain effort to breathe while from end
> to end of that valley of death came one long unceasing moan from the lips
> of brave men fighting and struggling for life.[35]

These are the dramatic words of Father William Doyle, a chaplain serving
with the 8th Battalion Royal Dublin Fusiliers, following the German gas
attack by the 2nd Bavarian Corps at Hulluch on 27 April 1916. This battalion was part of 16th (Irish) Division, a fresh but inexperienced New Army
formation which received the brunt of this assault.

Hulluch was just on the German side of the front line, about 1 mile north
of Loos. Two days before, a German deserter had alerted the British to a
possible attack and rats had been seen running into no-man's-land from
the enemy lines, which were only 120–300 yards away – a sign that gas was
probably about to be used in the area and some had leaked. There was also a
systematic preparatory enemy bombardment. All this meant that the Germans
had lost the element of surprise, the British troops were warned off and extra
friendly artillery was moved in to drive off any potential attack. Meanwhile,
the Germans prepared 3,800 gas cylinders along a 2-mile front.

On 27 April, there was a favourable wind and the weather conditions were
warm and calm and, following a short preliminary heavy bombardment at
0500 hours, the Germans launched the first of two chlorine gas attacks ten
minutes later. The cloud headed towards the 16th (Irish) Division and elements of the 15th (Scottish) Division and it was recorded that 'the quantity
of gas employed was very large'.[36] Gas alerts were called as primitive PH
gas helmets were pulled over British soldiers' faces and the extra guns fired
into enemy positions. Visibility was down to 3 yards and the gas could be
smelled 15 miles away. After thirty minutes, small groups of twenty to thirty
Germans started to probe British lines, their legs and feet showing under the
cloud, and shortly afterwards three German mines were blown and another
gas cloud followed.

Sadly, some members of the 9th Battalion Black Watch were caught without any protection as their commander thought that if the masks had been
used once they were useless, so he had ordered them to be removed. Some
Germans managed to reach the trenches occupied by the Dublin Fusiliers,
the Black Watch and 7th Battalion Royal Inniskilling Fusiliers, but they were
all driven out or killed after some short but intense fighting. Incredibly, all was
quiet by 0730 hours. Lieutenant Lyon of the 7th Battalion Leinster Regiment

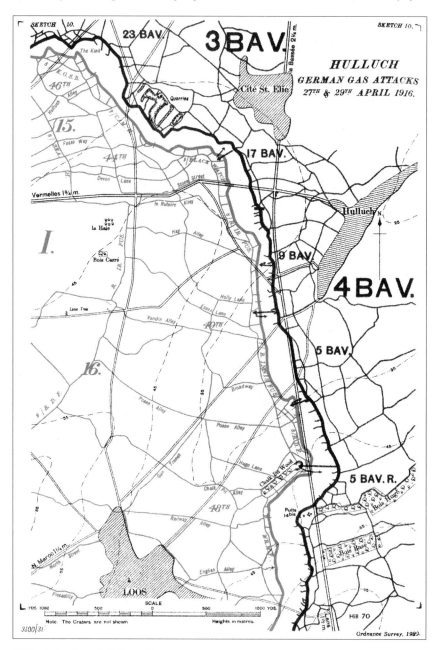

Hulluch, April 1916. (Edmonds)

had to arrange a burial for sixty men in one shell hole, 'they were in all sorts of tragic attitudes, some of them holding hands like children'.[37] Captain John Staniforth, also serving with the 7th Leinsters, commented, 'Every rifle, machine gun, cartridge, bandolier, telephone wire, and metal of any sort turns a dull arsenic green, with a corroding film.'[38]

The second gas attack occurred at 0345 hours on 29 April aimed at the 16th (Irish) Division again. Half an hour later the Germans were seen massing for an attack, so there was an effective British artillery barrage on their positions and then the wind changed. Their own gas caused casualties amongst them, blunting any significant chance of their success. However, there had been a large number of friendly casualties from the gas on both days, particularly on the 29th, despite rapid masking, because the PH 'sack' helmets were claimed to be inefficient and on the second attack, the gas had lingered. There were 1,260 British gas casualties over the two days and 338 died. Others were to die from the effects of this attack in later years.

An investigation on this Hulluch attack was instigated on 30 April because of the high casualties and concern about the effectiveness of the PH helmet respirators. It followed a 16th Division report that recorded, 'It is suggested that the Germans, knowing they were attacking an untried division in not very good trenches, hoped to clear those trenches with gas and by the bombardment.'[39]

At first, there was some headquarters' staff criticism of the Irish Division's gas drills – 'bad gas discipline' – because of the high level of casualties, before they realised the ineffectiveness of the troops' protection. It was discovered that the machine-gunners who were equipped with a newer box respirator were protected, so every effort was made to procure the new models, but that was too late for this terrible experience. The investigation concluded that the alarm had not been raised in time, the protective helmet was not put on quickly enough and had not been positioned properly on the soldiers beforehand and inspection of helmets and gas drills needed to be improved. Many soldiers had thought they had been 'gassed through their helmets', so they removed them prematurely. Apparently, 'wearers of PH helmets have been warned that when the helmet is worn in gas a prickly irritating sensation is to be expected in the eyes, nose and throat' – not an effect to engender confidence in the equipment.[40]

The Times reported, 'It was the first time this Irish Division had been in action, but the young soldiers were magnificently cool.'[41] Ironically, on the same day as the second attack Padraig Pearse, the Irish Nationalist, ordered the laying down of arms following the short Irish Easter Rising in Dublin. At the time, the rebellion was not generally supported and the Irish Nationalist leader, John Redmond, commented in the House of Commons:

> Is it not an additional horror that on the very day when we hear that the men of the Dublin Fusiliers have been killed by Irishmen on the streets of Dublin, we receive the news of how the men of the 16th Division – our own Irish Brigade, and of the same Dublin Fusiliers – had dashed forward and by their unconquerable bravery retaken the trenches the Germans had

won at Hulluch? Was there ever such a picture of a tragedy which a small section of Irish faction had so often inflicted on the fairest hopes and the bravest deeds of Ireland.[42]

The Germans communicated to the division on three placards, on 1 May. The first one stated, 'Irishmen! Heavy uproar in Ireland. English guns are firing on your wives and children.' The second broadcast the British and Indian Army disaster at Kut, Mesopotamia, 'Kut captured. 13,000 English Prisoners.' And the third, 'English guns firing on your Wives and Children. English Dreadnought sunk: English Military Bill Refused. Sir Roger Casement Persecuted. Throw your arms away. We will give you a hearty welcome.'[43]

The 8th Battalion Royal Munster Fusiliers responded to this propaganda by capturing them in a night raid and one of the responses was reputedly, 'In addition to being Irish Catholics, we have the honour to be Irish soldiers.'[44] I Corps and the 1st Army had held the line, but at considerable cost.

The Kink (11–14 May 1916)

The next significant action in Monro's 1st Army sector was the loss of 'the Kink' or 'Hussar Horn'. This part of the British line, just south-east of the Hohenzollern Redoubt, formed a small salient into the German positions 400 yards wide, but was overlooked south and north by the enemy. It had been the scene of severe fighting in the previous autumn, as part of the Loos offensive. The Kink was extremely exposed to enemy observation and fire and had 'the worst reputation of any place in the sector'.[45] There was daily enemy harassing fire, a great deal of mining and craters were dotted over the landscape, occupied by different sides.

The Germans wanted to seize the salient and their opposition this time was again I Corps. Opposing them in the front trenches were two brigades of the 15th (Scottish) Division. Although the British 170th Tunnelling Company was supposed to have gained local superiority, the Germans detonated two small mines in the first few days of May 1916 as part of their preliminary operations and the 18th Bavarian Regiment stood by to assault the Kink, straighten the lines and reduce the threat of future British mining. The attack was not expected.

The major bombardment and subsequent German attack took place on 11 May. The Germans confused the British by good use of artillery on different positions and 'the dust and smoke along the whole front had soon made observation impossible'.[46] Most of the attack became directed at two

THE LOSS OF THE KINK
11TH MAY 1916.

N

The
Dump
(Fosse 8)

3

BAV.

Hindenburg Trench

Cross Trench

Tirpitz Trench

Slag Alley

Zeppelin Alley

I BN. 8 BAV.

I BN.

23

BAV.

Potsdam Trench

Bill's Bluff

The Kink

Huszar Horn

Kaiserin Trench

B Coy.

C Coy.

Alexander Tr.

C Coy.

Crown Trench

A Coy.

Boyau 70

Anchor Tr.

Vigo St.

Clifford St.

Gordon Alley

Sackville Street

13 / R. SCOTS.

Boyau 96

Border Redoubt

Hulluch Alley

Crown Trench

10 / SCO. RIF.

45TH

15.

46TH

SCALE
YARDS 100   0   100   200   300   400   500 YARDS.

Heights in metres

British Trenches lost on the 11th. May.   - - - - -
British Front Line at the conclusion of the fighting
German Attacks on the 11 th. May

3100/31.

Ordnance Survey 1930.

Kink Salient, May 1916. (Edmonds)

battalions: 13th Battalion the Royal Scots and 10th Battalion the Scottish
Rifles, units from the two neighbouring brigades. For most of the day, the
trenches of the 13th Royal Scots were pummelled, 'the front line being almost
obliterated in many places'.[47] The bombardment intensified on the Kink at
1745 hours, coupled with German counter-battery fire. General McCracken
and his staff now realised that an attack was likely and so the divisional reserve

brigade was prepared to move forward and all machine-gun posts occupied. This was not going to be enough to stop the assault that was launched at 1800 hours. The Germans succeeded in occupying the Kink on a front of 600 yards long and 400 yards deep.

Their success had been achieved after producing what the Official Historian described as 'one of the heaviest concentrations of artillery on a small area in the war'.[48] It was the 13th Royal Scots who gave ground, but suffered the most in this catastrophic exposure to enemy fire. One shell had landed on battalion headquarters at 1600 hours, killing the commanding officer, adjutant and machine-gun officer and placing the whole command team out of action. Thereafter, there was no chance of any effective command and control within that battalion or any co-ordination of their defence. Half the unit was either dead or wounded because of the intense bombardment. The advancing Germans had little opposition and, as well as seizing the salient, succeeded in capturing thirty-nine miners. Their shells and gas had confused the British in depth, whilst British artillery fire could not accurately engage the enemy because of the dust and smoke.

Counter-attacks were attempted at 1830 hours, 2130 hours and in the dark at 0130 hours, but to no avail. The brave Scottish soldiers were simply mown down by accurate German machine-gun fire. Only a small portion was recaptured. By 0300 hours, the British lost all hope of seizing back the lost ground and, frustratingly, could only consolidate their new line. Of the division's 420 casualties, seventy-two were 'missing'. The Divisional History records that 'of the latter there is every reason to suppose that most, if not all, were buried during the bombardment'.[49]

A final effort was made to retake the Kink on 14 May, but again there were heavy casualties. The divisional commander called a halt to further attacks later that day and it was decided that the new line was stronger than the previous position. His decision was endorsed by Charles Monro.

Interestingly, no commanders were castigated for the loss of the Kink; there were no recriminations from Monro. Beckett and Corvi comment that Monro proved that he was 'a prudent, sensible commander, who did not expect his men or their commanders to do the impossible'.[50] This is a fair observation, but generals do not win any favours by losing ground.

Vimy Ridge (21–23 May 1916)

Another loss of ground occurred within Monro's 1st Army area, at Vimy Ridge on 21 May 1916. Vimy Ridge, just north of Arras, is best known for the courageous actions of the Canadian Corps in 1917, but it was also a hotly disputed area in the two previous years. The French 10th Army had fought and held the position until March 1916, when the British 3rd Army took over this section of the front.

The 9-mile long ridge dominated the ground with a westerly facing gentle slope, which allowed the Germans excellent arcs of observation and fire. Steep slopes to the east concealed German troops and their supporting artillery and mortar positions. The Allied lines were poorly constructed, described graphically in the Official History, 'There were few good communication trenches: most were unfit for use, all were undrained and utterly unsanitary. Dead bodies, months old, still lay unburied, and a vast amount of debris and rubbish covered the whole area.'[51]

Ideally, the British line should have been pulled back slightly to make best use of better defensive ground. However, after the blood lost and gains by the French in that sector before, there was no way that any local commander or Monro could readjust positions. This was another area of mining and counter-mining amongst the landscape of shell holes and hastily organised positions, and an underground clash went on with twelve Allied tunnelling companies in action. The British gradually established their mining supremacy after heavy casualties on both sides, and five Allied mines were blown on 15 May, leading to more forward craters to defend.

The new, temporary German commander, Freytag-Loringhoven, needed to destroy the British underground successes and planned an overland counter-attack:

> The casualties which we suffered by mine explosions and continual night attacks aroused in me lively anxiety … Things could not go on as they were … If by attack we could throw back the British over the position which we had held until the end of September 1915 and so rob them of all their mine shafts, and hold the position won, we should have tranquillity.[52]

Coincidentally, his attack on 21 May 1916 was opposed by another temporary commander – IV Corps leader, Henry Wilson, who was standing in as 1st Army commander because Monro had gone on leave on 9 May. Command and control arrangements were also adversely affected because there was a major changeover in that sector of army, corps, divisional and garrison responsibilities only twenty-four hours before the attack. It had only just switched from a 3rd Army to a 1st Army area of responsibility and critically, some of the artillery units were changing over as the German attack began. At short notice, Wilson's 47th (London) Division was to face the German assault in the area of Berthonval. The 47th was, of course, Monro's old divisional command from 1914, but its commander was not due back off leave until the day before the German attack and his deputy had 'refused Wilson's offer of reinforcements'.[53]

The British were not convinced that an enemy assault was imminent, despite the increase of German artillery and mortar fire in the preceding days. Intense German fire began at 0500 hours on 21 May and lasted six hours. There was then a pause until 1500 hours when it intensified again, hitting 47th Division's front-line battalions hard, but also reaching 8 miles to the rear. The whole area was covered in smoke and dust and the Germans even added tear gas to the mix to increase British confusion. This was probably the heaviest concentration of fire on the Western Front, so far in the war. Eighty German gun batteries were firing on a 1,800-yard front, hidden by the Vimy Ridge reverse slope and 70,000 German shells fell in four hours. 'All accounts agree that never had such a bombardment been seen and spectators could only wonder that there was any rifle fire from the 140th Brigade (47th Division) when the assault took place.'[54]

The German infantry ran forward at 1945 hours, following the blowing of a mine and the lifting of their barrage by 150 yards. The 140th Brigade had been surprised and destroyed and many of them became prisoners as they struggled out of their collapsed trenches. The enemy were less successful elsewhere, but local British counter-attacks failed during the early hours of the following morning. The Germans had seized part of Vimy Ridge. Wilson wrote, 'It is a nasty little knock, our casualties about 1,200 to 1,500. By a savage bombardment I have been knocked out of rotten trenches, which we only took over on Sunday morning.'[55]

Wilson wanted to launch a large counter-attack as soon as possible and planned one by three brigades for early on 23 May. Haig would not allow this to occur until full preparations had been made and Monro, back from leave, told him to defer the attack for twenty-four hours until he had enough artillery available in support. It was going to be difficult to hold the positions, even if they could be regained. Eventually, it was agreed to launch the counter-attack at 2100 hours on 23 May. Unfortunately, as if the Germans knew what was happening, the British forming up places were bombarded an hour before the proposed zero hour. One battalion lost 100 men immediately and was not in a fit state to advance, whilst elsewhere the decimated attacking force moved forward. The result was the wiping out of B Company of the 22nd Battalion Royal Fusiliers and a failed counter-attack. Monro called a halt to further assaults at 0030 hours on 24 May. Rather than devote more artillery to regain the position at a later date, it was decided that the priority had to be supporting the subsequent Somme offensive.

Henry Wilson's reputation suffered as a result of this 'nasty little knock', which had ended in a loss of ground and 2,475 British casualties, compared to the Germans' 1,350. This unfortunate event was the only significant action that Wilson had the opportunity to command as corps commander.

Sir Douglas Haig was unhappy with the situation and was not prepared to allocate more resources to a continued battle in the area, as this would divert valuable assets from the coming Somme offensive. He criticised Wilson's handling of the events of 21 May, though one of Wilson's biographers described it as 'sheer bad luck', which may have led to him never receiving higher command.[56] Haig was also unhappy about the performance of one of Wilson's brigadiers and wondered why both the divisional commander and Wilson had not taken action to rebuke him.

Wilson's position was not helped by a visit to his headquarters on 27 May 1916 by one of Haig's staff officers, who reported that the IV Corps staff were despondent and pessimistic. Wilson was reported as saying that French troops were 'better fighters than the British' and the 'Germans were better men than ours'.[57] Haig spoke to Monro on the same day and wrote in his diary, 'The IV Corps was the most efficient one in the Army when Sir H Wilson took over the Command. Since then it had much decreased in military value. He [Monro] must go into the matter at once, and get things right without delay.'[58]

Wilson believed that the visiting staff officer, Charteris, had had his leg pulled and misinterpreted his staff's attitude, appealing to Monro for assistance. However, Wilson came close to being sacked as a consequence of this visit. He was very fortunate that Monro stood by his IV Corps commander, reporting back to Haig that he wanted to retain his present staff and that Wilson had had a difficult situation to deal with at Vimy Ridge. Wilson stayed in command, but when Monro eventually left the 1st Army, Wilson was passed over for the command, despite Monro's recommendation. Monro had remained strongly loyal to his subordinate, despite the loss of ground and failure to retake it. GHQ's views were clear about the operation, 'With regard to the operations in progress on the Vimy Ridge, the Commander-in-Chief makes you to understand that he attaches considerable importance to the recovery and establishment of a satisfactory line, which can be maintained.'[59]

This would not do him any favours in the light of the next more significant reverse at Fromelles. Meanwhile, Monro continued to hold his army conferences to make sure his subordinates received clear direction. On 23 May, he re-emphasised the importance of strengthening the wire and the significance of digging dummy positions with good camouflage to assist deception. Haking and Kavanagh were not keen on constructing dummy positions, but Monro insisted that they proceeded.[60]

A small snapshot of Monro's views about the 1st Army area of responsibility is captured by *The Times* correspondent, Colonel Repington, on a visit to the headquarters at Chocques on 9 July 1916, just eight days after the start of the Somme battle. Monro told Repington that the Germans were exhausted, though their Guards units fought effectively and 'he thinks that the Boches are fighting well, but are decidedly tired, and, on the whole, are not fighting with their old fire'.[61] Monro was also proud of what his mining companies and raids had achieved. Repington finishes his account with the comment, 'Monro's mind and brain are as good as ever.'[62] At subsequent conferences in June, he insisted that co-operation should be improved between the infantry and the Royal Flying Corps, tunnelling companies and artillery, whilst improving gas drills; these were all professional efforts to improve the capability of his command.[63]

Fromelles (19–20 July 1916)

The renowned military historian Liddell-Hart had a very clear view about the Battle of Fromelles, written during the inter-war years:

> A most curious military delusion, for while simulated preparations for a large scale offensive would cause the enemy natural apprehension, the actual delivery of a narrow-fronted attack would disclose the bluff. One consequence was the shattering of the 5th Australian Division in an absurdly advertised attack at Fromelles.[64]

Fromelles, or Fleurbaix, is a little-known battlefield, though it is remembered in Australia as this was the first significant action in Western Europe by the Australian Imperial Force. The Australian Official History of this battle is seven times longer than the British account and there has long been an Australian perception that the British preferred to overlook the disaster. According to the author Lyn Macdonald, the battle 'created a breach between the Australian fighting troops and their British comrades, which would never be completely closed'.[65] In fact, there were two Allied divisions fighting under the command of Haking's XI Corps and Monro's 1st Army – the British 61st (2nd South Midland) Territorial Division, detached from Plumer's 2nd Army further north, and the 5th Australian Division. Their opposition was the 6th Bavarian Reserve Division, which included amongst its ranks a then unimportant Adolf Hitler.

The two Allied formations were inexperienced compared with the battle-hardened Germans and this was one of the factors that led to disaster. The battle only raged for a short time, but it was a period when an Australian division suffered the highest losses in one day during the First World War, with over 5,000 casualties. Nothing significant was gained. As Roger Lee has written in his excellent detailed study of British battle-planning at Fromelles, 'The short duration, heavy casualties and failure to hold any captured territory have made this one of the more controversial British attacks in a year marked by controversial and bloody infantry assaults.'[66]

Fromelles sat just north-east of Aubers Ridge, 6 miles south of Armentières, the scene of previous fighting, and the battle was fought on the night of 19 July to the morning of 20 July 1916. It was an extremely small action compared with the massive Battle of the Somme that lasted from 1 July to 18 November and involved an initial attack by British and French armies of over 100,000 men, of which there were over 60,000 British casualties on the first day. However, Fromelles was not a small engagement for the troops involved and it probably had an adverse impact on Monro's career and his future on the Western Front.

At the Somme, the aim was to punch a hole in the German lines by the third day, providing the opportunity for exploiting the breakthrough. There were some initial successes, due mainly to the intense artillery concentration of fire. However, these were only limited and after a series of small actions, a second British assault occurred at night on 14 July. As the Somme battle raged, Haig became concerned about German reinforcements, many of which were being moved into their lines from the north, opposite Monro's 1st Army, and a 'demonstration' was considered to prevent that movement. At this stage, Haig was receiving optimistic intelligence reports on the enemy, favouring more attacks. The New Zealand Division was used in the first attempt to stop German reinforcements moving over four nights from 9 July onwards, mainly with the use of artillery, but this had little effect and an assault was considered.

The two assaulting divisions at Fromelles were given little time to prepare, unlike the months of preparation before the Somme attack. However, in June corps commanders in both the 1st and 2nd Armies had suggested options for British attacks in their sectors and had conducted some contingency planning, following Haig's direction that 1st, 2nd and 3rd Army commanders were to prepare for operations, 'for misleading the enemy as to the real priority of the attack'.[67] Monro, who called a key planning conference on 8 June, had developed a number of deception and offensive plans using XI Corps and including an option to replace static immobile defensive posts of wood and iron in front of the 1st Army position with more portable defences, ready to move quickly before an attack. Monro and his corps commanders were debating the merits of the attack, deception, attrition and the potential opportunity of seizing ground.[68] He also submitted plans to GHQ of deception operations, using artillery, 1,900 gas cylinders, smoke, machine guns, raids and wire cutting across his whole front line. However, there was no clear guidance from Haig, who had the main attack on the Somme as his priority.

Even in May, Haking had been telling his divisional commanders of a potential assault in the sector. It is at this stage that Haking earned his perceived 'obsession with capturing Aubers Ridge'.[69] This is an accusation made by many of his contemporaries and historians, though the ridge was important as a piece of vital ground dominating the flat ground of the Fromelles area and allowing the Germans excellent fields of observation and fire.

Monro conducted another conference for his corps commanders on 14 June. There, they learned of the overall plan for the Somme and what their role may be. Monro made it clear that he favoured holding enemy trenches in order to fix them in position and avoid further German reinforcement of the Somme. There is no doubt that a great deal of option planning had taken place under Monro's command and that he had closely listened to Haking's plans and encouraged liaison with Plumer, though there were no final orders drawn up at this stage. At his next conference of 22 June, Monro acknowledged the lack of junior leaders and experienced planners available.

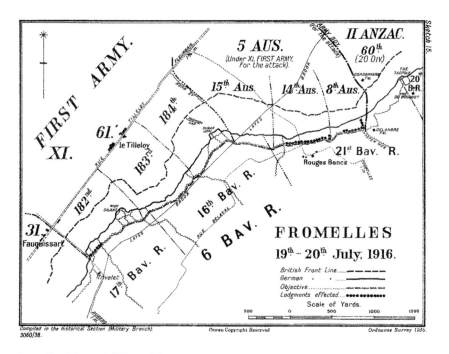

Fromelles, July 1916. (Edmonds)

Detailed planning was required and, 'Nothing should be left to chance.'[70] Lee comments that Monro's flexibility is 'evidence that Monro was more flexible in his command style than post-war critics have suggested'.[71]

Eventually, instructions were sent to Plumer on 5 July, which ordered the 1st and 2nd Armies to 'select a front on which to attempt a break'. Both army commanders believed that the boundary between their areas of responsibility had the best opportunity for success. On 8 July, following the offer of support from Plumer, Monro spoke to his corps commanders, telling them that 'the battle of the Somme was progressing favourably', and ordered Haking to develop his options for XI Corps.[72] The following day, Haking presented his concept of operations, described as 'an ambitious one, aiming at the capture – partly by means of a feint – of the Fromelles-Aubers Ridge, a mile behind the enemy's front'.[73] Haking chose Aubers Ridge as an objective, whilst Monro preferred objectives closer to the Somme – Hill 70 near Loos, or Vimy Ridge – as he believed that their capture, with the threat to Lille, would more adversely affect the enemy. Haking's plan was rejected by Monro on 12 July, but the situation was changing and pressure grew for an artillery demonstration opposite the 1st Army sector.

The following day, Major General Butler was sent from Haig's headquarters to talk to Monro and the chiefs of staff of the 1st and 2nd Armies (major generals Barrow and Harington). They agreed a demonstration with artillery, but also an infantry attack using two divisions from the 1st Army and one from the 2nd. This was in response to the news that more German units had been moved from the Lille area south to the Somme; they wanted this to stop. There followed 1st Army Order Number 100 of 15 July 1916, which stated the clear aim of the operation – 'To prevent the enemy from moving troops southward to take part in the defence of the Somme.'[74]

However, there was some contradiction in the orders; one line tells XI Corps to 'carry out an offensive operation' whilst another states that there should be the 'impression of an impending operation on a large scale'.[75] In addition, intelligence information on enemy dispositions and co-ordinating administrative requirements were minimal. Consequently, Lee criticises Monro and his staff for omitting such critical information, particularly as it 'was the largest of its supporting actions'.[76] However, Haking knew his commander and his intentions well, so it can be argued that Monro did provide enough detail for Haking to interpret and execute his own corps orders.

Secrecy was not required, because the demonstration needed to be impressive and obvious, so that the enemy treated the attack as a real threat; this was not known by the attacking troops and would not help the future number of casualties. In addition, the situation was not helped by Haking keeping his plans secret from neighbouring divisions, so they were not aware of their role once he attacked. The plan was to capture 6,000 yards of German front line, though this was reduced to 4,000 yards as Haking heard that less artillery than originally planned was going to be available and the number of attacking divisions was reduced to two.

Controversy occurred on 16 July, though only with hindsight as historians have tried to determine who was really responsible for the Fromelles blood-bath. On that day, Monro was informed by Butler that there was 'no urgent need for the XI Corps operation'.[77] Already, a smaller but similar attack had been launched by Haking just a few days earlier as a diversionary attack to the Somme, on 29 June at 'Boar's Head', when the 39th Division had been decimated for no gain. This became known as 'the day that Sussex died' and resulted in the destruction of three South Downs battalions of the Royal Sussex Regiment. The units had briefly penetrated the enemy lines and had then been ejected at a cost of over 1,000 casualties.

Haking sacked the divisional commander, but believed that the terrible experience improved the formation's fighting value; he seemed to learn nothing from the event. One staff officer later described Haking as 'really impossible, untruthful and a bully and not to be trusted'.[78] Another reason for not carrying out the attack at Fromelles came after Major Howard, one of Haig's staff, carried out a reconnaissance of the proposed attacking area with the Australian Brigadier General Elliott; they reputedly reported that 'the attack could hardly fail to end in disaster'.[79] Also, Butler proclaimed, 'Haig did not wish the infantry to attack at all unless the commanders were satisfied that they had sufficient artillery and ammunition not only to capture, but to hold and consolidate, the enemy's trenches.'[80]

Nevertheless, Haking remained confident of every success, despite the additional adverse factor of bad weather. Both Haking and Monro agreed that the troops were ready and would be disappointed if the attack did not occur – 'They were determined to maintain the proposed schedule.'[81] So Haig had left the commanders on the spot to make the decision, which was unanimous. A more recent general, Farrar-Hockley, was not impressed by Monro's decision:

> General Sir Charles Monro believed that the best way to do this (stop the Germans moving south) was a frontal attack in full daylight with singular lack of coordination between either of the attacking infantry forces or their artillery. He had the opportunity, as the weather was bad, to cancel the operation – Haig left the decision in his hands. But he lacked the moral courage to do so. Australian and English battalions advanced to their doom across the waterlogged ground.[82]

There was a considerable amount of British artillery firepower used in preparation for the attack; the final ratio of guns to objectives being greater than that on the first day of the Somme. The barrage began on 14 July, though the poor weather meant that accurate registration of fire was difficult and the situation was not helped by inexperienced artillerymen.

A delay to the attack occurred and Bean and Edmonds, both official historians of this battle, wrote that Monro had decided not only to postpone the operation, but to cancel it. In fact, Monro telegrammed Haig saying that he no longer wanted the attack to take place. However, again Haig encouraged the action, though he gave Monro the final decision:[83]

> The Commander-in-Chief wishes the special operation mentioned to be carried out as soon as possible, weather permitting, provided always that General Sir Charles Monro is satisfied that the conditions are favourable, and that the resources at his disposal, including ammunition, are adequate both for the preparation and execution of the enterprise.[84]

Monro had to obey this order and Barton describes this response by Haig as 'an insurance policy against future blame'.[85] There were a few hours' delay to zero hour because of bad weather which hampered accurate friendly artillery fire and air reconnaissance, but the attack went ahead.

With 5th Australian Division left and 61st (2nd South Midland) Division right, most battalions left their trenches from 1730 hours onwards on 19 July, in the light and on flat ground interspersed by awkward water features, and observed by the enemy from Aubers Ridge. As the friendly barrage lifted at 1800 hours, the German artillery and machine guns had easy targets to engage. Friendly fire landed on the Allied troops, the German positions had not been neutralised, the wire had not been cut, communications were poor and unable to react to changing circumstances and there was little knowledge of the enemy positions.

Casualties were heavy and one battalion of the Royal Warwickshire Regiment lost all of its officers. Within the hour it was clear that the 61st (2nd South Midland) Division's attack had failed and not reached its objectives, whilst on their left, the 5th Australian Division had fared slightly better. Further confusion ensued because the boundary between the two divisions cut through the 'Sugarloaf' raised feature and there was inconsistent reporting about progress being made. There were also extremely effective German counter-attacks, which is not surprising; the Allies did not want surprise for this attack, and beforehand the Germans had captured details of two operation orders and the artillery plan. A second Allied attack was planned for 2100 hours, but this was cancelled and units were withdrawn the following morning. The War Diary recorded, 'Under the circumstances, the Corps Commander does not think it feasible to renew the attack with these two divisions, though both are capable of continuing to hold the ground.'[86]

Overall, 7,000 casualties, mainly Australian, had been sustained across both divisions for no tactical gain, though it has been argued that the strategic objective of the attack, that of delaying German reinforcement to the Somme area from the north, had been achieved. This is reflected by Haig's diary comments immediately after the battle, '... the enterprise has certainly had the effect of obliging the enemy to retain reserves in that area'.[87] It is doubtful, however, that this was worth the huge sacrifice of life and the British Official History recorded that 'to have delivered battle at all betrayed a great under-estimate of the enemy's power of resistance'.[88] Even fellow 1st Army corps commander, Henry Wilson, called it 'a botch job'.[89] An enemy, Bavarian report was blunt in its assessment:

> Considering all these preparations and this concentration of forces, the attack ended in dismal failure ... On the evidence of its conduct of the action at Fromelles, the British command will never be capable of achieving a major breakthrough ... the British Army of today is a defensive army. It may succeed in denying victory to its adversary, but it can never be victorious itself.[90]

The *North German Gazette* of 3 August 1916 reported that the Allies' 'whole attitude showed they had over-estimated the effect of their heavy bombardment'.[91] Fromelles continued to be considered a great victory for the Bavarians, even after the war.

The debate continues on who or what was to blame for the failure. Edmonds comments, 'The pity of it was that the action need not have been fought, since the 1st Army had perfect liberty to cancel it,' but does not apportion blame.[92] 'Butcher Haking' is often identified as the main culprit and that verdict is not helped by his later comments that 5th Australian Division was not 'properly trained' and the 61st (2nd South Midland) Division 'lacked the offensive spirit', despite their undoubted bravery and sacrifice. However, evidence shows that Haking did appreciate the risks involved in the attack and understood the bigger picture, aggressive action being required to keep 'the Germans constantly alert, anxious and in considerable strength on their front lines. It prevents them from withdrawing troops for offensive or defensive purposes to some other parts of the line.'[93]

It was Monro who had the final decision on 18 July, encouraged from above by Haig and below from the overconfident Haking. Was this a 'lack of moral courage' or an inevitable decision considering the factors at the time?

Senior analyses the situation extremely well in his modern book on Haking and points out that the strategic plan, which was beyond Haking's control, kept changing and Monro was obviously 'lukewarm' about the attack. He was certainly indecisive – a characteristic which was not displayed elsewhere in his life.[94]

Brigadier General (Retired) H. E. 'Pompey' Elliott, who had commanded 15th Australian Brigade in the battle, gave a controversial talk fourteen years later and stated that Haking sheltered 'behind the weakness displayed by Monro, by Butler and even by Haig himself at this critical juncture', when Monro could have called off the attack.[95] Elliott has been a main source of reference for many accounts of the battle, yet Lee, after his extensive research on Fromelles, comments:

> Elliott, while a participant, was not an objective commentator on the battle … He was too far down the command chain to understand the full picture and the way the plan meshed together; he had insufficient time to famil-iarise himself with the battle.[96]

Inevitably, there is no one commander at fault. Each one in the chain of com-mand had a part to play in the poor planning and muddle – Haig, who was concentrating on the Somme and was not providing clear direction, Monro for his indecisiveness in this case and Haking's over optimism and enthusiasm to take the fight to the enemy.

Monro was partly to blame, despite the comment by his chief of staff, 'More than once he interfered in order to restrain the impetuosity of a sub-ordinate commander.'[97] The Official Histories place the emphasis of blame on Haking. This was due to the scale of and focus on the Somme battles and it has to be remembered that, from an Australian point of view, Monro was popular because he had the applauded record of reversing the more public, disastrous decisions at Gallipoli.

In the case of Fromelles, it is hard not to agree with Bourne's assess-ment that 'Monro simply abandoned his responsibilities … and his men paid the price'.[98] Monro had had two clear opportunities to cancel the attack. Interestingly, Barrow's perspective of Monro as 1st Army commander does not reflect this Fromelles analysis, though he does identify one weakness:

> General Monro was not an adventurous leader in the field, but he was a res-olute commander. When he saw clearly that the enemy should be attacked he would attack to the utmost limit of his strength. When he stood on the defensive he was prepared to hold ground with the utmost tenacity.[99]

Despite Fromelles, the relationship between army and corps commander was good; Haking respected Monro's authority and Monro recommended him as his successor in August 1916, though Haking only had temporary command for a few weeks before Horne took over the 1st Army.

Yet it was not just command decisions that were at fault at Fromelles. Indeed, Lee's detailed analysis concludes that, although there were planning mistakes, 'the principal cause of failure of the attack was the failure of the combat troops implementing the plan'.[100] The troops involved, including their unit and sub-unit commanders, were confused about the attack, they only had limited training and were inexperienced. They were not just, as the Australian myth suggests, a 'victim of incompetent British Generalship'.[101] Lee's battle-planning analysis concludes that the battle was operationally successful, achieving some of its objectives and effectively supporting the wider context of the Somme battles.

Nevertheless, the combination of losing ground at the Kink and Vimy Ridge and failing to succeed at Fromelles cannot have done Monro any good. Although they were not very significant actions on the Western Front, as a whole he had not been given the opportunities to demonstrate his full potential in command of the 1st Army. On 1 August 1916 he was summoned to Sir Douglas Haig, who told him that he was to become C-in-C India. Haig wrote in his diary, 'He did not at all want to go to India.'[102]

This was a severe personal blow. Monro had been one of the first four divisional commanders in France in 1914 and one of the few generals who had commanded at the corps and army levels on the Western Front. He did not want to leave France, the decisive theatre of the war, and said to his biographer and chief of staff, 'I was brought up never to question the decisions of my superiors and never to refuse any appointment offered me however much I dislike it.'[103] Barrow described Monro's posting from the 1st Army as 'a grievous loss … He was the soldier's friend and knew it.' He loyally described his commander as 'the emblem of strength, durability and steadfastness'.

However, Charles Monro was to excel in the Indian appointment for the next four years; he set sail in September 1916.

10

INDIA

It is a great comfort to me to have you in India.[1]

General Sir Charles Monro was no stranger to India, though the last time he had served there was as a major in 1898, following the Malakand and Tirah expeditions. Much had changed in the intervening years, as the voice of Indian nationalism began to be heard. These political changes were to continue during his four years as C-in-C and defence member of the Viceroy's Council.

He now held the highest military post in the most important jewel in the Empire's crown at a time when Indian troops had an important role in the war effort and had been deployed mainly to Mesopotamia and the Western Front. At the beginning of the war, the army in India stood at 236,000 men, of whom 77,000 were British troops. Many were earmarked for internal security duties, whilst the rest were organised into nine infantry and eight cavalry divisions. However, this large army, which had been reorganised by Kitchener at the turn of the nineteenth and twentieth century, was more suited to the North-West Frontier environment than any other; logistic and artillery support were very limited compared to European armies.

This weakness led to some crises, particularly in Mesopotamia. However, within three weeks of the war's declaration, 16,000 British troops and 28,500 Indians were on their way to France and by the end of India's experience of the war in Europe, Africa and the Middle East, its army had earned sixteen Victoria Crosses and ninety-nine Military Crosses, though at a cost of 36,000 soldiers killed and 70,000 wounded; the country had provided a very significant contribution to the war effort. Most British Army Regular troops were replaced in India by battalions of the British Territorial Force.

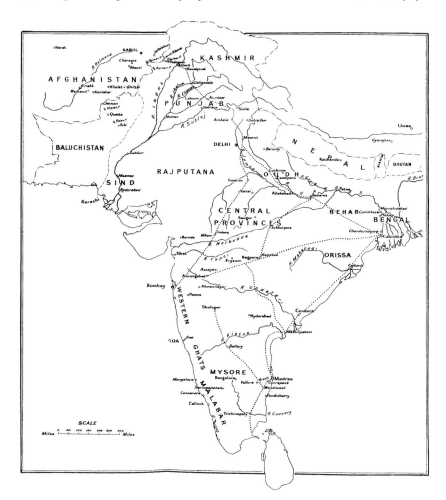

India. (Author's collection)

Initially, there was no recruiting or training organisation for reinforcements, so generating a larger and more efficient flow of recruits was a critical
task at which Monro was to excel at during the remaining two years of war.
He may initially have been a reluctant C-in-C, but he threw himself into his
new role with characteristic professionalism and sense of duty, despite a note
to a relative in August 1916:

> It has been rather a scramble trying to get things together for the shiny
> in a short time, especially as I cannot get into a stitch of kit which I wore
> before the War, not a garment will go round me. It is horrible, as you can
> understand I hate the prospect of going to India most heartily … Still, it
> cannot be helped as soldiers have to go where they are told.[2]

He expressed similar sentiment to *The Times* correspondent, Colonel Repington, just prior to his deployment, adding, 'there is no question at all of making any serious change in the administration of the Army in India'.[3] Repington reported that Monro did not seem to have been given any strategic direction and that he had 'a tough job in front of him'.[4]

As C-in-C he was to work very closely with the Viceroy of India, who had only arrived in the country seven months earlier. At 48, Frederic John Napier Thesiger, 1st Viscount Chelmsford, was eight years younger than the general. A qualified lawyer and volunteer infantry captain, he had spent from 1905 to 1913 as governor of Queensland, then New South Wales, in Australia. Like Monro, he was very much a product of the Victorian Establishment, coming from a well-known family and educated at Winchester College and Magdalen College, Oxford. His wife, Frances, was also an aristocrat from the Spencer-Churchill family.

He was the viceroy for all of Monro's time in India, departing in 1921, and is most well known for jointly instigating the Montagu-Chelmsford or 'Mont-Ford' reforms and overseeing India's first elections in 1920, though he has been described, rather unfairly, as 'little more than a nonentity'.[5] To some observers, he appeared more like a headmaster than a viceroy, 'an able man of fine presence, he was rather aloof and, though sympathetic to the aspirations of Indians, lacked the warmth of personality that appeals to them'.[6] Though he was honest, conscientious, hard-working and kind, he lacked a charismatic personality and imagination. His wife was described as dull, but she was the dominating partner.

Despite this, Chelmsford has to be credited for some reform and he gave Monro his support. Certainly, they worked together well, as observed by Ralph Verney, one of the viceroy's key staff officers, in 1918, 'I think it would be a great blow to His Excellency if the Commander-in-Chief were taken away now from India, they both get on so well together and know each other so well now.'[7]

Meanwhile, Monro's priority as he arrived in post was Mesopotamia.

Mesopotamia

Mesopotamia, now Iraq but then part of the Ottoman Empire, was within India's sphere of influence and in November 1914, the Abadan oil pipeline and nearby oilfields had been seized from the Turks by parts of India Expeditionary Force D. By the end of 1915, the Mesopotamia Expeditionary Force (MEF) had grown from one division to over 50,000 troops. After significant early successes in battles along the rivers Tigris and Euphrates, Major General Charles Townshend's 6th Division had overstretched itself, underestimated the enemy and been surrounded at Kut. Despite a series of relief attempts, the Kut garrison surrendered on 29 April 1916.[8] This was, arguably, the British Army's worse defeat since Cornwallis' surrender during the American Revolutionary War and, following the findings of the Mesopotamia Commission, it led to the resignation of the Secretary of State for India, Austen Chamberlain, in 1917.

In the meantime, command and control arrangements were changed to make Charles Monro report to the CIGS, Sir William Robertson, on Mesopotamia matters and responsible direct to the Army Council in London, rather than the Government of India, for the provision of supplies and personnel to the theatre. Following the sacking of previous Kut relief force commanders, the extremely competent General Sir Stanley Maude was now the commander in the field.[9] Whilst the CIGS preferred Maude's MEF to hold ground because of the post-Kut fragile nature of the campaign and the weak line of communications, Maude was suggesting that once his force was strong enough it should advance on Baghdad. He strongly believed that the MEF was preventing the Turks from reinforcing the Persian front. As in the Gallipoli situation, General Monro's opinion was sought, based on a personal visit.

It was made clear to both generals, from London, that the mission of the MEF was 'to protect the oil-fields and pipe-lines' and that 'no fresh advance to Baghdad can at present be contemplated' until lines of communications were significantly improved. In addition, it was stated that the seizure of Baghdad would not have any 'decisive effect on the War'.[10] Monro, accompanied by two key staff officers from Army Headquarters India, Brigadier General A. Skeen and Major General C. Richardson, arrived in Basra on 10 October 1916. He commented on what he saw:

> A glimpse of Basra gave one 'furiously to think'. It brought before one's eyes the appalling difficulties which the troops who went there first had to face – a road-less country, no water except by the river, no stone, no timber, no labour except the Arab nomads, terrific heat, very little transport and so forth.[11]

He spent the next ten days there. His visit was welcomed by Maude and it encouraged his army:

> His Excellency made an extended tour of the theatre of operations, and his advice and comments on various matters were of the greatest value

to myself personally, whilst the army hailed his visit with the liveliest satisfaction, feeling that he would assume his office with first-hand and sympathetic knowledge of our needs and difficulties.[12]

Maude's biographer wrote that Monro's visit 'served to assure them that the Mesopotamian Field Force was no longer a Cinderella, apparently looked upon with comparative indifference by Government Departments in Simla and Whitehall'.[13]

Monro travelled with Maude up the River Tigris, visiting and inspecting elements of the force, including the 13th Division, though his old Gallipoli injury meant that he was not too agile. Maude commented, 'What impressed him more than anything, I think, was the magnitude of the undertaking: In fact he said to me that this would be reckoned in history as about the biggest expedition of its kind that England had ever sent out.'[14]

Monro reported back to the CIGS on 19 and 26 October and his opinion was similar to Maude's. He stated that Maude's army was greatly improved and that there was no need for it to withdraw; it was providing a credible threat to the Turks. He wrote that General Maude had tight control of the situation, he was competent, his force was well administered and the logistic support was being steadily enhanced. He added that future aggressive action was feasible, writing, 'An entirely passive attitude would in my judgement

General Maude. (Author's collection)

be unprofitable and bad for the troops.'[15] Concurrently, Maude lobbied the CIGS for his support to advance.

The CIGS concurred with Monro's assessment, which allowed Maude freedom of action. Eventually, this would lead to the successful advance up the River Tigris and the capture of Baghdad the following year. Maude wrote:

> So we all set to work zealously, and by the time I left for the front after Sir Charles Monro's visit I felt that the foundations were secure and it was only a question then of building up our reserves of supplies before it would be safe to move. I was very glad when Sir Charles Monro came for it enabled him to see a good deal and it has been most helpful to our relations with India ever since.[16]

Monro again supported Maude's aspirations to capture Baghdad, without waiting for Russian success against the Turks, when he wrote to the CIGS in March 1917. 'This he argued, would politically enhance British prestige in the East, thus reducing anxiety as to the situation in Afghanistan or Persia, whilst simultaneously depriving the Turks of a concentration point from which to threaten Persia.'[17]

A great deal of prestige had to be recovered after the disastrous experiences of both Kut and Gallipoli. Once again, Monro had provided sound critical military strategic guidance to an important operation. His main role in Mesopotamia was to supply the required levels of personnel and materiel.

Other Theatres of Operations

Charles Monro was also responsible for other theatres of operations, now largely forgotten in the big picture of the First World War. Though less critical to the war effort, they were still important missions. The Turks were held back at Aden, whilst the Persian Government was supported in the south by a small Indian Army force, working with the Russians and commanded by Brigadier General Sir Percy Sykes. Concurrently, in south-east Persia a fellow Queen's (Royal West Surrey) Regiment officer, Brigadier General Reginald Dyer, was making his name defeating aggressive tribes in the region of the Persian–Balluchi border; he later wrote a book entitled *The Raiders of The Sarhad*, but he was to become infamous in 1919 for the Amritsar Massacre.[18]

There were other minor operations on the Indian borders at Mekran, against the Jhalawan tribes and also the Mohmands on the North-West

THE MESPOT DINNER.

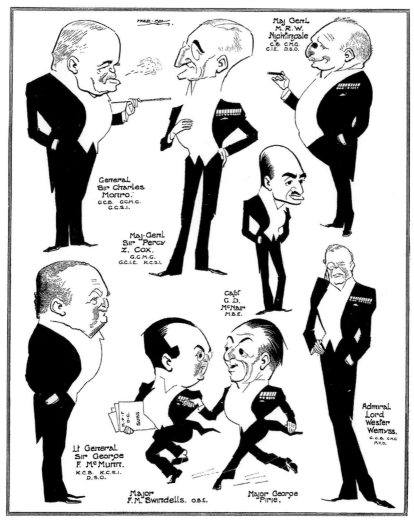

SOME OF THE MESPOT AND PERSIAN FORCES—BY FRED MAY

Caricature of General Sir Charles Monro. (*The Tatler*, August 1920)

Frontier. India's military efforts during the war were summarised by Monro in his despatch of 26 November 1918, which acknowledges the Indian effort:

> This despatch would not be complete without a special acknowledgement of the spontaneous and generous assistance afforded by Ruling Princes and Chiefs, as well as by the British and Indian communities throughout India, in the contribution of men, money and material towards the prosecution of the War.[19]

Indianisation

Monro's predecessor as C-in-C had been General Sir Beauchamp Duff, who had served in India for many years and was known as a sound staff officer and administrator, though not a dynamic leader. Unfortunately, his future was also affected by the Kut disaster and the subsequent Mesopotamia Commission Report. Indeed, his suicide in 1918 has been attributed to his sense of guilt.

The change in style of command was quickly illustrated. Monro, with his regimental duty background and operational experience on the Western Front, was not impressed with the fact that his predecessor's staff were still wearing peacetime uniform. Thus, en route to army headquarters at Simla, Monro gave them three days' warning to dress in service dress. Apparently, this caused chaos as officers raided tailors to try and find the right uniform in time!

Monro explained his priorities in India to Robertson in December 1916, as he wanted to improve efficiencies in a number of areas. This included the creation of inspection and training teams in the Indian Army and improvements to rationing, clothing and recruiting. He wanted to increase the number of troops available for operations, but urgently requested more rifles and machine guns from England. He also wanted to improve the higher control of the Indian Army, 'I hope by the constitution of an Army Council out here to accelerate business, but to do that we must have more senior officers as Adjutant-General and Quartermaster-General.'[20]

His next issue was the granting of the King's Commission to Indians. Since the Mutiny in 1857, all officers serving in the Indian Army had been British. Viceroy-commissioned officers (VCOs) did exist; they were Indians promoted through the ranks who acted as communicators between British officers and Indian other ranks, but they had little authority and were more junior than even a British second lieutenant. However, nationalists were demanding more recognition for educated Indians in the army, a process named 'Indianisation'.

Eventually, ten places were allotted to Indians at the Royal Military College, Sandhurst, provided they could afford it and pass the exams, whilst in due course in 1918, a military college was set up at Daly College, Indore. These two measures have been described as 'token gestures', though to many Europeans at the time the decisions appeared radical.[21] Indore was closed after a year and commissions were not available to the artillery, air force and technical corps. Nevertheless, the future first President of Pakistan passed out of Sandhurst and the first Indian C-in-C attended Indore.

Any change was a challenge, particularly if one reflects on the following incredulous note sent to the Secretary of State for India by the commander of the Indian Corps in France, General Sir James Willcox, earlier in the war:

The Indian is simply not fit to lead his men against Europeans ... It is the presence and natural instincts of the white man which the Indian officer can never replace ... The Indian has not the instincts which make leaders in modern war.[22]

However, the changing political environment was having an effect. The new Secretary of State for India, Edwin Montagu, described as a 'radical liberal', announced on 20 August 1917:[23]

The policy of His Majesty's government, with which the Government of India are in complete accord, is that of the increasing association of Indians in every branch of the administration, and the gradual development of self-governing institutions, with a view to the progressive realisation of responsible government in India as an integral part of the British Empire.[24]

Monro had already attempted to get Indian officers into service clubs against great European opposition, though he was described by Montagu as being interested in Indianisation but not enthusiastic, describing the demand for commissions as 'political'.[25]

Montagu needed the support of the military to execute his reforms, but Monro was not a great fan, as he said, 'When I am with Mr Montagu I feel that I am walking with a man who is steadily edging me towards a precipice and when he gets me near enough will push me over.'[26] Montagu was said to want an Indian 'Sandhurst' available to any qualified Indian, but Monro 'insisted that preference should be given to the sons of servicemen', thus limiting entrance qualification.[27]

These comments by Montagu about Monro's attitude are not entirely fair. Monro mentions his attitude to King's Commissions in two letters to Robertson in 1917. His comments are very clear and forward-looking, 'if we maintain too conservative an attitude towards well born Indians we shall ultimately drive them all into the opposition camp' and 'to avoid turning aristocracy into the camp of the malcontent' they must attend Sandhurst not an Indian college.[28]

Montagu was not an easy person to befriend, as illustrated in his obituary in *The Times* in 1924:

In his lovable and complicated character great subtlety of intellect was curiously mingled with great simplicity of mind. He had the trustfulness of a child. It was often betrayed and he suffered agonies of disappointment and surprise, but his confidence always returned, ready for the next encounter ... He never got tired of being sorry for people ...[29]

The Viceroy Chelmsford's relationship with Montagu was also fragile, as explained in a letter by Nita Verney, the wife of one of his close staff, in 1917:

> Montagu, our new Secretary of State, is, or was, an ultra radical and the Viceroy and his Council are rather in a state of nerves in case he pushes the new reforms too quickly after the splendid work of India in this War; they have got to come but must be set about gradually.[30]

However, whilst Monro may have been wary about Montagu's reforms, he did believe that the massive loyal Indian effort in the war and Indian advancement should be recognised and had discussed the commissioning issue with the Secretary of State for India, Austen Chamberlain, before he left England. The viceroy and Monro were in agreement for the way ahead and the king-emperor appointed the first nine Indian officers to British commissions on 5 August 1917.

However, because of the age of the first new Indian British officers, who were already VCOs, they were not practically able to compete with their British equivalents. It was still a great honour, though, and was an important step towards Indianisation, driven through by Monro. He had had to adopt a cautious approach, as explained by a 1917 despatch:

> Our object in formulating these proposals has been to place Indians of the fighting classes on a footing of equality with other subjects … Some may regard these proposals as conceding too much, others as not going far enough. The Commander-in-Chief is of the opinion, however, that they mark the extreme limit to which we can with safety proceed. In this opinion we entirely concur.[31]

It was still a token gesture, however. Between 1919 and 1921 only fourteen Indian gentlemen cadets were commissioned through the Royal Military College.[32] Monro's successor, Lord Rawlinson, would take Indianisation forward.

Recruiting

Monro's greatest contribution as C-in-C in India was probably to boost recruiting for the First World War effort. Promises were made to the population in order to improve recruitment during the war, including the commissioning opportunities already mentioned, whilst new classes of citizens were allowed to become soldiers for the first time with the support of government.

All this effort, begun before his arrival but energised by Monro, resulted in an incredibly successful tripling of the Indian Army from 155,000 men to 573,000 between 1914 and 1918. Punjabi Muslims, Sikhs, Rajputs, Gurkhas and Jats provided most of the troops traditionally, with smaller, but still significant, numbers of Dogras, Pathans, Hindustani Muslims and Ahirs, but 'seventy-five "new classes" were "tried" during the course of the war'.[33]

Instead of regiments being formed of set groups of classes, the new Territorial system meant that a unit was formed from mixed classes from a particular area. Less or new recruited groups included the Gujars and Gaur Brahmins from the south-east of the Punjab and Kachins and Chins of Burma. The latter resulted in a success story, '70th Burma Rifles coming into existence in September 1917 and being increased in less than a year to a regiment of four battalions'.[34] As Menezes has written, 'The myth of the martial races was exploded during the First World War.'[35]

The war effort needed more troops as soon as possible. Early in 1916, 28,000 men had been raised as a labour corps to serve on the Western Front, but even more were needed to substitute for high casualties around the world and in supporting roles. Incentives helped recruitment; by the end of 1916, Indian sepoys received free rations when not on operations for the first time, and pay and conditions were improved – practical improvements encouraged by the practical Monro. In addition, a Central Recruiting Board was established with local regional boards and second battalions of existing units were used as the basis for expansion. There was pressure from London; Robertson was grateful for the extra troops and units and wrote to Monro, 'India must contribute a great deal more than she has hitherto done. Meanwhile, I am sure you will peg away and get on with things.'[36] In another letter, he wrote, 'We want all the men we can get whatever their colour may be.'[37]

In July 1917, twenty-one new battalions began to be created and by the end of the year, '63,000 Punjabi Mussalmans were recruited out of a fit male population of 145,000, and 43,000 out of 112,000 Sikhs'.[38] This meant that two divisions could be sent to reinforce Mesopotamia, two divisions could be redeployed to Palestine and the Indian contribution to Egypt could be increased.

Also in 1917, the Indian Defence Act made all British European subjects between the ages of 16 and 18 join a cadet corps, whilst 18–41-year-olds were liable for military service in India. Those between 41 and 50 were obliged to join a Reserve. The *Evening Post* recorded, 'The Viceroy (Lord Chelmsford) reported to the necessity for concerted effort in assisting the

Empire to finish the war. General Sir Charles Monro (C-in-C) pointed out that it was intended that the new forces should relieve the regulars on garrison duty.'[39]

Barrow aptly describes Monro's achievements at this time:

> From the year 1917 onwards Sir Charles Monro, with the unfailing sup-
> port of the Viceroy (Lord Chelmsford) and the Government of India,
> was the chief inspirer and organiser of one of the most remarkable
> expansions in man-power and munitions outside Great Britain and the
> Dominions which have ever been known under a voluntary system
> of service.[40]

There is no doubt that he also had a great eye for detail, as illustrated by his 'Jobs to do' notebooks, now preserved in the National Army Museum.[41] A great deal of effort went into recruitment from the Punjab in 1916–18, driven by its lieutenant governor, Sir Michael O'Dwyer. He threatened conscription if there were not enough volunteers, telling the locals that it was their duty to join up; Great Britain's war was their war. Land and pensions were used as a reward for service and O'Dwyer played classes off against each other and used the commissioning incentive to encourage more recruits, '… the number to be granted will naturally depend in a great measure on the response to the call for recruits'.[42]

A total of 300,000 Indian recruits were enlisted in 1918, allowing reinforcement on various fronts and the opportunity to send more British troops to the Western Front. This was an amazing administrative achievement. The recruitment effort by Monro during the war was recognised by the CIGS, Field Marshal Sir William Robertson:

> The question of raising more native battalions was first taken up in 1916,
> when Sir Charles Monro became Commander-in-Chief, and, thanks to
> his cooperation and administrative ability, about one hundred and fifty
> battalions as well as other units were added to the Indian Army, being
> sent to Palestine or Mesopotamia as soon as ready. Indirectly, therefore,
> he had a notable share in the success of the Palestine campaign of 1918, in
> September of that year. The offensive was carried out against Damascus
> and Aleppo, and nearly four-fifths of the infantry belonged to these same
> Indian battalions, the bulk of the British infantry having before that time
> been hurried off post-haste to the West Front.[43]

He had also established a munitions board under Sir Thomas Holland, which had created further efficiencies in the Indian war effort.

The 'Snowdon' residence of the C–in–C, Simla. (Author's collection)

General Sir Charles Carmichael Monro received many accolades in 1919. In January, he was awarded the Knight Grand Cross of the Most Honourable Order of the Bath (the GCB), and this was followed by the Emperor of Japan's Order of the Rising Sun, Grand Cordon, in May and then the award of the Knight Grand Commander of the Star of India (GCSI). He also received a special mention in Field Marshal Haig's final despatch of the First World War – the first general to be mentioned after the final five army commanders of the Western Front.[44]

Ever the practical general, he also created a new institution in India for travelling troops – the 'Monro Soldiers' Canteen', originally established in Delhi. These were popular and cheap food army 'outlets' based at the main railway stations in India and operated by European ladies.

He had many challenges, partly due to the low quality of some of the officer class in India. Even at the end of 1917 he was complaining to Robertson, 'Some of the generals out here are not of much practical value … similarly our Royal Artillery brigadiers are old and antiquated in their principles of training.'[45] He was a hard taskmaster. Monro was working hard to achieve the efficiencies he had promised Robertson; at one stage he wrote, 'the night arrives long before the work in hand has been completed'.[46]

Political Background

All this success had been helped by a generally supportive political climate. Not only were the princely states on side, but also Jinnah, the Muslim League and the Indian National Congress were sympathetic to the war effort. Even Mahatma Gandhi, who still believed in British justice at this stage, had volunteered for medical service and encouraged recruitment, despite his record of protest through *satyagraha* (or 'truth force/firmness') becoming more widely known, incorrectly, as passive resistance. This Indian support to the war effort was admired by many, including the author John Buchan, who wrote, 'It was the performance of India which took the world by surprise and thrilled every British heart.'[47]

The Indian politicians realised the importance of the Indian contribution and the political control and social concessions that could be gained. However, not every political party was supportive, including the Ghadr (Revolutionary or Mutiny) Party. Based in San Francisco, it attempted to forge 'an armed revolution to end British rule in India with arms and explosives from abroad'.[48] Germany had hoped to stir anti-British imperialism and encouraged revolt in India, partly through the use of agents in Afghanistan, trying to portray the kaiser as a great supporter of the Muslim faith and the Ottoman Empire, and there were many Indians who had doubts about fighting the Turks for religious reasons.[49] In addition, care had to be taken with Hindus to ensure they had the appropriate religious procedures in place to avoid losing castes by 'crossing the black water'.[50]

Fortunately for the British, India as a whole remained loyal and was to provide significant military and financial support to the war effort. However, there were instances of Indian Army mutiny, which had to be dealt with. At Gallipoli in 1915, the commander of the 29th Indian Brigade did not trust his two battalions of Punjabi Muslims, so used them for logistic and communication support, rather than in the front line.

More critically, there was a mutiny in Singapore in 1915. There, the Muslim 5th Indian Light Infantry was about to move to Hong Kong when half of the unit mutinied and a number of officers, soldiers and Malays were murdered. It was rumoured that they would have to fight fellow Muslim Turks in Mesopotamia. Eventually, the mutiny was quashed and forty-seven mutineers were executed. The incident was kept quiet and the report was not published until the 1960s. Poor leadership was identified as the fault, though the troops had been subjected to anti-British preaching and the influence of Ghadrites, who had attempted to stir Indian rebellion in some of the colonies and in India. By the end of 1916, most of the Ghadrites, many of whom were Sikhs, were in custody and in the Punjab, forty-six were hanged and 200 jailed or deported.

Also, by that time, violence in Bengal had been controlled by new legislation and a competent new governor. Meanwhile, there was other anti-British political activity as Mrs Annie Besant and Bal Tilak founded separate Home Rule leagues, which generated over 30,000 supporters in each of their organisations within two years. However, there was no general popular support to these activities, though British prestige was badly affected by the Kut disaster, the failed Dardanelles expedition and casualties and lack of success on the Western Front. One particularly important achievement by nationalists from both the Indian National Congress and Muslim League at this time was to agree on proposals for constitutional changes within the Lucknow Pact, presenting an Indian political unified front.

There was careful management of the troops, replacing potentially disloyal units with loyal and dependable ones, whilst maintaining the British 'backbone'. Hence the need to retain British troops in India and to ensure they were part of every brigade. Monro had to keep in mind this careful mix of Indian class, religion and British influence as he improved the recruiting situation.

Probably the most significant political development in this period were the Mont-Ford Reforms, named after Edwin Montagu, the new Liberal Secretary of State for India from July 1917, and Lord Chelmsford, the viceroy. Montagu was a volatile and excitable character compared with Chelmsford's patient steadiness and Barnett has written unkindly that 'the stoical Chelmsford had little to do with them'.[51] A move towards political reform was indicated in 1915 and 1916, to encourage Indian support for the war. Their proposals were 'the most momentous utterance ever made in India's chequered history', according to Montagu's 1918 *Report on Indian Constitutional Reforms.*[52]

Chelmsford wanted to give India 'the largest measure of self-government compatible with the maintenance of the supreme authority of British rule'.[53] After consultation throughout India during 1918 by both personalities, the reforms were announced a year later, the Government of India Act became law in 1919 and changes enacted in 1921. The viceroy stated, 'The motto I would ask you to place before yourselves is *festina lente* [hastening slowly].'[54] This involved devolving central authority and introducing dyarchy to provincial governments within eight provinces. Some Indian ministers were created within a more democratic provincial structure, whilst other departments, such as law and order, were unchanged and worked direct to governors. Therefore, governors were partly autocratic, but partly responsible to a newly elected group, though they did not have to take ministers' advice. Dyarchy did not feature in central government, though three members of the Executive Council, which included Monro, were to be Indians. In addition, a Chamber of Princes was formed and the central legislature was made more democratic.

Montagu commented, 'The main principle is that instead of founding the Indian Government on the confidence of the people of England, we are gradually to found it on the confidence of the people of India.'[55]

Unfortunately, in 1919 the earlier measures were seen as too little too late by the nationalists – 'disappointing and unsatisfactory' – despite the first opportunity of limited responsible self-government. The Indian National Council generally supported the Mont-Ford Reforms, but demanded full responsible government within fifteen years. Matters were not helped, in their view, by the extension of repressive wartime emergency powers, known as the Rowlatt Acts, as the authorities feared the potential of a second Indian mutiny. There were also concurrent economic challenges with price rises and food and cloth shortages creating further dissatisfaction within the population. Meanwhile, the British were increasingly seen as superior and unwilling to offer further concessions to the Indian. The Amritsar District Magistrate summed the situation up:

> The soil is prepared for discontent by a number of causes. The poor are hit by high prices, the rich by a severe income tax assessment and the Excess Profits Act. Mohammedans are irritated by the fate of Turkey. From one cause or another the people are restless and ripe for the revolutionist.[56]

Gandhi began his rise to great influence in 1919 and launched a new campaign of national *satyagraha*, or non-co-operation, in February. *Hartals* (strikes) were called and that encouraged three weeks of riots in Delhi. More clashes between crowds and security forces came after a day of *hartals* across India on 6 April 1919, 'Black Sunday'. Gandhi was arrested, providing a catalyst for further violence in Bombay, Ahmedabad and Viramgam. However, these sporadic demonstrations were to be overshadowed by the Amritsar disaster in the Punjab.

Massacre at Amritsar

Amritsar served as a turning point for uniting the independence movements in India. The massacre of nearly 400 protesters and the wounding of at least 1,200 more in the Jallianwala Bagh (garden) by Brigadier General Reginald 'Rex' Dyer on Sunday 13 April 1919 was a pivotal event, which succeeded in turning most of the previously moderate Indians against the British Empire and its rule.[57] Without any warning, 1,650 rounds of .303 ammunition were fired at point-blank range at over 5,000 unarmed civilians.

It is still a controversial event. In 1997, the queen visited the site and expressed her regret and sadness and in 2013, the British prime minister also visited and wrote in the condolence book, 'This was a deeply shameful event in British history, one that Winston Churchill rightly described at the time as "monstrous".'[58] However, many Indians are unhappy that a formal apology has still not been made. This book will not attempt to retell the story, as there are many books that provide such detail; the interest here, is General Monro's role in the aftermath.

Reginald Dyer had been commissioned into the 1st Battalion of Monro's own regiment, the Queen's (Royal West Surrey) Regiment, in August 1885, six years after Monro was commissioned into the same unit, as a deliberate stepping stone to later service in the Indian Army. He had no personal connections with Surrey, but the regiment had a high reputation and joining was an excellent choice. As Collett has written, 'The fact that Dyer was accepted by them showed that he had passed out well from Sandhurst and that he was reckoned as a man of some promise.'[59]

He joined the Queen's in Ireland, when Monro was the adjutant, so they would have known each other relatively well. Monro would have monitored his progress as the 'junior subaltern' on behalf of the commanding officer, whilst Dyer reputedly used his sporting prowess to instruct Monro how to box. He was also caught up in the battalion's deployment to quell rioting in Belfast in 1886, as mentioned in Chapter 1. As in 1969, the troops were protecting the Roman Catholic population against Protestant Loyalist hardliners, in this case stirred up by Gladstone's first Home Rule Bill. This included the requirement for Dyer to deal with rioters whilst under pressure, though not in the same manner as he did in 1919.

Later in 1886, Dyer was transferred to the 2nd Battalion, based in Calcutta, India, but in the process of being sent on an operational tour in the Third Burma War. Burma had been occupied quickly by British forces and then run with brutal efficiency. Unfortunately, the ensuing insurgency was difficult to control so British forces were reinforced from India. This included Dyer's new battalion, which manned company and platoon outposts along a river. This was a hard-fought counter-insurgency little known today and British methods were tough compared with the modern softer approach, as illustrated by some of the commander's guidance – 'Resistance overcome without inflicting punishment on the enemy only emboldens him to repeat the game, and thus, by protracting operations, costs more lives than a sharp lesson boldly administered.'[60]

Perhaps it is hardly surprising that Dyer behaved the way he did in the Jallianwala Bagh. However, he earned a good reputation in Burma; he had been a brave, fit, hard-working and competent platoon commander, though he was also known for a fiery temper and was considered to be of middling ability. He transferred to the Indian Army in 1887 and by 1919 had gained a great deal of operational experience on the North-West Frontier and was then commanding 54th Brigade at Jullundur.

Initially, there was a mixed reaction to what Dyer had done, with some Europeans in India saying that he was the 'saviour of the Punjab'. Rudyard Kipling wrote that he was the man that saved India, and set up a fund for Dyer that raised £26,000, whilst O'Dwyer stated, 'I have no hesitation in saying that General Dyer's action that day was the decisive factor in crushing the rebellion, the seriousness of which is only now being realised.'[61]

Others had different views. The incident united opposition to British rule within India, and eventually many European countries and the United States of America condemned his action. Chelmsford believed that Dyer had been too efficient, but Dyer was admired by the Indian European community. Montagu was more uncomfortable with what Dyer had done and as debate on the issue continued, Chelmsford and his council became increasingly fed up of Montagu's 'interference'. Indians wanted revenge, and debates in both Houses of Parliament criticised his actions and led to the setting up of the Hunter Commission to investigate the incident. This would arrive in Delhi in October 1919, but not before another war had been fought, involving Dyer and his brigade – the Third Afghan War.

The Third Afghan War 1919

The Third Afghan War was a much smaller and shorter affair than the previous two. However, this time the Afghans took the offensive. By 1919 the First World War was over and weary Indian troops were returning home. Between 10 and 20 million Indians had died as a result of the 1918 influenza epidemic and there was intense pressure to demobilise elements of the Indian Army and British troops overseas. Indian frontier activity during the war had been mainly defensive, despite some tribal unrest, in order to conserve manpower and other resources; remarkably, Afghanistan had stayed neutral. This was despite the influence of a Turco-German mission in Kabul and their agitation for the Afghans to participate on their side. However, in 1919, the Indian internal unrest encouraged the insecure new Amir of Afghanistan, Amanullah, to proclaim a *jihad* and to launch an attack into India. 'The British forces on the Frontier were at the moment incomplete, much below establishment, and of somewhat inferior military value, owing to the despatch of the cream of the Army overseas in the course of the Great War just terminated.'[62]

In addition, the India-resident British Territorial Force units were trained for internal security, rather than conventional fighting and many Indian units were on 'block leave'. However, the British and Indian forces were better armed than the Afghans, with machine guns, mortars and armoured cars; they also had wireless sets, transport and air power. Amongst the air crews was the future 'Bomber' Harris.

As rebellion surged in the Punjab, Afghan troops made arrangements with border tribes and concentrated in the Khyber area. They posed a real threat, though as Monro wrote in an official report, 'We were particularly fortunate in having at hand so valuable a reinforcement as the British troops ex-Mesopotamia awaiting demobilisation.'[63] He had announced, 'The Commander-in-Chief regrets that he is compelled by a serious situation, which has arisen in India to ask you to volunteer to remain temporarily in India for a period not exceeding one month, or less if the situation demands it.'[64]

Some battalions were hastily pulled together from a mixture of volunteers, Territorials and conscripts who happened to be passing through India. Swiftly delaying demobilisation of both British and Indian troops was not a popular decision for those involved, but it was an extremely sound one.

Handling the units was tricky. Some officers and men were reluctant to 'volunteer' and were concerned about retaining their jobs when they returned home, and a few senior commanders were becoming concerned about discipline. As internal unrest was gradually brought under control, a caution was issued from Army Headquarters to the chain of command in early May, but for British eyes only:

> During the recent disturbances agitators have spread rumours of dissension amongst British troops with a view to persuade the ignorant and excitable Indian population that they may with impunity defy law and order … In order that despatch to the United Kingdom may proceed steadily without delay, it is essential that no foundation for such rumours be furnished to the Indian agitator class, who are very observant and watch closely the attitude of British troops.[65]

At one stage 800 Royal Army Service Corps personnel went on strike because they did not want to be deployed to the North-West Frontier, but wanted to be returned home. They were placated, but meanwhile in July there were concerns about the loyalty of 6 Composite Special Battalion at Deolali, ex-Mesopotamia veterans whose mobilisation had been deferred and who were also destined for the frontier. This was potential mutiny, though Monro did not want to inflame the situation at this fragile time, avoiding arrests if possible. This was sensible, as a number of other small groups of British troops failed to obey orders and one general reported, 'Their patience has reached the limit and they scoff at expressions of sympathy. They express utter indifference to safety of India or calls of patriotism.'[66]

In September, passions were aroused again because of discontent surrounding the prioritisation of who could be repatriated first. Twenty-five mutineer 'delegates' were received at Simla in early October 1919 and heard for two days. The adjutant general was present and Monro personally completed the proceedings. They agreed to a resolution and persuaded the mutineers that they had to continue serving. Monro shook hands with each man and 'met them with a combination of sympathy and firmness which had the effect of easing the situation'.[67] This little-known fragile 'mutiny' situation should not be blown out of proportion as the numbers involved were small. However, in an extremely unsettled India, Monro's headquarters appeared to have averted an even more serious internal situation.[68]

Returning to the Third Afghan War, Monro's plan at Army HQ at Simla was to strike towards Jalalabad, dividing the frontier tribes of Mohmands and Afridis, whom he had fought in the past, from Afghan support. The British force would then attack the Afghans. This army, which was mobilised in early May 1919, was divided between the North-West Frontier Force under the command of General Sir Arthur Barrett and the Balochistan Force, led by Lieutenant General R. Wapshire. The former grouping was split again at the end of May 1919 to form a third element, the Waziristan Force, under Major General S. Climo.

Incredibly, Monro managed to muster over 75,000 fighting troops to fight an Afghan army that, theoretically, was 50,000 strong plus additional support from border tribesmen; Monro was most concerned about the capabilities of the latter. The fighting was divided into three phases:

Fighting in the northern sector, May–June.
Fighting in the central and southern sectors, May–June.
Border tribes' unrest, June–August.

Monro's signed Order of the Day No 1, of 12 May 1919, proclaimed:

> The soldiers of the Empire, both British and Indian, have suddenly been called to defend from Afghan aggression the frontiers of India on which an unwarranted attack has been made without any warning or cause. His Excellency the Viceroy has therefore ordered troops to proceed at once to the Frontier to punish those who have had the temerity to violate Indian soil. Troops are now being assembled in large numbers for this purpose.

The Indian Princes and the Durbar of the State of Nepal have offered their troops to punish the enemy who so foolishly and treacherously trespassed in our territory.[69]

Initially, the British main effort was in the Khyber area, with the objective of Dakka, reacting to the Afghan invasion of the border area of Chitral and their capture of Bagh, only 25 miles from Peshawar, the capital of the North-West Frontier Province. The British quickly surrounded and isolated Peshawar, prior to arresting anti-British activists, which included the local postmaster.[70] However, the Afghan advance had not been well calculated, as their forces were initially sparse and passage through the passes was still affected by snow.

There were also successful low-level defensive actions by the Chitral Scouts and the Mehtar's Bodyguard. Fortunately, the Afghans lacked speed and surprise, allowing their enemies time to counter-attack, though the first attempt to dislodge the Afghans failed. However, the British captured Landi Kotal on 11 May and Dakka on 13 May, then defeated the Afghan Army on 17 May, effectively supported by Royal Air Force bombing. Air power proved useful and psychologically successful, as illustrated on 24 May, when a Handley-Page aircraft bombed Kabul.

Elsewhere, the Afghans' efforts were a little more successful. Tribal attacks occurred at Ali Masjid, where the Khyber Rifles performed badly and had to be disbanded and replaced by more reliable Indian troops.

Not all of the British action was efficient or well thought through on the ground. Earlier, at Dakka, the victory had been close run and Brigadier Baldwin was accused of exposing his troops to danger unnecessarily and was sent to the rear in disgrace. He was denied a court martial or court of enquiry and the evidence available suggests that he may have been used as a scapegoat.

However, both of his superior commanders arranged for him to be removed, also citing poor march discipline and wrongly splitting his force in the advance; this decision was supported by Monro. Eventually, Baldwin was interviewed by Monro, whom Robson writes, 'was clearly not in full command of all the facts'.[71] Also, Baldwin later wrote that Monro was 'utterly unfit to be Commander-in-Chief'.[72] However, from Monro's position at Simla, he had little choice but to support Barrett's views. Baldwin was a bitter man and Monro's trust in Barrett was clear, 'His profound experience of frontier warfare and his sagacious advice were at all times of the greatest value to Army Headquarters.'[73]

Meanwhile, in the centre the Afghan C-in-C, Nadir Khan, advanced down the Kaito Valley and the Waziristan militia supported him by mutinying. The British withdrew from most of Waziristan and Khan laid siege to 65th Brigade at Thal on 27 May. A relief column arrived on 1 June, which included Brigadier General Dyer's 45th Brigade. At this stage, the Amritsar massacre had not hit the headlines, due to the slow communication channels of the time and Dyer was not aware that, in early May, the Secretary of State for India had written to the viceroy suggesting that an enquiry was necessary to investigate 'the causes of and the treatment of the riots that have occurred in India'.[74] Also, before deploying he met General Barrett, as he was anxious. Barrett reportedly said to Dyer, 'That's all right, you would have heard about it long before this, if your action had not been approved.'[75]

As Dyer launched himself into action, as part of the Thal Relief Force, he felt reassured. He performed well in this role, immediately showing imagination by transporting logs as dummy guns on lorries, giving the enemy the impression that he was well equipped with artillery. He provided motivating leadership, moved his brigade quickly and drove his soldiers hard. He also made the most of attached aircraft for detailed reconnaissance and artillery in the assault. This was a successful operation by Dyer, providing a significant contribution towards the British victory in the Third Afghan War and he was mentioned in despatches. Monro relayed his thanks to Dyer:

> The efforts made by Brigadier-General Dyer from the time he arrived at Kohat were attended with full energy and competence. The manner in which he disposed of his troops, the full use he made of his artillery, the ardour he infused into his troops, denoted the hand of a Commander confident in his capacity and in his troops. Brigadier-General Dyer in this episode has given further evidence of power of Command.[76]

Meanwhile, in the south two infantry brigades and two cavalry regiments eliminated an Afghan force occupying Spin Boldak. Also, the Mohmands were beaten in two successful ambushes, though the Afridis were initially successful against Ali Masjid and there was rebellion in the Zhob Valley which lasted until August. The tribes had proved to be far more dangerous than the Afghan Army.

Whilst unrest on the frontier continued for a few months more, the end result for the Afghans was soon clear. The Amir wanted to negotiate a peace and an armistice was agreed on 3 June. Ironically, despite the Indian Army's military success, Amanullah's aggressive posture and relatively harmless peace agreement meant that the Afghans believed that they had achieved a political victory. Militarily, Monro had conducted a successful campaign, though he had been concerned about sustaining his limited resources, so the armistice was a relief to both sides.

Operations in Waziristan were to continue into 1920, following tribal success against Indian Army militia units. Monro directly controlled Major

General Climo's force and wrote afterwards, 'It became necessary to consider how best to bring the Waziristan tribes to book for the many wanton attacks they had made on our troops.'[77] Terms were published, whilst the British prepared to attack the Tochi-Wazirs and then the Mahsuds with 30,000 combat troops.

The striking force was commanded by Major General A. Skeen. Despite tribal ambushes and raids, his actions went according to plan and eventually the enemy were pacified, though this was not until November 1920 and regular troops had to be established in these fragile areas to keep the peace. Once again, General Monro had provided clear and firm leadership. It was towards the end of this engagement that there was a significant reaction to Brigadier Dyer's actions at Amritsar.

Dyer and Monro

Dyer had deployed to Waziristan, believing that his actions at Amritsar, which had included the infamous 'crawling order', had been condoned by his superiors.[78] O'Dwyer was vocally supportive; very shortly after the massacre he had sent the message, 'Your action correct. Lieutenant-Governor approves.'[79] Neither had General Barrett given him any cause for concern. The Punjab had been knocked into submission and the Sikh priests of Amritsar had made him an honorary Sikh for his swift and effective action, but Gandhi called for a Royal Commission of Inquiry and the All India Congress Committee sent a respected Indian moderate to England to support the request. Once Montagu knew more about what had happened he telegraphed to Chelmsford in early May 1919:

> Dyer's judgement and temper have in my opinion proved so unreliable that I am of the opinion that he cannot be fit to retain command. I consider in fact it very undesirable that he should continue in the Army of India.[80]

The viceroy initially defended Dyer, though he knew little of the detail at that stage. Dyer was popular with the Europeans in India and they believed that he had saved the country from a rebellion. Before the viceroy responded, he conferred with the Bishop of Lahore and General Monro, who agreed with Chelmsford's view. The viceroy wrote to Montagu:

> I have heard that Dyer administered Martial Law in Amritsar very reasonably and in no sense tyrannously. In these circumstances you will understand

why it is that the Commander-in-Chief and I feel very strongly that an error of judgement, transitory in its consequences, should not bring down upon him a penalty which would be out of all proportion to the offence and which must be balanced against the very notable services which he rendered at an extremely critical time. I should add further that Dyer took part in the recent operations at Thal and again distinguished himself as a military leader of great push and determination.[81]

On 2 August Monro personally congratulated Dyer at Army HQ Simla, for his performance at Thal, but made no mention of Amritsar, apart from instructing him to compile a report on the incident. This was unlike the adjutant general and quartermaster general, who had both openly supported Dyer up until the time of the inquiry. Again, Dyer was left with the impression that another key personality in the 'system' supported him and this led to later accusations that Monro turned his back on him. However, it can be argued that whilst Monro was quite rightly recognising Dyer's success at Thal, he made a sound judgement by maintaining his neutrality on Amritsar, prior to hearing the evidence. This was a tough line to take with a senior officer who had just excelled in an important operation, particularly as they knew each other from their subaltern days in the same regiment.

The ending of the Afghan War meant that there was increased pressure for an inquiry, but the Indian Establishment was still resisting one. Monro was reported as being particularly outspoken, 'It would only serve to call into question the authority of the army and its officers, and have a discouraging effect on all ranks.'[82] In the wider context of internal unrest, which had been quashed earlier in the year, both Monro and Chelmsford did not feel that an inquiry was necessary and Chelmsford's relationship with Montagu deteriorated as the latter established the Hunter Committee, which arrived in India in mid-October.

Lord Hunter, a Scottish Liberal lawyer with little knowledge of India, led a panel of four European and three Indian members to investigate the recent violence in India. General Monro had personally written to General Barrow, his past chief of staff with the 1st Army and his future biographer, encouraging him to be one of this group – an offer he accepted. This meant that he had a trusted and close friend within the committee. Barrow, who had also been at Staff College with Dyer, later summed up the Amritsar affair from his perspective, 'It is a story of racial hatreds, blinding passions, biased judgements, falsehoods, a story of which only a garbled version was allowed to reach the ears of the masses in this country.'[83]

The Hunter Committee sat for six weeks, taking evidence. It was 'to investigate the recent disturbances in Bombay, Delhi and the Punjab, their causes, and the measures taken to cope with them.'[84] Dyer provided his evidence on 19 November and said that if he had had more troops available he would have inflicted more casualties and, if his armoured cars were able to fit into the Jallianwala Bagh, he would have engaged the crowd with their machine guns. In his view, this was to 'create a wide impression' in the Punjab.

The committee produced seven volumes, though only one concerned Amritsar, as the others concentrated on the general disturbances. The report was published in May 1920. It criticised Dyer for failing to give the crowd sufficient warning before opening fire and then continuing to fire whilst the crowd was trying to escape. It also attacked his 'crawling order'. It stated:

> We can arrive at no other conclusion than that at Jallianwala Bagh General Dyer acted beyond the necessity of the case, beyond what any reasonable man could have thought to be necessary, and that he did not act with as much humanity as the case permitted.[85]

O'Dwyer was annoyed because he felt that the committee failed to link the threat of internal rioting with the recent Afghan aggression; he believed that Dyer's actions had successfully quelled further problems. However, the committee could not agree on its findings and split on racial lines. The three Indian members produced a minority report stating, 'The actions of the authorities were both brutal and counter-productive.'[86] In contrast, the majority agreed that live firing on rioters had been justified at Delhi, Ahmedabad, Viramgam, Lahore and Kasur, and criticised authorities at Gujranwala for not using similar force. Dyer was not criticised for opening fire and Barrow later wrote, 'With the reservation that he should first have given a warning, we can agree that Dyer was justified in dispersing the crowd by force.'[87]

The Indian Government received the report in early March 1920 and could not condone Dyer's actions, though it acknowledged that 'he acted with integrity of purpose'. Monro commented:

> His motives and intentions in a position of much difficulty were beyond cavil, but he showed a great lack of discretion in the situation with which he was confronted. We expect our generals to display greater wisdom and a wider sense of proportion in periods of crisis, and he showed himself to be lacking in these essentials.[88]

Meanwhile, Dyer had returned to Jullundur in January 1920 and asked for six months' home leave to rest, but this was denied on the 30th by Army HQ, unless he decided to relinquish command of his brigade. However, on the same day his morale was boosted by another message that stated, 'His

Excellency the Commander-in-Chief approves of Brigadier-General R. E. H. Dyer officiating in command of the 2nd Division vice Major General Sir Charles Dobell, appointed to exercise command Northern Command pending further orders.'[89]

This message seems incredible, following just two months after Dyer had delivered his evidence. This clearly illustrated that the army in India, under Monro, thought he deserved promotion and recognition for his recent performance in both Amritsar and the Third Afghan War. This appears to demonstrate extremely poor judgement by Charles Monro and uncharacteristic behaviour. Barrow defends Monro, stating that the appointment was only a temporary one and that the Army Council was never going to approve Dyer's promotion to major general; he was not of the right quality and he was not fit. However, on 14 February the order was effectively rescinded and Dyer, who was now quite frail and suffering from jaundice, was informed that a different brigadier general was to take the temporary command of the 2nd Division.

Monro had reversed his decision within two weeks. This was probably as some of the content of the committee's report was becoming available to him amidst a fragile political environment and political pressure. Prior to the report and Dyer's evidence, General Molesworth, who was on the adjutant general's staff, later recalled that all army headquarters supported Dyer, including Monro, and 'Monro now considered that Dyer had showed a lack of wisdom, a foolhardiness, a lack of sensitivity that was inexcusable. He therefore decided he could no longer protect Dyer from political pressure.'[90]

Ultimately, the army was the tool of the politicians and Monro had no choice but to make the decisions he did in his important position within the Indian administration. However, it is difficult not to come to the conclusion that his initial decision to promote Dyer, albeit temporarily, was a poor one. O'Dwyer expressed his view:

> The Government of India – of which the Commander-in-Chief is a member – were becoming increasingly alarmed by the spurious agitation worked up over the Punjab 'atrocities', were doubtless being pressed by Mr Montagu to make any concessions that would secure a 'calm atmosphere' for the Reforms, and adopted the usual, but ineffective, method of throwing some of their servants to the wolves.[91]

A separate report was published in February. Compiled independently by the Indian National Congress, it found the massacre was 'a calculated piece of inhumanity towards utterly innocent and unarmed men, including children, and unparalleled for its ferocity on the history of modern British administration'.[92] It demanded Dyer's impeachment, again illustrating the huge political pressure on the Indian Government to show remorse.

Before the Hunter Committee's report was published, Dyer was summoned to Delhi in March 1920 to be told that he was relieved of command. It came as a complete surprise to him that both the adjutant general and General Monro should make this decision and he replied to the former that, as he had never been tried, he should not be condemned. He said nothing to Monro, then returned dispirited to Jullundur, where he was ordered to stay. According to General Molesworth, Monro was also upset by the interview and said little, because until then he had supported Dyer. Subsequently, Dyer was advised by letter from the C-in-C to tender his resignation from the army; this was completed on 27 March 1920.

Dyer's biographer, Ian Colvin, claimed rather emotionally that Monro thought it necessary to be discourteous to Dyer. He also wrote that Monro had been persuaded to change his mind about the promotion issue by a prominent Indian politician. Barrow rebuked his comments, stating, 'This clumsy attempt to discredit Sir Charles Monro falls flat directly the rottenness of the foundation on which it is built is exposed to view.'[93] Certainly, Colvin's support of Dyer seems to lack appropriate evidence, though Monro's decision to promote Dyer is still extremely questionable.

Interestingly, Monro's order to return Dyer to England on sick leave was a lesser punishment than it could have been; Montagu would have preferred him to have been dismissed from the army in India and lose his pension. In fact, he was not aware of Monro's order until after Dyer was on his way home and was furious that he had not been informed, as it meant that Dyer could not be disciplined by the Cabinet. Chelmsford apologised to the Secretary of State for War, Winston Churchill, on Monro's behalf, 'He now realises that the course he adopted was precipitate and that this action should have been deferred until your approval of our Resolution had been received. He regrets the embarrassment he has caused you.'[94]

Monro realised that it was probably sensible to remove Dyer from India as soon as possible, seeming to take some of the pressure off the brigadier general and perhaps saving them both from further personal embarrassment within India. By making this decision, he avoided Dyer being in the country as the Hunter Committee's findings were published. This was a far shrewder and more pragmatic move than the earlier intent to promote Dyer.

Dyer arrived in England on 2 May to a generally supportive British public, but further controversy. He had still not seen the report and he sought Army Council views in order to rebut its findings, but it would not acquit him of his error of judgement, nor would it castigate Dyer further. Meanwhile, Churchill and Montagu were recommending his disciplinary dismissal, rather than voluntary resignation, though this was not suggested by Monro who, when consulted, wrote, 'I directed Dyer to resign command of his brigade. I do not recommend this officer for further duties and I informed him that he can expect nothing further in India. He should be ordered to retire; beyond this I have no further recommendation.'[95]

This judgement by Monro partly protected Dyer from further disciplinary measures back in England, as the Army Council debated the issue with Churchill. Eventually, on 7 July 1920 it was announced in Parliament that Dyer was to be retired on half pay and would not be employed further. Later, the House of Lords voted in his support and money was raised for him by the *Morning Post*. This antagonised Indians and led to Gandhi stating that 'co-operation in any form with the satanic British Government is sinful'.[96]

The issue raised its profile again in 1924 when O'Dwyer was involved in a libel case. Mr Justice McCardie, who did not have all the facts available on the issue, declared, 'I express my view that General Dyer, in the grave and exceptional circumstances, acted rightly, and in my opinion he was wrongly punished by the Secretary of State for India.'[97] This generated a great deal of embarrassing publicity for the government and continued to stoke dissatisfaction with British rule in India; Indians had seen how the British Houses of Parliament, the British public and Justice McCardie backed Dyer's aggressive actions.

Dyer died in 1927, though the controversy of Amritsar continues to this day.

1920

Monro had suffered a particularly challenging year in 1919 with the widespread disorder, Dyer and the Third Afghan War, and 1920 marked his last few months in office. Political unrest increased, stoked by the aftermath of the Amritsar massacre and the handling of Dyer. Chelmsford was accused of 'patient inaction' as non-co-operation grew, inspired by Gandhi's widening political influence; the monsoon failed and there were further strikes. Prominent Indians began to resign from government positions and most returned their British honours, whilst schools and law courts were boycotted. In addition, the Muslim Khilafat Movement spread its anti-British rhetoric.[98]

However, in the same year the country's first elections to the Imperial Legislative Council and Provincial Councils took place and the new Parliament of India was opened in February 1921.

There were a number of military issues to be dealt with. One of the more emotional ones was the mutiny by the Connaught Rangers, 'The Devil's

Own'. Monro knew this Irish regiment well, as it had served with distinction in Brigadier General Haking's 5th Brigade within his 2nd Division in 1914, on the Western Front. The regiment was also well known for its popular marching tune, 'It's a Long Way to Tipperary'. Barrow, Monro's original biographer, dismisses the mutiny incident as 'an unwarranted slur put on the name of a famous regiment which had a record of 129 years unbroken service'.[99] However, it was Barrow, heading Northern Command in India, who ordered the execution of 22-year-old Private (or Ranger) James Joseph Daly, in November 1920.

The Irish War of Independence began in 1919, but the 1st Battalion arrived in India in the November. Subsequently, in June 1920, some of the soldiers mutinied over the behaviour of the 'Black and Tans' in Ireland.[100] Ranger Joseph Hawes declared, 'We'll soldier no more for England', and the commanding officer could not dissuade the mutineers from their action. Eighty-eight men were involved and seventy-seven of them were imprisoned, but Daly, one of the ringleaders, was executed. Ironically, the battalion had fought against the Easter Rising in Dublin, back in 1916. The incident took place at Wellington Barracks and Solan Camp, Jullundur, as the soldiers refused to take orders from their officers, retained their weapons, changed the Union flag to an Irish Tricolour, put a guard on those who would not follow them and placed green, white and orange rosettes on their breasts. Other Irish regiments did not follow the Connaught Rangers' example, perhaps because the officers had better control and there were not the same characters available as ringleaders.

Monro's representative, Colonel Jackson, arrived at the barracks on 29 June, flying a white flag. He told the mutineers that the barracks would be retaken, that they were surrounded and could not escape. He had a battery of artillery, two loyal battalions and a company of machine-gunners supporting him, so the rebels had no choice but to be interned – at least there was a bloodless resolution. Their trial began in August; sixty-one soldiers were sentenced, with fourteen receiving the death sentence. However, the British political position in Ireland was softening and Monro commuted all of the death sentences, except that for Private Daly. He had led an attack on the armoury, where two soldiers had been killed. Daly was the last British soldier shot for mutiny. It can be argued strongly that Monro had no choice but to make him the scapegoat, 'Daly had to die, not for Ireland, but for India', setting an example to the local population, as political tensions remained high.[101] Chelmsford reinforced this perspective by stating, 'we should find ourselves in a position of great difficulty in the future with regard to Indian troops if, in the case of British soldiers, we did not enforce the supreme penalty where conditions justified it'.[102]

As the new Irish state was established the Connaught Rangers, along with five other Irish regiments, were disbanded in 1922. The following year, the remaining prisoners were released and in 1936 Ireland honoured the mutineers with pensions. The mutineers are still commemorated in Ireland at Glasnevin Cemetery and in a stained glass window in Galway Cathedral. Daly is remembered in the 'Ballad of the Mutiny of the Devil's Own':

> He was like a living angel, when walking out to die,
> This gallant Irish martyr, no tear did dim his eye.
> Although he died in Dagshai jail, 'twas for a noble deed,
> So I hope you'll pray for Daly from the County of Westmeath.[103]

Strategically, Monro had to deal with a great deal of criticism about the way India had fought the Great War. Immediately after its conclusion, the India Office had proposed a committee to examine the Indian military system and make it more efficient, recommending that this grouping should be based in India, reporting to the C-in-C. London disagreed, as it perceived the Indian Army as being part of the whole Empire's military force, the CIGS stating:

> The military forces of the Empire can no longer be adequately considered departmentally or even territorially … the Imperial General Staff alone can fix India's responsibilities to the Empire and co-ordinate the whole question of Imperial Defence in one comprehensive scheme.[104]

Montagu took the middle line and the New Army in India Committee reported to him, led by Viscount Esher. This was the same man who had helped shape the British armed forces before the First World War. He had also helped set up the Mont-Ford Reforms, but he was not interested in a separate Indian force and would not travel to India, because of his age. The members of the Esher Committee included the controversial Sir Michael O'Dwyer, but Montagu also appointed three Indians, representing the established aristocracy and commercial and professional groups. The first part of the report was submitted in November 1919 and it was heavily influenced by the results of the damning Mesopotamia Commission's report and the army's perceived inefficiencies, again many logistic and medical, during the Third Afghan War and Waziristan operations.

The Indian Army had been organised at the beginning of the twentieth century to fight on the frontiers of India and in a counter-insurgency role. This meant operating in small groups from secure bases, using basic equipment and weapons with only limited combat support and combat service support available – minimum artillery and engineers and basic medical and logistic support. In addition, the latest and most potent weapons available were operated by their British colleagues, rather than the Indian. This was a deliberate British insurance scheme to help counter any potential mutiny. Communications were also basic, though no one could deny Indian bravery and loyalty in battle. These weaknesses were identified in the Mesopotamia Commission's Report and highlighted again in the Esher Committee.

It was recommended that the administration of the Indian Army should be included in the Empire's overall military effort with closer connections between the War Office in London and the C-in-C in India. There should be a new deputy CIGS with Indian experience, though not necessarily ex-Indian Army, appointed as the military secretary at the India Office. The CIGS or his new deputy should be able to attend the Council of India and deal with the viceroy on imperial military matters, whilst the C-in-C dealt with Indian military matters, 'thus unity of military policy will at last be established between Great Britain and India'.[105] The recommendation was to simplify some of the army department and council membership and provide the C-in-C with a military council and a new CGS, although he would not be allowed to take command in the field.

However, Montagu did not want the C-in-C to have too much power, compared with civilian administrators and politicians. Perhaps his deteriorating relationship with Monro over the handling of Dyer contributed to this view. There were differing views on the way ahead in London and Delhi as India feared that some of its local autonomy might be taken away.

Eventually, numbers of cavalry and infantry troops were reduced, partly at the expense of a larger artillery force. More sappers were enlisted and 'the signal service expanded ten times'.[106] There were also improvements to pay, accommodation, hospitals, housing and pay to come. The committee wanted an army system that would be 'simple, economical and adaptable, without undue friction and disturbance'.[107] It realised that there was a need to raise the standard of living for both Indian and British officers and soldiers in India. There was little mention of Indianisation, as the Indian members of the committee could not agree on the way ahead on the issue, but the Indian Army would gradually be modernised and partially Indianised prior to the Second World War.

Rawlinson would take forward the findings of the Esher Committee and recommendations of the Legislative Assembly, along with the financial challenges to implement them, but Monro was still influencing proceedings when the Viceroy's Council was exposed to the findings in March 1920 and it arrived with the British Government in June. India wanted more autonomy and Monro, at the head of an overstretched force, gave the findings little support and feared it was 'calculated to force the hands of government'.[108] He believed that London did not listen to India's concerns when formulating strategy, and wrote:

> That policy should presumably bear some reaction to the latter's [India's] military strength, and if this be true, we ought to be in much closer touch with the Home authorities and some understanding should be arrived at with them as to the role within the Empire, which India may be called upon to discharge.[109]

He was also 'convinced that a small force properly staffed, adequately equipped, well trained, and with the correct proportion of ancillary services' would be better than a large, poorly equipped army.[110] Monro was being practical as ever, understanding India and the impractical expensive recommendations made by the Esher Committee; he had years of Indian experience, unlike Esher. Before he left India, he prepared a statement of facts in which he tried to explain that there were fundamental differences between the Indian and British soldier, which many people simply did not understand. Growing nationalism and financial limitations would not help the proposed

Sir Charles and Lady Monro, Simla. (British Library. Mss Eur D783/9)

changes and Indians and their government were increasingly unhappy about the prospect of supporting empirical operations overseas. Rawlinson was to reorganise the Indian Army in 1922.

Though he was highly respected by Chelmsford, Montagu and the British and Indian establishments, Monro did receive some public criticism for his time as C-in-C, some of which was aired in *The Times* in August 1920. He receives nothing but praise for his military decisions and his changes in recruiting and administrative measures in India during the First World War, though his handling, afterwards, of Dyer was questionable and not consistent. He is accused of not reorganising the Indian Army quickly enough after the war, as the same logistic, transport and medical weaknesses displayed during the Mesopotamia campaign were revealed again in the Third Afghan War and in Waziristan.

He was also criticised for over-centralisation within his Army HQ. However, he knew India and the army well and did the best he could to improve those inefficiencies within the resources available, without forcing an unrealistic pace of change. He knew the strengths and weaknesses of the Indian soldier well and continued to insist on high levels of training. He even managed to keep the Territorial Forces motivated when they were forced to stay mobilised. All his decisions were practical and measured and, as has been commented on before, 'He was never more at home than when he was talking to a private soldier.'[111] He was never one to boast or make a fuss of his important role.

On balance, Monro was a very successful C-in-C in India during a particularly fragile period. He was highly praised by India's foreign secretary, Sir Hamilton Grant, in the 1931 biography:

> At a time when the shadow of the fall of Kut and the debacle in Mesopotamia lay dark over India, the advent of Sir Charles Monro, with his cheery optimism, seemed to breathe new life into us all. Combining as he did, a breezy bonhomie and an unquenchable sense of humour with the iron discipline of his beloved regiment, The Queen's, he was the right man in the right place at the right time.[112]

Monro was very shrewd, honest, wise and loyal, and he brought the usually antagonistic military and civil administration staff together as a team. He is praised for working extremely hard, whilst maintaining good humour and calmness and helping to ensure that Afghanistan stayed neutral during the First World War because of his sensible military dispositions.

He also records that Monro did the best he could to direct the Third Afghan War and operations in Waziristan, considering the logistic and medical challenges which were beyond his control to improve at that stage. Monro 'exercised an extraordinary safe and steadying influence' and 'socially, Sir Charles and his charming lady were an enormous asset to us all in Simla and Delhi'.[113] Grant's views were echoed by his successor as Foreign Secretary in India, Sir Henry Dobbs. Rawlinson was able to take forward many reforms, due to Monro's earlier work.

In a letter to *The Times* newspaper adding to Monro's obituary in 1929, Field Marshal Lord Robertson acknowledged Monro's critical role when he was in India, praising him for sorting out the Mesopotamia campaign and for his recruiting and administrative successes. He wrote, 'Before he assumed the chief command the resources of India had not been utilised to anything like the extent of which they were capable.'[114] More recently, the eminent historian, John Terraine wrote about Monro in an essay about leadership and generals in the First World War, 'Monro has been called the best C-in-C of British India, even including Lord Roberts – which suggests a touch of class!'[115]

On the lighter side, Monro was known for keeping his staff at Army HQ motivated and amused. He preceded his staff's surnames with 'young' when he talked to them and encouraged the use of nicknames. He and Lady Monro were popular with the local children and kept pressure on his aide-de-camp by castigating him if he did not know the name of every British person or child he met in Simla. He also maintained his horse-riding and hunting skills, particularly as he found walking difficult after his Gallipoli accident. Both Sir Charles and Lady Monro were held in great affection by the people of Simla for their kindness, sympathy and 'dignified simplicity'.[116]

Monro resigned his post when he believed that he could no longer give of his best. He said, in a typically honest manner:

> It will be for the benefit of the Army that there should be a change. The past four years have not been marked out as a period of entire calm and any man is bound to suffer from the effects of continuous work for so long a time.[117]

Monro's time in India had been rewarding, but extremely tiring. One short biography recorded, 'In August 1920 Monro, worn down by the stress and sheer volume of work, resigned his post and returned to London on half pay.'[118] His regimental obituary printed in *The Times* reinforced this view, stating that he was 'worn out by the cares of office, sheer stress of work, and struggle against official routine'.[119]

However, he still displayed his sense of humour and was known for hating affectation. On one occasion, a staff officer brought him a military paper full of Latin quotations:

As he read the paper, General Monro kept up a flow of pungent comment and having finished, he wrote at the end of the type-script not, as usual, 'Seen', but 'Nullum sanguinem bonum'. Then turning to the staff officer and looking up slyly, he said with a nod: 'You see I, too, know Latin.'[120]

He relaxed in England, gave speeches and seems to have unveiled a remarkable number of First World War memorials, including his own regiment's at Holy Trinity Church, Guildford.

As Monro was about to leave India, he received a new unique additional appointment – colonel of his own regiment, the Queen's Royal Regiment (West Surrey). 'General Sir C. C. Monro, GCB, GCSI, GCMG, ADC Gen to The King, to be Colonel in succession to Major-General Sir E. O. F. Hamilton, KCB, who has resigned the appointment. 13th October 1920.'[121] He would hold this honorary appointment until the time of his death in 1929.

In outline, every infantry regiment has a colonel, which is an honourable ceremonial position and is an appointment rather than a rank. It is a great honour for either a senior serving or retired officer, who has usually served with the regiment in the past, and it requires the approval of the sovereign and the regiment's colonel-in-chief. He is informed about what is going on in the regiment and provides commanding officers with advice on matters concerning the overall welfare of the regiment and its institutions. He also visits the units of the regiment and ensures a continual strand in the regiment's *esprit de corps*. In addition, he provides a channel of informal and formal communication with other elements of the army and higher command. This was a great honour and a privilege for Charles Monro, who was returning to his roots, and he took this new role extremely seriously. He excitedly recorded, on hearing his appointment, 'Nothing personal could touch my heart so closely as such an honour.'[122]

At that time, his regiment consisted of two Regular and four Territorial Force battalions:

1st Battalion (Regular Army), based in Aldershot, then on counter-insurgency operations in Ireland during 1921.

2nd Battalion (Regular Army), on operations in Waziristan, then back to garrison duties at Lucknow, India.

4th Battalion (Territorial Force), based at Croydon.

5th Battalion (Territorial Force), based at Guildford.

22nd (County of London) Battalion, London Regiment (the Queen's), based at Bermondsey (Territorial Force).

24th (County of London) Battalion, London Regiment (the Queen's), based at Southwark (Territorial Force).

He also became the honorary colonel of the 23rd (County of London) Battalion the London Regiment (Territorial Force), which was to be connected to the 'other Surrey regiment', the East Surrey Regiment.

At this time he received a further two accolades. With effect from 30 December 1920, he became the 1st Baronet of Bearcrofts, Stirlingshire. This harked back to his family's origins in Scotland and was a hereditary appointment that would not be taken forward as he and Lady Monro had no children. Then in 1921, he was appointed King of Arms of the Order of the Bath. This was a unique honour from his grateful nation and he was the herald of the order until his death. The order is still the fourth most senior of the British Orders of Chivalry, after the Most Noble Order of the Garter, the Most Ancient and Most Noble Order of the Thistle, and the dormant Most Illustrious Order of St Patrick. It is an honour awarded to military and civil servants and the recipients are limited in number, but there was only one King of Arms.

His talents were not wasted after his exhausting time in India. Within two years, he was appointed the governor and C-in-C of Gibraltar, succeeding another First World War commander, General Sir Horace Smith-Dorrien, in September 1923.

11

THE FINAL YEARS

Gibraltar

Gibraltar was going to be General Sir Charles Monro's posting for his last five years of full-time service. Like India, the 'Rock' was familiar; here he had met his future wife and assumed his first brief staff appointment in 1898, twenty-five years before. British provincial papers recorded the event:

> General Sir Charles Monro, the new Governor-General, arrived here from England by the P&O liner *Caledonia* this morning to take up his duties. He landed at ten o'clock in beautiful weather, amid salutes of guns in the fortress, and was received by the civil, naval and military authorities, guards of honour being drawn from the Irish Guards and the 1st Buffs.[1]

Gibraltar had been captured from Spain by the British in 1704 and was (and arguably still is) one of the most important coastal fortresses in the world. From the Empire's perspective, Thackeray wrote, 'It is the very image of an enormous lion, crouched between the Atlantic and Mediterranean, and set there to guard the passage for its British mistress.'[2]

It controlled access to the Mediterranean and was critical as a logistic base and coaling station for the Royal Navy, assisting the projection of British power and vital for the strategic lines of communication to South Africa and through the Suez Canal to India and beyond. The Royal Navy regularly exercised its home and Mediterranean fleets there. It is only 3 miles long and ¾ mile in breadth and in 1923 its population was about 23,000 people, including a garrison of 5,000 men.

Monro represented the British monarch in Gibraltar and therefore was the head of state. He had a unique role as the governor, commanding the garrison

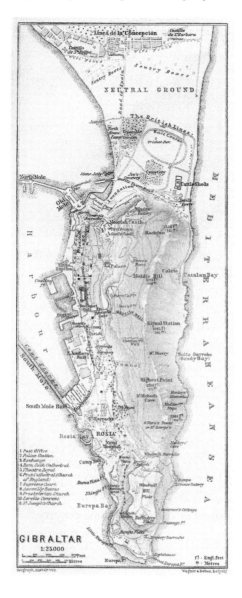

Left: Gibraltar. (Author's collection)

Below: The Arms of Gibraltar. (Will's)

and controlling legislation, but critically administering the Rock's government, aided by an Executive Council of four official and three unofficial members. Towards the end of his posting, the Executive Council consisted of:

The governor – General Monro.
The military officer next in seniority after the governor.
Colonial secretary – Major H. W. Young.
Attorney general.
Treasurer.
J. Andrews-Speed, A. C. Carrara and G. Gaggero (all Justices of the Peace).[3]

This advisory council was only established a year before Monro arrived and was a demonstration of British gratitude for loyal and effective service during the First World War. In addition, in 1921 the first local elections were held for a new city council, run by a chairman with five nominated members and another four elected by ratepayers; the latter group ended up as all being local members of the Transport & General Workers Union. However, its powers were limited to street maintenance, sewage, sanitation and water supply.

There was a call to create a majority of elected members to the city council in 1926, but this suggestion was rejected by Monro; at this stage, the Rock was a British fortress and there was little perceived institutional scope for further democracy. Gibraltarians were fiercely loyal to the Crown and not seen as a people that might rebel, one author writing that the population was 'so small, so cosmopolitan, so parasitic that it could not develop a real nationalist movement'.[4]

Gibraltar had important links to both Great Britain and its Empire and neighbouring Spain. In England, there was an economic boom immediately post-war with the 'roaring twenties', the 'Jazz Age' and 'Bright Young Things'. However, this was short-lived, as industrial and economic problems developed with depression and deflation, leading to the General Strike of 1926. By the mid-1920s, there were over 2 million unemployed in Great Britain, and in Europe communism and fascism were becoming very attractive to some populations.

Gibraltar also suffered from a poor economy, limited trade and unemployment, so Monro's appointment was not an easy one, as he steered the fortress's fortunes. The Gibraltar shipping trade, a key employer, declined markedly in the 1920s and the period has been described as 'years of grinding poverty for the Gibraltarian working class'.[5]

The worst economic year in Monro's time as governor was 1927, and there was a difficult coal-heavers' strike, which began in January 1928 because of their low wages. Riots occurred as a reaction to cheap labour being brought in from Morocco, and rioters were remanded on bail. Sir Charles acted as an arbitrator between the employers and the workers and the strike was brought to an end in April. Yet again, he demonstrated his tact and ability to relate to people.

Coincidentally, in the same month as Monro assumed governorship there was a *coup d'état* in Spain, bringing to power Captain General Miguel Primo de Rivera; he would remain Spain's 'paternalistic and Catholic fascist dictator' until 1930. He attempted to unite his disgruntled country with the cry, 'Country, Religion and Monarchy' with the support of both the Church and King Alfonso XIII. His repressive government imposed martial law and banned political parties and Primo de Rivera stated, 'Our aim is to open a brief parenthesis in the constitutional life of Spain and to re-establish it as soon as the country offers us men uncontaminated with the vices of political organisation.'[6]

To balance this repression, he did build some of the best roads in Europe at the time, established state-run hotels (the *paradores*), improved dams and electricity and arranged access for workers to negotiate more fairly with their bosses. He also dealt with a significant colonial rebellion against both Spain and France in Morocco. However, despite his achievements in his seven years of power, he helped create some of the social tensions that led to the Spanish Civil War of 1936.

Perhaps surprisingly, the relationship between Spain and Gibraltar in Monro's tenure was reasonably cordial. There was no threat of conflict with Spain; the British Empire was powerful, whilst Spain was politically fragile and was busy with a fight on its hands against Abd el-Krim in Morocco. Some political stability had been reinforced by the Hispano-Franco-British Declaration of 1907, guaranteeing a status quo in the Mediterranean between the three nations. Also, there were important trade links and a great deal of contraband smuggling across the border.

There was a close connection between the British and Spanish monarchies; King Alfonso XIII had been married in 1906 to Princess Victoria Eugenie of Battenberg, or 'Princess Ena', Queen Victoria's granddaughter. Spain had remained neutral during the First World War, but it had supplied Gibraltar with much needed water supplies and allowed essential Spanish workers to keep the dockyard working. Continued friendly relations were demonstrated by Monro in 1924, when he led a delegation from the Rock to meet Primo de Rivera on the latter's official visit to Algeciras.

Inevitably, since 1704 there had been tension and some misunderstanding concerning the border between Spain and Gibraltar and the argument waxed and waned about whom the Rock should belong to. The Spanish dictator even aired the possibility of swapping Gibraltar with the Spanish colony of Ceuta in North Africa and this received some support from the military in England, including Lord Kitchener, when the idea was first raised a few years before, though this idea was never developed.

The border was not policed in the same way as it is today with intermittent tough controls of movement, enforced by Spain; this did not come until the next Spanish dictator Franco's regime. Eventually, the border was closed from 1969 and not fully reopened until the author's service in Gibraltar in 1985. In fact, the British constructed the first fence in 1909, not for defensive purposes but 'constructed of steel and of an unclimbable pattern, about seven foot high, and topped with three strands of barbed wire, thus bringing the total height to nine feet'.[7] There was some dispute about what the fence was really for and which country's soil it had been built on.

In addition, the Gibraltar Chamber of Commerce and the *Gibraltar Chronicle* complained about some of the trade restrictions across the frontier in the 1920s. During this period, two fences were erected – one patrolled by the British, the other ¼ mile away in the 'neutral ground' by the Spanish. However, the situation did not halt workers crossing from La Linea, the adjacent Spanish town, on a daily basis; British officers riding across the border to join the Royal Calpe Hunt; wealthy Gibraltarians visiting their Spanish residences nor men attending Gibraltarian prostitutes resident in La Linea. There was a great deal of economic, social and cultural exchange between the two sides and when Primo de Rivera attempted to impose strict customs controls on the frontier, Gibraltarians and their Spanish civilian neighbours joined forces to cause a policy U-turn.

The Royal Calpe Hunt was a very popular pursuit for the new governor, who remained a keen horseman and had hunted throughout his life. The hunt has been described as 'an outstanding example of the friendly co-operation between Gibraltar and Spain which sadly no longer exists'.[8] It traced its origins to 1812, when a pair of foxhounds were imported to the Rock. Whilst the kennels were based in Gibraltar, the hunt took place across the border in the rugged countryside and cork woods of the Campo de Gibraltar area of Spain. Military officers and civilians from both sides of the frontier took part and the hunt gained 'royal' status in 1906 when the British King Edward VII became a joint patron with King Alfonso XIII.

The hunt's season was from November to March and it took place twice a week, pushing into Spain for up to 14 miles. During Monro's time as governor, the most famous master ran the hunt. This was Pablo Larios, or the Marquis of Marzales, who assumed the appointment in 1891 and held the post for forty-five years. He was a wealthy landowner in Spain and provided a civilian lead, at great personal expense, to a mainly military clientele. This arrangement seemed to work well on a practical level during Monro's time in Gibraltar, but his successor as governor, General Sir Alexander Godley, did not want a Spanish civilian running a military show, so had him removed. This caused quite a stir, attracting an article in *The Field* magazine and a division between those who supported Godley, the 'Godlies', and Larios' supporters, the 'Ungodlies'! It was left to the subsequent governor, with pressure from King George V, to reinstate Larios and remove the discord.

Monro encouraged his staff and other officers to participate in the hunt and ordered offices to be shut from 1030 hours on hunting days:

The governor inspects the troops. (National Army Museum, 1923–28)

During one hunt, a horse kicked out and caught the General on his bad leg. The kick did little harm, but the General addressed the rider in the vulgar vernacular of the Army, to the scandalised amusement of the ladies who were within the range of his penetrating voice.[9]

Monro also organised an annual dinner for the Royal Calpe Hunt at his residence, Government House,[10] and ran a lunch for the farmers whose land was hunted over. However, on one occasion when he was with the hunt, he was thrown to the ground by his horse, ending up on his back for three weeks and it took several months before he returned to normal duties.

Sir Charles took a great interest in the history, people and activities of Gibraltar. In 1926 he was instrumental in formalising the current arms of Gibraltar, which are based on a triple-towered castle with a golden key dependent from the centre, presented by the Spanish sovereigns, Ferdinand and Isabella, in 1502. Following his Despatch Number 171 of 28 September 1926 and approval by the secretary of state and the College of Arms, the arms were formalised and the words '*Montis Insignia Calpe*' (A Mountain Named Calpe) were included under the device.

He also helped to design the new market, smartened up the Trafalgar Cemetery and, following monkey raids on his dressing room, arranged for the Rock monkeys to be fed regularly. In addition, he kept some popular local traditions going, such as serving food alongside Lady Monro and senior officers to the older residents of the convent on Christmas Day. Both he and his wife were responsible for a great deal of entertaining, working very closely with the Royal Navy. This culminated with the reception of the Duke and Duchess of York, the future King George VI and Queen Elizabeth, on the last stage of their Empire tour in June 1927.

During his time on the Rock, Monro commanded various military units in his garrison and oversaw many parades and activities. There is one relatively unknown dramatic story about one of those infantry battalions, 2nd Battalion East Surrey Regiment. This relates to one of the young officers shooting dead the commanding officer in his office, on 7 April 1927. The unfortunate victim, Lieutenant Colonel James Fitzgerald, had transferred to the East Surreys from the disbanded Royal Irish Regiment and had taken command in 1924. His death is recorded in *The Journal of The East Surreys* in May 1927, but no comment was made about the circumstances, because it was felt to be too embarrassing, 'The death of Lieutenant Colonel James Stephens Fitzgerald at Gibraltar, is not only a great personal sorrow to all those who knew him, but an irreparable loss to the Regiment.'[11]

The subaltern responsible, Lieutenant Austin Duffield, receives no mention, though the same journal records all the ceremonial, shooting and sporting activity on the Rock and that Lieutenant Lawton had fractured his collarbone in a point-to-point race! The 'system' did not want to make a fuss of the event, but it was well-publicised by both the local *Gibraltar Chronicle* and national newspapers at home, 'Lieutenant Colonel Fitzgerald was shot in his office this morning. The matter is the subject of official investigation.'[12]

Lieutenant Duffield was the battalion weapon training officer, and walked into Lieutenant Colonel Fitzgerald's office and fired two rounds, one of which was meant for the commanding officer and one for himself, but one of the colonel's Sam Browne belt buckles reduced the lethality of the first bullet, so the second had to be directed at him as well. The colonel's last words before dying were shouted to his adjutant, 'Dowling he has shot me, place him under arrest.'

The reason why Duffield carried out this act is still wrapped in mystery. He refused to say anything during the trial and the defence plea of insanity was not accepted by the jury, which found him guilty. The judge sentenced him to death on 17 June 1927 and the Chief Justice's speech included the statement, 'It was a deliberate and considered killing of a defenceless man', and there was no doubt of his guilt.[13] Duffield said in a statement before the trial, 'Since our arrival in Gibraltar the CO has given up all idea of soldiering and it is better that one man should die than that the whole of the Regiment be ruined.'[14]

There was certainly animosity between the two characters – Fitzgerald was an Irish Roman Catholic, whilst Duffield was an Irish Presbyterian. Moreover, Duffield was known to be seeing the colonel's daughter; a fact that her father did not appreciate. Her name was not mentioned in court. There have been other contributory rumours concerning Fitzgerald's war service as a prisoner of war and his relationship with his captor Germans, and an unproven accusation that he had made homosexual advances towards other officers.

The local civilian population reacted strongly against the conviction because they felt that the sentence was too harsh, and they presented General Monro with a petition for Duffield's reprieve. There was also a petition from Belfast. Sir Charles obviously agreed to these appeals for leniency, as he commuted the sentence to penal servitude for life on 12 July 1927. His reason for this decision will probably never be known, but according to an account by a Brigadier Norman Brading, another East Surrey subaltern in Gibraltar during 1927 and a former aide-de-camp to Monro in his last period as governor, Brading questioned the general why Duffield had only received a life sentence:

> He [Monro] said, 'Well I actually can't tell you, but I was just as surprised as you were, and there it is. It has been given out that there hasn't been a hanging in Gibraltar for so many years, and politically they didn't want another one. But that was just tape. One day it will come out and we shall get to know about it.'[15]

It never has. Brading added that the battalion was 'very unhappy' because the commanding officer was not an East Surrey and he was disliked.

Duffield spent fifty-nine days in the Moorish Castle, then he was shipped to prison in England. He was released in 1937 and later joined the King's African Rifles and may have served in a Uganda regiment as a warrant officer. He reportedly became the editor of the *Uganda Herald* and it is claimed in one source that he earned the MBE![16]

There is no doubt that the now 68-year-old Sir Charles was highly respected during his governorship of Gibraltar. This was reflected by a report in newspapers at the time of his departure in 1928:

> General Sir Charles Monro, the Governor of Gibraltar, has been paid an unusual compliment by the Chamber of Commerce, which has sent a telegram to the Secretary of State for the Colonies, Mr Amery, asking that the Governor's term of office shall be extended owing to his 'general popularity'.[17]

The Governor's Palace. (Author's collection)

The Governor's Cottage. (Author's collection)

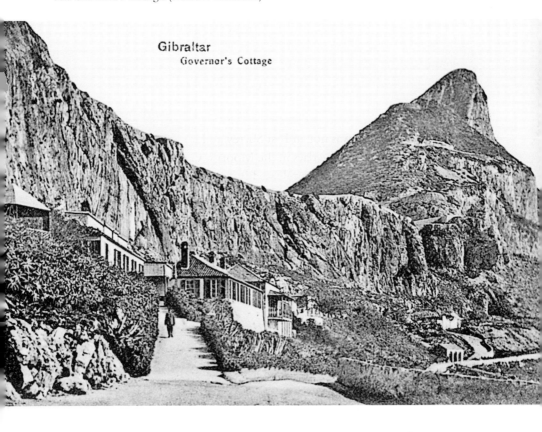

This request was not granted. However, as he left, the senior member of the Executive Council commented on his justice, tact, zeal, humanity, kindness and hospitality, whilst the board of directors of the Chamber of Commerce made some handsome presentations to Sir Charles and Lady Monro as they departed. The key director included the following words in his farewell speech:

> Your period of Governorship will be a memorable one indeed, for your unfailing kindness, your invariable tact in dealing with the many delicate matters that ever arise during the term of a colonial Governorship, and the really deep personal interest which both you and Lady Monro have ever taken in all that concerns Gibraltar and its population without distinction of class or creed.[18]

The general and his wife were presented with an enormous silver salver and a tea service. All this praise was accepted with his usual humility. Shortly afterwards, he wrote to a close friend:

> At any rate the curtain has fallen on my military career. I leave it with regret, but with the assurance held to a marked degree, that a real Guardian Angel has watched over the career of an inconspicuous officer, with loving care, and has thereby secured the advancement of this individual very far beyond his deserts.[19]

Last Duties

As the Monros departed on the P&O ship *Kaisar-i-Hind* back to England, they did not realise that he had only a year to live. They spent part of the 1928–29 winter in Alassio, Italy, and the general prepared to fill his life with six main tasks: governor and commandant of the Church Lads' Brigade; trustee of the Imperial War Museum; chairman of the Soldiers' & Sailors' Family Association and the Army Temperance Association; and finally, his favourite appointment of colonel of the Queen's Royal Regiment (West Surrey) and of the 24th London Regiment (Queen's).

He gave many speeches on these organisations' behalf. For example, he was vocally not impressed by the decision of the government to withdraw support from the Cadet Corps – a decision later reversed. He had highlighted their virtues of 'discipline, obedience, sacrifice and comradeship' and the immense contribution of ex-cadets to the First World War.[20]

He died in the early hours of 7 December 1929 at his home at 54 Eaton Square, London. He had developed cancer and underwent an unsuccessful operation on 30 November. Unusually for a retired officer, on 11 December he was given the honour of a full military funeral in Westminster Abbey, the same place that he was married. The Dean of Westminster officiated and the pall-bearers were General Sir George Barrow (his previous chief of staff and original biographer), General Sir Archibald Murray, General Sir Havelock Hudson, General Sir George Kirkpatrick, General Sir Robert Whigham, Lieutenant Colonel Sir Edward Altham, Lieutenant General Sir Thomas Scott and Lieutenant General Sir George MacMunn. The royal family was represented and the First Sea Lord, Marshal of the Royal Air Force and the Army Council were present. The large congregation included an incredibly long list of nobility and high-ranking officers from all three services; the late Sir Charles had 'touched' a great deal of the leaders of British Society and the Empire during his sixty-nine years of life.

A myriad of organisations that he had been connected with paid their respects. The 2nd Battalion the Queen's Royal Regiment (West Surrey) provided a guard of honour accompanied by its regimental colour and detachments from the Territorial 4th and 6th Battalions, along with men from the 22nd and 24th London Regiments (Queen's). Lady Monro had his favourite hymns sung and the Union flag on his coffin, provided by the trustees of the Imperial War Museum, was the same flag used at Earl Haig's funeral.[21] His sword, headdress and a wreath of white lilies lay on the Union flag. Regimental buglers sounded the 'Last Post' and 'Reveille' and senior non-commissioned officers from his regiment carried his coffin out of the abbey to the sound of the band of the Welsh Guards. He was buried in Brompton Cemetery.

The British Library contains a fascinating collection of Monro obituaries, collected by his wife and bound in leather with the initials 'CCM' on the cover.[22] On a lighter note, but recognising his enthusiasm for riding and hunting, the *Horse and Hound* magazine described him as a 'rare good sportsman and cheery companion'.[23] More thoughtfully, the *Army and Navy Gazette* reported:

Never spectacular in either his actions or decisions, Sir Charles Monro was little in the public eye, but he should be remembered as a single-minded servant of his country, possessed not only of wisdom and tact but of that high degree of moral course which is as rare in high places as among the common folk, as one who always put the welfare of his Service and his country before all personal considerations and was not afraid to risk misunderstanding and unpopularity by making what he considered just decisions.[24]

The grave of Sir Charles and Lady Monro, Brompton Cemetery. (Author's collection)

A great regimental friend and previous colonel of the regiment, General Sir E. O. F. Hamilton, paid a personal tribute to Sir Charles Monro in the *Surrey Advertiser* of 14 December 1929:

> As one of his oldest brother officers in The Queen's, as well as one of his oldest friends, I can testify to his popularity in the Regiment and to his excellence as a Regimental officer. He never sought popularity or public notice, but he gained both by his genial character and abilities.[25]

Pristinae Virtutis Memor
Vel Exuviae Triumphans

An Assessment

General Sir Charles Monro was an extremely competent and successful British Army officer, fiercely loyal to the Empire, his country, subordinates and his regiment. He was also highly decorated, though he was never famous and did not reach the ultimate rank of field marshal despite his achievements. He was also a loving husband, though he and Lady Monro had no children.

'He came, he saw, he capitulated' were the harsh words of Winston Churchill, following Monro's decision making at Gallipoli, and he would certainly not have endeared himself to the great politician over some of his actions relating to the fate of Brigadier General Dyer after the Amritsar massacre. Monro did not court popularity; he did what he thought was the right thing and it was a particularly brave decision to go against Kitchener's intent to continue fighting at Gallipoli and to stick to the plan of Dyer's retirement and extraction from India in the face of intense political pressure.

As a young officer, he experienced typical soldiering around the Empire in the late nineteenth and early twentieth centuries; he was inquisitive and developed an intelligent and practical style of command. He was always highly respected by both superiors and subordinates and he achieved high command, though he had not commanded an infantry battalion. He was also popular with soldiers despite his disciplinary nature and outwardly robust manner and he recognised and promoted talent.

Barrow, his first and until now only biographer, was certainly biased in his praise of his leader, however, he was close to him and did know him exceptionally well. He does, however, avoid too much adverse criticism and fails to mention some of the tricky situations that the general had to deal with. In particular, the challenges of 1916, when Monro was commanding the

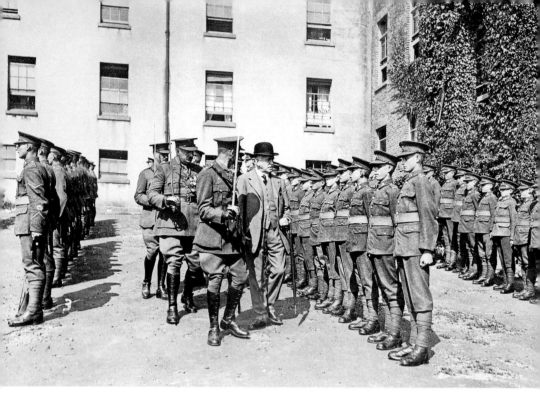

The colonel-in-chief inspects troops at Dover, 1926. (Surrey History Centre. QRWS 30ELIAGE 1-21-1)

1st Army and the uncharacteristic weak decisions made concerning the Battle of Fromelles, which are, remarkably, ignored. This has led some modern historians to comment that Monro was, 'a very limited general'; a comment that is unfair when one looks at Monro's wider contribution to the war effort.[1]

Monro did gain substantial command experience leading a division, corps and army at war and he also gave critical strategic leadership at Gallipoli, Mesopotamia, in the Third Afghan War and a number of smaller conflicts. However, despite succeeding Haig as both corps and army commander and being respected by him for his steadiness and judgement, he never seemed to gain complete trust from the latter and he was not given much opportunity to prove himself at corps and army level. Haig had not wanted him to command the 1st Army; he had other favourites.

He was particularly keen at improving training for war within a very conservative army establishment and was one of a few influential officers to recognise the value of machine guns and the importance of musketry and appropriate tactics. Throughout his career he encouraged innovation in training and his influence at Hythe before the war and the development of specialist training schools during the conflict are now virtually forgotten.

Another supreme success, which is all but forgotten now, is his immense impact in India as C-in-C. The efforts he made to raise extra troops in India, make the Indian Army more efficient and control the border areas receives little attention from historians – but it should do, as many 'behind the scenes' activities in conflict are often more important than some of the battles fought. He dealt with the Third Afghan War and Waziristan skilfully, making the best of the resources he was able to muster.

Barrow acknowledged that Monro had a very bluff and direct manner, but states that this hid an 'exceedingly reserved, sensitive, nervous and highly strung' character.[2] Few who did not know him well noticed these traits, but he was sympathetic and humane; note his handling of the Territorial Force units in India in 1919 when they wanted to return home and demobilise, and the Duffield affair in Gibraltar. This did not mean, however, that he did not believe in tough discipline. For example, he followed the other senior generals' attitude with his approach to desertion.

Perhaps his weakest characteristic was a reluctance to make calculated risks. The greatest commanders, who win critical battles, have to display this attribute. Barrow acknowledges that 'he was far from being an adventurer' and he did not take any action that was not cautiously thought through.[3] Rather, he was efficient, tactful and calculating and this was particularly ideal for assessing the Gallipoli and Mesopotamia situations and for his service in India and Gibraltar. He disliked any hint of amateurism, which was often evident in some British officers, and he admired German professionalism. These attributes were diverse compared to the publicity-seeking and tactless Haig or the womanising French; the press were not generally interested in a quietly efficient, professional, but less flamboyant commander.

He was not the perfect commander – who is? Though he was intelligent, loyal, efficient, kind, modest, popular, tactful, determined and decisive, he also lacked imagination and flamboyancy and did make a number of wrong decisions. However, his achievements, dominated by his common sense, far outweighed his faults. General Sir Charles Monro left an important mark on history and this should be recognised:

> He was the best type of British officer – brave, level-headed, unassuming, conscientious – and in a long and distinguished career devoted to the service of his country proved himself a leader of men and a wise and absolutely honest public servant.[4]

Modesty and a serious desire to do the duty set before him precluded his ever becoming as well known as his merit deserved, but he should be remembered with gratitude as a most able and single-minded servant of the State.[5]

THE CAREER OF GENERAL SIR CHARLES CARMICHAEL MONRO, BART., GCB, GCSI, GCMG

Year	Rank and Appointment	Location
1860 (15 June)		Birth at sea
1871–78		Pupil – Sherborne School
1878–79	Gentleman Cadet – Student	Royal Military College, Sandhurst
1879	Second Lieutenant – Platoon Commander, 1st Battalion the Queen's (Royal West Surrey) Regiment	Colchester
1881–86	Lieutenant – Adjutant, 1st Battalion the Queen's (Royal West Surrey) Regiment	Colchester and Ireland
1889–90	Captain, Student	Staff College, Camberley
1890–98	Captain, then Major (1898) – Company Commander, 1st Battalion the Queen's (Royal West Surrey) Regiment	Malta, India, Mohmand and Tirah expeditions
1898–99	Major	Brigade Major, Gibraltar; DAAG, Guernsey

Year	Rank and Appointment	Location
1899–1901	Major, then Brevet Lieutenant Colonel (1900) – DAAG	Aldershot, then 6th Division South Africa
1901–07	Lieutenant Colonel, then Colonel (1903) – Chief Instructor, then Commandant School of Musketry	Hythe
1907–11	Brigadier General – Brigade Commander, 13th Infantry Brigade	Dublin, Ireland
1912–14	Major General – GOC 2nd London Division	Southern England
1914 (August–December)	Major General – GOC 2nd Division	Western Front
1915 (December 1914–July)	Lieutenant General – GOC I Corps	Western Front
1915 (July–October)	General – GOC 3rd Army	Western Front
1915 (October–November)	General – C-in-C Mediterranean Expeditionary Force	Gallipoli
1915–16 (November–February)	General – C-in-C Eastern Mediterranean Forces	Gallipoli and Salonika
1916 (February–October)	General – GOC 1st Army	Western Front
1916–20 (October–August)	General – C-in-C India	India
1920	Retired	
1923–28	Governor	Gibraltar

Year	Rank and Appointment	Location
1928	Trustee Imperial War Museum in succession to Earl Haig. He was also Governor and Commandant of the Church Lads' Brigade, Chairman of the Soldiers' and Sailors' Family Association and the Army Temperance Association	
1929 (7 December)		Died – 54 Eaton Square, London

The Monro coat of arms.
(Author's collection)

The Honours and Awards of General Sir Charles Carmichael Monro, Bart., GCB, GCSI, GCMG

Year	Honour/Award	Comment
1906	Companion of the Bath (CB)	Ordinary Member of the Military Division of the 3rd Class
1915	Knight Commander of the Order of the Bath (KCB)	Additional Member of the Military Division of the 2nd Class
1915	French Legion of Honour	Grand Officer – 2nd Class
1916	Knight Grand Cross of the Most Distinguished Order of Saint Michael and Saint George (GCMG)	For distinguished services rendered in connection with the withdrawal of the Force from the Gallipoli Peninsula. He was mentioned in despatches four times during his career
1918–22	Aide-de-Camp General to the king	
1919	Japanese Order of the Rising Sun	Grand Cordon

Year	Honour/Award	Comment
1919	Knight Grand Cross of the Most Honourable Order of the Bath (GCB)	Additional Member of the Military Division of the 1st Class. Appointed King of Arms in 1921, a post held until his death
1919	Knight Grand Commander of the Star of India (GCSI)	As C-in-C India
1920–29	Colonel of the Queen's Royal Regiment (West Surrey)	
1921	Created 1st Baronet of Bearcrofts, Stirlingshire, Bath King-at-Arms and Knight of Grace of the Order of the Hospital of St John of Jerusalem	
1922–28	Honorary Colonel of 23rd Battalion, the London Regiment	
Other Medals	India Medal 1895–1902 (2 clasps: Tirah 1897–98 and Punjab Frontier 1897–98) Queen's South Africa Medal 1899–1902 (3 clasps: Driefontein, Paardeberg and Relief of Kimberley) 1914 Star clasp British War Medal 1914–20 Allied Victory Medal 1914–19; oak leaf clasp India General Service Medal 1908–35	

NOTES

Chapter 1

1   Lubbock (1955), p.181.
2   *Argus* newspaper, Melbourne, Monday, 19 March 1860.
3   Barrow (1931), p.268.
4   Information from current family members: Alastair Monro Gaisford and Dr Christina Goulter.
5   A tenth child, James, was born in 1854 but died as a baby.
6   School archivist information from *The Sherborne Register* and *Shirburnian* magazine.
7   Gourlay (1971), p.122.
8   Barrow (1931), pp.16 and 265.
9   Ibid. p.19.
10 Gourlay (1971), p.139.
11 School archivist information from *The Sherborne Register* and *Shirburnian* magazine.
12 www.sherborne.org/about us/a-brief-history.
13 Gourlay (1971), p.139.
14 Moore-Bick (2011), pp.19–20.
15 *The Western Gazette*, Friday, 1 July 1921.
16 Thomas (1961), p.151.
17 Barnett (1974), p.314.
18 Robbins (2005), p.3.
19 Turner (1956), p.243.
20 Yardley (1987), p.40.
21 Younghusband (1891), p.iv.
22 Ibid. p.6.
23 Hamilton, Ian B. M. (1966), p.12.
24 Younghusband (1891), p.13.
25 Heathcote (1978), p.17.
26 *Hart's Annual Army List* (1881), p.347. George was commissioned into the 101st (Royal Bengal Fusiliers) on 16 February 1878. He later served in the Worcestershire Regiment and was retired as a major in 1904.

27 Mockler-Ferryman (1900), p.40.
28 Shepperd (1980), p.79.
29 Heathcote (1978), p.18.
30 Thomas (1961), p.140.
31 Barrow (1931), p.20.
32 Mockler-Ferryman (1900), p.112.
33 Marshal-Cornwall (1973), p.2.
34 Thomas (1961) pp.143–44.
35 Ibid. p.132.
36 Barrow (1931), p.20.
37 The regiment has been amalgamated over the years and is now the Princess of Wales's Royal Regiment (PWRR). The author is a deputy colonel of the PWRR.
38 Foster (1961), p.59.
39 Irwin (2004), pp.32–35; Yardley and Sewell (1989), p.46.
40 Bond (1961), p.236.
41 Crowley, Wilson and Fosten (2002), p.42; Musketeer (1951), p.600.
42 Anonymous (1953), p.37.
43 Strachan (1997), Chapter 9.
44 Myatt (1981), p.56.
45 Bond (1962), p.115.
46 French (2005), p.21.
47 Davis (1906), Vol. VI, p.161.
48 Davis (1906), Vol. V, p.177.
49 Turner (1956), p.266.
50 Barrow (1942), p.41.
51 Robbins (2010), p.28.
52 Younghusband (1891), Chapter IV; War Office Report (1888), p.2.
53 Ibid. p.6.
54 Barrow (1931), p.20; Godwin-Austen (1927), p.227.
55 Younghusband (1891), p.154.
56 Ibid. p.240.
57 Young (1958), p.55.
58 Jeffery (2006), p.17.
59 Bond (1972), p.137.
60 Barclay (1958), p.176.
61 Report (1892).
62 F. N. Maude retired as a colonel, was a military author and ran the book reviews for the *Journal of the Royal United Service Institution*.
63 N. B. Inglefield was a key cricket player for the Royal Artillery.
64 Ibid. pp.6–7.
65 Bond (1972), p.126.
66 Godwin-Austen (1927), p.227.
67 Bond (1972), p.141.
68 Barclay (1958), p.176.
69 Robertson (1921), p.89.
70 Ibid. p.90.
71 Barrow (1942), p.46.

72 Holden Reid (1992), p.3.
73 Liddell Hart (1927), p.174.
74 Fuller (1935), pp.122–23.
75 Holden Reid (1992), pp.5 and 11.

Chapter 2

1   Davies (1906), p.179.
2   Modern parlance for brigade major is 'chief of staff'.
3   Barrow (1931), p.20.
4   Moon (1989), p.902.
5   Ibid. p.904.
6   Holmes (2005), p.81.
7   Beloc poem, 'The Modern Traveller' (1898).
8   Wilkinson (1976), p.174.
9   *The Works of Rudyard Kipling* (1994), p.440.
10 Birdwood (1941), p.77.
11 Messenger (1994), p.212.
12 Heathcote (1974), p.158.
13 Heathcote (1995), p.127.
14 Barthorp (1996), p.24.
15 Haswell (1967), p.110.
16 Skeen (2008 reprint 1932), p.2.
17 *Our Indian Empire* (1937), p.8.
18 Kipling (1994), p.418.
19 Shadwell (1898), pp.1, 3 and 25.
20 Tribal Analysis Center (TAC) (2009), p.1. The TAC is an independent
    cultural and geographical research organisation based in the USA. It
    specialises in the collection of data related to tribes in remote areas of the
    world. The analysts come from a wide range of academics and professionals.
21 Ibid. p.8.
22 Barrow (1931), p.22.
23 Manchester (1983), p.252.
24 Coughlin (2013), pp. XV and XII.
25 Ibid. (From the *Daily Telegraph* 9 October 1897) p.178.
26 Davis (1906), p.185.
27 Manchester (1983), p.253.
28 Haswell (1967), p.111.
29 Hobday (1898), p.110.
30 Churchill (1898 reprint), p.189.
31 Davis (1906), p.187.
32 Burkitt (1917), p.76.
33 Callwell (1911), p.8.
34 Miller (1977), p.273.
35 Callwell (1911), p.9.
36 Ibid. p.vii.
37 Ibid. p.151.
38 Hutchinson (1898), pp.224 and 226.

39 Statistics from Shadwell (1898), p.94.
40 *Regimental India* (undated), p.24.
41 Barthorp (1982), p.133.
42 Brazier (2010), pp.160/161.
43 Chichester and Burges-Short (1900), p.761.
44 Davis (1906), p.193.
45 Shadwell (1898), p.154.
46 Ibid. p.165.
47 Davis (1906), p.199.
48 Shadwell (1898), p.185.
49 Lieutenant Wallace Wright was to earn the VC serving with the 1st Battalion in Nigeria, just four years later. He also became a Member of Parliament.
50 Callwell (reprint 1990), p.289.
51 James (1898), p.217.
52 Callwell (1911), p.140.
53 Coughlin (2013), p.253.
54 Davis (1906), p.208.

Chapter 3

1   Conan Doyle (1903), p.11. Conan Doyle wrote one of the first, most popular books on the Boer War.
2   Farwell (2009), p.30.
3   Ibid. p.33. The word *helot* is used to describe a serf or slave. Its origin is from ancient Greece, where the occupied inhabitants of Helos were serfs of the Spartans.
4   Barnett (1974), p.338.
5   Carver (1999), p.12.
6   Cole and Priestly (1936), p.265.
7   Barnett (1974), p.340.
8   Hay (1942), p.116.
9   'The South African War of 1899–1900', *Royal United Service Institution Journal* (RUSI) (1901), p.1238.
10 Amery (1905), p.337.
11 *The London Gazette*, 8 December 1899, p.8258.
12 Hall (1999), p.60.
13 Lord Kitchener joining the ship at Gibraltar.
14 Gooch (2000), p.573.
15 Wessells (2000), p.45.
16 Barrow (1931), pp.23–24.
17 Ibid. p.24.
18 Caunter (Undated), p.12.
19 The National Archives, WO105/6. Kelly-Kenny Despatch.
20 Ibid.
21 Pakenham (1979), p.333.
22 Farwell (2009), p.206.
23 Selby (1969), p.178.
24 Wessels (2006), p.13.

25 Royle (1985), p.163.

26 Magnus (1958), p.164.

27 Farwell (2009), p.207.

28 Arthur (1920), pp.280–81.

29 Pakenham (1979), p.335.

30 Caunter (undated), p.16.

31 Conan Doyle (1903), p.250.

32 Pakenham (1979), p.335.

33 The National Archives, WO105/6 – Major General Colville's Report on Paardeberg, 3 March 1900.

34 Smith-Dorrien (1925), p.154.

35 'The Lessons of the Boer War and the Battle Working of the Three Arms', RUSI (1901), p.1242.

36 Ibid. p.1393.

37 Pakenham (1979), p.337.

38 The National Archives, WO105/6 – Kelly-Kenny Despatch.

39 Pakenham (1979), p.337.

40 Daniell (1951), p.201.

41 Stirling (1903), p.185.

42 Brazier (2010), p.167.

43 Stirling (1903), pp.230–231.

44 http://thercr.ca/history.

45 Magnus (1958), p.167.

46 De Wet (1902), p.57.

47 The National Archives, WO105/6 – Kelly-Kenny Despatch to Lord Roberts, 20 February 1900.

48 Ibid. Lord Roberts' Despatch on Paardeberg, 28 February 1900.

49 Pollock (1998), p.181.

50 Gibbs (1957), pp.228–29.

51 Arthur (1920), p.283.

52 Ibid. p.291.

53 The National Archives, WO105/6 – Field Marshal Roberts' Despatch, 31 March 1900.

54 Wessells (2000), pp.126–27.

55 Wessells (2006), p.13.

56 Baden-Powell (1903), p.33.

57 Eady (1930), pp.10 and 164.

58 Caunter (undated), p.18.

59 Farwell (2009), p.210.

60 De Wet (1902), p.56.

61 Ibid. pp.63 and 64.

62 Selby (1969), p.186.

63 Barrow (1931), pp.24–25.

64 The National Archives, WO105/6 – Kelly-Kenny Despatch to Lord Roberts, 3 March 1900.

65 Amery (1905), p.553.

66 Ibid. p.558.

67 De Wet (1902), p.69.

68   Stirling (1903), p.54.
69   Amery (1905), p.569.
70   Conan Doyle (1903), p.262.
71   Sixsmith (1976), p.40.
72   Pakenham (1979), p.375.
73   Barrow (1931), p.25.
74   Conan Doyle (1903), p.264.
75   Knight (1935), p.590.
76   De Wet (1902), p.70.
77   Ibid.
78   Ibid. p.73.
79   Pollock (1900), p.196.
80   Jackson (1999), p.103.
81   Ibid.
82   Wessells (2000), p.127.
83   Jackson (1999), pp.131–32.
84   Wessells (2000), p.175.
85   Belfield (1975), p.114.
86   Carver (1999), p.199.
87   Wessells (2000), p.128.
88   Ibid. pp.128–29.

Chapter 4

1   Amery (1903), pp.10–11.
2   Caunter (1901).
3   May (1901), pp.191 and 198–99.
4   Balck (1904), *Journal of the Royal United Service Institution*, Vol. XLVII, pp.1276–77.
5   Churchill (1901), *Journal of the Royal United Service Institution*, Vol. XLV, p.839.
6   Johnson (1960), p.48.
7   Barrow (1931), pp.26 and 31.
8   Stewart (1903), p.1.
9   'Always on the Bull', *Soldier* (January 1969), p.16.
10   Robertson (1921), p.23.
11   Stewart (1903), p.3.
12   *Journal of the Royal United Service Institution*, Vol. XLIX (July–December 1905), pp.1175 and 1182.
13   Details from the National Archives, WO76/356.
14   Known as the 'Mad Minute'. Every soldier was taught to place fifteen aimed shots in one minute onto a 4ft target at a range of 300 yards.
15   Macdonald (1987), p.98.
16   Myatt (1983), p.161.
17   Lucy (1938), pp.113–14.
18   Edmonds, Vol. 1 (1923–49), p.11.
19   Dunlop (1938), p.127.
20   Ibid. p.132.
21   Amery (1903).

22 Amery (1903), p.32.

23 Unfortunately, the round peakless cap, known as the 'Brodrick', was not popular, as it looked ridiculous! It was replaced by a German-style cap in 1904.

24 Barnett (1974), p.357.

25 Dunlop (1938), p.146.

26 Ibid. p.179.

27 Ibid. p.203.

28 Ibid. p.179.

29 Ibid. p.177.

30 Ibid. p.231.

31 Sheffield (2011), p.57.

32 Sixsmith (1976), p.53 and Viscount Esher, 'Journals and Letters 1', p.391.

33 Sheffield (2011), p.59.

34 Mayne (1903), p.223.

35 Haldane quotation from his autobiography, quoted in Dunlop (1938), p.235.

36 *Army Quarterly* (1947–48), p.50.

37 General Staff can be defined nowadays as a body of military professionals selected for their intellect and proven merit; an elite, who are educated in a programme of demanding, selective education and training. *British Army Review*, No 163 (Spring/Summer 2015), p.112.

38 Jeffery (1985), Introduction.

39 Coincidentally, the Regular Army of today is being reduced by 20,000 personnel.

40 For further information read *Stand To* magazine of the Western Front Association, September 2013, Fox p.41–45.

41 Barnett (1974), p.367.

42 *Army Quarterly* (1947–48), p.54.

43 *Field Service Regulations Part I Operations 1909* (reprint 1914), p.135.

44 Dunlop (1938), p.226.

45 Mayne (1903), pp.232–33.

46 Andrew (1906), p.38.

47 Callwell (1909), p.89.

48 *Infantry Training Manual 1905*, Foreword.

49 *Infantry Training Manual 1911*, pp.103–04.

50 The National Archives Kew, WO33/337 – The Russo-Japanese War up to 15 August 1904, p.78.

51 Jones (2012), p.205.

52 *The Nottingham Post*, 21 December 1901.

53 Now called 'Tactical Exercises without Troops' (TEWTs).

54 Spiers (1980), p.152.

55 *Training and Manoeuvre Regulations 1913*.

56 Barrow (1931), p.32.

57 Ibid. p.33.

58 *Royal United Service Institution Journal*, Vol. XLIX (July–December 1905), p.1281.

59 Jones (2012), p.53.

60 Ibid. p.54.

61 Ibid. p.55.

62   The National Archives, WO27/508 – IG Report for 1907, p.79.
63   French and Holden Reid (2002), pp.98–99.
64   Bowman and Connelly (2012); Simpson (1981), p.3.
65   Dunlop (1938), p.306.
66   *The London Gazette*, 29 June 1906, p.4460.
67   *The Army Review* (1911), p.91.
68   *Journal of the Society for Army Historical Research*, Vol. 59 (1981), p.94.

Chapter 5

1   Quotation from *The Army Quarterly*, Obituary (1930), p.237.
2   Details from *The New Army List*, 1910.
3   http://www.firstworldwar.com/bio/plumer.htm.
4   Barrow (1931), pp.15–16.
5   Wickes (1974), p.41.
6   Barrow (1931), p.37.
7   Ibid. p.38.
8   Ibid. p.37.
9   Ibid. pp.38–39.
10   Mary O'Hagan was born on 25 November 1879 and died on 28 August 1972.
11   Lady Alice O'Hagan was not able to maintain Towneley Hall and sold it to Burnley Corporation in 1901.
12   *The Times*, 1 October 1912.
13   Sir Bhawani Singh Bahadur had been the Maharaj Rana of the Rajput State of Jhalawar since 1899. He was keen on informing his subjects about Western culture. He was a member of the Royal Society of Great Britain, a keen astronomer, and built Kemball Public Library and Colwin's Girls' School.
14   *The Times*, Tuesday, 1 October 1912, lists all of the key guests and gifts in detail.
15   *The Manchester Courier*, 2 October 1912 – 'Society Weddings' section.
16   *The New York Times*, 2 October 1912 – 'Dog Attends Bride'.
17   *The Essex County Chronicle*, Friday, 4 October 1912.
18   Davis (1906), Vol. VI, p.142.
19   Detail from *Who Was Who* (1935), p.309.
20   *Oxford Dictionary of National Biography*, 1937.
21   Barrow (1931), p.40.
22   Ibid.
23   *The War Illustrated* (1916), p.1836.
24   Beckett and Corvi (2006), p.125.
25   For further details of the 1912 manoeuvres, read Simon Batten, *Journal of the Society for Army Historical Research*, Vol. 93, No 373 (Spring 2015), pp.25–47.
26   French (1919), p.298.
27   Dennis (1987), p.30.
28   French (1919), p.300.
29   French (1919), p.299.
30   Dennis (1987), p.262.
31   Ibid. p.23.
32   Ibid. p.24.

33 Beckett (2008), p.34.
34 Ibid. p.25.
35 Ibid. p.29.
36 The unit was considered deployable for foreign service if 75 per cent of its members volunteered.
37 Magnus (1958), p.233.
38 Dennis (1987), p.30.
39 Magnus (1958), p.290.
40 Maude (1922), p.vii.

Chapter 6

1   Barrow (1931), p.41.
2   Total German Army numbers available were about 1 million conscripts and 4 million reserves.
3   Liddell Hart article in *Purnell's History of the First World War* (1970), p.120. John Charteris had been one of Haig's personal staff officers in India, and had returned with him to the Aldershot Command in 1912 (the 'Hindoo Invasion'), author of *At GHQ*, published in 1931.
4   Sheffield and Todman (2004), p.46.
5   Holmes (1999), p.39. Quotation of Field Marshal Lord Chetwode.
6   Churchill (1937), p.84.
7   Terraine (1960), pp.15–16.
8   French and Smith-Dorrien loathed each other. Smith-Dorrien had been appointed by Kitchener, the Secretary of State for War. French had wanted Plumer to command II Corps.
9   Davies and Maddocks (1995), p.83 and Charteris (1931).
10 Archibald Murray was thought of as intelligent and able, but better as a senior staff officer than commanding in the field.
11 Sheffield and Bourne (2005), p.57.
12 Wyrall (1921), p.329.
13 HMSO (1935), pp.41–42.
14 *Catastrophe* by Max Hastings and *1914* by Allan Mallinson.
15 Simpson (2006), Chapter 1; Sheffield and Todman (2004), Chapter 5.
16 Barrow (1931), p.41.
17 Kipling (1997), p.30.
18 The National Archives, WO95/1283/1 – 20 August 1914; Wyrall (1921), p.xiv.
19 French (1919), p.36.
20 Terraine (1960), p.44. The 'Old Contemptibles' nickname was proudly taken up by the BEF.
21 Macdonald (1987), p.99.
22 Bloem (1930), p.75.
23 Ibid. p.108.
24 The National Archives, WO95 1283/1 – 24 August 1914.
25 *Staff Officers' Handbook* definition (2000), 6-4-50.
26 Wyrall (1921), p.28.
27 Sheffield and Bourne (2005), p.63.
28 French (1919), p.68.

29 The National Archives, WO95 1283/1 – 4th (Guards) Brigade record, 1930 hours, 25 August 1914.
30 Whitbread.
31 Sheffield and Bourne (2005), p.65.
32 Macdonald (1987), p.268.
33 Hamilton (1917), p.50.
34 Herbert (2009), p.17.
35 Kipling (1997), p.34.
36 The National Archives, WO95 1283/1 – 26 August 1914.
37 Brazier (2010), p.182.
38 French (1919), p.77.
39 Sheffield (2011), p.78.
40 Ascoli (1981), p.113.
41 Smith-Dorrien statement, Imperial War Museum, pp.8–9. For a fuller assessment of the dispute over French's comments about Smith-Dorrien and the latter's response, read Beckett (1993). Smith-Dorrien's statement was published as an internal 'Private and Secret' document in response to French's book *1914* at the end of 1919.
42 Wyrall (1921), p.43.
43 Sheffield and Bourne (2005), p.68.
44 Macdonald (1987), pp.233 and 235.
45 Ibid. p.235.
46 The National Archives, WO95 1283/1 – 28 and 29 August 1914.
47 Wyrall (1921), p.47.
48 Kipling (1997), p.37.
49 Ibid.
50 Terraine (1960), pp.181–82.
51 Spears (1930), p.415. A vital reference covering British and French relationships at the highest military levels in 1914.
52 Wyrall (1921), p.50.
53 Ibid. p.57.
54 Sixsmith (1976), p.76.
55 Wyrall (1921), p.63; French (1919), p.129.
56 Kipling (1997), p.41.
57 French (1919), p.132.
58 Ascoli (1981), p.155.
59 Wyrall (1921), p.67.
60 French (1919), p.145.
61 Sheffield and Bourne (2005), p.70.
62 The National Archives, I Corps War Diary.
63 Brazier (2010), p.184.
64 Wyrall (1921), p.84.
65 Kipling (1997), p.42.
66 French (1919), p.153.
67 Wyrall (1921), p.87.
68 Ibid. p.88.
69 The National Archives, WO95 1283/3 – 22 September 1914, 2nd Division War Diary.

70 Wyrall (1921), p.216.

71 Murland (2012), p.199.

72 Sheffield and Bourne (2005), p.73.

73 Carew (1964), p.217.

74 Conan Doyle (1916), pp.240 and 244.

75 French (1919), p.241.

76 Wyrall (1921), p.133.

77 French (1919), p.241.

78 Davies and Maddocks (1995), p.69.

79 The National Archives, WO95 1283/2 – 31 October 1914, 2nd Division War Diary.

80 He was succeeded by Brigadier General E. Bulfin, 2nd Brigade commander. Brigadier General Lord Cavan, commanding 4th (Guards) Brigade, took over 2nd and 3rd Brigades as well during this fast-moving, changing environment.

81 Barrow (1931), p.44.

82 French (1919), p.257.

83 Hussey, *British Army Review* (August 1994), p.81.

84 Beckett (2004), p.137.

85 Hussey (1994), p.82; Charteris (1931), p.53.

86 Macdonald (1987), p.391.

87 Sheffield and Bourne (2005), p.77.

88 Barrow (1931), p.45.

89 Wyrall (1921), p.152.

90 Wylly (1925), p.26.

91 Brazier (2010), p.186.

92 Wyrall (1921), p.153.

93 Macdonald (1987), pp.418–19.

94 Sheffield and Bourne (2005), p.81.

95 Barrow (1931), p.46.

96 Wyrall (1921), p.158.

97 Beckett and Corvi (2006), p.126.

98 French (1919), p.153.

99 LHCMA – Liddell Hart 15/6/5/13.

Chapter 7

1   Liddell Hart (1970), p.135.

2   Edmonds (1927), p.1.

3   Ibid. p.3.

4   Edmonds (1928), p.ix.

5   Senior (2012).

6   Daniell (1955), p.262.

7   Imperial War Museum, Letters of Sir Philip Game to his wife.

8   Haking (1914), p.463.

9   Senior (2012), p.1 and Imperial War Museum, Horne Papers, 23 January 1919.

10 Terraine (1998), p.46. For detailed study, read Farr, *The Silent General: Horne of the First Army* (2007), and Robbins, *British Generalship during the Great War* (2010).

11   Farr (2007), p.272.
12   Imperial War Museum – Horne letter to his wife, 25 December 1916.
13   Barrow (1931), p.46.
14   Ibid. p.47.
15   Ibid. pp.47–48 and Wyrall (1921), p.191.
16   Farr (2007), p.50. Horne letter to wife 25 January 1915.
17   The National Archives, WO95 590/1 – Letter from CGS to GOC,
     31 January 1915.
18   *London Gazette*, 12 February 1915.
19   The National Archives, WO95 590/1 – Monro report on Cuinchy dated
     27 January 1915, I Corps War Diary.
20   The National Archives, WO95 590/2 – Various correspondence, March 1915.
21   Sheffield and Bourne (2005), p.108.
22   The National Archives, WO95 590/4 – Whigham note to 1st and 2nd
     Divisions dated 7 March 1915.
23   Ibid. WO158/258 and 158/182.
24   Ibid. WO95/707 – IV Corps Diary, 'Rawlinson Remarks on 8th Division
     Scheme'.
25   Kingsford (1916), p.187.
26   The National Archives, WO158/258 – Horne's orders, 6 March 1915.
27   Edmonds (1927), p.115.
28   The National Archives, WO95 590/4 – I Corps War Diary.
29   Simpson (2006), p.12.
30   The National Archives, CAB 24/2/1 – Note by CIGS, 5 January 1916.
31   Horne letter to wife, 29 April 1915.
32   The National Archives, WO95/5 – Confidential note from Horne to Monro,
     23 March 1915.
33   Ibid. Monro letter to GHQ, 23 March 1915.
34   The National Archives, WO95 950/1 – War Diary, 7 May 1915.
35   Sheffield (2011), p.113 and the National Archives, WO95/6 – 13 April 1915,
     Brigadier Rice order to divisions and brigades.
36   Edmonds (1928), p.5.
37   The National Archives, WO95 950/6 – 'General principles for the attack'.
38   Edmonds (1928), p.13.
39   Prior and Wilson (2004), p.85.
40   Hancock (2005), p.26.
41   The National Archives, WO95 591/1 – 7 May 1915.
42   Edmonds (1928), p.20.
43   The National Archives, WO95 591/1 – 17 May 1915, Haking report.
44   Neillands (2007), p.140.
45   Edmonds (1928), p.28.
46   Bristow (1995), p.107.
47   Hancock (2005), p.128.
48   Senior (2012), p.36.
49   Ibid. p.37.
50   Sheffield (2011), p.115.
51   Sheffield and Bourne (2005), p.123.
52   Simpson (2006), p.14.

53 See Farrar-Hockley for further insight.

54 Beckett and Corvi (2006), p.75.

55 Sheffield and Todman (2004), p.71.

56 Ibid. p.72.

57 Gough (1931), p.85.

58 Ibid. p.88.

59 Neillands (2007), p.151. Letter dated 11 May 1915.

60 Gough (1931), p.87.

61 Wylly (1925), p.97.

62 Gough (1931), p.87.

63 Edmonds (1928), p.65.

64 Ibid. p.68.

65 Horne letters, Farr (2009), p.58.

66 Wylly (1925), p.98.

67 Barrow (1931), p.49.

68 Gough (1931), p.90.

69 Simpson (2006), p.15 and the National Archives, WO95/591 – I Corps No 356, 1 June 1915.

70 Neillands (2007), p.164.

71 Hughes and Seligman (2000), pp.255–56.

72 Prior and Wilson (1992), p.96, quoting Rawlinson diary, 13 July 1915.

73 The National Archives, WO95/359 – Monro letter to CGS, 15 July 1915.

74 Ibid. 3rd Army War Diary, 6 July 1915.

75 Ibid. Letter Foch to GHQ, 25 July 1915.

76 Travers (2003), p.53. From Imperial War Museum Maxse Papers, 69/53/6, 'Secret, Notes of Conference', 4 August 1915, by Sir Charles Monro.

77 The National Archives, WO95/359 – Notes on Army Conference, 4 August 1915.

78 Bombers were grenade throwers.

79 Barrow (1931), p.49.

80 Messenger (2005), p.249.

81 Robbins (2005), p.86.

82 Samuels (1992), p.159.

83 Robbins (2005), p.86, quoting Imperial War Museum Maxse Papers 69/57/7 – Brigadier General R. J. Kentish to Maxse, 21–22 February 1917.

84 Hesketh-Prichard (1994), p.1.

85 Ibid. p.4.

Chapter 8

1 Churchill (1931), p.515.

2 Moorehead (1974), p.291.

3 Barrow (1931), p.52.

4 Records of casualty figures vary in official accounts.

5 Barnett (1974), p.385.

6 Liddell Hart (1970), p.135.

7 Repington (1920), p.83.

8 Parliamentary Debates, 20 March 1917.

9   Travers (2002), p.138.
10 Aspinall-Oglander (1932), p.245.
11 Ibid. p.268.
12 Ibid. p.328.
13 Ibid. p.384.
14 Moorehead (1974), p.284.
15 Hamilton (1966), p.336.
16 www.firstworldwar.com/source/ashmeadbartlettletter.htm
17 National Library of Australia, Murdoch letter dated 23 September 1915.
18 Hamilton (1966), p.397.
19 The National Archives, CAB 24/1/47 – Hamilton Memorandum 26 November 1915.
20 Ashmead-Bartlett (1928), p.251.
21 Cameron (2011), p.186 and Australian War Museum, Bean Papers 3ERL 606, Item 18.
22 Travers (2002), p.225.
23 Syk (2012), p.89.
24 Lloyd-George (1938), p.314.
25 Robertson (1921), p.269.
26 Hamilton (1920), p.235.
27 Barrow (1931), pp.61–62.
28 Hamilton (1966), p.405.
29 Aspinall-Oglander (1932), p.386.
30 *Official History*, 'Military Operations Gallipoli', Vol. II, Maps and appendices (1932), pp.69–70.
31 Keyes (1941), p.273.
32 Travers (2002), p.204.
33 Hankey (1961), p.456. Hankey was an aide to Lloyd George and secretary to the War Cabinet and Imperial War Cabinet. He became Baron Hankey in 1938 after a distinguished career as a senior civil servant and became a government minister.
34 Imperial War Museum – C. E. Callwell letter to A. Lynden-Bell, 22 October 1915.
35 LHCMA, Robertson 3/2/29 – Telegram from Birdwood to Kitchener, 21 October 1915, 11.15 p.m.
36 LHCMA, Robertson 3/2/29 – Telegram Birdwood to Lord Kitchener, 4 November 1915.
37 Imperial War Museum Documents – A. Lynden-Bell, typescript account, pp.1–2.
38 Churchill (1931), p.489.
39 Imperial War Museum Documents – A. Lynden-Bell, typescript account, p.2.
40 LHCMA, Hamilton 7/4/10 – Pawnay letters to wife, 4 November 1915.
41 Churchill (1931), p.489.
42 Godley (1937), p.194.
43 Syk (2012), p.98.
44 Ibid.
45 Aspinall-Oglander (1932), p.400.
46 Ibid. p.401.

47   Barrow (1931), p.69.

48   Aspinall-Oglander (1932), p.400.

49   LHCMA, Robertson 3/2/29 – Telegram from Monro to Kitchener, 31 October 1915, 7.50 p.m.

50   Churchill (1923), p.490.

51   Bean (1924), p.785.

52   Imperial War Museum – A. Lynden-Bell, letter to C. E. Callwell, December 1915.

53   Keyes (1941), p.286.

54   Birdwood (1941), p.279, and LHCMA, Robertson 3/2/29 – Telegram Monro to Kitchener, 2 November 1915, 5.55 p.m.

55   LHCMA, Robertson 3/2/29 – Telegram Monro to Kitchener, 2 November 1915, 5.55 p.m.

56   Aspinall-Oglander (1932), pp.404–05.

57   Ibid. p.405.

58   Churchill (1923), p.491.

59   Coates (2000), Stationery Office reprint of 1918, Part II, p.184.

60   Birdwood (1941), p.279.

61   Barrow (1931), p.78.

62   *The National Review*, No 74/443, 'The Aftermath, the Evacuation of the Dardanelles' by Major Orlo Williams MC (1920), p.657.

63   Magnus (1958), p.362.

64   *The National Review*, No 74/443, 'The Aftermath, the Evacuation of the Dardanelles' by Major Orlo Williams MC (1920), p.660.

65   Barrow (1931), p.80.

66   The National Archives, CAB 24/1/38 – Memorandum on the Conduct of the War, 8 November 1915.

67   Pollock (1998), p.456. (*The Times*, 22 November 1915.)

68   Birdwood (1941), p.280.

69   Coates (2000), p.187.

70   Birdwood (1941), p.281.

71   Ashmead-Bartlett (1928), p.263, and LHCMA, Robertson 3/2/29 – Kitchener to prime minister, 15 November 1915, 4.10 p.m.

72   LHCMA, Robertson 3/2/29 – Kitchener to prime minister, 17 November 1915, 3.40 p.m.

73   LHCMA, Robertson 3/2/29 – General Staff Conclusions by Lieutenant General A. J. Murray, dated 22 November 1915, p.11.

74   Ibid. p.251.

75   Barrow (1931), p.91.

76   LHCMA, Robertson 7/2/13 – Letter Callwell to Robertson, dated 1 December 1915.

77   Aspinall-Oglander (1932), p.418.

78   Moorehead (1974), p.302.

79   Aspinall-Oglander (1932), p.416.

80   Barrow (1931), p.82.

81   Aspinall-Oglander (1932), p.422.

82   Farr (2007), p.71.

83   Aspinall-Oglander (1932), p.429.

84 Keyes (1941), p.286.

85 Ibid. p.292.

86 Moorehead (1974), p.305.

87 Aspinall-Oglander (1932), p.436.

88 *The London Gazette*, 7 April 1916 – Monro Despatch, 6 March 1916, p.3780.

89 Ibid.

90 Ibid. p.3784.

91 Barrow (1931), p.103.

92 *The Manchester Courier*, Saturday, 18 December 1915.

93 Ibid.

94 LHCMA, Hamilton 17/32 – Scrapbook, dated 15 March 1916.

95 LHCMA, Hamilton 21/4 – Sellar to Hamilton, dated 11 April 1916. *Parti pris* can be translated as 'prejudice' or 'bias'.

96 Lord Chancellor in the British Cabinet from 1914 to 1915.

97 LHCMA, Hamilton 21/4 – Hamilton to Sellar, dated 12 April 1916.

98 LHCMA, Hamilton 7/9/6 – Letter dated 9 January 1919.

99 LHCMA, Hamilton 17/2 – Personal scrapbook. Letter to *The Times* dated 15 October 1931.

100 For further information on Lady Hamilton's efforts read Celia Lee's biography.

101 Lee (2001), p.175.

102 Wylly (1925), p.153.

103 Coates (2000), Stationery Office reprint of 1918, Part II, p.202.

Chapter 9

1   Barnett (1974), p.392.

2   Sheffield (2011), p.139

3   Travers (2003), p.105. Sacking was known as being 'degummed' or 'stellenbosched'.

4   Edmonds (1932), p.33.

5   Travers (2003), p.105.

6   Barrow (1942), p.165.

7   Barrow (1931), pp.106–07.

8   Ibid. p.107.

9   Dewar and Boraston (1922), p.65.

10 Ibid. p.70.

11 Ibid. pp.107–08.

12 Ibid. p.393.

13 The National Archives, WO158/19 – Notes on Operations, 16 January 1916.

14 Beckett and Corvi (2006), p.130.

15 Senior (2012), p.75.

16 Senior (2012), p.80.

17 Holmes (2004), p.312.

18 Barrow (1931), p.112.

19 Denman (1992), p.72.

20 The National Archives, WO95/165 – 30 July 1916.

21 The National Archives, WO OAM 97 – French to Army Commanders, 28 October 1915.

22 Senior (2012), p.81.

23 Ibid. p.82.

24 Edmonds (1932), p.242.

25 *The London Gazette*, 29 May 1916, Third Supplement.

26 Later General Sir Guy Williams in the Second World War.

27 170th Tunnelling Company was manned by civilian sewer workers from Manchester and miners detached from some Welsh infantry regiments.

28 Mine 'A' was 7,000lb of ammonal, Mine 'B' 3,000lb of blastine and 4,000lb ammonal and Mine 'C', of two charges, 10,550lb of ammonal. Middleton-Brumwell (1923), p.35.

29 Middleton-Brumwell (1923), p.39.

30 Ibid. p.176.

31 *The London Gazette*, 28 March 1916, Supplement 29527, p.3410.

32 Kiggell to Monro, National Archives, WO158/46), 25 March 1916.

33 Middleton-Brumwell (1923), p.43.

34 *The London Gazette*, 29 May 1916, Third Supplement.

35 http://www.royaldublinfusiliers.com.

36 The National Archives, WO158/269.

37 Denman (1992), p.69.

38 Ibid.

39 The National Archives, WO158/269 – Report 2–4 May 1916.

40 Ibid.

41 *The Times*, 1 May 1916.

42 http://www.royaldublinfusiliers.com.

43 Grayson (2012), p.104.

44 Ibid.

45 Edmonds (1932), p.205.

46 The National Archives, WO95/163 – Enquiry dated 26 May 1916. Lieutenant General Kavanagh, 21 May 1916.

47 Stewart and Buchan (1926), p.70.

48 Edmonds (1932), p.207.

49 Stewart and Buchan (1926), p.72.

50 Beckett and Corvi (2006), p.132.

51 Edmonds (1932), p.212.

52 Cave (1996), p.54.

53 Collier (1961), p.234.

54 Edmonds (1932), p.217.

55 Callwell (1927), p.283.

56 Callwell (1927), p.300.

57 Blake (1952), p.145.

58 Sheffield and Bourne (2005), p.188.

59 The National Archives, WO95/162 – 1st Army War Diary.

60 Ibid.

61 Repington (1920), p.270.

62 Ibid.

63 The National Archives, WO95/164.

64 Liddell Hart (1930), pp.261–62.

65 Macdonald (1983), p.165.

66 Lee (2015), p.3. This excellent book studies the BEF planning process from orders issued at the strategic level down to those given on the front line.

67 Sheffield and Bourne (2005), p.118.

68 WO95/162, 1st Army War Diary, 1100 hours, 8 June 1916.

69 Lee (2010), p.88.

70 WO95/162, 1st Army War Diary, 1100 hours, 8 June 1916.

71 Lee (2015), p.88.

72 Cobb (2007), p.15.

73 Bean (1929), p.331.

74 Lee (2010), p.95.

75 Lee (2015), p.96. Extract from 1st Army Order Number 100.

76 Ibid. p.97.

77 Edmonds (1938), p.124.

78 Pedersen (2004), p.36.

79 Bean (1929), p.346.

80 Ibid. p.347.

81 Barton (2014), p.170.

82 Farrar-Hockley (1964), p.200.

83 It should be noted that Bean is criticised by some modern historians, including Barton, for not accurately referring to available German references to the battle. This helped to perpetuate ANZAC myths.

84 Bean (1929), pp.349–50.

85 Barton (2014), p.173.

86 The National Archives, WO95/165.

87 Sheffield and Bourne (2005), p.208.

88 Edmonds (1938), p.134.

89 Senior (2012), p.108.

90 Barton (1914), p.395.

91 The National Archives, WO95/165.

92 Edmonds (1938), p.134.

93 Lee (2015), p.71. From Haking's notes from 1st Army Conference, May 1916 – XI Corps War Diary.

94 Barton (1914), Chapter IV.

95 Cobb (2007), p.176.

96 Lee (2015), p.6.

97 Barrow (1931), p.113.

98 Beckett and Corvi (2006), p.135.

99 Ibid. p.112.

100 Lee (2015), p.200.

101 Ibid., foreword by Sheffield.

102 Sheffield and Bourne (2005), p.215.

103 Barrow (1931), p.114.

Chapter 10

1 LHCMA, Robertson 8/1/66 – Letter Robertson to Monro, 1 August 1917, p.8.

2 Barrow (1931), pp.122–23.

3 Repington (1920), p.318.

4   Ibid.

5   Bence-Jones (1982), p.221.

6   Moon (1989), p.972.

7   Verney (1994), p.117.

8   For the full story of Kut, read Crowley (2009), *Kut 1916*.

9   Previously 13th Division's commander at Gallipoli.

10 Barrow (1931), pp.155–56.

11 Ibid.

12 *The London Gazette*, 10 July 1917, p.6938.

13 Callwell (1920), p.247.

14 Ibid. p.248.

15 Robertson (1921), p.74.

16 Barrow (1931), p.159 and Repington (1920), p.595.

17 Syk (2012), p.157. Quoting telegrams from C-in-C India to CIGS on 1 and 4 March 1917.

18 Dyer (1921).

19 *The London Gazette*, 26 November 1918, p.13907.

20 LHCMA, Robertson 8/1/52 – Letter Monro to Robertson dated 28 December 1916.

21 Gupta (2002), p.228.

22 Farwell (1989), p.251.

23 Barnett (1972), p.143.

24 Cohen (1990), p.74.

25 Montagu (1930), pp.201 and 352.

26 Draper (1981), p.31.

27 Menezes (1999), p.313.

28 LHCMA, Robertson 8/1/61 – Letters from Monro to Robertson dated 15 June 1917 and 2 November 1917.

29 Barnett (1972), p.144.

30 Verney (1994), p.71.

31 Heathcote (1995), pp.210–11.

32 Ibid. p.215.

33 Cohen (1990), p.69.

34 Lucas (1926), p.199.

35 Menezes (1999), p.286.

36 LHCMA, Robertson 8/1/53 – Letter Robertson to Monro dated 12 January 1917.

37 LHCMA, Robertson 8/1/80 – Letter Robertson to Monro dated 23 November 1917.

38 Ibid. p.250.

39 *Evening Post*, Vol. XCIII, Issue 47, 23 February 1917, p.7.

40 Barrow (1931), p.118.

41 National Army Museum, NAM-7207-19-1.

42 Cohen (1990), p.72. O'Dwyer speech of 4 May 1918. O'Dwyer was an extremely robust lieutenant governor of the Punjab, who was both respected, but feared and disliked by Indian nationalists. His methods and attitude, including vocal support for Dyer's actions at Amritsar, led to his assassination by Shaheed Udham Singh on 12 March 1940.

43   Robertson (1921), p.317.
44   *The London Gazette*, 8 April 1919, p.4709.
45   LHCMA, Robertson 8/1/77 – Letter Monro to Robertson dated 2 November 1917.
46   LHCMA, Robertson 8/1/61 – Letter Monro to Robertson dated 15 June 1917.
47   Keay (2001), pp.470–71.
48   Menezes (1999), p.267.
49   For further information on the German mission to Kabul, read Stewart (2014).
50   Farwell (1989), p.236.
51   Barnett (1972), p.147.
52   Ibid. p.146.
53   Bence-Jones (1982), p.223.
54   Keay (2001), p.473.
55   Barnett (1972), p.148.
56   Moon (1989), p.988.
57   379 dead and 1,200 wounded, though some references claim that there were many more casualties.
58   *The Times*, 21 February 2013, p.21.
59   Collett (2005), p.29.
60   Ibid. p.38.
61   Farwell (1989), p.285.
62   Sheppard (1955), p.109.
63   *The London Gazette*, 12 March 1920, p.3272.
64   British Library, Putkowski Telegram 26239, Army Headquarters (AHQ), Simla to General Officers Commanding (GOC) Brigades, 14 April 1919, L/MIL/17/5/3079.
65   British Library, Putkowski Telegram 7928-7-A-1, Admin Staff, SCP to GOCs Divisions: Mhow; Bangalore, GOCs Brigades: Karachi, Jubbulpore, Jhansi and Secunderabad Infantry, 2 May 1919, L/MIL/17/5/3080.
66   British Library, Putkowski Telegram 9950-4-A1, GOCSCP to AG, Simla, 21 September 1919, L/MIL/17/5/3084.
67   Heathcote (2003), pp.175–76.
68   For further information, read Putkowski on https://www.marxists.org/history/etol/revhist/backiss/vol8/no2/putkowski2.html.
69   British Library (African and Asian Studies), Mss Eur D783.
70   Peshawar remains a very volatile area even today; an example being the massacre of children in a school by the Taliban in December 2014.
71   Robson (2004), p.72.
72   Ibid. p.73.
73   *The London Gazette*, 12 March 1920, p.3285.
74   Collett (2005), p.301.
75   Ibid. p.305.
76   Coates (2000), p.152.
77   *The London Gazette*, 7 December 1920, p.12130.
78   Miss Marcia Sherwood, a schools' superintendent, had been beaten by thugs in Amritsar a few days before the massacre. On 19 April, Dyer ordered that

all Indians passing the spot had to crawl along the whole lane or be strung up and whipped. The rule lasted for five days.

79 Furneaux (1963), p.88.
80 Collett (2005), p.323. From Chelmsford and Montagu Papers in the British Library.
81 Ibid. pp.323–24.
82 Draper (1981), p.146.
83 Barrow (1942), p.227.
84 Collett (2005), p.333.
85 Barrow (1931), p.192.
86 Lloyd (2011), p.xxxi.
87 Barrow (1931), p.190.
88 Ibid. p.201.
89 Furneaux (1963), p.128.
90 Collett (2005), p.348. From Montagu Papers, Trinity College, Cambridge.
91 Furneaux, p.129.
92 Ibid. p.137.
93 Barrow (1931), p.218.
94 Draper (1981), p.206.
95 Collett (2005), p.360. From Montagu Papers, Trinity College, Cambridge.
96 Farwell (1989), p.290.
97 Furneaux (1963), p.166.
98 The Khilafat Movement were angry about the Western powers' treatment of Turkey after the war.
99 Barrow (1931), p.213.
100 These were temporary constables, mainly ex-soldiers supporting the Royal Irish Constabulary. Their name came from the mix of military and police uniforms they wore. Their harsh methods of operation made them infamous.
101 http://www.historyireland.com, published in *20th-Century / Contemporary-History*, Issue 1 (Spring 1998), News, Revolutionary Period 1912–23, Vol. 6.
102 Ibid.
103 http://www.irish-society.org.
104 Heathcote (1995), pp.233–34.
105 Ibid. p.236 and Esher Committee Report.
106 Roy (2013), p.111.
107 Gupta and Deshpande (2002), pp.182–83.
108 Ibid. p.200.
109 Ibid.
110 Ibid. p.208.
111 Barrow (1931), p.239.
112 Ibid. p.222.
113 Ibid. pp.223–24.
114 *The Journal of the Queen's Royal Regiment*, Vol. III (May 1930), p.83.
115 Terraine (1998), p.46.
116 Barrow (1931), p.251.
117 Ibid. p.244.
118 *Oxford Dictionary of National Biography*, Monro, p.3.
119 *The Journal of the Queen's Royal Regiment*, Vol. III (May 1930), p.80.

120 Ibid. p.83.

121 *The London Gazette*, 22 October 1920, p.10262.

122 Barrow (1931), p.249.

Chapter 11

1   *The Western Morning News and Mercury*, Wednesday, 9 September 1923.

2   Baedeker (1911), p.53.

3   *The Dominions Office and Colonial Office List* (1928), p.289.

4   Garratt (1939), p.151.

5   Stockey (2009), p.45.

6   Robinson (1970), p.28.

7   Hills (1974), p.391.

8   *The Spectator*, 1 November 2014.

9   Barrow (1931), p.255.

10   Known as 'The Convent'.

11   *The Journal of the East Surrey Regiment*, Vol. II, No 32 (May 1927), p.2.

12   *Gibraltar Chronicle*, 7 April 1927.

13   *Gibraltar Chronicle*, Criminal Sessions, 22 June 1927.

14   Ibid. 21 April 1927.

15   Brading (date unknown), extracts.

16   *Gibraltar Magazine*, August 2013, p.5.

17   *Aberdeen Press and Journal*, 1928.

18   Barrow (1931), p.257.

19   Ibid. p.259.

20   Barrow (1931), p.259.

21   Lady Mary Monro, Dame Commander of the Order of the British Empire (DBE – awarded in 1919) died on 28 August 1972 (aged 92). She was a keen supporter of service-related charities. This included being president of the Not Forgotten Association from 1952–57 (a charity founded in 1920 for the comfort, cheer and entertainment of wounded ex-servicemen in hospital after the Great War), and she was a patron of Lady Grover's Hospital Fund for Officers' Families. Both charities still operate.

22   British Library, Asian and African Studies, Mss Eur D783/7.

23   *Horse and Hound*, 14 December 1929.

24   *Army and Navy Gazette*, 12 December 1929.

25   *Surrey Advertiser*, 14 December 1929.

Chapter 12

1   Beckett and Corvi (2006), p.139.

2   Barrow (1931), p.266.

3   Ibid.

4   Obituary, *The Army Quarterly*, January 1930, p.238.

5   LHCMA, Liddell Hart 15/6/5/13 – Obituary.

BIBLIOGRAPHY

Books

Amery, L. S., *The Problem of the Army* (London: Edward Arnold, 1903).

Amery, L. S., *The Times History of the War in South Africa 1899–1902* (London: Samson Low, Marston & Co. Ltd, 1905).

Andrew, Major A. W., *Rifle Fire and the Higher Individual Training of the Soldier* (London: W. Thacker & Co., 1906).

Anonymous, *The History of the Queen's Royal Regiment* (Aldershot: Gale & Polden Ltd, 1953).

Arthur, Sir George, *Life of Lord Kitchener, Volume I* (London: Macmillan & Co. Ltd, 1920).

Ascoli, David, *The Mons Star* (London: Harrap Ltd, 1981).

Ashmead-Bartlett, E., *The Uncensored Dardanelles* (Hutchinson & Co. Ltd, 1928).

Aspinall-Oglander, Brigadier General C. F., *Military Operations, Gallipoli. Vol II. May 1915 to the Evacuation and Maps and Appendices* (London: William Heinemann Ltd, 1932).

Aspinall-Oglander, Cecil. *Roger Keyes* (London: The Hogarth Press, 1951)

Baden-Powell, Major B. F. S., *War in Practice* (London: Isbister & Co. Ltd, 1903).

Baedeker, Karl, *The Mediterranean* (Leipzig: Karl Baedeker Publisher, 1911).

Baldwin, Stanley Simm, *Forward Everywhere Her Majesty's Territorials* (London: Brassey's, 1994).

Barnett, Correlli, *The Collapse of British Power* (London: Eyre Methuen, 1972).

Barnett, Correlli, *Britain and Her Army* (London: Penguin Books, 1974).

Barrow, General Sir George, *The Life of General Sir Charles Carmichael Monro* (London: Hutchinson & Co. Ltd, 1931).

Barrow, General Sir George, *The Fire of Life* (London: Hutchinson & Co. Ltd, 1942).

Barthorp, Michael, *The Frontier Ablaze: The North-West Frontier Rising 1897–98* (London: Windrow & Greene, 1996).

Barthorp, Michael, *Afghan Wars* (London: Cassell & Co., 2010).

Barton, Peter, *The Lost Legions of Fromelles* (London: Constable, 2014).

Bean, C. E. W., *The Story of ANZAC, From 4 May 1915 to the Evacuation of the Gallipoli Peninsula* (Sydney: Angus & Robertson, 1924).

Bean, C. E. W., *The Australian Imperial Force in France 1916* (Sydney: Angus & Robertson Ltd, 1927).

Beckett, Ian F. W., *The Judgement of History* (London: John Donovan Publishing Ltd, 1993).

Beckett, Ian F. W., *Ypres: The First Battle, 1914* (Harlow: Pearson Education, 2004).

Beckett, Ian F. W., *Territorials – A Century of Service* (Plymouth: DRA Publishing, 2008).

Beckett, Ian F. W., and Steven J. Corvi, *Haig's Generals* (Barnsley: Pen & Sword, 2006).

Belfield, Eversley, *The Boer War* (London: Leo Cooper, 1975).

Bence-Jones, Mark, *The Viceroys of India* (London: Constable, 1982).

Birdwood, Field Marshal Lord, *Khaki and Gown* (London and Melbourne: Ward, Lock & Co. Ltd, 1941).

Blake, Robert, *The Private Papers of Douglas Haig 1914–1919* (London: Eyre & Spottiswoode, 1952).

Bloem, Walter, *The Advance from Mons* (Solihull: Peter Davies, 1930).

Bond, Brian, *The Victorian Army and the Staff College 1854–1914* (London: Eyre Methuen, 1972).

Bowman, Timothy, and Mark Connelly, *The Edwardian Army: Recruiting, Training, and Deploying the British Army 1902–1914* (London: Oxford University Press, 2012).

Brading, Brigadier N. B., *A Gibraltar Drama* (publishing details not known).

Brazier, Kevin, *The Complete Victoria Cross* (Barnsley: Pen & Sword, 2010).

Bristow, Adrian, *A Serious Disappointment* (London: Leo Cooper, 1995).

Burkitt, Reverend H. J., *The History of the Queen's (Royal West Surrey Regiment)* (Guildford: AC Curtis & Co. Ltd, 1917).

Callwell, Colonel C. E., *The Tactics of Today* (Edinburgh and London: William Blackwood and Sons, 1909).

Callwell, Colonel C. E., *Tirah 1897* (London: Constable & Co. Ltd, 1911).

Callwell, Colonel C. E., *Small Wars* (London: Greenhill Books, reprint 1990 of 1906).

Callwell, Colonel C. E., *Field Marshal Sir Henry Wilson* (London: Cassell & Co. Ltd, 1927).

Callwell, Major General Sir C. E., *The Life of Sir Stanley Maude* (London: Constable & Co. Ltd, 1920).

Cameron, David W. *Gallipoli – The Final Battles and Evacuation of Anzac* (Newport, Australia: Big Sky Publishing, 2011).

Carew, Tim, *The Vanished Army: The British Expeditionary Force 1914–1915* (London: William Kimber & Co. Ltd, 1964).

Carver, Field Marshal Lord, *The National Army Museum Book of the Boer War* (London: Sidgwick & Jackson, 1999).

Caunter, Major J. E., *The Campaign in the Free State* (Royal Military College. Yorktown: A Bradford – Albion Works, undated *c.* 1901).

Cave, Nigel, *Vimy Ridge, Arras* (Barnsley: Pen & Sword, 1996).

Charteris, Brigadier-General John, *At GHQ* (London: Cassell & Co. Ltd, 1931).

Chichester, Henry Manners, and George Burges-Short, *The Records and Badges of Every Regiment and Corps in the British Army* (Aldershot: Gale & Polden Ltd, 1900).

Churchill, Winston S., *The Story of the Malakand Field Force* (Bibliobazaar, 1898, modern reprint).

Churchill, Winston S., *The World Crisis 1915* (London: Thornton Butterworth Ltd, 1923).

Churchill, Winston S., *The World Crisis 1911–1918* (London: Thornton Butterworth Ltd, 1931).

Churchill, Winston S., *Great Contemporaries* (London: Thornton Butterworth Ltd, 1937).

Clark, Alan, *The Donkeys* (London: Hutchinson, 1961).

Coates, Tim, *Defeat at Gallipoli: The Dardanelles Commission Part II, 1915–16* (London: The Stationery Office, 2000).

Coates, Tim, *The Amritsar Massacre: General Dyer in the Punjab 1919* (London: The Stationery Office, 2000).

Cobb, Paul, *Fromelles 1916* (Stroud: Tempus Publishing Ltd, 2007).

Cohen, Stephen P., *The Indian Army* (Delhi: Oxford University Press, 1990).

Cole, Major D. H., and Major E. C. Priestley, *An Outline of British Military History 1660–1936* (London: Sifton Praed & Co. Ltd, 1936).

Collett, Nigel, *The Butcher of Amritsar* (London: Hambledon & London, 2005).

Collier, Basil, *Brasshat* (London: Secker & Warburg, 1961).

Conan Doyle, Arthur, *The Great Boer War* (London: Thomas Nelson & Sons, 1903).

Conan Doyle, Arthur, *The British Campaign in France and Flanders 1914* (London: Hodder & Stoughton, 1916).

Coogan, Tim Pat, *The IRA* (London: Collins, 1970).

Corfield, Robin, *Don't Forget Me, Cobber: The Battle of Fromelles* (Melbourne: Miegunyan Press, 2009).

Coughlin, Con, *Churchill's First War* (London: Macmillan, 2013).

Crowley, Lieutenant Colonel P. T., *Afghanistan, the Three Wars* (Canterbury: Princess of Wales's Royal Regiment, 2002).

Crowley, Lieutenant Colonel P. T., Lieutenant Colonel L. M. Wilson and Bryan Fosten, *The Infantry Regiments of Surrey* (Kent: Geo. J. Harris, 2002).

Crowley, Colonel P. T., *Kut 1916* (Stroud: Spellmount, 2009).

Daniell, David Scott, *Cap of Honour: The Story of the Gloucestershire Regiment 1694–1950* (London: George G. Harrap & Co Ltd, 1951).

Daniell, David Scott, *Regimental History: The Royal Hampshire Regiment, Volume III 1918–1954* (Aldershot: Gale & Polden Ltd, 1955).

Davies, Frank, and Graham Maddocks, *Bloody Red Tabs* (London: Leo Cooper, 1995).

Davis, Colonel John, *The History of the Second Queen's Royal Regiment, Volume V* (London: Eyre & Spottiswoode, 1906).

Davis, Colonel John, *The History of the Second Queen's Royal Regiment, Volume VI* (London: Eyre & Spottiswoode, 1906).

Denman, Terence, *Ireland's Unknown Soldiers* (Dublin: Irish Academic Press, 1992).

Dennis, Peter, *The Territorial Army 1907–1940* (Royal Historical Society: The Boydell Press, 1987).

Dewar, George A. B., and Lieutenant Colonel J. H. Boraston, *Sir Douglas Haig's Command, December 19, 1915 to November 11, 1918* (London: Constable & Co. Ltd, 1922).

Draper, Alfred, *Amritsar: The Massacre that Ended the Raj* (London: Cassell, 1981).

Dunlop, Colonel John, *The Development of the British Army 1899–1914* (London: Methuen, 1938).

Dyer, Brigadier General R. E. H., *The Raiders of the Sarhad* (London: HF & G Witherby, 1921).

Eady, Major H. G., *Historical Illustrations to Field Service Regulations, 'Operations' 1929* (London: Sifton Praed & Co. Ltd, 1930).

Edmonds, Brigadier General J. E., *History of the Great War Based on Official Documents, Volume 1* (Historical Section of the Committee of Imperial Defence, 1923–49).

Edmonds, Brigadier General J. E., *Military Operations, France and Belgium, 1914* (London: Macmillan & Co. Ltd, 1922).

Edmonds, Brigadier General J. E., *Military Operations, France and Belgium, 1915* (London: Macmillan & Co. Ltd, 1927).

Edmonds, Brigadier General J. E., *Military Operations, France and Belgium, 1915* (London: Macmillan & Co. Ltd, 1928).

Edmonds, Brigadier General J. E., *Military Operations, France and Belgium, 1916* (London: Macmillan & Co. Ltd, 1932).

Edmonds, Brigadier General J. E., *Military Operations, France and Belgium, 1916, Volume II* (London: Macmillan & Co. Ltd, 1938).

Evans, Marix, *Encyclopaedia of the Boer War 1899–1902* (Oxford: ABC–CLIO Ltd, 2000).

Farr, Don, *The Silent General: Horne of the First Army, A Biography of Haig's Trusted Great War Comrade-in-Arms* (Solihull: Helion, 2007).

Farrar-Hockley, Anthony, *Goughie* (London: Granada Publishing Ltd, 1975).

Farwell, Byron, *Armies of the Raj* (London: Viking, 1989).

Farwell, Byron, *The Great Boer War* (Barnsley: Pen & Sword, 2009).

Foster MC, Major R. C. G., *History of the Queen's Royal Regiment, Volume IX* (Aldershot: Gale & Polden Ltd, 1961).

French, David, and Brian Holden Reid, *The British General Staff Reform and Innovation c. 1890–1939* (London: Frank Cass, 2002).

French, David, *Military Identities* (Oxford: University Press, 2005).

French, Viscount, *1914* (Boston and New York: Houghton Mifflin Company, 1919).

Fuller, J. F. C., *The Army in My Time* (London: Rich & Cowan, 1935).

Furneaux, Rupert, *Massacre at Amritsar* (London: George Allen & Unwin Ltd, 1963).

Garratt, G. T., *Gibraltar and the Mediterranean* (London: J. Cape, 1939).

Gibbs, Peter, *Death of the Last Republic: The Story of the Anglo-Boer War* (London: Frederick Muller Ltd, 1957).

Godley, General Sir Alexander, *Life of an Irish Soldier* (New York: EP Dutton & Co. Inc., 1937).

Godwin-Austen, Brevet Major A. R., *The Staff and the Staff College* (London: Constable & Co. Ltd, 1927).

Gooch, John, *The Boer War Direction, Experience and Image* (London: Frank Cass, 2000).

Gough, General Sir Hubert, *The Fifth Army* (London: Hodder & Stoughton, 1931).

Gourlay, A. B., *A History of Sherborne School* (Dorset: Sawtell's of Sherborne Ltd, 1971).

Grayson, Richard S., *At War with the 16th Irish Division, 1914–1918, the Staniforth Letters* (Barnsley: Pen & Sword, 2012).

Gupta, Partha Sarathi, and Anirudh Deshpande, *The British Raj and its Indian Armed Forces 1857–1939* (Delhi: Oxford University Press, 2002).

Haking, Brigadier-General R. C. B., *Company Training* (London: Hugh Rees Ltd, 1914).

Haking, Colonel R. C. B., *Staff Rides and Regimental Tours* (London: Hugh Rees Ltd, 1908).

Hall, Darrell, *The Hall Handbook of the Anglo-Boer War* (South Africa: University of KwaZulu Natal Press, 1999).

Hamilton, Ernest W., *The First Seven Divisions* (London: Hurst & Blackett Ltd, 1917).

Hamilton, Ian B. M., *The Happy Warrior* (London: Cassell, 1966).

Hamilton, Sir Ian, *Gallipoli Diary* (London: Edward Arnold, 1920).

Hancock, Edward, *Aubers Ridge* (Barnsley: Pen & Sword, 2005).

Hankey, Lord, *The Supreme Command* (London: George Allen & Unwin Ltd, 1961).

Hart, Peter, *Gallipoli* (London: Profile Books Ltd, 2013).

Hart's Annual Army List (1881, 1882, 1902, 1909).

Hastings, Max, *Catastrophe – Europe Goes to War* (London: William Collins, 2013).

Haswell, Jock, *The Queen's Royal Regiment (West Surrey)* (London: Hamish Hamilton, 1967).

Hay, Ian, *The British Infantryman* (Edinburgh: Penguin Books edition, 1942).

Heathcote, T. A., *The Indian Army* (London: David & Charles, 1974).

Heathcote, T. A., *The Story of Sandhurst* (RMAS, 1978).

Heathcote, T. A., *The Military in British India* (Manchester and New York: Manchester University Press, 1995).

Heathcote, T. A., *The Afghan Wars 1839–1919* (Staplehurst: Spellmount, 2003).

Herbert, Lieutenant Colonel the Honourable Aubrey, *Mons, Anzac and Kut* (Barnsley: Pen & Sword, 2009).

Hesketh-Prichard, Major H., *Sniping in France* (London: Leo Cooper, 1994).

Hills, George, *Rock of Contention: A History of Gibraltar* (London: Robert Hale & Co., 1974).

HMSO, *History of The Great War – Order of Battle of Divisions, Part 1 – The Regular British Divisions* (London: HMSO, 1935).

Hobday, E. A. P., *Sketches on Service during the Indian Frontier Campaigns of 1897* (London: James Bowden, 1898).

Holmes, Richard, *The Western Front* (London: BBC Worldwide Ltd, 1999).

Holmes, Richard, *Tommy, the British Soldier on the Western Front 1914–1918* (London: Harper Collins, 2004).

Holmes, Richard, *The Little Field Marshal* (London: Cassell edition, 2005).

Holmes, Richard, *Sahib: The British Soldier in India* (London: Harper Collins, 2005).

Hughes, Matthew, and Matthew Seligman, *Leadership in Conflict 1914–1918* (Barnsley: Leo Cooper, 2000).

Hutchinson, Colonel H. D., *The Campaign in Tirah* (London: Macmillan & Co. Ltd, 1898).

Jackson, Sir William G. F., *The Rock of the Gibraltarians: A History of Gibraltar* (London: Associated University Presses, 1987).

Jackson, Tabitha, *The Boer War* (London: Channel 4 Books, 1999).

James, Lionel, *The Indian Frontier War* (London: William Heinemann, 1898).

James, Robert Rhodes, *Gallipoli* (London: BT Batsford Ltd, 1965).

Jeffery, Keith, *The Military Correspondence of Field Marshal Sir Henry Wilson* (The Bodley Head, for the Army Records Society, 1985).

Jeffery, Keith, *Field Marshal Sir Henry Wilson: A Political Soldier* (Oxford University Press, 2006).

Johnson, Franklyn Arthur, *Defence by Committee* (London: Oxford University Press, 1960).

Jones, Spencer, *From Boer War to World War* (University of Oklahoma Press: Norman, 2012).

Keay, John, *A History of India* (London: Harper Collins, 2001).

Keyes, Admiral of the Fleet Sir Roger, *The Fight for Gallipoli* (London: Eyre & Spottiswoode, 1941).

Kingsford, Charles Lethbridge, *The Story of the Duke of Cambridge's Own (Middlesex Regiment)* (London: Country Life, 1916).

Kipling, Rudyard, *The Works of Rudyard Kipling* (Ware: The Wordsworth Poetry Library, Wordsworth Edition Ltd, 1994).

Kipling, Rudyard, *The Irish Guards in the Great War: The First Battalion* (Staplehurst: Spellmount, 1997).

Knight, Captain C. R. B., *Historical Records of the Buffs* (London: The Medici Society Ltd, 1935).

Laffin, John, *British Butchers and Bunglers of World War One* (Stroud: Alan Sutton Publishing, 1988).

Lee, Celia, *Jean, Lady Hamilton 1861–1941: A Soldier's Wife* (London: Mackays, 2001).

Lee, Roger, *The Battle of Fromelles 1916* (Sydney: Big Sky Publishing, 2010).

Lee, Roger, *British Battle Planning in 1916 and the Battle of Fromelles* (London: Ashgate, 2015).

Liddell Hart, Captain B. H., *The Remaking of Modern Armies* (London: John Murray, 1927).

Liddell Hart, Captain B. H., *The Real War 1914–1918* (London: Faber & Faber Ltd, 1930).

Liddell Hart, Captain B. H., *History of the First World War* (London: Cassell & Co. Ltd (Pan), 1970).

Lloyd, Nick, *The Amritsar Massacre* (London: IB Tauris, 2011).

Lloyd George, David, *War Memoirs of David Lloyd George, Volume 1* (London: Odhams Press Ltd, 1938).

Lubbock, Basil, *The Colonial Clippers* (Glasgow: Brown, Son & Ferguson Ltd, 1955).

Lucas, Sir Charles, *The Empire at War, Volume V* (London: Oxford University Press, Humphrey Milford, 1926).

Lucy, John, *There's a Devil in the Drum* (London: 1938, reprint 2009).

Macdonald, Lyn, *1914: The Days of Hope* (London: Penguin, 1987).

Macdonald, Lyn, *Somme* (London: Michael Joseph, 1983).

McGilvray, Evan, *Hamilton & Gallipoli* (Barnsley: Pen & Sword, 2015).

Magnus, Philip, *Kitchener – Portrait of an Imperialist* (London: John Murray, 1958).

Mallinson, Allan, *1914 – Fight the Good Fight* (London: Bantam Press, 2013).

Manchester, William, *The Last Lion, Winston Spencer Churchill* (Boston, Toronto: Little Brown & Co., 1983).

Marshal-Cornwall, General Sir James, *Haig as Military Commander* (London: BT Batsford Ltd, 1973).

Maude, Alan H., *The 47th (London) Division 1914–1919* (London: Amalgamated Press Ltd, 1922).

May, Lieutenant Colonel E. S., *A Retrospect on the South African War* (London: Sampson Low, Marston & Co., 1901).

Mayne, Lieutenant Colonel C. B., *The Infantry Weapon and its Use in War* (London: Smith, Elder & Co., 1903).

Menezes, Lieutenant General S. L., *Fidelity and Honour* (Delhi: Oxford University Press, 1999).

Messenger, Charles, *For Love of Regiment* (London: Leo Cooper, 1994).

Messenger, Charles, *Call-To-Arms: The British Army 1914–18* (London: Cassell, 2005).

Middleton-Brumwell, P., *History of the 12th Eastern Division in the Great War 1914–1918* (London: Nisbet & Co. Ltd, 1923).

Miller, Charles, *Khyber* (New York: Macmillan Publishing Company, 1977).

Mockler-Ferryman, Augustus F., *Annals of Sandhurst* (London: William Heinemann, 1900).

Montagu, Edwin S., *An Indian Diary* (London: Heinemann, 1930).

Moon, Sir Penderel, *The British Conquest and Dominion of India* (London: Duckworth, 1989).

Moore-Bick, Christopher, *Playing the Game* (Solihull: Helion & Company, 2011).

Moorehead, Alan, *Gallipoli* (London: NEL/Mentor Edition, 1974).

Murland, Jerry, *Retreat and Rearguard 1914* (Barnsley: Pen & Sword, 2011).

Murland, Jerry, *Battle on the Aisne 1914* (Barnsley: Pen & Sword, 2012).

Myatt, Frederick, *The British Infantry 1660–1945* (Poole, Dorset: Blandford Press, 1983).

Neillands, Robin, *The Great War Generals* (London: Robinson, 1998).

Neillands, Robin, *The Death of Glory* (London: John Murray Publishers, 2007).

Pakenham, Thomas, *The Boer War* (London: Abacus version, 1979).

Pederson, P. A., *Fromelles* (Barnsley: Leo Cooper, 2004).

Pollock, John, *Kitchener* (London: Constable, 1998).

Pollock, Major A. W. A., *With Seven Generals in the Boer War* (London: Skeffington & Son, 1900).

Prior, Robin, and Trevor Wilson, *Command on the Western Front* (Barnsley: Pen & Sword, 2004).

Purnell's History of the First World War (Bristol: BPC Publishing Ltd, 1970).

Rawson, Andrew, *The 1914 Campaign* (Barnsley: Pen & Sword, 2014).

Repington, Colonel C. á Court, *The First World War 1914–1918, Personal Experiences: Volume 1* (London: Constable and Co. Ltd).

Rhodes James, Robert, *Gallipoli* (London: BT Batsford Ltd, 1965).

Robbins, Simon, *British Generalship on the Western Front 1914–1918* (London & New York: Frank Cass, 2005).

Robbins, Simon, *British Generalship during the Great War: The Military Career of Sir Henry Horne 1861–1929* (England & USA: Ashgate Publishing Ltd, 2010).

Robertson, Field Marshal Sir William, *From Private to Field Marshal* (London: Constable & Co. Ltd, 1921).

Robinson, Richard A. H., *The Origins of Franco's Spain: The Right, the Republic and Revolution 1931–1936* (University of Pittsburgh Press, 1970).

Robson, Brian, *Crisis on the Frontier* (Staplehurst: Spellmount Ltd, 2004).

Rogan, Eugene, *The Fall of the Ottomans* (London: Allen Lane, 2015).

Roy, Kaushik, *The Army in British India* (London: Bloomsbury Publishing plc, 2013).

Royle, Trevor, *The Kitchener Enigma* (London: Michael Joseph, 1985).

Samuels, Martin, *Doctrine and Dogma* (London: Greenwood Press, 1992).

Selby, John, *The Boer War: A Study in Cowardice and Courage* (London: Arthur Barker Ltd, 1969).

Senior, Michael, *Haking: A Dutiful Soldier* (Barnsley: Pen & Sword, 2012).

Shadwell, Captain L. J., *Lockhart's Advance through Tirah* (London: William Clowes & Sons Ltd, 1898).

Sheffield, Gary, *Forgotten Victory: The First World War: Myths and Realities* (London: Headline Book Publishing, 2001).

Sheffield, Gary, *The Chief: Douglas Haig and the British Army* (London: Aurum Press Ltd, 2011).

Sheffield, Gary, and Dan Todman, *Command and Control on the Western Front* (Staplehurst: Spellmount, 2004).

Sheffield, Gary, and John Bourne, *Douglas Haig: War Diaries and Letters 1914–1918* (London: Weidenfeld & Nicolson, 2005).

Sheppard, Major E. W., *The Study of Military History* (Aldershot: Gale & Polden Ltd, 1955).

Shepperd, Alan, *Sandhurst: The Royal Military Academy* (London: Country Life Books, 1980).

Simpson, Andy, *Directing Operations: British Corps Command on the Western Front 1914–18* (Stroud: Spellmount Ltd, 2006).

Simpson, Keith, *The Old Contemptibles: A Photographic History of the British Expeditionary Force August–December 1914* (London: George Allen & Unwin, 1981).

Sixsmith, E. K. G., *Douglas Haig* (London: Weidenfeld & Nicolson, 1976).

Skeen, General Sir Andrew, *Lessons in Imperial Rule* (London: Frontline Books, 2008).

Smith-Dorrien, Horace, *Memories of Forty-Eight Years' Service* (London: John Murray, 1925).

Spears, Sir Edward, *Liaison 1914* (London: Eyre & Spottiswoode, 1930).

Spiers, Edward M., *Haldane: An Army Reformer* (Edinburgh: University Press, 1980).

Spiers, Edward M., *The Late Victorian Army 1868–1902* (Manchester: Manchester University Press, 1992).

Stewart, Jules, *The Kaiser's Mission to Kabul* (London/New York: IB Tauris, 2014).

Stewart, Lieutenant Colonel J., and John Buchan, *The Fifteenth (Scottish) Division 1914–1919* (Edinburgh & London: William Blackwood & Sons, 1926).

Stirling, John, *Our Regiments in South Africa 1899–1902* (Edinburgh & London: William Blackwood & Sons, 1903).

Stockey, Gareth, *Gibraltar, 'A Dagger in the Spine of Spain'?* (Brighton, Portland: Sussex Academic Press, 2009).

Strachan, Hew, *Politics of the British Army* (Oxford: Clarendon Press, 1997).

Syk, Andrew, *The Military Papers of Lieutenant General Frederick Stanley Maude 1914–1917* (Army Records Society, The History Press, 2012).

Terraine, John, *Mons* (London: Pan Books Ltd, 1960).

Terraine, John, *White Heat: The New Warfare 1914–18* (London: Sidgwick & Jackson, 1982).

Terraine, John, *1914–1918 Essays on Leadership & War* (Dorset: Oakdale Printing Company Ltd, the Trustees of the Western Front Association, 1998).

Thomas, Hugh, *The Story of Sandhurst* (London: Hutchinson, 1961).

Travers, Tim, *Gallipoli* (Stroud: Tempus Publishing Ltd, 2002).

Travers, Tim, *The Killing Ground* (Barnsley: Pen & Sword Military Classics, 2003).

Tribal Analysis Center, *Mad Mullahs, Opportunities, and Family Connections: The Violent Pashtun Cycle* (Williamsburg, Virginia, 2009).

Turner, E. S., *Gallant Gentlemen* (London: Michael Joseph, 1956).

Verney, David, *In Viceregal India 1916–1921* (Exeter: Short Run Press, 1994).

Wessells, Andre, *Lord Roberts and the War in South Africa 1899–1902* (London: Sutton Publishing Ltd, for Army Records Society, 2000).

Wessells, Andre, *Lord Kitchener and the War in South Africa 1899–1902* (London: Sutton Publishing Ltd, for Army Records Society, 2006).

Wet, Christiaan Rudolf de, *Three Years War (October 1899–June 1902)* (Westminster: Archibald Constable & Co. Ltd, 1902).

Wickes, H. L., *Regiments of Foot* (Reading: Osprey Publishing Ltd, 1974).

Wilkinson, Theon, *Two Monsoons* (London: Duckworth, 1976).

Wood, Field Marshal Sir Evelyn, *Winnowed Memories* (London: Cassell & Company, 1918).

Wylly, Colonel H. C., *History of the Queen's Royal Regiment, Volume VII* (Aldershot: Gale & Polden Ltd, 1925).

Wyrall, Everard, *The History of the Second Division 1914–1918* (London: Thomas Nelson & Sons Ltd, 1921).

Yardley, Michael, *Sandhurst – A Documentary* (London: Harrap Ltd, 1987).

Yardley, Michael, and Dennis Sewell, *A New Model Army* (London: WH Allen, 1989).

Young, Lieutenant Colonel F. W., *The Story of the Staff College 1859–1958* (Aldershot: Gale & Polden Ltd, 1958).

Younghusband, Captain G. J., *The Queen's Commission* (London: John Murray, 1891).

Articles

'Always on the Bull', *Soldier Magazine* (January 1969).

'The Army Council and its Origin', *British Army Review*, No 19 (HMSO, October 1964).

Balck, Major, 'The Lessons of the Boer War and the Battleworking of the Three Arms', *Journal of the Royal United Service Institution*, Vol. XLVII (London: JJ Keliher & Co. Ltd, 1904).

Barclay, Brigadier C. N. article in, *The Army Quarterly and Defence Journal*, Vol. LXXVI (London: April & July 1958).

Batten, Simon, '"A School for the Leaders": What Did the British Army Learn from the 1912 Army Manoeuvres', *Journal of the Society for Army Historical Research*, Vol. 93, No 373 (Spring 2015).

Bird, Major W. D., 'Infantry Fire Tactics', *The Journal of the Royal United Service Institution*, Vol. XLIX (July–December 1905).

Bond, Brian, 'Edward Cardwell's Army Reforms 1868–74', *The Army Quarterly and Defence Journal*, Vol. LXXXIV (London: William Clowes & Sons Ltd, 1962).

Bond, Brian, 'Prelude to the Cardwell Reforms 1856–68', *The Journal of the Royal United Service Institution*, Vol. CVI (London: RUSI, 1961).

Churchill, Winston L. Spencer, 'Some Impressions of the War in South Africa', *Royal United Service Institution Journal*, Vol. XLV (1901).

'Early History of the Army School of Musketry in Hythe, Kent', Muzzle Loaders Association of Great Britain *Black Powder Magazine* (Winter 2007).

Fox, 'A Curious Hybrid: The Special Reservist 1908–1914', *Stand To Magazine*, No 98 (September 2013) Western Front Association.

Holden Reid, Brian, 'War Studies at The Staff College 1890–1930', *Strategic & Combat War Studies Institute: The Occasional* (1992).

Hussey, John, 'A Hard Day at First Ypres', *British Army Review*, Issue 107 (August 1994).

'Hythe and Its School of Musketry', Leslie Stewart article pp.479–84. Reprint pp1–3. *Cassell's Magazine*, No 27 (1903).

Irwin, Lieutenant General Sir Alistair, 'What is Best in the Regimental System' *Royal United Service Institution Journal* (October 2004).

Maud, Lieutenant Colonel P. D., 'Lord Haldane's Reorganisation of the British Army 1905–1912', *The Army Quarterly*, Vol. LV (October 1947 and January 1948).

Monro, Major General C. C., 'Fire and Movement', *The Army Review* (July 1911).

Musketeer, 'Infantry Problems and Traditions', *Journal of the Royal United Service Institution*, Vol. XCVI (1951).

Myatt MC, Major F., 'The Cardwell System', *British Army Review* (1981).

'Obituaries', *The Army Quarterly*, Vol. 19, No 2 (January 1930).

'Obituary, General C.C. Monro' *The Journal of the Queen's Royal Regiment*, Vol. III, May 1930.

Simon Courtauld article, *The Spectator* (1 November 2014).

Spiers, Edward, 'Reorganisation of Infantry of the Line', *Journal of the Society for Army Historical Research*, Vol. 59 (1981).

'The South African War of 1899–1900', *Royal United Service Institution Journal*, Vol. XLV (1901).

Vincent, Colonel Sir Howard, 'Lessons from the War for Immediate Application', *The United Service Magazine*, Vol. XXIV (October 1901–March 1902).

'The Von Lobell Annual Reports on the Changes and Progress in Military Matters in 1904', *Royal United Service Institution Journal*, Vol. XLIX (1905).

Williams MC, Major Orlo, 'The Aftermath, the Evacuation of the Dardanelles', *The National Review*, No 74/443 (January 1920).

Newspapers and Periodicals

The Aberdeen Press and Journal (Wednesday, 28 March 1928).

Argus, Melbourne (1860).

Army and Navy Gazette (12 December 1929).

The Essex County Chronicle (Friday, 4 October 1912).

The Essex Newsman (Saturday, 3 August 1912).

Evening Post (Vol. XCIII, Issue 47, 23 February 1917).

Gibraltar Chronicle (1927).

Gibraltar Magazine (June 2009, August 2011 and August 2013).

Horse and Hound (14 December 1929).

The Journal of the East Surrey Regiment, Vol. II (August 1925–May 1931).

The London Gazette (8 December 1899; 7 April 1916; 28 March 1916; 29 May 1916; 10 July 1917; 26 November 1918; 8 April 1919; 12 March 1920; 22 October 1920 [p.10262]; 7 December 1920).

The Manchester Courier (2 October 1912 and 18 December 1915).

The National Review (January 1920).

The New York Times (2 October 1912).

The Nottingham Post (Saturday 21 December 1901).

Surrey Advertiser (14 December 1929).

Soldier (January 1969).

The Times (Tuesday 1 October 1912; Wednesday 2 October 1912; 1 May 1916; Thursday 21 February 2013).

The Western Gazette (Friday 1 July 1921).

The Western Morning News (9 September 1923).

Papers

Holden Reid, Brian, 'War Studies at the Staff College 1890–1930' (HMSO, Strategic & Combat Studies Institute, 1992).

The Liddell Hart Centre for Military Archives (LHCMA):
    Hamilton 7/2/47, 7/4/10, 7/9/6, 17/2, 17/32, 21/4.
    Howell 9/3/5, 9/3/6, 9/3/7.
    Liddell Hart 15/6/5/13.
    Montgomery-Massingberd 8/32, 8/33.
    Robertson 3/2/29, 7/2/39, 8/1/51 to 8/1/54, 8/1/56, 8/1/58, 8/1/60, 8/1/61, 8/1/77.

National Army Museum (NAM):
    NAM-7207-19-1 – Notebooks of General Monro 1916–17, 'Jobs to be done' notebooks.
    NAM-7207-20 (1923–28) – Gibraltar Photograph Album.
    NAM-1958-06-40 – General Monro's medals on mounted card.
    NAM-1978-10-110 – Papers of Lieutenant General Sir Walter Campbell KCB on Gallipoli extraction.

British Library (Asian and African Studies):
 Mss Eur D783 – Letters, scrapbooks and photographs of Sir Charles Monro,
 C-in-C India 1916–20, and Lady Monro. Monro collection: papers of
 General Sir Charles Carmichael Monro (1860–1929), mainly comprising
 letters, scrapbooks and photographs compiled by himself and Lady Monro,
 whilst he was serving as C-in-C India 1916–20.

Imperial War Museum:
 Letters of Sir Philip Game to his wife – PWG 9 and 11, 1915 and 1916.
 Letters of Sir Henry Horne to his wife – Horne Papers, 25 December 1916,
 23 January 1919.
 C. E. Callwell letter to A. Lynden-Bell, 22 October 1915.
 A. Lynden-Bell, typescript account, pp.1–2.
 A. Lynden-Bell, letter to C. E. Callwell, December 1915.
 Maxse Papers, 69/53/6. Secret, Notes of Conference, 4 August 1915 by Sir
 Charles Monro.

The National Archives Kew (Public Records Office):
 War Office (WO) 27/508 – IG Report for 1907.
 War Office 33/337 – The Russo-Japanese War up to 15 August 1904.
 War Office 76/356 – 'Record of Officers' Services 1893'. 'Succession of
 School of Musketry'.
 WO95/162-167 – 1st Army War Diary.
 War Office 95/359 – 3rd Army War Diary.
 War Office 95/588-591 – I Corps War Diary.
 War Office 95/1283 – 2nd Division War Diary.
 War Office 158/17, 18, 19, 21 – General Staff Notes on Operations.
 War Office 158/46 – Letter Kiggell to Monro, 25 March 1916.
 War Office 153/128 and War Office 158/258 – Neuve Chapelle.
 War Office 158/269 – 'Gas Attacks by the Enemy'.
 War Office 105/6, 20, 23 – Various Boer War correspondence.
 CAB 24/1/38 – Memorandum on the Conduct of the War.
 CAB 24/1/47 – Memorandum General Sir Ian Hamilton.
 War Office Report of the Examination for Admission to the Staff College
 held in June 1888 (HMSO).
 War Office Report on the Final Examination at the Staff College held in
 December 1891 (HMSO).
 R. Whitbread, private papers, IWM Department of Documents 8/30/1.

Miscellaneous Documents

The Dominions Office and Colonial Office List (London: Mercer, Harding & Gent
 Waterlow & Sons Ltd, 1928).
Field Service Regulations, Part I, Operations (HMSO, 1909, Reprint 1914).
Hart, Lieutenant General H. G., *The New Army List* (London: John Murray, 1910).
Infantry Training Manual 1905, General Staff, War Office (HMSO).

Infantry Training Manual 1911, General Staff, War Office (HMSO).

Our Indian Empire, training manual (Crown Copyright Reserved, 1937).

Oxford Dictionary of National Biography (1937).

Regimental India 1825–1947, The Queen's Royal Surrey Regimental Association (Sandwich: The Press on the Lake, undated).

The Sherborne Register.

The Shirburnian magazine.

Staff Officers' Handbook 2000 (HMSO).

Training and Manoeuvre Regulations 1913, General Staff, War Office (HMSO).

The War Illustrated (1916). Gallery of Leaders.

Who Was Who 1897–1916 (London: A & C Black Ltd, 1935).

Television

Blackadder Goes Forth (Series Four, *Blackadder*) (BBC, 2000).

Websites

http://www.sherborne.org/about us/a-brief-history

http://thercr.ca

http://www.royaldublinfusiliers.com

http://www.mlagh.com

http://www.firstworldwar.com/bio/plumer.htm

https://www.marxists.org/history/etol/revhist/backiss/vol8/no2/putkowski2.html

http://www.irish-society.org

http://www.historyireland.com

INDEX

Also by the same author …

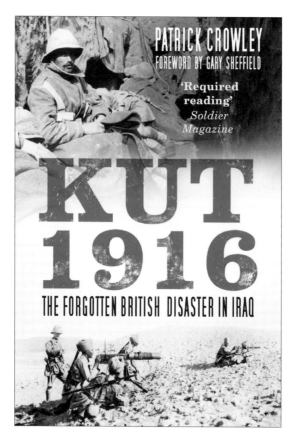

978 0 7509 6606 1

The destination for history
www.thehistorypress.co.uk